Content-Based Second Language Teaching and Learning

An Interactive Approach

MARJORIE HALL HALEY

George Mason University

THERESA Y. AUSTIN

University of Massachusetts

Boston   New York   San Francisco
Mexico City   Montreal   Toronto   London   Madrid   Munich   Paris
Hong Kong   Singapore   Tokyo   Cape Town   Sydney

Series Editor: *Aurora Martínez Ramos*
Series Editorial Assistant: *Katie Freddoso*
Senior Marketing Manager: *Elizabeth Fogarty*
Composition and Prepress Buyer: *Linda Cox*
Manufacturing Manager: *Andrew Turso*
Editorial-Production Coordinator: *Mary Beth Finch*
Editorial-Production Service: *Shepherd, Inc.*
Electronic Composition: *Shepherd, Inc.*

For related titles and support materials, visit our online catalog at www.ablongman.com

Between the time Website information is gathered and then published, it is not unusual for some sites to have closed. Also, the transcription of URLs can result in unintended typographical errors. The publisher would appreciate notification where these errors occur so that they may be corrected in subsequent editions.

Library of Congress Cataloging-in-Publication Data

Haley, Marjorie Hall, 1952–
    Content-based second language teaching and learning : an interactive approach / Marjorie Hall Haley, Theresa Y. Austin.
      p. cm.
    Includes bibliographical references and index.
    ISBN 0-205-34427-5
    1. Language and languages—Study and teaching. 2. Interaction analysis in education.
  3. Language arts—Correlation with content subjects. I. Austin, Theresa Y. II. Title.

P53.447.H35 2004
418'.0071—dc22
                                                           2003057967

Printed in the United States of America.

10 9 8 7 6 5 4 3   08 07 06

Brief Contents

Contents

CHAPTER FOUR

Evaluating and Creating Interactive and Content-Based Assessment 116

CHAPTER FIVE

Interactive Listening and Reading   150

CHAPTER SIX

Foregrounding Oral Communication   188

CHAPTER SEVEN

Foregrounding Written Communication   233

CHAPTER EIGHT

An Interactive Approach for Working with Diverse Learners   276

CHAPTER NINE

Integrating Technology in an Interactive, Content-Based Classroom   300

SECTION III: FOCUS ON COMPREHENSION 349

CHAPTER TEN
Comprehension Exercises 349

A shift in the demographics of the United States, coupled with special attention to our nation's educational goals and standards, has created a fertile opportunity for addressing teacher preparation and the needs of pluralistic schools of the twenty-first century. Teacher preparation plays a vital role in providing both pre- and in-service teachers with an understanding of cultural, linguistic, cognitive, and related variables, and their effects on the teaching-learning process.

> All elementary and secondary school students currently in the United States will be living in and contributing to an increasingly diverse society and interdependent community of nations in the 21st century. To realize their personal, social, and long-term career goals, individuals will need to be able to communicate with others skillfully, appropriately, and effectively. The challenge of contemporary education is to prepare all students for life in this new world, including those learners who enter schools with a language other than English. (ESL Standards for Pre-K–12 Students, p. 1)

Once you begin teaching, it is very likely that you will find yourself in any given school year standing in front of a class comprised of students who have different a) languages, b) academic levels, and c) linguistic proficiency levels. The major goal of this book is to assist in the preparation of teachers in English as a Second Language (ESL), bilingual education, and foreign/second/world languages to work with students in grades K–12. The second goal is to provide rich examples of effective interactive instructional strategies and assessment practices in content-based classroom settings.

Whenever a book is coauthored, there is a question about the voice that should be used to convey information. Some editors believe that the book should be from a third-person perspective, a narrator who is neutral and omnipresent yet unidentifiable. Others opt for including the authors by personal names and making it explicit where each is expressing a particular point. We have opted for a happy mixture of the two. In this book we have tried to allow each author's voice to speak directly to you, giving you an opportunity to examine both our perspectives throughout the text. You will read sections in which we write from the same position. At other times we will write from different positions to reflect contrasting points of view, namely *psycholingustic* and *sociocultural*. (These will be described in further detail in chapter 1.) These positions will allow you to experience thinking from different points of view that coexist in our profession, i.e., language education, today. We hope this will allow you the space to consider what each position has to offer and how you may wish to apply this information to your teaching.

ORGANIZATION OF AN INTERACTIVE APPROACH TO CONTENT-BASED SECOND LANGUAGE TEACHING AND LEARNING

An Interactive Approach to Content-Based Second Language Teaching and Learning consists of three sections and ten chapters: Section I is Language, Language Learning, and Language Acquisition. This section includes chapter 1, How Languages Are Learned and Acquired. This chapter examines the core principles of psycholinguistics and sociocultural perspectives as they relate to teaching and learning.

Section II is Interactive Instructional Practice in Content-Based Settings. This section includes chapter 2, Methods and Approaches in Language Teaching; chapter 3, Planning for the Standards-Based Classroom; chapter 4, Creating Interactive and Content-Based Assessment; chapter 5, Interactive Listening and Reading; chapter 6, Foregrounding Oral Communication; chapter 7, A Focus on Written Language Communication; chapter 8, An Interactive Approach for Working with Diverse Learners; and chapter 9, Integrating Technology in an Interactive, Content-Based Classroom.

Section III is a Focus on Comprehension. This section includes chapter 10, Comprehension Exercises.

CHAPTER ORGANIZATION

This text is intended to be *interactive*. One of our objectives in writing this book is for the reader to interact, reflect, and respond to the book's contents. Space is provided for you to write in the text and we urge you to revisit your responses throughout the time you are reading. The first page of each chapter presents the features and what you will be examining.

Each chapter is organized by most or all of the following sections or features:

1) **Think/Pair/Share**—Designed for you to interact with a classmate, partner, or colleague, tap your schemata (background knowledge), or engage in thoughtful discussion.
2) **Setting the Stage**—Frames the content of the chapter and provides both theoretical and research-based underpinnings.
3) **Video Clips**—Some chapters will include video clips of teachers demonstrating effective practices that accompany the text. These may be accessed from the text's Web site at www.ablongman.com/hallhaley1e. Additionally, there is an accompanying activity for each video clip.
4) **Reflect and Respond**—Activities written to allow you time to *reflect* on what you have read and to *respond* to a question that helps aid your comprehension.
5) **Discuss and Reflect**—Questions that focus on the content of the chapter. Space is provided for you to answer these questions and for you to reflect on your responses.
6) **Ask Yourself These Questions**—Broad questions for which you will want to begin formulating answers before you begin your teaching career

7) **What Do Teachers Think?**—These are "voices from the field." ESL or foreign/second language classroom teachers (K–12) were interviewed or asked to write their views on topics specific to the topic of the individual chapter.

8) **Field-Based Experience**—Offer suggestions for activities to be undertaken in a classroom or school setting. These are opportunities to practice what you have read.

9) **Case Study**—Case studies created to demonstrate the main focus of the chapter. You are asked to read and then respond to questions based on the case study.

10) **Action Research**—Practical action research project that can be completed during student teaching/internship or field experience. They will help you create meaningful questions that can be examined through an investigatory process.

11) **Additional Resources**—List professional organizations, Web sites, and national and international professional journals.

12) **Application Activity**—A suggested activity for you to try during student teaching/internship or field experience.

13) **Glossary of Terms**—A quick reference to terms used throughout the chapter.

PURPOSE AND AUDIENCE

This book is written for use as a textbook in teacher education programs for preservice and inservice English as a Second Language (ESL) and foreign/world language teachers. We have attempted to address the needs of a wide audience: undergraduate preservice, graduate preservice, and inservice ESL and foreign/world language teachers.

Undergraduate preservice and graduate preservice teachers—this book should serve you well primarily as a methodological resource. We have written the book based on the assumption that you have an introductory background in second language acquisition theories and research. Furthermore, we assume that you will have field experiences as part of your teacher education program and therefore you will be able to participate in live classroom settings and use and observe what you learn in the book.

Inservice teachers—the book is intended to provide you with extra resources, new ideas, and perhaps a fresh perspective on interactive teaching in content-based language classes.

For the purposes of this text we define ESL teachers as those who work with students for whom English is *not* their first language. These students are often referred to as English Language Learners (ELLs), English to Speakers of Other Languages (ESOL), language minority students, or Limited English Proficient (LEP). Foreign/second/world languages refers to *all* languages, including English that are studied and taught as an addition to one's first language. This responds to the changing political and social contexts in education in the United States.

We want to point out that there are similarities and differences between learning a language that is encountered and used outside the classroom setting (a second language setting) and learning a language that is used for a short time frame in schooling and not for any significant amount of time outside that environment (foreign).

Since these two settings reflect two extremes, undoubtedly there are situations that fall in between, where a subsequent language may be used in certain sectors of one's community but not shared by everyone. For example, if our current national educational goals are met, foreign language education in the elementary schools will move away from being considered a sporadic and enrichment activity to being a core subject in the curriculum. When this happens, we will see a K–12 developmental cycle of learning that may allow foreign/second/world language learners to become bilingual in similar ways to ESL learners who are expected to be able to learn subject matter through their second language and to adjust to cultural differences in their adaptation to the cultures where English is spoken.

So in jointly addressing the commonalties and differences, we hope we will foster in our profession the acceptance that we are all language educators who can learn from each other. Furthermore, as we live in a world with populations in contact with each other, as well as changing demographics in the United States, we begin with the assumption that all our classrooms will be diverse, with learners from a variety of backgrounds. With this in mind, we embrace an approach that will strive to help all learners achieve.

Where Should You Begin?

When you begin this book, you initiate a journey to interact with some ideas we have compiled for you through our own experiences as language educators. We have assembled them in such a way so as to have you investigate your own thinking about language and language learning as well as to share what is currently in practice.

While we have envisioned an order of chapter progression, we encourage you to start with the areas that you have a need to know. What you will find is that there are links to ideas presented in previous or succeeding chapters. We provide these in order for you to construct a coherent view of these materials for your own purposes. If we are successful, you will be able to read this book many times from different points and obtain different perspectives each time you read it.

Chapter 10 consists of comprehension exercises and activities for each of the book's nine other chapters. These are written so that after you have completed a chapter and the exercises contained in it, you can self-assess as a means of determining what you learned. These exercises will help you to synthesize information covered in each chapter and reflect on your construction of knowledge.

Reflection.   Our histories can help reveal historical influences on how we came to this profession and our notions about it. By writing *your* reflections you may learn about your own reasoning process and beliefs. Take a few minutes to consider the following:

1. What brought you to the profession of language education? How do you see yourself currently in this profession? For example, an advocate for immigrant populations as a future ESL teacher, a seasoned bilingual teacher, a foreign language teacher educator, a male in a profession that has been considered female-dominated, a cultural ambassador, a person for whom learning languages has been exciting and easy, etc.?

2. Where do you see yourself in the future? A elementary school teacher of foreign languages, a high school ESL teacher, or a university language teacher educator?

3. Where do you want to begin? Start by listing your major questions about our profession and comparing your list to our chapters. Is there any item missing? Add it by visiting our Web site at www.ablongman.com/hallhaley1e.

4. We have designed this book to serve as a resource. You may assume that with this type of reading you will have lots of questions, and we hope that this book will serve you well as you look for answers here.

Acknowledgements

An Interactive Approach to Content-Based Second Language Teaching and Learning is a product of combined teaching, research, thinking, and commitment to second language education. We are indebted to our many colleagues around the globe who offered encouraging words and who value the intent of the book. For those whose opinions we have been fortunate to receive: Ginger Collier, Robert Terry, Joan Isenberg, Ryuko Kubota, Elizabeth Henning, Jerri Willett, Debbie Zacarian, Alvaro Quintero Polo, and Barbara Hruska, we offer our sincere appreciation.

We are particularly grateful to the many bilingual, ESL, and foreign/second language teachers who gave so generously of their time and input: Connie Thibeault, Reyna MacMillan, Marty VanOpdorp, Lynn Fulton Archer, Sonia Miller, Pat Rentz, Catherine Egan, Janeath Casallas, Char Spitler, Alvaro Quintero, Joyce Illif, Lu Xu, Katerina Ites, Janeath Velasquez, and many more.

We would like to thank the reviewers of the manuscript: Irma N. Guadarrama, University of Houston; John McFadden, California State University; and Maria E. Medrano, National University.

Special thanks go to: Amanda Seewald for her tireless efforts in copy editing and moral support; Maggie Gonzales, office manager for the Center for Multilingual/Multicultural Education at George Mason University, whose reassurances were always welcomed and needed; Kathy Seaholm, my graduate research assistant, who was so effective in helping with extensive literature searches, and graduate research librarian at GMU, Sarah Sheehan. Without a doubt we need to thank our families (my daughter, Esther) and spouses, (Donald and Mark) for their unflagging support throughout our creative process.

Marjorie Hall Haley
Theresa Y. Austin

CHAPTER ONE

HOW LANGUAGES ARE LEARNED AND ACQUIRED

THIS CHAPTER WILL FEATURE

- How our assumptions shape our understandings about
  - language and language learning
  - teaching language
- Core principles that form the foundations of our text:
  - An Interactive Approach to Content-based Teaching and Learning

YOU WILL EXAMINE

- Sociocultural theories and practices
- Psycholinguistic theories and practices

INTRODUCTION: SETTING THE STAGE

We begin with our own assumptions about language and language learning as a way of showing that these assumptions underpin our practices, both unexamined and examined. As the field is constantly changing, we want to stress that this process of questioning one's assumptions and reconstructing them on the basis of new knowledge is a key to maintaining updated instructional practices that are responsive to our learners. Consideration of these important issues that influence culturally responsive language learning and instruction need to be included in order to help teachers and learners address and transform social and cultural inequities that affect their ability to succeed.

Teachers who view themselves as life-long learners of teaching; who engage in sustained critical reflection and inquiry into their own knowledge and practice; who recognize that in teaching, it depends; and who can articulate what it depends on will develop complex, flexible, conceptual understandings of themselves, their students,

---

THINK, PAIR, SHARE

Before you begin reading this chapter, consider the fact that everyone—from the mother who speaks to a child, to a linguist who systematically cracks an unknown code, to a news columnist who decries the deterioration of the standards of language use—has an idea of what constitutes language. We ask that you begin by articulating your beliefs in the following activity.

1. When I think of *language*, I mean:

   _____

   _____

2. When I think of *learning*, I mean:

   _____

   _____

---

their classrooms, and their schools, and will be able to use their knowledge in different ways, for different purposes, and in different instructional context, enabling them to provide truly effective teaching practices. (Johnson, 1999, p. 12)

Language teachers helping learners and themselves overcome previously held prejudices and stereotypical attitudes will promote better cross-cultural interactions. This necessary examination will develop understanding, tolerance, and respect between cultures and a more sophisticated ability to negotiate cultural differences. As second/foreign language teachers, you will need to be well prepared to instruct in a demographically and technologically rapidly changing world where cultures are increasingly interacting through various media. If we do not learn to handle these global connections we will be faced with failures that Urbanski (1988) describes:

> The problem with today's schools is not that they are no longer as good as they once were. The problem with today's schools is that they are precisely what they always were, while the world around them has changed significantly. Schools must be restructured as centers of inquiry and reflection, not of unexamined tradition.
> (As cited by Huber, Kline, Bakken, & Clark, p. 184)

In the following sections we [the author] narrate our histories of language learning and teaching. We share our values and beliefs that we regard as important to learning and teaching. We'll begin with Marjorie.

When Marjorie started teaching, her interest in languages grew out of a fascination with words and sounds, accents and dialects. Growing up as a child whose parents are from diverse backgrounds afforded her opportunities to be raised in a culture of people of many colors, dialects, and accents. She narrates her story here:

> My interest in languages grew out of a fascination with words and sounds, accents and dialects. Growing up as a child whose parents are new England Canadian French/Naragansett Native American and Virginia African American/Cherokee Native American afforded me the opportunities to be raised in a culture of people of many colors, dialects, and accents.
>
> I began formally studying a foreign language (French) in the mid-'60s just as the Audio Lingual Method (ALM) was being proclaimed as "cutting edge" methodology. ALM focused predominantly on grammatical form within a sentence-level context. Along with ALM came the advent of language labs and small records which students could purchase for a nominal price, thus allowing extra practice outside of the classroom. Will any one of us who experienced ALM ever forget the dialogues we were required to memorize? At that time studying a foreign language was not only an elective but students were "selected" to take those classes—the major requirement was that one have an overall C average and no lower than a B average in English. Consequently, students enrolled in foreign languages were there, for the most part, because they wanted to be and not because they were required.
>
> After three years of French, I decided that Spanish was another language I wanted to learn and to know something about the culture, so I took fourth level French and first level Spanish. I soon realized that my French was a tremendous boost in my ability to do well in Spanish. After all, they were both Romance languages and what I didn't know I could sometimes figure out just by looking at the words. I should mention that my secondary teachers came from different methodological backgrounds. My Spanish teacher, new to the profession and in her second year of teaching, had been trained in ALM, while my French teacher, a veteran classicist, was most comfortable using Grammar Translation. He did not believe in interaction among students, rather reading and translating were the basis of his instructional strategies.
>
> In the fall of 1970 I found myself entering College where I confidently declared Spanish as my major and French as my minor. With my high school classroom experiences and opportunities I assumed that reading and speaking in both Spanish and French more than qualified me for such an undertaking.
>
> Much to my surprise I was enrolled in classes with native speakers and students who had traveled and lived in countries of the target languages. My Spanish and French were both very "bookish" and my confidence suffered a great blow. It was then that I decided to take extra courses and to immerse myself in the presence of both peers and professors who spoke Spanish and French. I approached my student teaching during the fall of my fourth year with great enthusiasm. Only after a few short weeks, I knew teaching was my niche and I wanted to excel at it. My undergraduate teacher training program far exceeded my expectations—my professors were supportive and always willing to help me improve my teaching. By 1974 I began my first teaching position with a public school system on the east coast of the United States. I taught Spanish, French, and Foreign Language Appreciation (FLA).
>
> For the next few years I sought opportunities to travel abroad. My first trip was to visit Seoul, South Korea. It was during the time I first understood the relevance of pedagogy. While in my own classes I would experiment with an interactive, more student-centered approach—communicative language teaching approach. Communicative language teaching allows students to be actively involved in information-exchange

tasks that they can complete by working in pairs or small groups. This approach was very successful and my students and I both were learning a lot and having fun. During my academic years, I would pay particular attention to instructional strategies used by university professors and teaching assistants.

I organized my classes so that students were not just memorizing dialogues and regurgitating drills. My students were quite anxious to practice new activities and they were very appreciative of having real and concrete ways to construct meaning with the language. During each of these summers my own language skills increased exponentially. My self-confidence returned and once again I felt an amazing degree of comfort and ease in being able to move in and out of mixed cultures and languages—understanding cultural mores and social norms. What I didn't realize at that point was that I had been completely drawn into making teaching a lifetime career.

I would happily spend the next fourteen years teaching at the secondary level. From my high school and university experiences as a language learner to my years as a language teacher, I have witnessed second/foreign language instruction move to a focus on communicative proficiency—the ability to communicate in the target language in real-life contexts.

My notions about teaching are derived from:

- my experiences as a student in secondary education and graduate-level teaching and
- my experiences as a teacher/professor secondary education and graduate-level teaching.

As a secondary second/foreign language teacher I felt very confident in knowing how to maintain my ability to be a highly effective teacher. I attended conferences, presented workshops for staff development, and wrote curriculum guides for my school district. Additionally, I stayed closely connected to graduate-level coursework where I constantly sought to stay abreast of current methods/trends/pedagogy.

The same holds true for the past fifteen years I have spent at the university level. I am actively involved in several teacher action research studies in which I invite students and former students to participate. I continue to question and reflect on my own practice. Finally, I am always looking for ways to share my experiential background with teachers and colleagues, hoping that they too will enlighten me with their diverse views and experiences.

Teaching has been a small window to the world through which I have been able to "see" the powerful impact it can have on the lives of students. While teaching at the secondary level and striving with adolescents working to learn a second/foreign language, it was a given that my role would be teacher, mentor, surrogate mother, counselor, confidant, and friend. I accepted those roles as part of my job description. What came as a surprise was moving from teaching at high school levels to teaching graduate students—amazingly, I find myself assuming those identical roles. And I do so with great pride. I champion the causes of teachers who are stressed beyond belief, who work under unimaginable circumstances, and who absolutely love what they do. My self-imposed charge is to continue providing them with the tools, enthusiasm, and "stick-to-it-ness" that is required of every teacher. Second/foreign language teachers' classrooms are indeed a microcosm of the world for it is there that students actualize the commonalities of language and culture that connect us all.

Theresa's career evolved from her interests in languages from her own family's linguistic and cultural background: Louisiana Black English and French Creole, and

Okinawan and Japanese. As a person of multiracial ethnicity as well as multicultural, moving in and among different groups of relatives and communities piqued her interest in how her different affiliations as a member required language use shifts. As a Spanish major and Japanese minor at the university, she started teaching through tutoring Spanish and English as a second language in private classes. Then as a graduate student, she moved into teaching at the university and college level. During this time frame she taught adult literacy classes in Spanish and English as a Second Language (ESL), and elementary foreign languages. She tells her story below:

As a successful learner of Spanish, I felt that everyone could learn a language if they put enough individual effort into it. I conveniently forgot how my experiences living in a Spanish speaking country had given me a sense of urgency to learn the language to talk to classmates, relate to people, and to understand my new environment. When I began formal study in a high school, Spanish was familiar not "foreign." With relative ease I completed my book exercises, memorized the dialogues, and took the fill-in-the-blank tests. I even joined the honors club in Spanish to continue studying after school. This success lead to my declaring myself a Spanish major at the university. While my high school years had proven that I had been successful, my placement as a freshman into a university course at the fifth semester level shook my confidence. At this level, I was expected to read short stories and essays and write term papers in Spanish. Moreover, unlike my high school, the classes were conducted entirely in Spanish. After considerable struggle, meeting tutors for extra help, I survived the first two years of heavy reading and writing in Spanish literature and culture. Determined to become a better learner, I opted for the traditional junior year abroad to study in Spain. This study abroad experience plunged me into a formidable life-changing experience that cemented my bond to the Spanish-speaking world and gave me confidence to see myself as a Spanish language user. When I returned, my writing and speaking abilities had grown tremendously. I felt emboldened to continue for my master's degree in the same department. Shortly after my admission to the graduate program, I was offered a teaching assistantship (TA) to instruct in lower division courses.

Previous to my appointment as a TA, I had tutored students in English as a foreign language and Spanish. However, when I began teaching in a formal classroom, I no longer had the freedom to base my instruction on what the learners indicated as their needs, which up to then had been to fulfill language assignments at school. In the Spanish and Portuguese Department at my university at the time, methodology wars were occurring between two approaches being advocated by different professors: the Direct Approach and Programmed Instruction through audio-lingual based exercises. Proponents of each claimed superiority due to their "scientific" procedures, which emphasized oral over written language and which made them superior to the translation method of just learning to translate written texts. While both methodologies defined language as consisting of rules of syntax, morphology, and phonology, each placed different emphasis on different aspects of language and levels of thinking. The Programmed Instruction methodology began with phonological drills and exercises to insure that the learner replicate the sounds and structures of the language in the correct manner. Rules for phonological and morphological structures were explained formally in English and all students were expected to fill in written and oral exercises to practice the discrete and otherwise unrelated structures that were taught in an identified sequence, progressively moving from simple to more complex linguistic structures. The curriculum was organized by contrastive sounds, tenses, and complements; there was little connection to actual writing or speaking. Memorization was key to success. While the direct method, as implemented in our department, shared the similar notions of moving from simple to complex structures, emphasis was on immersing the student in Spanish from the beginning. The idea was to allow the students to experience a controlled encounter with the targeted structure, then to inductively determine the rule governing the structure. Since students were called upon individually to respond to a question, they had to actively listen to the teacher to make sense. It was argued that this was more authentic and involved higher order thinking analysis and synthesis than Programmed Instruction. Both approaches rewarded accuracy in reproduction of the structures and vocabulary in the assessments consisting of filling in the blanks ("Supply the appropriate X tense"), substitution of morphology ("Change present to the present perfect"), or responding in writing to oral questions. Rarely in the beginning two years were students expected to do any reading of extended texts in the target language beyond the dialogs, or write extended texts beyond a paragraph. In the Direct Approach, the instructor was required to use the target language throughout the class and attempt to maintain students' use. While in the Programmed Instruction approach, the instructor used English to explain and organize the class and the target language was used in the drills.

The wars were political and had consequences in the department, as whoever took sides on these methodologies were aligning themselves with one or the other of the professors who upheld each. Eventually one side prevailed and those who did not accept this were not given renewed contracts to teach. I was fortunate as I learned how to teach using both methodologies and thereby ensured my employability. I enjoyed learning how to explain the constituent parts of language structures and getting students to practice to produce these upon my request. At that time I perceived my students' accuracy in these controlled situations as a sign of being a "good" learner and assumed that this meant that they could handle encounters with people who spoke the target language. Likewise, it was assumed that those who failed to accurately produce the forms at 65 percent or higher on our exams were just poor learners and were failed. Since we were not held accountable for the numbers of failures or successes, rather just to maintain the standards of the department, I never wondered about the efficacy of my own practice in promoting learning. I enjoyed teaching and enough students gave me the impression that they did too. My student evaluations were good and I was rehired to teach until I graduated.

Before I graduated, I had the opportunity to teach adult ESL students and teachers who wanted to learn Spanish. From my successful university teaching experiences, I assumed I knew what "language" was and how to teach it. After all, I learned two different methodologies and I was an expert at explaining the structures. What I hadn't learned became more visible to me as I encountered differences between my students' needs and their perceptions of language and language learning.

Adults in my ESL classroom came from at least seven different nations, speaking at least one or two other languages. They arrived in my class after having already worked full days as laborers, maids, clerks, housewives, and mothers. I had such a variety of learners: some without even elementary schooling, some with two years of postsecondary. Most were males with a sprinkling of females included in the population. Most had less than secondary education experiences and came from Mexico or Central America. In the first meeting of my "United Nations" class, I had fifty students to teach and still more were walking in late as they were admitted to the class. I was told that the cutoff point was sixty-five. This shocked me because I came from university classes that were considered over-enrolled at 25.

Through teaching ESL to adults, I learned that my methods failed them. Their needs to negotiate their lives in an often hostile English environment required more than just helping them to understand the structure of English in isolated and unrelated sentences. They were not motivated to get a grade since there were no grades. They were motivated to survive and progress in a world they could chose to participate in marginally or fully, depending on the flexibility of the community and their own investment in learning. They needed to learn to build "new" identities as English users, to use the resources in their communities, to find better paying jobs, to further their education, to find safe housing and to build a social life that were all relevant and meaningful to them. If I were to be successful in this teaching setting, I had to learn to meet these needs of this diverse population in language, literacy, and cultural adaptation.

The other event that pushed my professional development even further than my formal studies was the opportunity to help teachers in the Los Angeles Unified School District learn Spanish to be able to teach their bilingual students. I was contracted to help design, implement, and evaluate a language program for teachers who at that time were being paid to learn Spanish. Again, I was faced with a challenge—teaching mature men and women who were experienced teachers. They were seasoned teachers who took pride in their ability to teach. Many saw their main issue as not having the language skills to communicate with their students. As we started with the same assumption, the program developers constructed a linguistically-based curriculum. This time I felt that I was very familiar and comfortable with twenty-five learners who had to be motivated to serve their students. I assumed a shared purpose "to become bilingual" but what I discovered rather early on was a heterogeneity in commitment and conflicting purposes. My learners had many assumptions about their students, how they should be taught, and what they should learn. But most of all they were vocal and adamant about their own needs. I could see that language learning sequence had to again be contextualized to the demands of their profession, be situated in the limited amount of time that they had to learn, and relevant to how they could best learn after their long school day. Their assumptions about the "other" culture of their students and its relationship to learning needed to be examined critically. As well, teaching content areas such as science, art, physical education, and music was a part of their daily schedules. So here again, my linguistic curriculum and my Direct Method of teaching had to be reconceptualized if I were going to be successful with my learners.

Reflecting on both of our stories, we agreed that second and foreign language teachers can profit from viewing teaching as social interaction, subject to the influences and forces of the societies in which it takes place. What we have tried to illustrate in this section are some of the moments when the notion of a "language" and "language learning" warranted careful deliberation to respond to different purposes in learning and different situations, which may be multiple and compete with each other. We indicated through our narratives that our experiences as learners and teachers were influenced by political and ideological factors in our particular geographic areas and we reflected on what directions we would take. Similarly, all language teachers will shape their beliefs about their work and in the everyday methods they use in their classrooms under political influences of some kind and will need to critically reflect on alternatives. To be able to analyze our actions, construct justifications for taking that action, and to consider alternative ways to instruct are essential processes for continual professional development and fulfillment of our commitment in a democratic society to teach *all* learners. We would like to highlight that our assumptions about these issues grow out of our past teaching and learning experiences, which tend to shape what we consider "normal" and what is to be expected in the language classroom. As a start to critically understanding our assumptions and where they come from, we provided part of our histories as language educators in particular institutions that provided us with certain types of support and constraints.

By demonstrating that interpretations of linguistic theories have been predominant in shaping what should be taught and how, we will demonstrate a need to include a discussion of other social and cultural theories that also provide significant directions for conceiving language and language learning. Noticeably missing from both of our narratives were influences that have subsequently caused us to address issues of racism, poverty and social justice (e.g., sexism, classism, sexual orientation biases). In the past, these issues were not given much consideration though it was clear even then that they influenced how learners interacted with members of targeted language communities (Cummins, 2000; Kozol, 1991; Nieto 1992).

In schools across the nation, all teachers of second language learners, particularly bilingual and ESL, face formidable instructional tasks: In addition to helping students learn structures of language, they are also responsible for helping learners adapt to both classroom and societal cultures, solve problems in their daily lives, and develop their intellectual, emotional, and social well-being. Students must also learn how to behave in literate ways to acquire knowledge and demonstrate their abilities through the second language across all subject matter.

It is important for all language teachers to gain an understanding of how language plays a role in shaping learners' thinking and construction of knowledge, how language is a reflection of our identity, and how language works as a way to develop our relationships with the groups into which we are socialized.

THE INTERACTIVE APPROACH: MAKING LEARNING MEANINGFUL

Interactive Learning in Content-Based Language Classes

From a technical viewpoint, it is widely acknowledged that conducting an analysis of learner needs will allow teachers to gather student background information often prior to or at the beginning of instruction. However, in K–12 academic settings for both second and foreign language learners, many states dictate a framework for instruction that guides the range of student learning in terms of sequence and scope. While surveys of students' interests can indicate tentative directions for instruction, creating language learning opportunities with a substantial connection to their communities and their learning in content areas can build literacy and further learning both about language and about content areas. For these reasons, interactive learning opportunities with content and student collaboration in the classroom provide a means for handling more complex language.

REFLECT AND RESPOND

1. In what ways have your notions of language been influenced by your language learning or teaching experiences? Look back on your responses at the beginning of this chapter and try to identify their origins.

   _____

   _____

2. As we evolve as professionals, the progress made in our field opens up new perspectives and concepts to consider when learning and teaching language. Which perspectives and concepts are new to you?

   _____

   _____

3. Write about other personal, professional, political, or ethical issues you face as a language educator.

   _____

   _____

Content-Based Language Learning

One teaching practice that draws on Stephen Krashen's theory of second language learning is integrated language and content instruction, or content-based learning. (You will read more about Krashen's theory later in this chapter.) Krashen's emphasis that success in acquiring a second language depends on focusing on meaning rather than form, on language input being just slightly above the proficiency level of the learner, and in an environment that has ample opportunity for meaningful interaction fits well with the content-based learning approach, which provides conditions similar to those present in first language acquisition (Crandall, 1992).

Custodio and Sutton (1998) showed how **content-based instruction (CBI)** could be used effectively in their own classrooms. Custodio, a middle school ESL teacher, used a **sheltered content model** for developing language with an introduction to U.S. history and culture. Students read historical fiction covering events from the explorations of Christopher Columbus to recent immigration to the United States. Biographies, nonfiction, textbooks, drama, poetry, and multimedia supplemented students' learning. The students experienced many advantages by learning social studies through a variety of language materials: (a) oral and written language skills developed in an integrated way, (b) students experienced the past by imagining what life was like in different places and times, and (c) interdisciplinary activities such as map studies, timelines, art projects, music, and current events could tie into the sheltered content model.

Sutton, a high school ESL teacher, used theme-based units focusing on young adult literature. Novels were selected relating to the students' cultures, varied reading levels, interests, and the degree to which the literature could connect with mainstream language arts classes. For example, the class read a novel, *Letters From Rifka*, about a Russian Jewish immigrant at the turn of the century. Then students learned literary terms, wrote about themes in the book, practiced journal writing and dictionary use, and had meaningful discussions about their own immigration experiences and compared them to those in the novel. The CBI approach in ESL classes can serve as a bridge to mainstream classes providing several important advantages such as: (1) promoting higher-level thinking, (2) allowing for meaningful discussion of students' cultures as reflected in the literature, and (3) reinforcing thinking through manageable amounts of reading, writing, listening, and speaking skills.

A Synthesis of Sociocultural and Psycholinguistic Theories and Practices

Our interactive approach to learning and teaching embraces the teacher's position to choose, through principled decision making, an eclectic method for improving opportunities for learning in his or her classroom. Instructional strategies that have a common focus on using meaningful experiences from the students' own lives to enhance second language learning include such activities as engaging students in dialogue journals, collaborative learning, monitoring how their communication is proceeding individually and as a group, and language inquiry tasks that incorporate content-based language learning. These are derived from theories on learning, the role language plays in content learning, and linguistic theories.

This chapter will focus in part on instructional practices that have evolved from theories on how language is learned based upon interdisciplinary sources contributed by educational theorists, social cognitivists, and sociolinguists, as well as philosophers, anthropologists, and sociologists. Though we will provide examples of how teaching innovations of the last ten to fifteen years have focused on interactive learning that benefit students, we make brief mention of earlier practices in teaching before the focus on the learning process was established. Other sources may be consulted to explore the earlier history of language teaching (Brown, 1987; Hancock & Scebold, 1999; Grenfell, 1999).

Influence of Cognitive Researchers

Since psychology has played an important role in the research on learning, it has been one of the most powerful disciplinary bases in education (Rivers, 1964). As the influence of scientific approaches to human behavior has spread, it also has contributed to our understanding of language learning.

In the late 1950s behaviorist psychology (Skinner, 1957) influenced approaches to language instruction through the work of language educators such as Lado (1964) and Bull (1965, 1972). In this model of language learning, students were to be given a sequence of discrete linguistic patterns that they practiced both in the classroom and language laboratories through many repetitive drills, and memorized dialogues until the patterns became habitual. Learners were expected to accurately reproduce the sound system, **morphology** and **syntax** without error. The linguistic patterns were identified in terms of complexity and learners were expected to proceed hierarchically adding each structure to their repertoire without returning to the same pattern after it was "learned."

The Communicative Approach to learning was introduced as research on the learning of language developed (**pycholinguistics** and **applied linguistics**) and as the research on language as communication in a social context gained acceptance (**sociolinguistics** and **semiotics**). One of the main discoveries from psycholinguistic research was a developmental sequence of language learning that did not support the organization and presentation of linguistic items in classrooms. This discovery indicated that learning of forms was not linear, rather more recursive. Research efforts moved on to identify what types of input would best facilitate the learning process.

An early theorist in the psycholinguistic field was Stephen Krashen, who proposed two distinct processes in developing ability in a second language: (a) acquisition, in which people acquire language as they engage in natural meaningful interaction, and (b) learning, in which people engage in a conscious process of study and attention to form and error correction, usually in formal language classrooms (Lightbown & Spada, 1993a). Krashen viewed language acquisition as the more important process, citing that many speakers are competent without having learned rules, while other speakers may know rules but be unable to apply them correctly when focusing attention on meaningful interaction. Lightbown and Spada (1993a) noted that it has proved to be very difficult to test this hypothesis, and acquisition and learning "would need to be defined more sharply, and controlled and manipulated experimentally" (p. 27). In spite of the difficulty of proving Krashen's hypothesis, it is possible to gather information with the research questions coming from his theory, based on numerous classroom practices to help formulate views on useful teaching strategies.

An applied linguist, Michael Long, another proponent of the interactionist view, agreed with Krashen on the necessity of **comprehensible input:** that learners need to understand messages and that both comprehension and acquisition occur when the linguistic input contains forms and structures that are just slightly beyond the learner's current level of ability (Lightbown & Spada, 1993a). In linguistic shorthand, this is expressed as **i + 1.** Some examples of interactional language learning that he studied between native and nonnative speakers are (a) comprehension checks—Do you understand? (b) clarification checks—Could you say that again? and (c) self-repetition or paraphrase—repeating the sentence partially or entirely.

Lily Wong Fillmore (1991) another applied linguist, contributed a wider view by demonstrating how social, linguistic, and cognitive processes are interconnected in language learning. Social processes occur in settings in which learners have the opportunity to observe language being used in the target language (TL) in natural communication so that eventually learners figure out how the language is structured and used.

Linguistic processes refer to "ways in which assumptions held by the speakers of the target language cause them to speak as they do in talking to learners—in other words, to select, modify, and support the linguistic data they produce for the sake of the learner" (p. 54). Wong Fillmore defined the cognitive processes in capsule form:

> [W]hat the learners have to work with are observations of the social situations in which the language was produced, and streams of vocal sounds produced by speakers according to complex and abstract systems of grammatical and social rules that systematically and symbolically link up sounds, meaning representations, and communicative intentions. What they must do with these data is discover the system of rules the speakers of the language are following, synthesize this knowledge into a grammar and then make it their own by internalizing it. (p. 56)

Wong Fillmore described the major difference between first- and second-language acquisition in terms of first language learning relying more heavily on the human being's species specific capacity to learn languages through a **language acquisition device (LAD);** whereas second language acquisition relies more heavily on general cognitive skills, which are generally well developed by the time individuals learn a second language. Wong Fillmore claimed that "[t]he degree of involvement of these two types of mechanisms is reversed, however, for second-language learning" (p. 58). Further, in second language acquisition, after general cognitive mechanisms are consolidated and assembled, then the LAD device comes into play to synthesize the information into a **"competence grammar"** (p. 59). Although this effort at theory building cannot be proved or disproved, it underscores the importance of social interaction and meaningful experiences in second language acquisition and learning.

Barry McLaughlin (1995), a psycholinguist, also embraces several principles that support second language learning as a social interaction process: (a) "Language is used to communicate meaning," (b) "Language flourishes best in a language-rich environment," and (c) "Children should be encouraged to experiment with language" (pp. 6–8). Teachers must check for feedback from students to see if they understand what is being said. Engaging in practices such as paraphrasing, modeling, and asking questions that clarify meaning can indicate to the teacher how much is being understood by the learner.

The next principle McLaughlin stresses is the idea that teachers should present an environment filled with a variety of books and other printed materials so that students can explore and expand their thinking and use of language. In addition, teachers can model clear speaking, elaborate on the child's speech, explain unfamiliar vocabulary, and stimulate social interaction among children by encouraging them to ask each other for help so that they can practice using language and increase their competency to reflect their learning.

Another meaningful way for children to express themselves is by writing child-generated texts that are based on the students' own cultural experiences. The last principle suggested by McLaughlin focuses on allowing children to experiment with language by not correcting all errors, because mistakes are part of a normal stage in language development that children go through to figure out the patterns and rules of a language. Instead of correcting in a formal manner, teachers can model correct language and expand or rephrase what the child has said. Moreover, students use formulas or chunks of words put together without understanding how they function in the language. Feedback from other children provides the necessary information for students to learn whether they are using the formulas in the appropriate way. So it is actually beneficial to be tolerant of children's mistakes and to support them by supplying correct forms until they can produce language on their own.

McLaughlin's principles (1992) have significance for teaching in several ways. First, teachers need to be aware of cultural differences, to know the patterns involved in second language (L2) learning, and to provide a "variety of instructional activities— small-group work, cooperative learning, peer tutoring, individualized instruction, and other strategies that take the children's diversity of experience into account" (p. 8). Second, all of these teaching strategies involve more social interaction between students and teachers and, as McLaughlin suggests, viewing cultural diversity not as a "problem" but as an "opportunity" to challenge the educational system to become more innovative, which would benefit mainstream students as well as culturally and linguistically diverse students.

From the study of systematic language variation (sociolinguistics), research from another perspective emerged. Language is seen more as both a product and process of becoming members of a social group in a particular context. In addition to geographic differences affecting language variation, economic class, political, age, race, ethnicity and gender also influenced which variation of language and how people learned to communicate. To become members of a social group, **communicative competence** needed to be developed (Canale & Swain, 1980). While applied and psycholinguistic research at the time tended to concentrate on syntax, morphology, and phonological development of a "standard" language, sociolinguistics examined the social reasons for language variations in communication that involved vocabulary, pronunciation, communication styles (rhetorics), and interactional styles in particular social events.

The communicative approach in teaching evolved, influenced by the notion that the act of using language for authentic purposes required the learner to negotiate meaning by functioning in a social interaction that was culturally situated. Thus not only linguistic input, but appropriate socio- and cultural interaction was necessary to be communicatively competent. Consequently, achievement in communication also had to be defined.

Communicative competence, which includes grammatical, sociolinguistics, discourse, and strategic competence, means that students are expected to demonstrate their knowledge about the rules of language, social norms for language use through performing communicative acts, and to use strategies for developing and maintaining conversations or written discourse. Errors are not only allowed but viewed as evidence of active learning. Furthermore, the machine-like and individualistic nuances of an input-negotiation, and output metaphors were challenged by those who identified social contexts (both of the wider community as well as the unfolding events in the classroom) of having substantial influence on language learning. In this way, **language socialization** and development constrasted with the individual mentalistic **language acquisition** model.

Research exploring the connection between socialization to language and learning how to think also emerged as an area significant to language learning. From a level of interaction, Vygotsky's (1987) notions were introduced to explain how development occurs. On a wider level of interaction, notions from social theories also came into our field as language came to be seen as tools for negotiating social, economic, and political power hierarchies that shape and are shaped by language use and development.

According to Vygotsky's sociocultural perspective, language and culture play a critical role in human development (Eggen & Kauchak, 1999). Through social interaction people create knowledge in using their first language, and this use of language helps guide their joint activity in particular settings, allowing for ways of thinking to be shared and learned. Many of Vygotsky's concepts have proven very readily applicable to second language education; two of which are **private speech,** or the self-talk that guides thinking and action, and the **zone of proximal development,** which refers to the range of tasks that a child cannot do alone but can accomplish with assistance. Using these concepts the teacher has three main tasks: (a) assess and gauge the student's ability to understand within the context of a realistic, tangible, and concrete problem; (b) select learning activities and facilitate steps that enhance the chances for learner success; and (c) provide instructional support by scaffolding. Scaffolding includes providing modeling, thinking aloud practice when solving steps to a problem, asking students questions to focus attention and suggesting alternatives. For students with prior literacy, it also includes using prompts and cues such as providing a list of questions to guide students to important information in writing or reading assignments highlighting similarities and differences in rhetorically structuring arguments, cohesive and coherence building, tone and audience considerations for lexical choices. While Vygotsky researched first language development, his contributions have been taken up by researchers in the bilingualism and second language field and more recently in the foreign language field (Lantolf, 2000; Hall, 2000; Takahashi, Austin, & Morimoto, 2000; Ohta, 2001).

In further examining classroom life, research from critical theorists allowed us to see classrooms not as neutral objective laboratories, but rather places where social dynamics and hierarchical power relationships influence who learns, what is learned, and how learning counts for whom and by whom (Fairclough,1989; Gee,1992; Pennycook, 1998). Any use of language necessarily incorporates cultural referents (from the past) and the negotiation of meaning has an impact on the future use of communication. Through socialization into groups within a particular culture, learners may recognize the diversity of choice to use these referents (Bakhtin, 1981). Nonetheless not all variations of language are respected or valued. Often variations with "cultural capital," a currency or value in a particular dominant social group (Bourdieu, 1986), are used to exclude or disenfranchise members of the community who use other varieties (Hooks, 1991; Smitherman, 1995; Bourdieu, 1986; Fairclough, 1989). For this reason, critical research examines the consequences of such social forces, particularly for students who are often considered "unsuccessful." As well as the socioliguistic framework, language is considered as a tool of "action and power" in shaping social relations and worldviews.

These sociocultural theories have deep resonance for pedagogical practice. For learners in a second language classroom, learning language is not just an individual mental event to gain communicative competence or even linguistic knowledge. The process entails a socialization towards the dominant culture's ways of using language and literacy, which could often present conflicts or mismatches with the student's home cultures and languages. Too often the student is faced not with adding a new language, but with replacing one with another. The response to learning then could manifest itself by the learner's assimilation, accommodation, or resistance to instruction. Research has proliferated in identifying the mismatches and conflicts in order to help teachers provide more culturally responsive instruction to diverse students. While much of the second language acquisition research is aimed at the beginning level of learners, studies from the critical perspective examine how later successful learners are identified and the conditions in which they are seen as "successful" or not. The characteristics of their struggles and interactions within institutions are studied to find out how they became successful.

THE ROLE OF INTERACTION IN LANGUAGE AND LITERACY LEARNING

When people interact they do so for a purpose and in ways that are socially conventionalized for personal development and interpersonal cooperation. Language and nonverbal cues are an important part of the communication system used for these interactions. Language is learned and used through interactions in which people establish their identity and maintain relationships, and avoid or negotiate conflicts and learn. Through language use, people construct and transmit knowledge about their world, sometimes intentionally, sometimes unintentionally, and uncritically. Nonverbal signs include **visual, olfactory, gestural,** and **kinesthetic cues** that are recognized as meaningful and can influence meaning. Some of these nonverbal cues can signal the first expressions of feelings. Darting glances, a fixed gaze, as well as silence and movement all convey potential meanings in context. When ways of believing, relating, and sharing knowledge through language become agreed upon and used by a community, the language use becomes part of the creation of the membership process. The interaction with cultural and social conventions in first languages (L1) allows for learners to appropriate these in contexts where they are being supported (Wolfram, Adger, & Christian, 1999). The interaction may trigger internalization of language, and then interaction with more skillful members of the same community can foment language development (Vygotsky, 1987). Thus all communication is culturally embedded and at the same time, because of the activity of its members, new conventions of language and knowledge are created over time. One significant illustration of such conventions is literacy. Interaction with literacy is similarly dependent on cultural and social conventions being appropriated as well and occurs in homes, schools, and the community (Au, 1995; Egan-Robertson, 1998). For this reason, identifying appropriate goals, creating supportive conditions, and activities to promote language development through interactivity are important concepts for teachers to understand. This will be further developed in Chapters 3 and 4.

THINK, PAIR, SHARE

Answer the following questions with a partner.

Call to mind how your interactions using a language affect your learning of that language, your image of yourself, your representation of what you know, and your understanding of that culture. List a few of the ways that your interactions with the language, with people who use the language, and your reflections have affected your language learning.

1. What kinds of interactions lead to more learning or impeded your learning? How?

   _____

   _____

2. How might being literate affect how you approach language learning?

   _____

   _____

INTERACTION AND ROLES OF FIRST (L1) AND SECOND LANGUAGE (L2)

Because learners of a subsequent language (L2) already have conventions in their first language (L1) background, these can be their potential resources. Major questions you may want to consider are:

- How can I use resources from the students' L1 that can help students learn L2?

- How can I create meaningful and relevant activities to facilitate using the L2 for a sustained period of interaction with L1 so that learners take on new roles, gain access and practice in these roles, improve their skills in using language and literacy for authentic purposes, and gain apprenticeship in critical thinking processes to act on improving their world?

Why language study ← - How can we critically help students to focus attention on the role of language in these activities—at discourse, pragmatic, syntactic, morphological, and lexical levels?

We have drawn upon five attributes of interaction that have been explored in both the applied linguistic and psycholinguistic literature as well as sociocultural research:

Meaningful interaction
Authentic interaction
Relevant interaction
Reflection and Action
Feedback

Meaningful Interaction

From an applied linguistic framework, linguistic input in the target language has been shown to become comprehensible through interaction; that is, when a person attempts to make information known to another and attempts to make sense of information that has been expressed by others. An active learner who has a purpose in a particular inter-action and who must use language to communicate that purpose negotiates meaning. It is assumed that if both interlocutors share similar information, a need for communi-cation will not exist. Applied linguistic research by Pica, Young, and Doughty (1987) has identified that "gap" as necessary to precipitate communication between two inter-locutors, and investigated different types of negotiation tasks that required overcoming this comprehension gap. Because not all interaction leads to intentional learning of a targeted goal, the interaction's direction and what is accomplished through the inter-action became the object of applied linguistic research in the late '80s and '90s. Through successive attempts to communicate, if the linguistic input becomes noticed and comprehensible, interaction can help learners attend to and acquire structures in a second language (Swain, 1995; Chaudron & Parker, 1990; Skehan, 1996).

Sociocultural research consists of studies that situate and analyze human behavior in a social context. The studies we draw from examine communication from various dis-ciplines, particularly from sociolinguistics, anthropology, ethnomethology, philosophy, and critical studies. Contextualized studies of communication include relevant histories of the interlocutors, their relationships, site and time of their interactions, and power relations in a particular culture. As well, studies from these fields are part of an inter-pretative paradigm in which an interaction's direction and what is accomplished is always seen from a view that is partial, from a particular perspective, and often contradictory.

These interpretations of interactions are partial as they conform to aspects of what each field has accepted for guiding interpretations. Common to these studies is the attempt to understand naturally occurring communication from the participants' per-spectives. Because interaction is researched from the perspectives of the participants, what each participant attends to in conversation reveals different aspects of what is on going at a particular time and space. Multiple perspectives from any interaction are inevitable. The same interaction may afford learners different outcomes depending on their orientation to, receptivity to, and interaction with the context of the unfolding interaction.

For teachers, working with learners to establish a common focal point through dialogue that seeks mutuality will need to provide learners with opportunities to artic-ulate their personal meanings and viewpoints (Schön, 1983). Working from learners' perspectives will help the teacher to determine which interactive moments lend them-selves to what kind of teaching and for whom (Tharp & Gallimore, 1991). These judgment calls occur in planning, throughout implementation of lessons, and after-ward, and need to be monitored and reflected on.

Authentic Interactions

In recognizing the importance of **authenticity** in interactions, psycholinguistic and applied linguistic research in second language has identified certain characteristics which promote linguistic competencies (morphosyntactic). These foster the learners' automatization and restructuring of linguistic information by helping them notice the gap between their current levels of production and subsequently make changes. Loschky and Bley Vroman (1993) suggest that instruction

teaching

1. make tasks that require the natural use of certain essential grammatical features in communication;
2. provide time for noticing gaps in knowledge of grammar;
3. provide sufficient and task appropriate feedback to help noticing the featured form by focusing learner's attention.

Face-to-face interactions with a target language also offer the opportunity to learn how to deal with one's own spontaneous oral communication and to negotiate oral communication from others. Therefore strategic communication skills may develop as interaction is sustained and becomes more successful. Strategic competencies are fostered by interactions where an exchange is encouraged to overcome gaps in information by such activities as:

- using background knowledge (schemata)
- combining semantic and pragmatic based strategies
- stretching what is known to compensate for what is not known

Authentic interactions from a sociocultural perspective would be those in which problem-posing, inquiry, and creative solutions are possible for the learner to understand how language functions to present various perspectives on the world, to voice one's position, and to act in one's own interests and in the interests of one's community. Rather than being a pedagogic exercise to rehearse linguistic skills, authentic interactions here would have the learners involved in purposeful social action using language that potentially offers them opportunity to transform their reality. (We'll see examples of authentic interactions in the chapters on listening and literacy development, oral language, and written language.)

Relevant Interaction

Through an analysis of functions and notions deemed important to the settings in which the learners are expected to interact, teachers decide the relevance of interactions for learners. From a psycholinguistic framework, teachers may carry out needs assessments to identify the learners' needs. Programs of instruction have been created to prepare students in such areas as academic language, language for specific purposes, foreign language exploratory programs, and language for literary analysis. (For curriculum design or syllabus design, see Widdowson, 1978; Mumby, 1978; Nunan, 1988, and others.) Analyses such as these generate programs of study intended to prepare learners to use language in context. Analyses may also be used in the design of activities or tasks that approximate challenges similar to those faced in the setting of interaction. See task-based instruction (e.g., Crooke & Gass, 1993; Crookall & Oxford, 1990; Nunan, 1989).

The main impetus is to create very similar experiences or simulate them through games in order to allow for linguistic practice. An area in which intensive focus has been placed is academic language and literacy developed through content areas (Chamot & O'Malley, 1987). Strategies to building linguistic and learning skills through content areas will be addressed in the upcoming chapters. The challenge exists in creating increasingly cognitively demanding opportunities to build language ability through content study.

From a critical sociocultural framework, relevant interactions would be those used to encourage the construction of knowledge and identities as language learners who are able to act on their own behalf. In particular, relevant interactions would extend the learner's current ability with supportive feedback until the learner could use the language independently and work collaboratively for the interests of their communities.

Relevant interaction in critical literacy would mean not merely replicating the language genres but examining them and using them to find alternatives to social reproduction of hierarchies based on differences such as ethnicity, race, gender, and class. Reading, writing, speaking, and listening are not seen as independent skills, rather as mutually supportive of cognitive and social development and thus interdependent in a particular cultural context. Achievement occurs when learners appropriate the symbol systems (e.g., oral, written, visual) to imagine and compose different and transformative futures.

We included our narratives in the "Setting the Stage" section earlier in this chapter to show how we became apprentices entering into a culturally sanctioned way of participation by joining this professional culture of language education. Since cultures provide different semiotic tools[1] for its members, trying to join any culture will require understanding what these tools are, how they are used, and for what purposes. Oral and written communication are a part of these tools. Also, as literacy instruction forms the major socialization events in schools, researchers from this line of investigation have analyzed how schooled literacies in English as a first and second language function to create hierarchies in relation to the different languages and literacies that learners bring with them, dismissing, and excluding nonstandard practices (Hooks, 1991; Tollefson, 1995; Durgunoglu, 1998). Cummins (2000) and Willett (1991) explore alternatives to ensuring success that are more inclusive and supportive of students in multilingual and multicultural communities.

In research from **critical studies,**[2] the historical and local locations of the participants from diverse communities are highlighted to show connections between the present classroom language learning realities and their connections to broader social economic and political realities—in essence, how inequities persist because of

---

[1] Semiotics is the study of signs that are used to represent meaning. These historically have connotations and interpretations. Signs and their referents are united by a culture's attaching meaning between these. Thus learning to be a member of a culture means learning to attach significance to some representations and not others. Danesi (2000) claims that learning these associative thinking processes takes "considerable amount of time to develop in the SL." (P. 67)

[2] We use critical studies here to encompass four areas of research: critical cultural studies (e.g., Bourdieu, Hall, Hooks, Lather), critical pedagogy (e.g., Freire, Giroux, Macedo, Nieto, Walsh), critical literacy (e.g., Auerbach, Benesch, Cushman, Fairclough, Luke, Norton) and critical language studies (e.g., Corson, Rampton, Pennycook). While all share a research agenda to uncover the use of power through different semiotic analyses, each focuses on different arenas of inquiry, communication systems, instructional practices, literacy that enables one to see and use power relations constructed through printed or oral practices. Their agenda may differ from goals of deconstructing symbols and myths, creating emancipatory interventions in teaching and learning or highlighting the power of ideology and how it works through language and literacy. Each type of critical study contributes to different areas from communication and sociology to education and language and literacy studies.

unquestioned institutional practices (McLaren, 1993). Precisely because second language and foreign language learners step into a context whose hierarchies are unknown, critical literacy and language awareness would help them uncover these histories and assumptions. As well through critical pedagogy, learners would study how to use language and literacy to change pressing social conditions in their class, school, and communities.

Reflection and Action

A final aspect of interaction is the relationship between reflection and action. From psycholinguistic research, metacognition, and metalinguistic awareness results form a dialectical relationship between learners' experiences and their reflection. Developing skills in these important cognitive processes allows for learners to develop better self-awareness and control, automaticity, and ability to make changes in their linguistic behaviors. In other words, by becoming aware of one's thinking, feelings, and actions, students can use their efforts for greater monitoring and control of these processes. Over time these may potentially lead to full automatization of processes that can help learning language and literacy. To develop this type of reflection, instructing learners about cognitive and metacognitive strategies is important. In fact, it is not surprising that from this viewpoint, students would be encouraged to engage in hypothesis testing and generate feedback through their interaction with others, which would enable them to notice gaps between the levels of their current skill as compared to the higher level needed for reaching mastery of the target language. Then with overt attention to these gaps, learners plan their response to gain greater mastery.

As part of Vygotsky's theory of learning, **social constructivism** holds the tenets that knowledge is constructed through meaningful interaction between what one already knows and what is new. The kinds of past experiences as well as the ways these experiences are organized influence the construction process. Reflection plays a major role in organizing and converting past experiences into knowledge. Critical studies would promote a reflection that is then turned towards using the new understanding to change oppressive conditions.* In this way, learners are also developing identities as active in the construction of more equitable communities.

Feedback

Rather than attending to correct language forms to evaluate the learners' language ability, feedback is given to help learners complete tasks. The high frequency of language use and the interactional demands influence the learner's ability to learn the discourses in the classroom to participate meaningfully in the communicative practices of the wider communities. If feedback is limited to linguistic forms, learners will begin to value the accuracy of forms over the functionality of these forms to convey their thoughts and build further knowledge. If feedback balances the need to encourage learners to express their thoughts as they learn to manage their language production, learners become aware of

* *Praxis*: "a theory informed action."

REFLECT AND RESPOND

1. *Communicative competence* means

   _____

   _____

2. Give one example of *private speech*

   _____

   _____

3. Make a list of three activities that might be useful to teachers for ensuring that every learner's identity is celebrated

   _____

   _____

the need to refine their language use as a means of communicating their feelings, understanding and new knowledge to a variety of audiences for a variety of purposes. Thus they are shaping their own identities through communication.

SECOND LANGUAGE TEACHING STRATEGIES

One of the major issues in second language learning is the debate over traditional teaching methods versus innovative teaching methods. Thomas and Collier (1999) defined traditional teaching methods as "classes that are more text-book driven and very teacher-controlled, where students have few opportunities to interact with each other" (p. 8a). Consider the following finding in a report by a U.S. Department of Education-sponsored national study:

> Direct observations reveal that teachers do most of the talking in classrooms, making about twice as many utterances as do students. . . . In over half of the interactions that teachers have with students, students do not produce any language. . . . When students do respond, typically they provide only simple information recall statements. This pattern of teacher–student interaction not only limits a student's opportunity to create and manipulate language freely, but also limits the student's ability to engage in more complex learning. (Ramirez, Yuen, & Ramey, 1991, p. 8)

This model of instruction in which a teacher asks a question, the student responds, and the teacher evaluates the response is a very different discourse than more

THINK, PAIR, SHARE

After reading this chapter, complete the following activity with a partner.

1. After reading this chapter, this is what I think is most important about language learning, sociocultural, and psycholinguistic theories.

   _____

   _____

2. After reading, here is what I learned from my partner. Listen to what your partner has written and write down what you learned from her or him.

   _____

   _____

recent **dialogic** approaches developed in the last ten to fifteen years that focus on learning practices facilitated by instruction. According to Thomas and Collier (1999):

> [C]urrent approaches focus on interactive, discovery, hands-on learning. Teachers in these classes often use cooperative learning, thematic interdisciplinary lessons, literacy development across the curriculum, process writing, performance and portfolio assessment, microcomputers, critical thinking, learning strategies, and global perspectives infused into the curriculum. (P. 8a)

These current instructional practices offer an interesting way to incorporate variety into the classroom learning process, thus stimulating motivation. Ongoing staff development can help teachers to implement these techniques.

SUMMARY

Many disciplines contribute insights for language instruction. In the past, psychology has held a firm lead in generating directions for educational practices. However, in the past thirty years, fields that have distinct theoretical bases in the fields of applied linguistics, anthropology, sociology, and philosophy have contributed to the research on language, language learning, and teaching. Language educators in particular can benefit from understanding how to draw on these disciplines to make classroom contexts more supportive of diverse learners.

We have shown that every language lesson, classroom, program, and policy departs in some way from a set of beliefs about language and language learning. No single learning theory accounts for all the variety that exists in the ways language learners develop ability in a subsequent language and literacy. This underscores how complex human behavior is, and how complex the purposes for language use are: for learning language, constructing knowledge, and forming identities.

Both psycholinguistic research and sociocultural research provide bases for informing our decisions about teaching. While the literature from psycholinguistic research attempts to provide universal rules about second language acquisition and factors of mental processes or stages that an individual may undergo, the research from socio-cultural perspectives identifies the particularities of learning in an identified social context. Seen from sociocultural lenses, learning language is first and foremost a learner in a social, dynamic, and interactive context. Principles derived from sociocultural research help teachers examine how to mediate learners' active development in collaborative, inclusive classrooms.

For this reason, as teachers we must use, observe, and develop professional judgment in our application of any particular theory. Our success with real learners in a given context is impacted by our decisions to be responsive to their struggles and to do so in an informed manner that builds our theories of language and language learning for success.

EXERCISES AND ACTIVITIES
DISCUSS AND REFLECT

1. The communicative language teaching approach borrowed similar organizational sequences, namely simple-to-complex, from a behaviorist model. However, this approach replaced linguistic structures with language functions; e.g., self-introductions, forming questions, making requests, apologizing. In what ways do you see learning from this approach being advantageous or disadvantageous when compared to a behaviorist classroom? In what ways are the learners in the two models similar?

2. Undeniably there are similarities and differences between second language acquisition and learning, and foreign language learning and acquisition. On the basis of your response contrast the two with respect to:
   - where learners come into contact with the language
   - who learners are
   - who determines learners' needs
   - their overall education attainment and their length of language study
   - developmental stages identified
   - how variability across learners is recognized and responded to
   - how errors are handled
   - what level of language developed; for example, words, structure, pronunciation, discourse
   - how and when academic content is learned through the language
   - how curricula are set up
   - what consequences for lack of success exist?
   - other

ASK YOURSELF THESE QUESTIONS

1. How do your notions about *language learning* versus *language acquisition* impact your instructional strategies or assessment?

2. In what ways do the sociocultural theories resonate or not with your current or future pedagogical practice?

3. What is *linguistic knowledge* and how does/will it impact your teaching?

WHAT DO TEACHERS THINK?

Why is it important for language teachers to know about language acquisition and language learning? We all wonder why it is necessary to take courses whose focus is primarily based on theories and research. Further, we continually ask ourselves, "What does this have to do with teaching?" As a veteran eighteen-year teacher, I feel amply experienced to attest to the importance of not only understanding language acquisition and language learning, but being able to apply those theories to practice. As a teacher, we should be able to determine where our students are, both cognitively and socially. It is important to know what is learnable at what point in time. This is, of course, more easily said than done. Lightbown (1998) notes that the heterogeneity of classes is a well-known reality and developmentally targeted teaching would be very difficult to organize. Ellis (1997) points out that second language acquisition (SLA) research findings do not provide straightforward guidance for the teacher and probably never will. They are not generally presented in ways accessible or meaningful to teachers, and SLA research agendas do not necessarily match the areas in which teachers are most concerned.

However, SLA research does offer a wide variety of concepts and descriptive accounts which can help teachers interpret and make better sense of their own classroom experiences, as well as provide ideas for classroom use. For example, SLA research has provided descriptive accounts of the course of interlanguage development showing that, while learners follow relatively invariant routes of learning, these routes are not linear and during phases of interlanguage restructuring apparent regression occurs. My background and knowledge of language learning and language acquisition have served me well. I am absolutely convinced that having this knowledge base has greatly contributed to my ability to skillfully apply theory to my everyday practice.
Michelina H. Main, ESL Teacher, San Antonio, Texas

FIELD-BASED EXPERIENCES

In your school district or school, find out if any teacher is engaged in trying an innovation in her classroom. Find out how language is being defined in this innovation. What theories are used to support her instructional decision making? What is she learning about her students' language and literacy development, their identities as learners, and their progress in learning subject matter? What are the discoveries she made about her innovation? Share what you have learned in class.

CASE STUDY

Gisela Zuniga has been a kindergarten–third-grade bilingual/ESL teacher for the past ten years in an urban school district that receives many return migrant students from Puerto Rico. Depending on limitations of the family's finances, many students spend varying amounts of the academic year in Puerto Rico and other stretches of time in the city. Gisela's school district has decided to officially eliminate Transitional Bilingual Education but will extend ESL services. In all formerly bilingual classes, the district's plans are to include more native speakers of English, the majority of whom are speakers of African American Vernacular English. Since Gisela will be teaching kindergarteners, she is excited about the possibility of building a dual language program with the bilingual teachers of her school and the teachers in the mainstream. Despite some conflict about the amount of time that was supposed to be dedicated to direct ESL instruction, both the bilingual teachers and the principal worked out a rationale that explained how English as a medium of instruction would be used to build comprehension with both groups—and as a bonus, how students would learn Spanish. After an assembly where information was available to parents in Spanish and English, the principal announced that all parents of kindergarteners could choose either to enroll in the dual language or all-English medium classroom. To his surprise, the majority of the parents, both Spanish speaking and English speaking, chose the dual language program. There were barely enough students in the English-only medium to constitute a class.

Gisela's plan to have an entire class in which at any moment a child could be learning through his or her second language, made her more conscious about her need to plan how she was going to choose English and Spanish for her instruction and how she was going to help her students become at ease and flourish in their second language environment. Gisela decided to use themes that could help student build positive identities through their language use. Her themes were *Me, My Family, My Neighborhood*, and would serve to meet ESL, language arts, art, and social and physical education development objectives. She selected highly colorful materials that would let students learn how to describe themselves, family, and friends through reading and making charts, posters, postcards, and maps. Her goal was to help students formulate questions about their communities that served as inquiry projects to map the city neighborhood by neighborhood. Gisela thought this would help her students connect their lives to school experiences and the school with their communities. This was the beginning for doing more exploration and for using language learning to communicate this learning to different audiences.

1. What are some arguments for using the strengths of students' past language learning experiences upon which to build proficiency in another language and literacy?

2. What advice would you give Gisela in making her classroom welcoming to both groups of students?

3. What suggestions would help Gisela in monitoring her language use in lessons in English for her English speakers and for her English language learners (ELLs)?

4. What suggestion would help Gisela in monitoring her language use in Spanish for her Spanish speakers and English speakers?

5. What other issues may arise given her mobile student population and the language varieties that she has represented in her community?

ACTION RESEARCH

As both ESL and foreign language teachers are challenged to create ways to actively engage students in meaningful instruction that develops their self-esteem, language, and content knowledge as well as values and thinking abilities, an action research project collaboratively undertaken with students can be a highly meaningful endeavor. Read the following list of potential projects. Being able to proficiently engage in oral and written language by the end of language study is probably one of the most motivating and empowering experiences students can have. These projects set in motion a dynamic use of language as social action.

Read the following list of potential projects.

1. Legacy curricula: building up to leave something behind
   - What would students want to change in their school, community, state? Brainstorm, categorize. Decide what resources would be needed and what constraints you would have. Discuss which would be achievable. Plan how to achieve, and document the process.
   - Invite others to help solve a problem.
   - Build something, such as a project, toy, game, or brochure.

2. Global interconnectedness
   - Exploration into the economies in the classroom, school or community. Students may question what is valued, how is it structured, how it works, who decides distribution, how did they get it, and how it can be changed.
   - Ecologies school: What limited resources are in danger of extinction, depletion? Any resources not recognized? How are they used? How can they be replaced, replenished, conserved? How and why?
   - Community's exploration of range of entertainment: Students think about their daily lives and the types and locations of their entertainment—video, movies, comics, music, dance. What entertainment comes from which countries? How are they distributed, promoted? They may select one and examine: What values are shared, not shared, and by whom? Do some people benefit and not others? What are the consequences? What can we do about them?

3. Creative arts
   - Compile and record a list of plays, games, rhymes, riddles that the students know. Create booklets for each category. Have students perform, then record either oral or written, then replay or reread the entries for the class, other classes, parents, the community. Then store in the class or school library.
   - Find out what literature, poetry, and novels students will be introduced to in higher grade levels. Then help students create their own literature around similar themes, genres, to share in a culminating performance for their classmates, higher grades, and community.

- Students identify what designs they are interested in: e.g., dress, architecture, automobiles. Have them find a design that they appreciated and try to analyze what features were included. They then learn to plan new designs using these features and a graphic organizer. How are these features influenced by cultures' social groups, geography, weather, economies, power, etc.? Students would collaborate on generating ideas for new designs to deal with the variables that have influenced these designs and communicate these to different community groups affected by these designs to get their responses.

4. Rewriting history project
    - What people don't know about . . . but want to learn. Read the essays or analyze interviews to find out what is admitted as unknown. Compile a list of the areas, group into categories, and decide which will be investigated. Identify a plan to answer questions: sources of information, who will gather which, decide format for the presentation of the project, and time frame.
    - What people think they know about. . . . (Reread the list of what people don't know and compare to what was learned.)
    - What people have to know. . . . (Read the list of the questions that were answered, name the ways information was gathered and how analysis was carried out. Class members in audience will recognize what was well done and help think of ways to increase the quality of the project findings or presentation.)

5. Tying language to your future career/specialization—acting like a specialist
    - Explore what language is typical for a specific profession.
    - Inquire about community institutions, public or private, willing to employ your students.
    - Look for a career: What types of communication are needed?
    - Find out what is done at the job and what types of communication occur there.
    - Find out the institutional hierarchy—who's in charge and who does what types of communication?
    - Decide what you want to become and why.
    - Inquire into how to prepare for such a job.

As you tailor your instruction to specific learners, keep track of your instructional practices and the types of struggles that you encounter. Have students write about their struggles in their project log book (distinct from their dialogue journals). On a periodic basis, use a class session for students to work in groups in reading, categorizing, and compiling the responses into a single chart. Determine the priority of the concerns raised and dedicate time to brainstorming solutions or suggestions. Have each student decide upon an individual solution as well as a class solution. Discuss benefits and drawbacks of the solutions that have been proposed for the group. Allow the class to decide on which one benefits the whole class and does not exclude anyone.

Foreign language teachers may need to decide in which language each phase is conducted so as to allow students ease of expression but also access to practice using the target language for such decision making.

ADDITIONAL RESOURCES

Ovando, C., & Collier, V. (1998). *Bilingual and ESL classrooms: Teaching in multicultural contexts*. Boston: McGraw-Hill.

Brown, D. (2001). *Teaching by principles: An interactive approach to language pedagogy*. White Plains, NY: Longman.

GLOSSARY OF TERMS

applied linguistics   the study of structure and variation of language

authenticity   bearing a direct resemblance to reality, also refers to actions that are intrinsically motivated (vanLier, 1996)

communicative competence   refers to knowledge or capability relating to the rules of language use

competence grammar   having to do with correct sentences of a language

comprehensible input   aural reception of language that is just a little beyond the learner's level

content   subjects in a curriculum, e.g., history, math, science

content-based instruction (CBI)   the concurrent study of language and subject matter

critical studies   examines influence of race, ethnicity, class and gender and relations of power

cues   indicators or signals

culturally responsive   instruction or materials that respond to the cultural diversity of the learners

dialogic   through discussion to invite and enable students/peers to engage in collaborative inquiry, extend knowledge to improve a situation

gestural   to show or express by using gestures

kinesthetic   movement

language acquisition   represents 'unconscious' learning that takes place when the emphasis is on communication

language acquisition device (LAD)   Chomsky (1965) concluded that children are born with some kind of special language processing ability

language socialization   learners are socialized through language as they are socialized to use language

morphology   the study of structure and form of words in a language

olfactory   sense of smell

private speech   Vygotskian concept that refers to the verbalized thinking that guides one's own mental activity

psycholinguistics   the study of the influence of psychological factors on the development, use, and interpretation of language

semiotics   the theory and study of signs and symbols, especially as elements of language

sheltered content model   language-sensitive content instruction

social constructivism   a learning theory that holds that truth, meaningfulness, and knowledge are created by and create social realities

sociolinguistics   the study of language and linguistic behavior as influenced by social and cultural factors

syntax   the study of the rules in which words or other elements of sentence structure are combined to form grammatical sentences

zone of proximal development   an instructional conversation in which the teacher listens carefully to grasp the students' communicative intent, and tailors the dialogue to meet the emerging understanding of the learners (Ovando & Collier, 1998)

REFERENCES

Au, K. H. (1995). Multicultural perspectives on literacy research. *Journal of Reading Behavior*, 27(1), 85–100.

Bakhtin, M. (1981). The Dialogic Imagination: Four essays of M. M. Bakhtin, trans. Caryl Emerson & Michael Holquist; ed: Michael Holquist. Austin: University of Texas Press.

Bourdieu, P. (1986). The forms of capital. In J. G. Richardson (ed.), *Handbook of theory and research for the sociology of education* (pp. 241–258). New York: Greenwood.

Brown, H. D. (1987). *Principles of language learning & teaching*. Englewood Cliffs, NJ: Prentice Hall Regents.

Bull, W. E. (1965). *Spanish for teachers; Applied linguistics*. New York: Ronald Press.

Bull, W. E. (1972). *Spanish for communication* [by]. [and others] Editorial advisor: George E. Smith. Boston: Houghton Mifflin [1971–74, v. 1, c1972]

Canale, M. & Swain, M. (1980). Theoretical bases of communicative approaches to second language teaching and testing. *Applied Linguistics, 1*(1), 1–47.

Chamot, A. & O'Malley, J. (1987). The cognitive academic language learning approach: A bridge to the mainstream. *TESOL Quarterly, 12,* 227–249.

Chaudron, C. & Parker, K. (1990). Discourse markedness and structural markedness. *Studies in Second Language Acquisition, 12*(2), 43–64.

Chomsky, N. (1965). *Aspects of the theory of syntax.* Cambridge, MA: MIT Press.

Crandall, J. A. (1992). Content-centered learning in the United States. *Annual Review of Applied Linguistics, 13,* 111–126.

Crookall, D., & Oxford, R. (1990). *Simulation, gaming, and language learning.* New York: Newbury House.

Crookes, G., & Gass, S. (1993). *Task and language learning: Integrating theory and practice. Vol 1.* Clevedon, UK: Multilingual Matters.

Cummins, J. (2000). *Language, power, and pedagogy. Bilingual children in the crossfire.* Clevedon, UK: Multilingual Matters.

Custodio, B., & Sutton, M. J. (1998). Literature-based ESL for secondary school students. *TESOL Journal, 7*(5), 19–23.

Durgunoglu, A. Y. (1998). Acquiring literacy in English and Spanish in the United States. (pp. 135–145). In A. Y. Durgunoglu & Verhoeven (eds.). *Literacy development in a multicultural context.* Mahwah, NJ: Lawrence Erlbaum.

Egan-Robertson, A. (1998). Learning about culture, language, and power: Understanding relationships among personhood, literacy practices, and intertextuality. *Journal of Literacy Research, 30*(4), 449–487.

Eggen, P. D. & Kauchak, D. P. (1999). *Educational psychology: windows on classrooms.* Upper Saddle River, NJ: Merrill.

Ellis, R. (1997). *The Study of second language acquisition.* Oxford University Press.

Fairclough, N. (1989). *Language and power.* New York: Longman.

Gee, J. P. (1992). *The social mind: Language, ideology, and social practice.* New York: Bergin & Gravey.

Grenfell, M. (1999). Language: Construction of an object of research. In M. Grenfell & M. Kelly (eds.), *Bourdieu: Language, culture and education. Theory into practice.* Bern: Peter Lang.

Hall, J. K. & Verplaestse, L. S. (eds.). (2000). *Second and foreign language learning through classroom interaction.* Mahwah, NJ: Lawrence Erlbaum.

Hancock, C. R., & Scebold, C. E. (1999). Defining moments in foreign language and second language education during the last half of the twentieth century. In D. Birckbichler & R. M. Terry (eds.) (pp. 19–50), *Reflecting on the past to shape the future.* Lincolnwood, IL: National Textbook Company.

Hooks, B. (1991). Narratives of struggle. In P. Mariani (ed.) (pp. 53–61), *Critical fictions: The politics of imaginative writing.* Seattle, WA: Bay Press.

Huber, T., Kline, F.M., Bakken, L., & Clark, F. (1997). Transforming teacher education including culturally responsible pedagogy. In J. E. King, E. R. Hollins, & W. C. Hayman (Eds.), *Preparing teachers for cultural diversity.* (pp. 129–145). New York: Teachers College Press.

Kozol, J. (1991). *Savage Inequalities.* NY: Crown Publishers.

Lado, R. (1964). *Language teaching: A scientific approach.* New York: McGraw-Hill.

Lantolf, J. (ed.) (2000). *Sociocultural theory and second language learning.* Oxford, UK: Oxford University Press.

Lightbrown, J. M., & Spada, N. (1995). *How languages are learned.* London: Oxford University Press.

Loschky, L. & Bley-Vroman, R. (1993). Grammar and task-based methodology. In G. Crookes and S. Gass, editors, *Tasks and Language Learning: Integrating theory and Practice* (pp 123–167). Clevedon, England: Multilingual Matters.

McLaren, P. L. (1993). *Schooling as ritual performance: Towards a political economy of educational symbols and gestures* (2, ed.) London: Routledge.

McLaughlin, B. (1992). *Myths and Misconceptions about Second Language Learning: What Every Teacher needs to Unlearn* (Educational Practice Report No. 5) Washington, DC: Office of Educational Research & Improvement (ERIC Doc. Reprod. Service No. ED 352806).

McLaughlin, B. (1995). *Fostering Second language development in young children: principals & practices.* (Educational Practice Report.) Washington, DC: Office of Educational Research & Improvement. (ERIC Document Reproductive Service No. ED 386932).

Mumby, J. (1978). *Communicative syllabus design.* Cambridge, UK: Cambridge University Press.

Nieto, S. (1992). *Affirming diversity: The sociopolitical context of multicultural education.* New York: Longman.

Nunan, D. (1988). *The learner-centred curriculum: A study in second language teaching*. Cambridge, UK: Cambridge University Press.

Nunan, D. (1989). *Designing tasks for the communicative classroom*. Cambridge, UK: Cambridge University Press.

Ohta, A. (2001). *Second language acquisition processes in the classroom. Learning Japanese*. Mahwah, NJ: Lawrence Erlbaum.

Pennycook, A. (1998). The right to language: Towards a situated ethics of language possibilities. *Language Sciences, 20*(1), 73–87.

Pica, T., Young, R., & Doughty, C. (1987). The impact of interaction on comprehension. *TESOL Quarterly 21*(4), 737–58.

Ramirez, J. D., Yuen, S. D. & Ramey, D. R. (1991). *Longitudinal study of structured English immersion strategy, early-exit, and late-exit transitional bilingual education programs for language-minority children*. San Mateo, CA: Aguirre International.

Rivers, W. (1964). *The psychologist and the foreign language teacher*. Chicago: University of Chicago Press.

Schön, D. (1983). *Educating the reflective practitioner: Toward a new design for teaching and learning in the professions*. San Francisco: Jossey-Bass.

Skehan, P. (1996). A framework for the implementation of task-based instruction. *Applied Linguistics, 17*(1), 38–62.

Skinner, B. F. (1957). *Verbal behavior*. New York: Appleton-Century Crofts.

Smitherman, G. (1995). Students' right to their own language: A retrospective. *English Journal, 84*, 21–27.

Swain, M. (1995). Three functions of output in second language learning. In G. Cook & B. Seidlhofer (eds.) (pp. 125–144), *Principle and practice in applied linguistics*. Oxford: Oxford University Press.

Takahashi, E., Austin, T., & Morimoto, Y. (2000). Social interaction and language development in a FLES classroom. In J. K. Hall & L. S. Verplaestse (eds.) (pp. 139–59), *Second and foreign language learning through classroom interaction*. Mahwah, NJ: Lawrence Erlbaum.

Tharp, R. G., & Gallimore, R. (1991). The instructional conversation: teaching and learning in social activity (Research Report 2). Washington, DC: Office of Educational Research and Improvement. (ERIC Document Reproductive Service No. ED 341254).

Thomas, W. P., & Collier, V. P. (1999) Accelerated Schooling for English Language Learners. *Educational Leadership, 56* (7), 46–49.

Tollefson, J. W. (Ed.)(1995). *Power and inequality in language education*. Cambridge, UK: Cambridge University Press.

van Lier, L. (1996). *Interaction in the language curriculum*. New York: Longman.

Vygotsky, L. S. (1987). Thinking and speech. In R. W. Rieber & A. S. Carton (eds.), *The collected works of L. S. Vygotsky, Volume 1: Problems of general psychology*. New York: Plenum Press.

Widdowson, H. G. (1987). *Teaching language as communication*. Oxford, UK: Oxford University Press,

Willett, J. (1991). Defining tensions and managing stress in pluralistic communities. In M. Foster (ed.), Readings on equal education. Vol 11. *Qualitative Investigations into Schools and Schooling*. AMS Press.

Wolfram, W., Adger, C. T., & Christian, D. (1999). *Dialects in schools and communities*. Mahwah, NJ: Lawrence Erlbaum.

Wong Fillmore, L. (1991). Second language learning in children: A model of language learning in social context. In E. Bialystok (ed.) (pp. 49–69), *Language processing in bilingual children*. Cambridge, UK: Cambridge University Press.

CHAPTER TWO

A CRITIQUE OF METHODS AND APPROACHES IN LANGUAGE TEACHING

THIS CHAPTER WILL FEATURE

- Behaviorist methods
- Rationalist methods
- Functional approaches
- Humanistic approaches

YOU WILL EXAMINE

- A critique of methods and approaches
- Ways to incorporate content-based and interactive teaching
- Diverse notions of language as social action and power
- Interactionalist/constructivist learning for constructing identities and knowledge through language use

INTRODUCTION: SETTING THE STAGE

The twentieth century witnessed enormous controversy over language methodology. This controversy was not just a phenomenon. Kelly (1976) described a gradual evolution of language teaching over twenty-five centuries that is characterized by frequent shifts in focus, practice, and purpose. These shifts in perspectives have led to both positive and long-term change. Grittner (1990) cites concern over the unfortunate recurrence throughout our history of "evangelistic movements that suddenly emerge, capture the attention of many teachers, cause an upheaval in methods and materials, and then—just suddenly—fade from view" (p. 9). The common premise behind the search for a unitary approach to learning and teaching seems to be that there exists an ideal method

THINK, PAIR, SHARE

Before you begin reading this chapter, complete the following activity with a partner.

1. Before reading, here is what I know about methods and approaches in language teaching:

   _____

   _____

2. Before reading, here is what I learned from my partner:

   _____

   _____

which, once discovered, will unlock the door to language proficiency for all learners and will make the learning process swift and effortless (Omaggio Hadley, 1993).

The purpose of this chapter is to critique a variety of methods and approaches in language teaching. The methods and approaches outlined will be accompanied by: characteristics, interactive and content-based applicability, interactive and content-based activities, alignment with ESL Standards, accommodations for diverse learners, and suggestions for assessment practices. The chapter is aligned with the national standards for teaching English language learners published by Teachers of English for Speakers of Other Languages (TESOL). *The ESL Standards for Pre-K–12 Students* is available to read or order online at www.tesol.org. (To read, click on "standards and initiatives" under "advancing the profession of TESOL." To order a copy, click on "publications and products." The standards provide clear guidelines for supporting English language learners in content-based, interactive classroom settings.

In this book we have chosen the concepts of *content-based* and *interactivity* as our two organizing principles for discussing issues related to language teaching and learning. In general, content-based ESL teachers seek to develop the students' English language proficiency by incorporating information from the subject areas that students are likely to study (Echevarria et al, 2000, p. 6). Whatever subject matter is included, for effective content-based instruction to occur, teachers need to provide practice in academic skills and tasks common to mainstream classes (Adamson, 1990; Mohan, 1990; Chamot & O'Malley, 1994; Short, 1994). Content-based instruction is easily aligned with the ESL standards. Three of the nine standards come under the goal of students being able to use English to achieve academically in all content areas.

Interactivity involves both students and teachers actively involved in co-constructing new knowledge and negotiating meaning. As a teacher you must provide instruction that allows students to practice the language in a content-based setting. Instead of teachers talking and students listening, interactive classes should be structured so that students are producing language and developing complex thinking skills. Interactive instruction is reciprocal—it involves active engagement by both teacher and learners.

It must be noted that neither content-based or interactive provides a curricular model nor a methodological prescription in and of itself. However, it is certainly possible to derive various implications from them for instruction. The rationale for creating a highly interactive class is based on the centrality of peer interaction for stimulating the second language acquisition process (Brown, 1994; Faltis, 1997; Wong Fillmore, 1989, 1991).

Selecting appropriate methods and approaches for content-based teaching may at first seem like a daunting task. Allowing the subject matter to control the selection and sequencing of language items means that you have to view your teaching from an entirely different perspective. You are first and foremost teaching geography or math or science; secondarily you are teaching language (Brown, 2001).

METHODOLOGY AND DEFINITIONS

Richards and Rodgers (1986) contend that there is a fundamental difference between a philosophy of language teaching at the level of theory and principles and a set of procedures derived from them (p. 15). **Methodology** is a system of principles, practices, and procedures applied to any specific branch of knowledge, whereas, **pedagogy** is defined as the art or profession of teaching. Other important terminology and their definitions include:

1. **Approach:** a set of theoretical principles
2. **Method:** a procedural plan for presenting and teaching the language
3. **Technique:** strategies for implementing the methodological plan.

What is the most effective way to teach a second/foreign language learner? Which methods, approaches, and techniques reflect content-based and interactive teaching? Why is it important to distinguish between, *approach*, *method*, and *technique?* Does the way we were taught impact the way we will teach? The answers to the questions are varied. Perhaps they may best be answered by beginning with an introspective reflection.

As you continue to read this chapter on methods and approaches, you will find it useful to refer to definitions of various Learning Styles, the *ESL Standards for Pre-K–12 Students* (found at www.tesol.org), and Multiple Intelligences (found below). You will also find an in-depth unit lesson plan that you can incorporate most of the methods and approaches described in the chapter.

LEARNING STYLES

A learning style is a general approach a learner uses to learn a new language (Scarcella & Oxford, 1992, p. 61). Oxford (1990) and Scarcella and Oxford (1992) identified five key elements of language learning styles:

1. *Analytical-global*—demonstrates the difference between a detail-oriented learner and a holistic one. This learner focuses on grammatical details and enjoys looking up words in the dictionary, rather than trying to guess their meaning.

REFLECT AND RESPOND

1. What methods, approaches, and techniques were used by your second/foreign language teachers in school at the elementary, secondary, or college level?

   _____

   _____

2. Were those methods, approaches, and techniques content-based and/or interactive? In what ways?

   _____

   _____

3. Write a brief description of how those methods, approaches, and techniques were effective.

   _____

   _____

HOWARD GARDNER'S EIGHT MULTIPLE INTELLIGENCES

Bodily/Kinesthetic	The ability to use one's mental abilities to manipulate and coordinate movements of one's physical body
Interpersonal/Social	The ability to recognize and understand others' feelings and interact appropriately with other people
Intrapersonal/Introspective	The ability to perceive one's own feelings and motivations for planning and directing one's life
Logical/Mathematical	The ability to detect patterns, calculate, think logically, and carry out mathematical operations
Musical/Rhythmical	The ability to recognize, compose, and remember tonal changes, rhythms, and musical pitch
Naturalist	The ability to recognize and classify natural surroundings, such as flora and fauna or rocks and minerals
Verbal/Linguistic	The ability to effectively manipulate language to express oneself and allows for the use of language as a means to remember information
Visual/Spatial	The ability to perceive and manipulate images in order to solve problems

2. *Sensory preferences*—demonstrates the physical, perceptual ways of learning. These may be visual, auditory, and hands-on (kinesthetic). Visual learners prefer visual cues or an opportunity to read information. Auditory learners like conversations and hearing the lesson's content. Kinesthetic learners do well in environments in which they can physically move around or are provided with manipulatives that aid in comprehension.

3. *Intuitive/Random and Sensory/Sequential Learning*—demonstrates the type of organization a learner prefers in the presentation of material. Intuitive/Random frequently think in a somewhat abstract way—nonsequential or random. Sensory/Sequential learners prefer to learn in an ordered step-by-step linear progression.

4. *Orientation to closure*—demonstrates those learners who need to reach conclusions and will tolerate ambiguity. These learners are often characterized by wanting the rules spelled out for them.

5. *Competition-cooperation*—demonstrates those learners who benefit from competing against or cooperating with their peers. Competitive learners are often motivated by the thrill of winning. Cooperative learners enjoy working with others in a collaborative manner.

SOURCE: Scarcella and Oxford (1992)

The methods and approaches described in this chapter offer a brief glimpse into our profession's language teaching repertoire. While some methods and approaches will fit nicely with ESL content-based interactive teaching, others will not. Some methods and approaches are more suited for foreign language teaching. The language profession has reached a point of maturity that enables it to recognize that the complexity of language learners in multiple worldwide contexts demands an eclectic blend of tasks, each tailored for a particular group of learners studying for particular purposes in a given amount of time (Brown, 2000). The language profession has realized that there never was and probably never will be a method for all. The focus in recent years has been on the development of classroom tasks and activities that are consonant with what we know about second language acquisition, and are also in keeping with the dynamics of the classroom itself (Nunan, 1991). We begin by examining the Behaviorist Methods, which have primarily been used in foreign language instruction and are not as adaptable to content-based ESL teaching and learning. The Behaviorist Methods are examined first because they represent the historical beginnings of language methodology. It is important to study the Behaviorists because they provide the point of departure for understanding language teaching and learning.

TRADITIONAL BEHAVIORIST METHODS

Behaviorist theory suggests that all behavior is viewed as a response to stimuli. Second/foreign language teaching philosophies and trends have been greatly modified over the course of the last few decades. The shift from written grammatical perfection to oral proficiency has given rise to the advent of the communicative language teaching revolution. Before the 1970s, there were three methods, which constituted the most common approaches to foreign language teaching: the Grammar-translation Method, the Direct Method, and the Audiolingual Method (Omaggio Hadley, 1993).

Grammar-translation Method

The **Grammar-translation Method** has been described by Omaggio Hadley (1993) as a "mental disciple," wherein the teacher seeks to strengthen students' minds through the exploration of literary works and extensive grammatical analysis of the structure of the target language.

- **Characteristics:** Teachers initially present students with an outline of the grammatical structure, including all its exceptions, or a bilingual list of vocabulary. Students complete exercises to demonstrate comprehension of the rules. These exercises include translation in some cases. As a secondary goal of instruction, the grammatical structures of the student's native and the target language are compared and contrasted. Most class instruction consists of conversation *about* the language, not *in* the language. Rarely are there opportunities to develop listening and speaking skills in the target language using this method.

- **Interactive and content-based applicability** are *not* the focus in Grammar translation. Students are instructed to concentrate on translating learning grammar rule and memorizing bilingual word lists, with little or no emphasis on interactive or oral skills.

- **Interactive and content-based Activities** are, for the most part, nonexistent. Students work individually, primarily engaged in reading and writing tasks. A content-based activity might include: Students read text in math, science, or social studies and discuss its meaning.

- **ESL Standards:** Goal 2, Standards 1 and 2

- **Diverse Learners.**

  LEARNING STYLES
  Analytic-global—Learner focuses on grammatical details and enjoys looking up words in the dictionary, rather than trying to guess their meaning.
  Sensory/sequential—Learner prefers to learn in an ordered step-by-step linear progression.
  Orientation to closure—Learners need to reach conclusion, will not tolerate ambiguity, and want rules spelled out for them.

  MULTIPLE INTELLIGENCES
  Logical Mathematical—Learners detect patterns, calculate, think logically, and carry out mathematical operations.
  Visual/Spatial—Learners perceive and manipulate images in order to solve problems.

- **Assessment:** (1) Students are asked to write the definitions of a list of vocabulary words taken from a math, science, or social studies text. (2) Students read a text and are asked to answer a set of comprehension questions. (3) Students are asked to say or write the rules for making nouns plural in English.

NOW VIEW THE VIDEO CLIP ON THE GRAMMAR-TRANSLATION METHOD

1. Describe how the teacher is using the Grammar-translation Method.

   _____

   _____

2. How might the teacher use an interactive activity for this lesson?

   _____

   _____

3. What are two suggestions for ways this lesson might be conducted differently?

   _____

   _____

Direct Method

The second method in the behaviorist category is the Direct Method. The **Direct Method** is modeled after the way in which children acquire their first language, by listening to it in large quantities.

■ **Characteristics:** Students may learn using classroom objects and miming the actions of the teacher. Specially constructed pictures depicting life in the target cultures are developed to enable the teacher to present meaning without translating.

■ **Interactive and content-based applicability** include having students exposed to simple discourse from the beginning of instruction and involving them in question-and-answer exchanges with the teacher. Since translating is strictly forbidden, students are encouraged to paraphrase in order to express themselves. Phonetic notation is frequently used in this method of instruction, as correct pronunciation is a key goal of instruction. Grammar rules are generally taught through inductive methods; however, when such rules are explicitly taught, explanations are provided in the target language. Immersion in the target language brings about the process of natural acquisition. Recalling knowledge from this type of learning requires less cognitive activity and more of a reflex reaction in linguistic ability (Brown, 1994).

■ **Interactive and Content-Based Activities**
   1. *Reteach a Topic*—Divide the class into groups (no more than five members per group). Assign a topic to each group to "teach" to the rest of the class, which will prepare them to succeed on an upcoming assessment/assignment. Have each group design a poster portraying the topic. The groups may also create

---

◖▪▭▪◗   NOW VIEW THE VIDEO CLIP ON THE DIRECT METHOD

Activity for viewing the video clip:

1. What characteristics of the Direct Method are clearly demonstrated in the video clip?

   _____

   _____

2. In what way is the Direct Method similar to or different from your own experiences as a second/foreign language learner?

   _____

   _____

3. What **application activity** does the teacher use? Is it effective? Why? Why not?

   _____

   _____

---

a game to practice the particular topic. Upon completion, each group will have five minutes to present the topic to the rest of the class with their poster during which time they "reteach" the class.

2. *Tic-Tac-Toe*—Draw a tic-tac-toe board on a transparency (or chalkboard). Cut out Xs and Os from a transparency. Number each square from the tic-tac-toe board to make placing of the Xs and Os easier. Divide the class into two teams: Xs and Os. Each person from a group chooses a number. From the number comes a question on current vocabulary, culture, grammar, or verbs. If the answer is correct, they get to cover the spot. If the answer is incorrect, the other group gets an opportunity to answer the question and take the spot.

3. *Alphabet Huddle*—Divide the class into teams. Explain that the teams must come up with a list of words that begin with the letter demonstrated by the teacher. The group with the most words wins. The game is called "huddle" because the groups tend to gather closely together so the others will not hear them.

- **ESL Standards:** All Goals and all Standards

- **Diverse Learners:**

  LEARNING STYLES
  Sensory preferences—
  Visual learners prefer visual cues or an opportunity to read information.
  Auditory learners like conversations and *hearing* the lesson's content.
  Kinesthetic learners do well in environments in which they can physically move around or are provided with manipulatives that aid in comprehension.
  Intuitive/Random learners think in an abstract way—non-sequential but random.

Sensory/Sequential learners prefer to learn in an ordered step-by-step linear progression.

Competition–cooperation—Competitive learners are often motivated by the thrill of winning. *Cooperative* learners enjoy working with others in a collaborative manner.

■ **Assessment:** All of the interactive activities listed above can be used as formal or informal assessments. Other assessments for the Direct Method might include performance-based activities in which students are asked to build, draw, demonstrate, or sing. Also, as the teacher you might conduct a miscue analysis and comprehension assessment (see chapter 5) as students read a text. This could also incorporate the use of learning logs.

Audiolingual Method (ALM)

The third method in the behaviorist category, the **Audiolingual Method (ALM)** (also named the Aural-Oral, Functional Skills, New Key, or American Method) evolved from the school of structural, or descriptive, linguistics. ALM was popular from the 1940s through the 1960s. It is based on structural linguistics and behavioristic psychology and places heavy emphasis on spoken rather than written language, stressing habit formation as a mode of learning.

■ **Characteristics:** This method adopts what is called a "natural order" to second language acquisition: listening, speaking, reading, and writing. ALM textbooks consist of three sections: the dialogue, **pattern drills,** and application activities. In this method, students are conditioned in oral discourse before grammatical structures are analyzed (Omaggio Hadley, 1993). The target language should be taught without reference to the first language. Students learn through stimulus–response techniques. Pattern drills are to precede any explanation of grammar. The natural sequence, *listening, speaking, reading,* and *writing,* should be followed in learning the language (Chastain, 1976).

■ **Interactive and Content-Based Applicability:** ALM focuses on stimulus–response pattern drills and memorization of dialogues. The teacher *always* corrects errors.

■ **Interactive and Content-Based Activities**
   1. Students work on *transformation drills,* which require the students to make substitutions in their responses. Change a declarative statement to an interrogative: "You have the pens." "Do you have the pens?"
   2. *Application activities* include dialogue adaptations, guided oral presentations, and conversation stimulus activities in which students repeat memorized material to meet minimal communicative needs.

■ **ESL Standards:** Goal 1, Standard 1; Goal 1, Standard 3; Goal 2, Standards 1, 2, and 3; Goal 3, Standard 3

■ **Diverse Learners:**

   LEARNING STYLES
   Sensory Preferences—auditory learners like conversations and hearing the lesson's content.

NOW VIEW THE VIDEO CLIP ON THE AUDIOLINGUAL METHOD (ALM)

1. Describe how the teacher uses *pattern* and *transformation drills.*

   _____

   _____

2. What characteristics of ALM are clearly demonstrated in the video clip?

   _____

   _____

3. In what ways is the teacher using this method effectively?

   _____

   _____

Sensory/Sequential learners prefer to learn in an ordered step-by-step linear progression.

MULTIPLE INTELLIGENCES
Logical/Mathematical learners can detect patterns, calculate, think logically, and carry out mathematical operations.
Verbal/Linguistic learners effectively manipulate language to express themselves and allow for the use of language as a means to remember information.

■ **Assessment:** Have students listen to or read a text selected from newspaper or magazine on the topic being covered. Ask students to self-assess by retelling or describing the story. This can be done working with partners or individually.

Second language acquisition theorists of the late 1960s and early 1970s rejected behaviorists' views of language learning in favor of **rationalist** and **mentalist** perspectives. Ellis (1990) describes two mentalist perspectives on teaching that contrasted quite strongly with one another.

RATIONALIST AND MENTALIST METHODS

Cognitive Anti-Method

■ **Characteristics:** Ellis (1990) describes the following major theoretical characteristics underlying the **Cognitive Anti-Method,** articulated by Newmark (1966)

REFLECT AND RESPOND

1. In your experiences of learning/acquiring a second/foreign language, were any of the Behaviorist Methods used? Describe those experiences.

_____

_____

2. Of the three methods described above, which do you find most appealing? Why?

_____

_____

3. Describe the instances in which you still see remnants of these three methods in use today.

_____

_____

and Newmark and Reibel (1968): (1) "Second language learning is controlled by the learner rather than by the teacher" (Ellis 1990, p. 35). The learner is engaged in problem solving, using the input as data from the which the system of language is discovered. (2) Learners have an innate ability to learn languages. Their language acquisition capacity is qualitatively like that of a child. (3) One need not pay attention to form in order to acquire a language. Linguistic analysis is not necessary for language learning, and grammatical rules and explanations are not useful in the classroom. (4) Learners do not acquire linguistic features one by one but acquire language globally. There is, therefore, no need to sequence instruction through selection and grading of the input. (5) Errors are inevitable and should be tolerated. Learners will eventually discover and correct their own errors and, therefore, do not have to receive error correction from the teacher. (6) L1 interference will disappear with more exposure to the target language. (Ellis, 1990, pp. 35–37)

■ **Interactive and content-based applicability** is quite evident, because the Cognitive Anti-Method is based on having students acquire language globally. Students are actively engaged in problem solving and critical thinking.

■ **Interactive and Content-Based Activities**
   1. _The Accident_—You have been in an accident. Describe what happened to the police officer. When a spectator says that you are lying, convince the police officer that you are not.
   2. _Can I Borrow That?_—Ask your friend or brother/sister to let you borrow some article of new clothing. She/he is somewhat reluctant to lend it to you but you really feel that you need it today. You try to persuade her/him to change her/his mind.

3. *Lip Syncs*—Begin by playing a song and having the students list the words they recognize. Next, allow the students to divide themselves into groups and choose a song. Have students provide the music and the transcripts of the songs. Give the students time to prepare their "concert" and ample time to practice.

- **ESL Standards:** All Goals and all Standards

- **Diverse Learners**

    LEARNING STYLES
    Analytical-global—detail-oriented learner
    Sensory preferences—visual, auditory, and kinesthetic
    Intuitive/Random and Sequential Learning—demonstrate the type of organization a learner prefers in the presentation of material
    Orientation to closure—learners who need to reach conclusions and will not tolerate ambiguity
    Competition–cooperation—learners who benefit from competing against or cooperating with their peers

    MULTIPLE INTELLIGENCES—ALL MULTIPLE INTELLIGENCES

- **Assessment:** (1) *Running Records*—as student reads, the teacher checks off words that were read correctly and codes those words student has trouble with. (2) *Portfolio*—teacher and student together collect various examples of student's work and assess how the student has developed over time.

Cognitive-Code Method

A basic principle underlying cognitive methodology was that meaningful learning was essential to language acquisition, and that conscious knowledge of grammar was critical.

- **Characteristics:** The **Cognitive-Code Method's** characteristics are the following: (1) The goal of cognitive teaching is to develop in students the same types of abilities that native speakers have. (2) In teaching the language, the teacher moves from the *known* to the *unknown;* that is the student's present knowledge base (cognitive structures) must be determined so that the necessary prerequisites for understanding new material can be provided. (3) Text materials and the teacher must introduce students to situations that will promote the *creative use of the language.* (4) Because language behavior is constantly innovative and varied, students must be taught to understand the rule system rather than be required to memorize surface strings in rote fashion. (5) Learning should always be *meaningful;* that is, students should understand at all times what they are being asked to do.

- **Interactive and content-based applicability** advocates learning by the direct association of foreign words and phrases with objects and actions, without the use of the native language by teacher or student. Students learn to understand the target language by listening to it a great deal and learn to speak it by associating speech with appropriate action.

REFLECT AND RESPOND

1. In your experiences of learning/acquiring a second/foreign language, were either of the Rationalist and Mentalist Methods used? Describe those experiences.

   _____

   _____

2. Of the two methods described above, which do you find most appealing? Why?

   _____

   _____

3. Describe the instances in which you still see the applications of these methods in use today.

   _____

   _____

- Interactive and Content-Based Activities
  1. *The Interview*—Ask students to imagine interviewing a famous person in history. Have students write out ten interview questions. Each student then interviews a classmate he or she does not know well. Each partner must answer in the target language. The interviewer should take notes and create a poster describing the other person. The interviewer will then present the partner to the class using the poster.
  2. *Fairy-Tale Fantasies*—Divide students into groups of four. Assign each group a work area and give them a sack full of props. Students are to act out an original fairy tale using the items from the sack. They are to use all the items as well as any others they may choose. Each group is allowed to pass one prop they don't want to another group. Students then present their *fairy-tale fantasy*.
  3. *Word Connection*—Partner rally-practice math, science, or social studies vocabulary by giving a category to two partners and they must come up with as many words as possible by taking turns (rallying back and forth). This can increase to two sets of partners for even more practice.

- **ESL Standards:** All Goals and all Standards

- **Diverse Learners**
  Learning Styles—All Learning Styles
  Multiple Intelligences—All Multiple Intelligences
- **Assessment:** (1) Informal Reading Inventory. (2) Check for comprehension through students' use of vocabulary in speaking, reading, and writing in answering questions at the various levels of proficiency.

FUNCTIONAL APPROACHES

There is an array of functional teaching approaches that can be employed in the second/foreign language classroom. Among the most popular and recent are Cognitive Academic Language Learning Approach (CALLA), Total Physical Response (TPR), Total Physical Response Storytelling (TPRS), and The Natural Approach.

Cognitive Academic Language Learning Approach (CALLA)

CALLA is an instructional model that was developed to meet the academic needs of students learning English as second language in American schools. The CALLA approach is targeted at language minority students at the advanced beginning and intermediate levels of English language proficiency. CALLA was created to provide assistance for ESL students and thereby enable them to succeed in school with transitional instruction. CALLA was originally developed to meet the academic needs of three types of ESL students:

1. Students who have developed social communicative skills through beginning level ESL classes or through exposure to an English-speaking environment, but have not yet developed academic language skills appropriate to their grade level;
2. Students who have acquired academic language skills in their native language and initial proficiency in English, but who need assistance in transferring concepts and skills learned in the first language to English; and
3. Bilingual English-dominant students who have not yet developed academic language skills in either language.

■ **Characteristics:** The CALLA model has three components and instructional objectives in its curricular and instructional design: topics from the major content subjects, the development of academic language skills, and explicit instruction in learning strategies for both content and language acquisition. Teachers explicitly teach learning strategies at the same time that they develop language and content knowledge. The learning strategies therefore provide students with extra support for the negotiation of content-area instruction in the second language.

Chamot and O'Malley (1994, pp. 60–64) have identified three types of learning strategies:

1. Metacognitive Strategies
   Advance organization
   Organizational planning
   Selective attention
   Self-management
   Monitoring comprehension
   Monitoring production
   Self-evaluation

    2. Cognitive Strategies
       Resourcing
       Grouping
       Note-taking
       Elaboration of prior knowledge
       Summarizing
       Deduction/induction
       Imagery
       Auditory representation
       Making inferences
    3. Social/Affective Strategies
       Questioning for clarification
       Cooperation
       Self-talk

Chamot and O'Malley recommend beginning CALLA lessons with ESL science, which provides many natural opportunities for hands-on discovery learning. ESL mathematics is next, because in the upper grades math is highly abstract and has a more restricted language register than science. Social studies is third, and English language arts the fourth subject introduced because of the complex level of reading and writing required as well as underlying cultural assumptions (Chamot & O'Malley, 1994; O'Malley & Chamot, 1990).

■ **Interactive and Content-Based Applicability:** Two basic premises in CALLA are that content should be the primary focus of instruction and that academic language skills can be developed as the need for them emerges from the content (O'Malley & Chamot, 1994).

■ **Interactive and/or Content-Based Activities**
    1. *Math*—Students working in groups learn to use a calculator for converting various monetary currencies.
    2. *Science*—In a cooperative learning activity, students explore various global weather patterns using the Internet.
    3. *Social Studies*—Students create graphic organizers depicting countries and capitals.
    Note: See Table 2.1 for sample lesson plan.

■ **ESL Standards:** All Goals and all Standards

■ **Diverse Learners**
    Learning Styles—All Learning Styles
    Multiple Intelligences—All Multiple Intelligences

■ **Assessment:** (1) Cloze activity; (2) Retelling of text; (3) Portfolio

■ **Interactive and Content-Based Applicability:** This method is highly interactive and through its use of notional-functional concepts, i.e., activities and strategies

TABLE 2.1   CALLA Lesson Plan

ENGLISH AS A SECOND LANGUAGE

Teacher_____School_____

Grade(s) 7 & 8 Level(s) Intermediate Class Description: ESL Content Science

PLANNING PHASE

Performance Objectives

1. Observe differences and similarities in fingerprints
2. Develop a system to classify prints into similar groups
3. Discover the usefulness of grouping objects according to similarities and difference

Lesson Outline:

Theme/Topic/Content: Fingerprints and a Classification System
National Standards: 1.1 Students will use English to participate in social interactions
                 1.2 Students will interact in, through and with spoken and written English for
                 personal expression and enjoyment

TEACHING PHASE

(1) Preparation

Warm-up Activity:
Ask students what they know about fingerprint patterns. Copy this information on the board. Class will discuss notion of classification.

(2) Presentation

Activities:
a. Students work in pairs and remove items from kit
b. Rub student's thumb with graphite pad
c. Peel off one piece of tape, being careful not to touch the sticky surface and press it in place over the thumb pad
d. Carefully remove the tape and press it into the 3x5 index card
e. Compare student's print with the partner's print for similarities and differences. What kind of patterns do they see? Referring to a handout, help students give names to the different patterns.

Four Skills
Listening Activity: Students follow directions.
Speaking Activity: Students participate in discussions and offer results.
Reading Activity: Students find information in reference materials.
Writing Activity: Students summarize findings.

(3) Practice

a. Use classified section of the newspaper to provide application of classification
b. Vocabulary review: Sentence completion and word search
c. Practice sentence completion and word search

Continued

TABLE 2.1   *(continued)*

(4) Evaluation

a. Review lesson to allow students to evaluate their success
b. Discussion and writing in learning logs

(5) Expansion/Extension

Thinking skills discussion: Debrief students by asking higher order thinking skills' questions.

Other Activities:

Follow-up: Each student will
record all food/beverages consumed over a four-day period.
Transfer information from diary to pyramid chart
Write a summary about food/beverage consumption
Write sentences about choices. Identify patterns of classification.

that engage the learner according to preferences and needs, will focus on students using language for real and meaningful purposes.

- **Interactive and Content-Based Activities**
  1. Information sharing activities
  2. Task-based activities
  3. Simulations
  4. Role plays

- **ESL Standards:** All Goals and all Standards

- **Diverse Learners**

  Learning Styles—All Learning Styles
  Multiple Intelligences—All Multiple Intelligences

- **Assessment:** All of the interactive and content-based activities above can be used as assessment activities.

Total Physical Response

Total Physical Response (TPR), developed by James Asher, is based on the theory that second language acquisition is similar to a child's first language acquisition. That is, as a baby, our first involvement in language is through responding to commands our parents give us. Only after about one to two years do we begin, as toddlers, to produce comprehensible utterances in our first language. Reading and writing are introduced only after we have been speaking the language for an additional two to three years, and we enter school. According to Asher (1969), "Total Physical Response involves having students listen to a command in a foreign language and immediately respond with the appropriate physical action." TPR follows the premise that the human brain has a biological program for acquiring any language—including the sign language of the deaf.

■ **Characteristics:** The general principles of TPR are: (1) Listening comprehension develops before speaking. (2) Understanding should be developed through movements of the student's body. (3) Language learners should not be forced to speak. As students internalize language through listening comprehension, they will eventually reach a readiness to speak. An individual will spontaneously begin to produce spoken language. (4) TPR is a listening–speaking approach. (5) The teacher says each command and then models the action several times. The teacher gives the command and signals to students to perform the action. (6) **Contiguity Principle**—A command is immediately followed by the corresponding action and body movement. (7) **Frequency Principle**—Commands, grammatical structures, and vocabulary are repeatedly linked to their referent. (8) **Feedback Principle**—There is a cause-and-effect relationship between the uttered command and the action that follows.

■ **Interactive and Content-Based Applicability:** TPR is also highly interactive since by its definition it involves having students listen and react to a series of commands. The strategy lends itself nicely to content-based instruction since the teacher can vary the commands according to themes or topics being covered. TPR is a highly effective approach in an American Sign Language (ASL) class.

■ **Interactive and Content-Based Activities**
   1. *Telling Time*—Students stand in a circle with one student in the middle. The student in the middle calls out a time in the target language. The students in the circle use their arms as hands on a clock and "become the clock," mimicking correct arm arrangements to indicate the called time.
   2. *Simon Says*—Students play Simon Says in the target language.
   3. *Clothing Game*—This can be played in teams or as a whole class. The object is for students to identify what clothing is worn where, e.g., in what country. The teacher has large placards placed around the room with the names or pictures of places. A description of clothing is read aloud and students must go stand in front of the appropriate picture.

■ **ESL Standards:** Goal 1, Standard 3; Goal 2, Standards 1, 2, and 3; Goal 3, Standard 2

■ **Diverse Learners**

LEARNING STYLES
SENSORY PREFERENCES:
Visual learners prefer visual cues or an opportunity to read information.
Auditory learners like conversations and hearing the lesson's content.
Kinesthetic learners do well in environments in which they can physically move around or are provided with manipulatives that aid in comprehension.

MULTIPLE INTELLIGENCES
Bodily/Kinesthetic—uses mental abilities to manipulate and coordinate movements of one's physical body
Musical/Rhythmic—recognize, compose, and remember tonal changes, rhythms, and musical pitch

NOW VIEW THE VIDEO CLIP ON TOTAL PHYSICAL RESPONSE (TPR)

1. How does the teacher engage the students' attention?

   _____

   _____

2. How can this lesson be used in both an English as a Second Language and/or a foreign class?

   _____

   _____

3. In what way(s) is this a content-based lesson?

   _____

   _____

Verbal/Linguistic—effectively manipulate language to express oneself and allow for the use of language as a means to remember information

Visual/Spatial—perceive and manipulate images in order to solve problems

- **Assessment:** (1) Role play; (2) Simulations; (3) Student self-assessment

Total Physical Response Storytelling

Total Physical Response Storytelling (TPRS), developed by Blaine Ray in the 1980s, uses storytelling to utilize and expand acquired vocabulary through stories that students can hear, see, act out, retell, revise, and rewrite. There is an intensive use of the target language with emphasis on communication and limited direct grammatical correction. Ray (1997) notes that TPRS stories need movement and a problem. They need to be "bizarre, exaggerated and personalized."

- **Characteristics:** Using traditional TPRS techniques to learn basic vocabulary, the teacher then uses that vocabulary to develop a mini-story. The teacher narrates the story using pictures, puppets, or student actors. As the narration develops, the teacher encourages students to fill in words or act out gestures. The teacher will often deliberately make mistakes and seek student correction, asking short answer, open-ended questions. Students retell the story to a partner. The teacher then encourages the students to develop a larger story from the mini-stories, which are in turn retold and revised by the students. In its most advanced phase, the students develop original stories, which they write, illustrate, and act out.

■ **Interactive and Content-Based Applicability:** TPRS is another highly interactive and content-based strategy because of its defining characteristics. Teachers can adapt and include wide varieties of content-specific themes and topics. The focus is on communication of content.

■ **Interactive and Content-Based Activities**
1. Teacher presents a mini-story using puppets, pictures, or student actors, which students then retell and revise.
2. Students use new and old vocabulary to create original stories, which they illustrate with pictures. (This may also be done on the computer.)
3. Students present new stories with pictures.

For additional information on TPRS go to: http://www.tprstorytelling.com or http://www.blaineraytprs.com

■ **ESL Standards:** Goal 1, Standard 3; Goal 2, Standards 1, 2, and 3; Goal 3, Standard 2

■ **Diverse Learners:**

LEARNING STYLES
SENSORY PREFERENCES:
Visual learners prefer visual cues or an opportunity to read information.
Auditory learners like conversations and hearing the lesson's content.
Kinesthetic learners do well in environments in which they can physically move around or are provided with manipulatives that aid in comprehension.

MULTIPLE INTELLIGENCES
Bodily/Kinesthetic—uses mental abilities to manipulate and coordinate movements of one's physical body
Musical/Rhythmic—recognize, compose, and remember tonal changes, rhythms, and musical pitch
Verbal/Linguistic—effectively manipulate language to express oneself and allow for the use of language as a means to remember information
Visual/Spatial—perceive and manipulate images in order to solve problems

■ **Assessment:** (1) Cloze; (2) Role play; (3) Self-assessment

Natural Approach

The **Natural Approach** was proposed by Tracy Terrell and Stephen Krashen in the late 1970s as a method of teaching second language that emphasizes the centrality of the acquisition process. Techniques in this approach focus on providing a context in the classroom for natural language acquisition to occur, with acquirers receiving maximum "comprehensible input" (Krashen, 1985), and establishing the best conditions possible for reducing the affective factors that may inhibit students' second language acquisition (Krashen, 1982). Initially, the focus of instruction should be on communication and not on form; therefore classroom activities should elicit communicative dialogue from students. Since linguistic creativity develops apart from routine

---

NOW VIEW THE VIDEO CLIP ON TOTAL PHYSICAL RESPONSE STORYTELLING (TPRS)

1. Describe the sequence of activities the teacher used in this video clip.

   _____

   _____

2. What are alternative activities the teacher might use for this lesson?

   _____

   _____

3. Compare/contrast TPR with TPRS.

   _____

   _____

---

responses (Krashen, 1981), such as those used in ALM, an immersion situation encourages the expansion and creative use of vocabulary.

Terrell (1977) provided the following guidelines for classroom practice in the Natural Approach:

1. *Distribution of learning and acquisition activities.* Most, if not all, classroom activities should be designed to evoke communication.
2. *Error correction.* According to Terrell, there is no evidence to show that the correction of speech errors is necessary or even helpful in language acquisition.
3. *Responses in both L1 and L2.* Terrell suggested that initial classroom instruction involve listening comprehension activities almost exclusively, with responses from students permitted in the native language.

■ **Characteristics:** Terrell (1977) summarized the main characteristics of the method as follows: (1) Beginning language instruction should focus on the attainment of immediate communicative competence rather than on grammatical perfection. (2) Instruction needs to be aimed at modification and improvement of the student's developing grammar rather than at building that grammar up one rule at a time. (3) Teachers should afford students the opportunity to *acquire* language rather than force them to *learn* it. (4) Affective rather than cognitive factors are primary in language learning. (5) The key to comprehension and oral production is the acquisition of vocabulary.

■ **Interactive and Content-Based Applicability:** Because the Natural Approach is based on language acquisition, it is both interactive and has a high degree of content-based applicability.

**NOW VIEW THE VIDEO CLIP
ON THE NATURAL APPROACH**

1. Describe the sequence of activities. Is it effective? Why? Why not?

   _____

   _____

2. What authentic realia is the teacher using? For what purpose(s)?

   _____

   _____

3. What has the teacher done to ensure that this segment of the lesson is interactive and content-based?

   _____

   _____

- **Interactive and Content-Based Activities**
  1. *Mystery Items*—Students are shown a variety objects with different textures (e.g., sponge, brick, cotton). These are displayed on a table. Students hear a description of an unidentified object (e.g., its use, physical appearance). They must determine what is being described.
  2. *Pictionary*—Divide the class into two teams. One member of each teams goes to the board and draws a vocabulary word or term for the other team members to guess. Whichever team member raises his or her hand first and guesses the right answer, wins.
  3. *Stand Up If* . . .—Use this activity to practice math operations. Assign each student a number. Ask students to stand up if "you are a multiple of 4."

- **ESL Standards:** All Goals and all Standards

- **Diverse Learners:** All Learning Styles and all Multiple Intelligences

- **Assessment:** (1) Open-ended problems; (2) Hands-on projects; (3) Experiments; (4) Portfolio

HUMANISTIC APPROACHES

Community Language Learning

Charles Curran (1976) developed the **Community Language Learning (CLL)** approach, which stresses the role of the affective domain in promoting cognitive learning. The basic theoretical premise is that the human individual needs to be understood

REFLECT AND RESPOND

1. In your experiences of learning/acquiring a second/foreign language, were any of the Functional Approaches used? Describe those experiences.

   _____

   _____

2. Of the four approaches described in question 1, which do you find most appealing? Why?

   _____

   _____

3. Describe the instances in which you still see the applications of these approaches in use today.

   _____

   _____

and aided in the process of fulfilling personal values and goals. The teacher acts as the "knower/counselor" whose role is basically passive. She or he should provide the language necessary for students to express themselves freely and to say whatever it is they want to say. The goal is the creation of a cooperative learning community in which students are responsible for each other. Usually the class is comprised of six to twelve learners seated in a close circle. The teacher or teachers stand outside the circle. The students begin conversation in the L1 and the knower/counselor translates in the L2. These sentences are generally tape-recorded. Following seven to nine sentences, the students and knower/counselor work with this generated material. Students may be asked, "Do you remember anything we said?" Students may ask questions at any time. There is very little error correction. Techniques used are designed to reduce anxiety in the group and to promote free expression of ideas and feelings.

- **Characteristics:** There are five learning stages:

  Stage 1. Students use their native language to discuss anything they would like with other students in a circle. The teacher places a hand on each individual student's shoulders and quietly whispers a translation into that student's ear. As the student repeats what the teacher whispers, the student's pronunciation is recorded. This is repeated student by student until the entire dialogue is translated. The tape recording is used later in instruction.

  Stage 2. "Self-assertive stage"—Students try to communicate orally in the target language without assistance from the teacher.

  Stage 3. "Birth stage"—This is the continuation of independence from the teacher, where only another student, not the student speaking, requests assistance from the teacher.

Stage 4. "Adolescent" or "reversal" stage—Students become comfortable enough to welcome corrective feedback from the teacher or others.

Stage 5. "Independent" stage—The flow of dialogue has been transformed to free interaction between students and the teacher. In this stage, everyone is supportive in offering one another ways of improving speech. The trust level is at its highest, and students do not find such corrective feedback intimidating.

■ **Interactive and Content-Based Applicability:** Interactivity is most prominent in the fifth stage, during which students are actively engaged in using real-life language, which, if guided properly by the teacher, can be both meaningful and contextualized. Similarly, the teacher can direct students' conversations in such a manner that content is very specific.

■ **Interactive and Content-Based Activities**
   1. *Two-Minute Presentations*—Students may give a news report, tell a joke, tell how to do something, talk about a favorite hobby, describe their dream house.
   2. *Clues*—A short mystery is read to the class. The students are divided into small groups. Each group is given a list of clues that will solve the mystery. They discuss among themselves. The group that solves the mystery first explains it to the class and receives bonus points.
   3. *Guess Who I Am?*—Each student in a group of four has the name of a famous person taped on his/her back. The group has ten minutes to ask each other questions and determine their identities. After time has been called, each member of the group tells who he/she thinks he/she is and why.

■ **ESL Standards:** All Goals and all Standards

■ **Diverse Learners**

   LEARNING STYLES—VISUAL, AUDITORY, AND KINESTHETIC
   MULTIPLE INTELLIGENCES
   Interpersonal/Social—ability to recognize and understand others' feelings and interact appropriately with other people
   Intrapersonal/Introspective—perceive one's own feelings and motivations for planning and directing one's life
   Verbal/Linguistic—ability to effectively manipulate language to express oneself and allow for the use of language as a means to remember information

■ **Assessment:** All of the interactive/content-based activities listed above can be used as assessment activities.

The Silent Way

The second humanistic approach is the **Silent Way,** which was introduced by Caleb Gattegno (1976) is based on the premise that the teacher should be silent as much as possible in the classroom and the learner should be encouraged to produce as much target language as possible. There is no use of the students' L1 during formal presentations of lessons. Students begin with practicing sounds. These are derived from the teacher pointing to color-coded graphemes on charts that cover all visual representations of the phonemes in English. The charts introduced pronunciation models and grammatical paradigms. Elements of the Silent Way, particularly the use of color charts and the colored Cuisenaire rods (small colored rods of varying lengths) grew out of Gattegno's previous experience as an educational designer of reading and mathematics programs. The rods are used to introduce vocabulary (e.g., numbers, adjectives, colors), and syntax (e.g., tense, word order, noun/adjective agreement). The Silent Way assumes that learners are solely responsible for what they learn. The teacher's role is to guide students by giving single-word stimuli or short phrases, once or twice. Students are encouraged to enhance their understanding and pronunciation among themselves.

■ **Characteristics** include (1) Learning is facilitated if the learner discovers or creates rather than remembers and repeats what is to be learned. (2) Learning is facilitated by accompanying/mediating physical objects. (3) Learning is facilitated by problem solving involving the material to be learned. (4) Learning tasks and activities encourage and shape students' oral responses without direct oral instruction from unnecessary modeling by the teacher. (5) The teacher models a word, phrase, or sentence and then elicits student responses.

■ **Interactive and Content-Based Applicability:** This approach is limited in interactive instructional strategies for both teacher and learner. Students do not work with authentic and/or culturally-based materials, nor do they hear much authentic native speech. There is little to no opportunity for students to use the language for real-world purposes.

Interactive and Content-Based Activities: The following is an example of sequential interactive activities that may be used with The Silent Way:

1. Teacher empties rods in a pile on table.
2. Teacher indicates that rods should be picked up and a correct utterance made.
3. All the students in the group pick up rods and make utterances. Peer-group correction is encouraged.
4. Teacher indicates that a student should give the teacher the rods called for.
5. Teacher then indicates that the students should give each other commands for the calling of rods. Rods are made available to all students.
6. Students are encouraged to experiment with the language.
7. The teacher only speaks to correct an incorrect utterance if a member of the group does not detect the error.

■ **ESL Standards:** Goal 1, Standards 2 and 3; Goal 2, Standard 1: Goal 2, Standard 3; Goal 3, Standard 2; Goal 3, Standard 3

■ **Diverse Learners**

LEARNING STYLES
Analytical/global
Sensory preferences
Competition–cooperation

MULTIPLE INTELLIGENCES
Logical/mathematical
Verbal/Linguistic
Visual/Spatial

- **Assessment:** (1) Portfolio; (2) Cloze; (3) Essay writing

Suggestopedia

The third approach, **Suggestopedia,** is also known as *Suggestive-Accelerative Learning and Teaching (SALT)* and the *Lozanov Method.* It began in Bulgaria with Georgi Lozanov (1978). Lozanov, a psychotherapist and physician, believes that relaxation techniques and concentration help learners tap their subconscious resources and retain greater amounts of vocabulary and structures. One of the primary tenets of this approach is to provide an environment that will allow students to escape the limitations and restrictions of traditional classroom environments.

- **Characteristics** include soft lights, baroque music, cheerful room decoration, comfortable seating, and originality in material presentation. This relaxation allows the student to be open to learning a second/foreign language. Since Lozanov regards anxiety as a hurdle that impedes language learning, he proposes two teaching principles to break down the sociopsychological constraints of a traditional learning environment. (1) *Infantilization*—which is designed to help students recapture the kind of learning functions experienced as children. (2) *Pseudopassivity*—refers to a relaxed physical state of heightened mental activity and concentration (Chastain, 1988, p. 104).

- **Interactive and Content-Based Applicability:** While the dialogue-based approach does provide some interactivity between teacher and students, it is greatly limited in that all materials are pedagogically prepared. Furthermore, because Lozanov recommends implementing this approach only in its original and complete version, it may not be easily adapted to a typical K–12 classroom setting.

- **Interactive and Content-Based Activities**
  1. Relaxation
        Physical relaxation
        Mental relaxation
        Suggestive set-up (pleasant learning experience is reactivated)
  2. First or active concert: (Optional) students are encouraged to visualize images.
  3. Second concert: Students listen to dialogue read by teacher with baroque music on in the background.
  4. Activation phase: Students engage in role plays.

- **ESL Standards:** Goal 1, Standards 1 and 3; Goal 2, Standards 1, 2 and 3; Goal 3, Standards 1, 2 and 3

- **Diverse Learners:**
  LEARNING STYLE—SENSORY PREFERENCES

MULTIPLE INTELLIGENCES
Intrapersonal/Introspective
Bodily/Kinesthetic
Verbal/Linguistic

- **Assessment:** (1) Self- or peer assessment; (2) Group project

Rassias Method

The fourth in the Humanistic series is the **Rassias Method,** which is also referred to as the *Dartmouth Intensive Language Model (DILM)*. This was developed by Dartmouth professor John A. Rassias in the late 1960s after being asked to put together an eight-week immersion program for Peace Corps volunteers. Since that time the method has been refined and enlarged. It is now used in over 80 languages at over 600 institutions worldwide.

The goal of the Rassias Method is to make the learner feel comfortable and natural with the language in a short period of time. This is done through a specific series of teaching procedures and dramatic techniques, which are designed to eliminate inhibitions and create an atmosphere of free expression from the very beginning.

- **Characteristics:** Some of the characteristics and classroom techniques are described as theatrical rapid-paced, unrestrained, theatrical, highly creative, imaginative, and necessitate great quantities of enthusiasm. Positive reinforcement is immediate and dramatic.

This method is often used for training business executives from international companies who are seeking training in both language and culture. These courses are usually short and intensive. Materials are animated and presented within a physical framework.

The Rassias Method also includes scheduling small support groups to work through structured activities, which assures that the material presented is reinforced in real-life, contextualized settings. This encourages and enhances individualized pacing and instruction.

- **Interactive and Content-Based Applicability:** The Rassias Method has components that are both defined by interactive and content-based. This places the learner at center stage and while this may be highly desirable for some, for others the impact on the affective domain is far too risky.

- **Interactive and Content-Based Activities**
  1. *Pacing or rhythmical learning*—Teachers use predesignated portions of the lesson in sequential order, sometimes with music or tonal patterns.
  2. *Choral repetition*—Whole class or sections of the class repeat(s) after the teacher or student leader.

- **ESL Standards:** All Goals and all Standards

REFLECT AND RESPOND

1. In your experiences of learning/acquiring a second/foreign language, were any of the Humanistic Approaches used? Describe those experiences.

   _____

   _____

2. Of the four approaches described in question one, which do you find most appealing? Why?

   _____

   _____

3. Describe the instances in which you see applications of these four methods in use today.

   _____

   _____

- **Diverse Learners:** All Learning Styles and all Multiple Intelligences
- **Assessment:** (1) Portfolio; (2) Oral or written interview; (3) Hands-on project; (4) Experiment

WHAT IS LANGUAGE?

As we have seen in the previous section, an examination of the variety of methodologies reveals assumptions about the relationship of the learners to the methods and about promoting uniform sequential learning. In summary, all proposed dividing language into discrete linguistic structures, parceling them out in a single way that supposedly benefited equally all learners who would ideally respond in similar ways to the methodology regardless of context. One underlying assumption for all these methodologies was that there was a single unified language that needed to be learned and that all learners follow similar paths in learning. Here we examine "What is language?" from various perspectives.

Second Language: Linguistic Theories and Psycholinguistic Theories

Since the 1980s, the most significant challenge to the prevalent mentalistic notions of language (structural linguistics and generative linguistics) has come from fields of research that view language as a social practice and not a skill or competence that is "universal." Rather, it views language as discourse specific to local cultural interactions between people who use and interpret it (e.g., interactionalists, constructivists,

THINK, PAIR, SHARE

Before you begin reading the final section of the chapter, complete the following with a partner.

1. Write down your own definition of language. (e.g., structure, use, interpretation, skills, modalities, genres)

   _____

   _____

2. What sources back up your definition? (e.g., dictionaries, textbooks, prior experience in language classes, linguistics course)

   _____

   _____

3. How might your definition shape your curriculum?

   _____

   _____

critical theorists). These perspectives come from sociolinguistics, anthropology, education, sociology, and psychology. Each discipline has generated theories to define language as a complex phenomenon that is constructed by and constructs culture, social structure, and thinking in specific settings. Theorizing from the sociocultural perspective helps us see the linkages between language, culture, thinking, socialization, and power as affecting language, literacy development and bilingualism.

For second language teachers, language as defined by these theories offers a view into what cultural and social perspectives are missing from textbook or curricula representation of language as communication. That is, the actual varieties used by members of a social group are not often included. As a quick review through many foreign language texts will indicate, little variation in use exists according to age, gender, class, race or ethnicity, or geographical region. At most, there will be comments on vocabulary differences between countries with similar national languages. The field of sociolinguistics (Halliday, 1994; Schiffrin, 1994) offers information that can help learners become sensitive to language diversity in interactions both in their communities and imagined future communities.

The field of sociolinguistics in particular examines how language use by various social groups not only helps identify membership but also constitutes membership. Often this occurs almost without reflection or conscious effort. The values, beliefs, and behaviors of a group become codified in ways members use that language; use becomes a signifier for identity. Often because language use can create social boundaries and inequities, knowing language use is viewed as social action from this perspective. People make judgments about intelligence, character, and truth based on language use. At times this is assumed as natural and often goes unquestioned. As language functions in a social world, hierarchies exist and exert pressure on the people whose variations are not given status. For this reason, examining how power operates through language use is significant yet often ignored in language classrooms—when, in fact, language use is, by nature, political and subject to economies as well. Bourdieu (1990) asserted that all language use can be seen as instances of "cultural capital" and those that have access to certain varieties will be valued. Furthermore, in the area of critical language awareness, language is analyzed to make explicit how ideology functions to position people in relations of power and knowledge (Fairclough, 1989).

ESL field research in these areas has influenced classroom practices and language instruction (Pennycook, 1989; Allwright, 1992).

Another field whose research we draw upon as a basis for informing instructional practice is social psychology. A "social interactionist" perspective on learning has been represented primarily in language field by those whose work has roots in the writings of Lev Vygotsky (1962).

The last but perhaps most familiar field is anthropology. Here we primarily select those studies that use ethnographies to research language as discourse and literacy practice over extended periods of time to give us an in-depth view of how day-to-day life unfolds in particular cultures.

Sociocultural Theories

As linguistic theories and psycholingistic theories remove language from social, political, and economic contexts, sociocultural theories strive to do the opposite. What counts as "language" is highly contextualized and particular to interactions in settings. Inasmuch as psycholinguistic theories see language as individual mental representations that each person universally acquires, sociocultural theories see language as social. Being social suggests that it changes over time and varies according to human activity in social contexts that are being created by language, and contexts that are also enacted or called into being by language. In other words, language is a means for regulating activity and interaction. It represents the objects and events that make up human experience. Words are our tools for reflecting on our experiences and communicating that thinking. Language thus can construct social contexts.

For many teachers, a sociocultural perspective probably is the least familiar because it is informed by theories that come from sociological, anthropological, and philosophical research, in addition to interactional sociolinguistics.

While many foreign language teachers of beginning and intermediate levels strive to teach the educated variety of the language rather than particular vernaculars, many second language educators frequently help learners navigate between vernaculars and the language of learning academic subjects.

In addition, language from this perspective also includes its symbolic nature and its use in the construction of knowledge and identities. This means that language is used to "become and act as a social being." In this view of language as action, participants interact together through language and other communicative signs to build their sense of being a person, to build knowledge about the world and their relation-ships to each other and the world. Let's examine several of these theories.

Sociolinguistics

In contrast to the generativist's concern to understand one underlying mental repre-sentation of language, the sociolinguist sets out to understand the many varieties of language use in human social life. Sociolinguists work to map out what differences exist in language use between codes that signal affiliations across social classes, race, gender, ethnicities, generations, and regions. Some examine solely the linguistic fea-tures that signal memberships according to the ways people use language within a par-ticular speech community (Labov, 1972; Rickford & Zentella, 1981), while others study the features of cross-cultural communication

For second language teachers, you may ask why an understanding of language variation is essential. Second language learning usually occurs when learners find the language they are studying in use in their community where many levels of vari-ation are encountered. For example, the peers with whom the learners are interact-ing will undoubtedly have their age group's variety of language or second language. Differences will be encountered in terms of what is considered boy/girl speech, male/female speech, working class/middle class language use, differences in ethnic talk, polite/impolite speech, and home community/academic/school community talk. In addition, the region in which the learner studies will provide a layer of regional variants.

Status of the Language Variation: Status of the Speaker

When the learner uses a stigmatized variety, either because it is the home language or peer language, negative consequences may occur in institutions that do not share the same values (Hornberger, 1996). For example, during the reign of the Roman Empire, Latin was considered the most important second language to acquire. As different lin-guistic groups came into contact with each other and the political and economic spheres of influence became dominated by certain groups, the language of the domi-nating groups were given higher status in relationship to the languages of lower sta-tus groups. As a result, the disenfranchisement of certain groups prevented them from receiving equitable and quality public institutional services.

Native American languages were considered inferior to English by the federal government. Therefore many native children were stripped of their first language, removed from their tribal lands, and forced into all-English education to force assimilation.

Even within a single nation, capital regions tend to have higher status than regions distant from the capital. In terms of foreign language learning, certain lan-guages enjoy "snob appeal" while others are accorded less status. (For myths about "better" languages, read Bauer and Trudgill, 1998; about standard languages, read Thomas, 1991; about bilinguals, read Krashen, 1999.) International economic plun-dering by colonial nations replicated their hierarchies in their colonies, which were layered over the hierarchies that existed prior to colonization. In general, the groups that controlled the educational, legal, and political systems controlled the use of their choice of status. Thus, many mainstream English speakers view varieties such as code switching (refers to using a combination of one or more languages simultaneously to convey meaning) Ebonics, or Chicano English as inferior versions of the standard. However, this situation is changing as varieties of language become nativized (e.g., Krachu), or stigmatized varieties gain in stature or popularity (e.g., Ebonics, code switching). This means that the Englishes of the world have contexts in which each is considered the standard, just as do the Spanishes of the world. This area of sociolinguistic research is called language planning and language policy (Phillipson, 1992).

Language as Dynamic and Changing versus Static and Monolithic

Even in the most widespread forms of bilingual education, transitional bilingual education was perceived as compensatory education that would phase out the use of mother tongue instruction as soon as English proficiency could be established. (We will discuss other models of programs in Chapter 3.) The very existence of bilingual education was challenged by right-wing groups as unAmerican and undemocratic. Groups such as U.S. English and English First waged a relentless and well-funded publicity campaign to discredit even these meager efforts. They argued to dismantle bilingual programs by replacing them with ESL or English immersion (see Macedo, 1994). From their perspective having another language was a deficit that needed to be replaced /filled by English instruction only. Despite the support of major professional organizations and researchers (e.g., TESOL, National Reading Association, and National Association for Bilingual Education), the general public still remains uninformed about the merits of bilingualism and bilingual education (Lambert, 1984; Valdes & Figueroa 1996).

Cummins speaks of additive and subtractive bilingualism. Subtractive bilingualism occurs where the native languages of bilingual students are systematically replaced by a second language and the learners are discouraged from using or identifying with their mother tongues and cultures. Additive bilingualism occurs when the mother tongue and the second language are learned without one displacing the other. At the same time, the learning of the second language opens up potential for greater appreciation and use of the mother tongue and culture as basis for growth. (Agar, 1994; Wolfram, 1999; Ernst-Slavit, 2003.)

Another type of sociolinguistics examines how people interact to construct social worlds through their talk. Interactional sociolinguists attempt to analyze the varieties and functions of language that groups use to accomplish different types of activities. Variation according to gender, women's and men's talk, race, ethnicity, social class, region, institutions, and bilingual speakers have all been examined for their use in constituting communities of speakers. Other areas included in the study of sociolinguistics are the use of verbal, paralinguistic, extraverbal, and nonverbal communication. This means that attitude is conveyed through signs that accompany oral language or through lexical choice and imagery in written texts. Also, changes in

THINK, PAIR, SHARE

When we consider language as action, we are taking into account how our utterances and writings are ways in which we act in a cultural way with others. This extends to explaining what is said or not said when, where, or how.

1. Consider the three following scenes:
   a. A teenager talking to peers in a telephone conversation
   b. A four-year-old asking that his mother buy him a new toy
   c. A young woman presenting a speech on economic development to male investors over fifty years old

   Answer this in pairs: What types of talk we would overhear if we could listen in on each of their conversations?
   Listen to the answers that your colleagues give. Give three reasons to explain why there may be varieties of responses from your colleagues.

2. If you were to help learners of your language handle the listening requirements of these conversations, how would you prepare them?
3. If your purposes were to disrupt (talk back to) the messages that were being communicated by the first person in each of the three examples, how might your listening be different? Consider:
   • your ability to recognize and use power relationships that sanction the use of certain rhetorical forms as possible and authoritative
   • your ability to recognize and use buzz words/discourse of a group
   • your ability to recognize and use language to do things to relate to people; e.g., solidarity/distance, improve your image, show membership attempt, to get them to give membership, to act as an authority/victim

This exercise illustrates that discourse between people in any setting will illustrate and constitute their knowledge, relative power, and status to each other. We will be able to see this through the talk that occurs as the relationship builds across turns. Social power, dominance patterns, symmetry, and mutual responsiveness are processed in any interaction. In everyday life, we can see the importance of analysis of discourses as a way to account for learners' attitudes towards language, motivations for language study, cognitive and affective (emotional) influences on learners' construction of knowledge, and their identities.

adjustment of purpose, topic, and attitude change the interlocutor's orientation to contexts that emerge out of communication. These influence what information is included and how it is organized.

Social linguistics was coined by James Gee in 1990 to include the study of ways of speaking, believing, and acting that are signaled and perpetuated through different language practices. Using critical sociological theories (Bourdieu, 1990, Fairclough, 1989), Gee demonstrates through discourse analysis how social worlds are constructed through and by texts. Different kinds of language use are called

REFLECT AND RESPOND

Answer the following questions. Share your answers with a partner.

1. Review how you defined language. How might you modify your definition after reading this section?
2. How might a learner's desire and effort to learn a language be affected by interaction with
   a. members of the target language group.
   b. messages perceived about language use by the wider society.
   c. the group they orient to as peers.
   d. their family and community ties.
3. While linguistic diversity is a natural part of every community, foreign language educators have relegated diversity to only the upper levels of language study in literature or culture classes. Beginning students and intermediate students are often taught language without recognition that variation exists. How might you address this oversight?
4. Because certain varieties are stigmatized and others valued, how might you equitably prepare your second language learners to use their variety to add other varieties to their repertoire?
5. What notions of "language" do you find difficult to accept?

upon in social activity in a community. For example, while some may think reading is the same decoding process no matter what the context or content, literacy is seen from a sociocultural framework as being multidimensional and multifunctional. Literacy involves speaking, listening, reading, writing, and thinking. Being literate calls on the person not only to decode the words on the page but relate the implications of the text to the literate person's actions in the world. For example, reading a newspaper comics section is not the same as reading the editorial page. Interpreting the meaning of the notion of front page news versus fine print of a contract or advertisement calls on knowledge about why information is presented in this way as well as what is being concealed or emphasized—a practice that varies across cultures.

From this discussion of sociocultural perspectives, language is defined not only in terms of its structure but by its use in human activity to symbolize, represent and create knowledge, identify, legitimize, and control. "Language as social action" is commonly used to refer to how language seems to "work."

SUMMARY

In this chapter we have provided you with a variety of methods and approaches that will not only enhance classroom instruction and help meet the national standards, but also address varieties of language levels. The methods and approaches presented in this chapter in no way suggest that teachers must subscribe to any particular one—

THINK, PAIR, SHARE

After reading this chapter, complete the following activity with a partner.

1. After reading this chapter, this is what I think is important about methods and approaches in language teaching.

   _____

   _____

2. After reading, here is what I learned from my partner. Read or listen to what your partner has written, and write down what you learned from your partner.

   _____

   _____

quite the contrary. What we recommend is that as a classroom teacher, you will adopt an "eclectic" approach/method—one that is fluid and constantly changing, depending upon the circumstances of your learners. The authors have decided that an interactive and content-based approach allows for various methods and techniques to be used by teachers to meet the needs of diverse learners.

As well, we introduced new lenses to you for understanding different perspectives of language that demonstrate the many facets that are actually operating in any social encounter. Since the teacher is no longer the authority figure around whom all activity is centered in a second-language classroom, teachers need to provide an appropriate environment in which students can work with each other on academic tasks (Ovando & Collier, 1998).

The intent of this chapter was to provide you with a menu of choices from which you will consider what aspects of language, learning, and tools of the trade (methods, techniques) you will use in structuring a space best for your learners.

EXERCISES AND ACTIVITIES

DISCUSS AND REFLECT

1. Identify two methods and/or approaches which you feel most closely benefit your students and why. Who is left out? Why? What can be done to scaffold the learning of those left out?

2. Why is it important to develop a teaching repertoire that includes a variety of methods and approaches? How will you expand your teaching repertoire to include a variety of methods and approaches?

ASK YOURSELF THESE QUESTIONS

1. Will/do I teach the way I was taught? How will I teach better than the way I was taught?

2. In selecting appropriate methods and approaches that work best for me, how can I make certain that students are benefiting from content-based and interactive instructional strategies?

3. How will/do I know if my chosen methods or approaches are working? What support or resources will I need to ensure success?

WHAT DO TEACHERS THINK?

Go to a Web site and listen to second/foreign language teachers who have recorded their views on methods and approaches in language teaching. See "Additional Resources" for examples.

FIELD-BASED EXPERIENCES

Select two second/foreign language teachers to observe for two weeks. Keep a journal with the following information: (a) Identify methods and approaches used; (b) Are the methods and approaches being used content-based and interactive? (c) Do students respond well to the chosen methods and approaches? (d) Do the teachers vary their methods and approaches by level of language being taught, time of day, number of students, composition of each class? Describe.

CASE STUDY

Mr. Ho is a middle school ESL teacher. This is his fifth year of teaching. This year he is facing his most challenging assignment—he has five classes. He teaches ESL A (beginning literacy), ESL B (intermediate level), ESL Transitional, and an ESL content math/science split-level class. The textbooks used by his school district are being discontinued and are out of date and not appealing to either him or the students. The district program of study and state framework do not address the needs of culturally and linguistically diverse learners. Because of this, Mr. Ho has decided to try and liven up these old texts by injecting methods and approaches that are very content-based and interactive and are culturally and linguistically sensitive.

1. If you were to team teach with Mr. Ho, discuss some ideas that you could collaborate on with him to use for engaging a heterogeneous group and discuss how and why these would benefit the students. Suggest approaches that may help Mr. Ho engage his students and discuss why and how they might be helpful to him.

2. As an experienced teacher, what might you offer Mr. Ho in support of thinking differently about his approach to teaching? How can Mr. Ho think differently about his approach to teaching by using a variety of methods instead of subscribing to one way?

ACTION RESEARCH

1. Create a survey instrument of no more than ten questions in which you ask teachers their views on methods and approaches of teaching second/foreign languages. These can be open-ended questions, multiple choice, or yes-no. Once you have the results, share this with your classmates or colleagues. Does a diversity of approaches serve all students? Where do students need to be supported?

2. Given the approaches or methods you have chosen to use, design an action research project that will allow you to monitor how these approaches will affect your diverse students attaining success.

ADDITIONAL RESOURCES

Cummins, J. (2000). *Language, power and pedagogy.* Clevedon, UK: Multilingual Matters.

Dave's ESL Café: *www.eslcafe.com/index.html*

Hakuta, Kenji. (1986). *Mirror of language: The debate on bilingualism.* New York: Basic Books.

Internet TESL Journal: *www.aitech.ac.jp/~iteslj*

Lightbown, P. M., & Spada, N. (1995). *How languages are learned.* London: Oxford University Press.

National Clearinghouse for English Acquisition: *www.ncela.gwu.edu/newsline*

National Clearinghouse on Bilingual Education: *www.ncbe.gwu.edu*

Reid, J. M. (Ed.). (1998). *Understanding learning styles in the second language classroom.* Upper Saddle River, NJ: Prentice Hall.

APPLICATION ACTIVITIES

1. As part of your field experience, student teaching internship, or in your own classroom, select three methods or approaches. What learning experiences (methods/approaches) have been used? How will you make the bridge between what students were used to and what you plan to use for approaches/methods? Practice teaching a fifteen-minute segment of a class once each day for a week. Keep notes on what worked well for whom and what didn't and for whom. Ask the students how they liked/disliked the method/approach and why.

2. Create a professional development portfolio by including the following: a personal narrative on your philosophy of teaching; your approaches/methods techniques; interactive and content-based activities based on certain methods and approaches.

Unit Plan

Description of Class:

Third Grade
22 students—9 boys and 13 girls
6 ESOL students, level A1, (5 boys, 1 girl) who have a combination of push-in and pull-out. Four speak Spanish, 1 speaks Farsi (the girl), 1 speaks a Philippine dialect. Three of the Spanish speakers and Philippine student have good verbal skills, but lag behind the other students in reading and writing. The Farsi speaker is behind in both verbal and written skills, and the student from the Philippines works very hard to stay on par with the other native speakers, aside from a noticeable accent.

Title:

The Wonderful World of Whales

Suggested Grade Level: Third grade

This lesson follows the Virginia Standards of Learning for grade 3:

Science

Scientific Investigation, Reasoning and, Logic
3.1 The student will plan and conduct investigations in which
  • questions are developed to formulate hypotheses:
  • predictions and observations are made;
  • data are gathered, charted and graphed;
  • objects with similar characteristics are classified into at least two sets and two two subsets;
  • inferences made and conclusions drawn;
  • natural events are sequenced chronologically; length is measured to the nearest centimeter;

Life Processes

3.4 The student will investigate and understand that behavioral and physical adaptations allow animals to respond to life needs. Key concepts include
  • Methods of gathering and storing food, finding shelter, defending themselves, and rearing young; and
  • Hibernation, migration, camouflage, mimicry, instinct, and learned behavior.

Living Systems

3.5 The student will investigate and understand relationships among organisms in acquatic and terrestrial food chains. Key concepts include
  • Producer, consumer, decomposer;
  • Herbivore, carnivore, omnivore; and
  • Predator-prey.

English

Oral language
3.1 The student will use effective communication skills in group activities.
  • Ask and respond to questions from teachers and other group members
  • Explain what has been learned
3.2 The student will present brief oral reports.
  • Speak clearly
  • Use appropriate volume and pitch

- Organize ideas sequentially or around major points of information
- Use clear and specific vocabulary to communicate ideas

Reading/literature

3.5

- Organize information or events logically. Use information to learn about new topics.
- Write about what is read.

3.7

- The student will write descriptive paragraphs.
- Develop a plan for writing.
- Focus on a central idea
- Group related ideas
- Include descriptive details that elaborate the central idea.
- Revise writing for clarity.
- Edit final copies for grammar, capitalization, punctuation, and spelling.

Technology

The student will develop basic technology skills.

- Develop a basic technology vocabulary that includes cursor, software, memory, disk drive, hard drive, and CD-ROM.
- Select and use technology appropriate to tasks.
- Develop basic keyboarding skills.
- Operate peripheral devices.
- Apply technologies to strategies for problem solving and critical thinking.

Content Area

The content area is science.

Using whales as a theme, language arts, science, and technology objectives can be integrated into the unit of study.

Overall Description:

The purpose of this unit is to get the student acquainted with the characteristics of whales, their habitat, the differences between whales and fish, and the vocabulary involved. Students will do research to learn more about a whale of their choosing, and to complement their language arts unit, they will write, edit and publish a simple paragraph about their findings.

Unit Objectives:

- Students will be able to describe the general characteristics of whales, such as size, shape, color, weight, and eating habits, and whether they are baleen or toothed whales.
- Students will be able to name at least five different types of whales.
- Students will be able to compare and contrast the similarities and differences between a whale and a fish.
- Students will understand the differences between feeding in toothed whales and baleen whales.
- Students will be able to explain how whales communicate with each other for feeding and danger.
- Students will understand how human activity can endanger whales.
- Students will use technology tools to collect, analyze, and display data.

Materials for the unit:

- Pictures of whales, size chart of whales, books about whales, video - *In the Company of Whales*
- Computers with Internet access, paper, pencils, stapler or spirals for binding books

- Chalk, Crayons, markers, and/or colored pencils for illustrating
- Measuring tape
- Combs, toothbrushes, and pepper, parsley, assorted small items of food (to demonstrate the difference between baleen and toothed whales)

Classroom environment:

- One or more computer stations within the classroom with printing capability or access to a computer lab
- TV with VCR
- Internet access is required for some of the project
- Chalkboard or overhead projector and screen for group presentations

Books:

Tokuda, W., & Hall, R. (1992). *Humphrey the Lost Whale, A True Story.* Hiean International Publishing.

Moore Kurth, L. (2000). *Keiko's Story: A Whale Goes Home.* Brookfield, MA: The Milford Press.

Wax, W., & Rowland, D. (1990). *10 Things I Know About Whales.* Chicago: Contemporary Books, Inc.

Bonner, N. (1992). *Whales of the World.* New York: Sterling Publishing Co. Inc.

Web Resources:

http://www.aqua.org

http://www.learningpage.com/pages/menu_wkshts/facts_oceans.html

http://www.whaleresearch.org/

http://www.seaworld.org/WhalesK3/all_about_whalespre2.htm

http://www.zoomwhales.com/subjects/whales/

http://www.panda.org/kids

http://www.enchantedlearning.com/subjects/whales

Week-Long Unit Activity:

The students will choose a whale that they would like to learn more about. They will research their whale on the Internet using the Web sites provided. They will then write, edit, and publish a simple paragraph about their whale. Illustrations and/or clipart will be encouraged. This will complement what they are studying in Language Arts. Students will give a short summary about their findings in front of the class. We will combine the reports of all the students to make a comprehensive book about whales, and each student will receive a copy.

Lesson Plans

Divided into five 90-minute units

Day One:

Unit Introduction

The teacher will have a KWL chart on the board. The students will be asked to contribute a fact they know about whales. We will be reading *Humphrey the Lost Whale, A True Story* by Wendy Tokuda and Richard Hall out loud.

After the book is read, the students will be asked if there is anything they would like to learn about whales, or anything they are interested in finding out more about. (The story may create some questions in their minds.) This will be written on the W (Want to Know) section of the KWL chart, and will be kept up until the unit is completed.

Objectives:

Students will be able to describe the basic characteristic of whales.

Students will be able to name at least five types of whales.

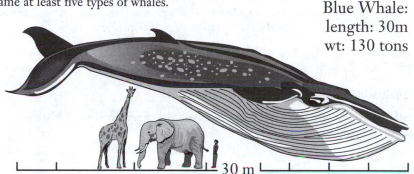

Blue Whale:
length: 30m
wt: 130 tons

30 m

Lesson:

Basic characteristics of whales.

Whales belong to the group of animals called cetaceans. They are mammals, which means that they are warm blooded, give live birth, feed their young milk, breathe air, and have hair on their bodies. There are about 75 species of cetaceans. Whales vary greatly in size. Baleen whales (also known as the great whales) are larger than toothed whales with the exception of the sperm whale, which can grow up to 65 feet in length. The blue whale is the largest animal on land or sea reaching a length of up to 110 feet and weighing nearly 200 tons. The heart of a blue whale is about the size of a small compact car, and the blood vessels are so large that a person could insert his or her arm through them.

Materials:

Books, chart of different types of whales with size comparisons, tape measure, sidewalk chalk.

Activity:

Divide the class into groups of three to four students. Give each group a bucket of sidewalk chalk and a tape measure and take them outside to a hardtop area such as the basketball court, an empty parking lot, etc. Have the students make a life-size drawings of whales using the chalk. Have the students stand inside the drawings. Estimate how many people could stand inside the different types of whales.

Evaluation/Assessment: Students will be judged on class participation. At the end of class students will be asked for a fact for the *Know* column of the KWL chart.

Day Two:

The differences between the whales and fish

Objectives:

Students will be able to name at least five differences between whales and fish.

Lesson:

How are fish and whales different? Let's consider the following questions.

- How do they breathe?
- How do they swim?
- How are their young born?
- What kind of skin do they have?
- Where do they live?
- How do they eat?
- Can fish be trained?

Activity:

(This activity will continue for the length of the unit.) Students will decide which type of whale they would like to learn more about for their research project. Students will be grouped by the whale they pick, with no more than four students to each group. Using the Internet resources and Web sites provided they will follow the rubric to develop their project.

Materials:

Computer(s) with Internet access and a printer, paper, colored pencils, markers, crayons

Evaluation/Assessment:

Students will complete a Venn diagram with the characteristics of whales and fish, discovering which features apply to both.

Day Three:
Baleen and toothed whales

Objectives: Students will understand the differences between feeding in toothed whales and baleen whales.

Lesson:

Different species of whales use different techniques to hunt and eat. There are two basic types of feeding methods:

- Toothed whales such as killer and sperm whales hunt large prey such as fish and squid, which they grab with their teeth. Of the 78 species of cetaceans in the world, 67 have teeth.
- Baleen whales have no teeth. They feed on small organisms in the water, or small fish such as herring and sardines, which they filter out of the water with sieve-like baleen plates. Only 11 species of cetaceans are baleen whales, including humpbacks, greys and blues.

Materials:

Small combs, tongs, large margarine tubs, carrot slices, parsley flakes, sprinkles

Activity:

1) Divide class into groups (four students per group would be ideal).
2) Give each group a container, a comb, and a pair of tongs. Explain that the comb represents baleen and the tongs represent teeth.
3) Fill containers halfway with water.
4) Sprinkle parsley flakes in each container. The parsley flakes represent krill. Ask students to experiment by using the tongs, or running the comb through the water. Which collects parsley flakes better?
5) Next, drop a few carrot pieces into the container. The carrots represent fish and other larger animals. Killer whales use teeth to catch fish and other prey. Have the students experiment with the comb and tongs. Which collects carrots better?
6) Use the following food items (or any others you can think of!), and have students determine if they would need baleen or teeth to eat them: pepper, cake sprinkles, small uncooked pasta, crackers, nuts, whole fruit, sesame seeds, and sunflower seeds.

Evaluation:

Informal evaluation in which the teacher will be going from table to table and watching the process. At the end of the experiment students will offer information on their findings.

Day Four:
Echolocation

Objectives:
Students will understand how whales use echolocation to find their food.

Lesson:
Although many whales have good underwater vision, the waters of the ocean may be dark or murky, especially very far down below the surface of the water. Whales make up for this inability to see underwater by using echolocation, or sonar. (Bats and some other marine mammals also use echolocation.)

Toothed whales use echolocation to sense objects. This is especially important in looking for food. Sound travels four times faster in water than in air, and much farther. In echolocation, a high-pitched sound (which sounds like clicks) is sent out by the whale. These powerful clicks or pings are produced in air sacs in their foreheads. As the whale approaches its target, it sweeps its head back and forth and saturates the area with clicks. The sound bounces off the object and some returns to the whale. The whale interprets this returning echo to determine the object's shape, direction, distance, and texture. Many of the sounds used in echolocation are high-pitched and inaudible to the human ear.

Activity:
Materials: fabric strips for blindfold

Procedure:
To teach the concept of echolocation, take the class outside and have them form a circle with one student in the center blindfolded. Another student enters the circle, but is not blindfolded. This is basically an adaptation of the game Blind Man's Bluff. The student calls out the name of the blindfolded student who in turn tries to tag him or her. Variations can have multiple students in the circle, students who move around, and louder or quieter voices.

Evaluation:
Students will be judged on class participation and observation.

Day 5:
Save the Whales

Objectives:
Students will understand how human activity can endanger whales.

Lesson:
Until the late 1960s, members of the whaling industry actively harvested (killed and processed) whales for a living. Watching whales has replaced hunting them as a booming business.

- Why is it important to protect whales?
- What do you think should be done to protect them?
- What other animals do you know of that are nearly extinct?

Activities:
Unit Activity/Research Project

The students will finish their research on whales. The groups will take turns presenting their findings with the rest of the class.

Evaluation/Assessment:

Research project will be evaluated for assessing comprehension and participation.

ESOL Adjustments:

Materials

Several books were chosen for their ease of reading for English language learners (ELLs). While containing similar content, their reading difficulty is at a comfortable level for these students.

Vocabulary

The level of the vocabulary will be difficult for the ESOL students, but will be a challenge to the non-ESOL students as well. The list of vocabulary words and definitions will remain posted on the wall throughout the unit.

Content

The content will be presented with charts and visuals to assist with comprehension. Assessment will be by all methods, instead of just written methods, to make the evaluation process more fair to second language learners.

Push in/Pull out

For the unit project, which will be the most difficult part of the unit for these students, the ESOL teacher will be pushing in to assist with the lesson. The students will be grouped and the teacher will try to plan so that there are only one or two ESOL students to each of four. The exposure to L2 and the assistance of the native speakers will make the project possible. The ESOL teacher will also assist with the paragraph writing.

The selection of books includes a few which are more simple than the others and would be perfect for second language learners.

Technology incorporated into the lesson:

- Students will use the Internet to search for information about a specific whale.
- Students may use word processing to write their paragraph.

Methods used:

CALLA: This lesson works well with the CALLA five stage instructional cycles, since it follows the lesson plan. It starts with preparation, which is motivation, or student apperception, and tries to bring students' prior knowledge into the lesson. It continues with presentation, which is the actual teacher-centered 25% of the lesson. The practice cycle is similar to the selected activity, which involves active use of new information. The Evaluation cycle is my assessment, which match my objectives, and the expansion is the future use of this material, and the way it relates to the other subjects.

I will also incorporate cooperative learning, and TPR in a content based student-centered environment.

Linguistic points:

Four skills incorporated in this lesson:

- Listening: Following directions, peer groups, cooperative learning.
- Speaking: Presenting their research findings in front of the class, class participation, group work.
- Reading: Reading stories, online information, research.
- Writing: Writing a paragraph on their findings.

Grammar structures

Students will reinforce the basics of writing a paragraph that they are learning about in language arts.

Students will create a simple paragraph by:

- Developing a topic sentence.
- Including simple supporting facts and details
- Using reference materials from the Internet

VOCABULARY WORDS:

BALEEN: Row of long fibrous plates made of keratin that grow from the roof of the mouth of ten species of whales. Whales use baleen to filter small food organisms from the water.

BELUGA: A toothed white whale that lives in Arctic waters and in the St. Lawrence River

BLOW: A big puff of air that a cetacean blows out of its blowhole(s). When a whale exhales, water vapor in its breath condenses and sometimes you can see a blow

BLOWHOLE: The nostril(s) of a cetacean. Toothed whales, including porpoises and dolphins, have one blowhole while baleen whales have two.

BLUBBER: The thick layer of fat that whales have to insulate their bodies in cold arctic water

BREACHING: A behavior observed in cetaceans that involves thrusting most or all of the body out of the water, and landing with a large splash

BULL: An adult male whale

CALF: A baby whale

CETACEANS: A marine mammal of the order cetacea, which includes whales, dolphins, and porpoises

COW: An adult female whale

DORSAL FIN: The fin on the back of a cetacean

ECHOLOCATION: Orienting, navigating, or finding food using echoes from sounds cetaceans make

FLIPPERS: The limbs of a cetacean

FLUKES: The horizontally oriented tail fin of a cetacean. The flukes are fibrous and do not have bones to support them.

KRILL: General term used to describe small, shrimplike crustaceans eaten by baleen whales

MIGRATION: The back and forth travel of whales from warm oceans to cool oceans

ORCA: Another name for the killer whale

PLANKTON: Small, marine animals and plants that drift in the oceans with the currents

POD: A group of whales

TAIL SLAPPING: cetacean behavior where the animal slaps its tail on the surface of the water, making a loud noise

WHALEBONE: Another name for baleen

Follow-up:

Tie this unit on whales in with a field trip to a local aquarium. Whales will be used as a theme in language arts.

Name: _____

KWL
Chart on Whales

What I Know About Whales	What I Want to Know about Whales	What I have Learned About Whales

Name: _____

Venn Diagram

The differences and similarites between whales and fish

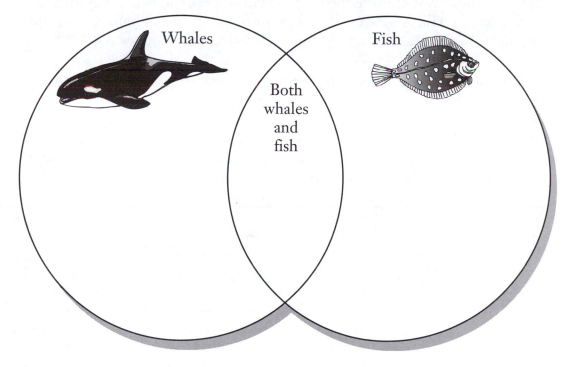

Swimmers
Live in Water
Have fins
Warm blooded
Cold blooded
Have hair

Breathe air with lungs
Breathe with gills
Nurse young
Do not care for young
Are mammals
Can be trained

Name: _____   Class: _____

Threats to Whales

Concern over the extinction of some species of whales has lead to a ban on whaling in almost one-third of the world's oceans. Despite these measures, whales remain at risk. These risks are a result of the effects of human activities. Learn more about these threats and their causes by completing this activity.

Access Whale Lessons   Lesson Three: Threats to Whales   2. Threats to Whales

Threat	Details About This Threat
Commercial Hunting	
Pollution	
Algal Blooms	
Ozone Depletion	
Global Warming	
Whale Watching	

GLOSSARY OF TERMS

audiolingual method (ALM)   places heavy emphasis on spoken rather than written language, stressing habit formation as a mode of learning

approach   a set of theoretical principles

behaviorist   based on Skinner (1957): human learning and animal learning are similar; all behavior is viewed as a response to stimuli

cognitive academic language learning approach (CALLA)   an instructional model that was developed to meet the academic needs of students learning English as a second language in American schools

cognitive anti-method   language learning is controlled by the student not by the teacher

cognitive code method   goal is to develop in students the same types of abilities that native speakers have

communicative language teaching   a functional approach which rests upon the premise that the target language should be taught through its use as a form of communication

community language learning   stresses the role of the affective domain in promoting cognitive learning

contiguity principle   a part of TPR in which a command is immediately followed by the corresponding action and body movement

direct method   modeled after the way in which children acquire their first language

feedback principle   a part of TPR in which there is a cause-and-effect relationship between the uttered command and the action that follows

frequency principle   a part of TPR in which commands, grammatical structures, and vocabulary are repeatedly linked to their referent

grammar-translation method   instruction is mostly *about* the language, not *in* the language

mentalist   described by Ellis (1990) as two contrasting perspectives on teaching: one was based on principles of first-language acquisition and is characterized by "natural" learning in the classroom. The opposing view is that learners must understand and analyze rules of language in order to build competence.

method   a procedural plan for presenting and teaching the language

methodology   system of principles, practices and procedures applied to any specific branch of knowledge

natural approach   a method of teaching second language that emphasizes the centrality of the acquisition process. Techniques in this approach focus on providing a context in the classroom for natural language to occur

pattern drills   based on grammatical structures usually presented in a dialogue, e.g., verb tenses or subject/verb agreement

pedagogy   the art or profession of teaching

rassias method   also referred to as the Dartmouth Intensive Language Model (DILM). Highlights a specific series of teaching procedures and dramatic techniques, which are designed to eliminate inhibitions and create an atmosphere of free expression

rationalist   based on the belief that students learn to understand a language by listening to it in large quantities and, likewise, students learn to speak a language by speaking it, especially when the speech is associated with an appropriate action

silent way   based on the premise that the teacher should be silent as much as possible in the classroom and the learner should be encouraged to produce as much target language as possible

suggestopedia   also known as Suggestive Accelerative Learning and Teaching (SALT) and the Lozano Method. Learning the language takes place through suggestion when students are in a relaxed environment.

technique   strategies for implementing the methodological plan

total physical response (TPR)   based on the theory that second language acquisition is similar to a child's first language acquisition. Involves having students listen to a command and immediately respond with the appropriate physical action

total physical response storytelling   uses storytelling to utilize and expand acquired vocabulary through stories that students can hear, see, act out, retell, revise and rewrite.

transformation drills   students make substitutions while practicing grammatical or syntactical forms, including person-number substitutions, patterned response drills, singular–plural transformations, and tense transformations

REFERENCES

Agar, M. (1994). *Language shock. Understanding the culture of conversation.* New York: Quill.

Allwright, D. (1992). Interaction in the language classroom: Social problems and pedagogic possibilities. In *Language teaching in today's world.* Vol. 3 of the proceedings of the 1989 International Symposium on Language Teaching and Learning, 32–53. Paris: Hachette.

Asher, J. (1982). *Learning another language through action: The complete teacher's guide* (2d ed.). Los Gatos, CA: Sky Oaks Production.

Asher, J. (1969). *Motivating children and adults to acquire a second language.* Rowley, MA: Newbury House.

Bauer, L., & Trudgill, P. (1998). *Language myths.* London Penguin.

Bourdieu, P. (1990). *The logic of practice.* Cambridge, UK: Polity Press.

Brown, H. D. (1980). *Principles of language learning and teaching.* Englewood Cliffs, N.J.: Prentice Hall.

Brown, H. D. (1994). *Principles of language learning and teaching* (3d ed.). New Jersey: Prentice Hall Regents.

Brown, H. D. (2001). *Teaching by Principles: An interactive approach to language pedagogy.* (2nd ed.) White Plains, NY: Longman.

Chamot, A. U., & O'Malley, M. (1994). *The CALLA handbook: Implementing the cognitive academic language learning approach.* New York: Longman.

Chastain, K. (1976). *Developing second language skills: Theory to practice* (2d ed.) Chicago: Rand McNally.

Chastain, K. (1988). *Developing second language skills: Theory and practice* (3d ed.). New York: Harcourt Brace Jovanovich.

Curran, C. (1976). *Counseling learning in second languages.* Apple River, IL: Apple River Press.

Diller, K. C. (1978). *The language teaching controversy.* Rowley, MA: Newbury House.

Ellis, R. (1990). *Understanding second language acquisition.* London: Oxford University Press.

Ellis, R. (1994). *The study of second language acquisition.* London: Oxford University Press.

Ernst-SLavit, (2003). *The hidden world of bilingual paraeducators: Lessons from the field.* Paper presented at the American Educational Research Association annual conference, Chicago, IL.

Fairclough, N. (1989). *Language and power.* Essex, England: Longman Group.

Fairclough, N., ed. (1992). *Critical language awareness* (pp. 33–56). London: Longman.

Faltis, C. J. (1997). *Join fostering: Adapting teaching for the multilingual classroom* (2d ed.). Upper Saddle River, NJ: Prentice Hall.

Gattegno, C. (1976). *The common sense of foreign language teaching.* New York: Educational Solutions.

Gee, J. P. (1990). Social linguistics and literacies: Ideology in discourse. Bristol, PA: Taylor & Francis.

Grittner, F. (1990). Bandwagons revisited: A perspective on movements in foreign language education. Chapter 1 (pp. 9–43) in D. Birchbichler, ed., *New Perspectives and New Directions in Foreign Language Education Series.* Lincolnwood, IL: National Textbook Company.

Halliday, M. A. K. (1994). *An introduction to functional grammar* (2d ed.). London: Edward Arnold.

Kelly, L. G. (1969). *Twenty-five centuries of language teaching.* Rowley, MA: Newbury House.

Kelly, L. G. (1976). *Twenty-five centuries of language teaching: 500 BC–1969.* Rowley, MA: Newbury House.

Krashen, S. (1995). *Insights and inquiries.* Hayward, CA: Almany Press.

Krashen, S. (1999). *Condemned without a trial. Bogus arguments against bilingual education.* Portmouth, NH: Heinemann.

Krashen, S., and Terrel, T. (1993). *The Natural Approach: Language acquisition in the classroom.* Oxford UK: Pergamon Press.

Krashen, S. (1981). *Second language acquisition and second language learning.* Great Britain: A Wheaton.

Krashen, S. (1982). *Principles and practice in second language acquisition.* New York: Pergamon Press.

Krashen, S. (1987). *Principles and practice in second language acquisition (2d ed.).* Upper Saddle River, NJ: Prentice Hall.

Labov, W. (1972). *Language in the inner city.* Philadelphia, PA: University of Pennsylvania Press.

Lambert, W. E. (1984). An overview of issues in immersion education. In *Studies on Immersion Education: A Collection for United States Educators,* (pp. 8–30). Sacramento, CA: California Department of Education.

Lozanov, G. (1978). *Suggestology and outlines of Suggestopedy.* New York: Gordon and Breach.

Macedo, D. (1994). *Literacies of power: What Americans are not allowed to know.* Boulder, CO: Westview Press.

Newmark, L. (1966). How not to interfere in language learning. In E. Najam (ed.), *Language learning: The individual and the process*. International Journal of American Linguistics.

Newmark, L., & Reibel, D. (1968). Necessity and Sufficiency in Language Learning. *International Review of Applied Linguistics in Language Teaching, 6*, 145–164.

Omaggio Hadley, A. (1993). *Teaching language in context*. (2d ed.). Boston Heinle & Heinle.

O'Malley, J. M. & Chamot, A. U. (1990). *Learning strategies in second language acquisition*. Cambridge, UK: Cambridge University Press.

Ovando, C., & Collier, V. (1998). Bilinqual and ESL classrooms: Teaching in multicultural contexts. Boston: McGraw-Hill.

Oxford, R. (May 1990). Strategy training for language learners: Six situational case studies and a training model. *Foreign Language Annals, 23*, 3 197–216.

Pennycook, A. (1989). The concept of method, interested knowledge, and the politics of language teaching. *TESOL Quarterly, 23*, 4, 589–618.

Phillipson, R. (1992). *Linguistic imperialism*. Oxford, UK: Oxford University Press.

Ray, B. (1997). *Fluency through TRP Storytelling: Achieving real language acquisition in the classroom*. Berkeley, CA: Command Performance Language Institute.

Richard-Amato, P. (1996). *Making it happen: Interaction in the second language classroom*. White Plains, NY: Longman.

Richards, J., & Rodgers, T. (1986). *Approaches and methods in language teaching: A description and analysis*. Cambridge, UK: Cambridge Press.

Scarcella, R., & Oxford, R. (1992). *The tapestry of language learning*. Boston: Heinle & Heinle.

Schiffrin, D. (1994). Interactional sociolinguistics. In D. Schiffrin (ed.) (pp. 97–136), *Approaches to discourse*. Cambridge, MA: Blackwell.

Shrum, J., & Glisan, E. (2000). *Teacher's handbook: Contextualized language instruction* (2nd ed.). Boston: Heinle & Heinle.

Stern, H. (1983). *Fundamental concepts of language teaching*. London: Oxford University Press.

Stevick, E. W. (1989). *Success with foreign languages: Seven who achieved it and what worked for them*. New York: Prentice Hall.

Terrell, T. (1977). A Natural Approach to Second Language Acquisition and Learning. *The Modern Language Journal, 61*, 325–337.

Thomas, G. (1991). *Linguistic purism*. New York: Longman.

Valdés, G. & Figueroa, R. (1996). *Bilingualism and testing: A special case of bias*. Norwood, NJ: A. Abler Publishing Corp.

Vygotsky, L. (1962). *Thought and language*. Cambridge, MA: MIT Press.

Wong Fillmore, L. (1989). Teachability and second language acquisition. In R. Schiefelbusch & M. Rice (eds.). (pp. 33–42), *The teachability of language*. Washington, DC: National Clearinghouse for Bilingual Education.

Wong Fillmore, L. (1991). Second language learning in children: A model of language learning in social context. In E. Bialystok (ed.) (pp. 49–69), *Language processing in bilingual children*. Cambridge, UK: Cambridge University Press.

Zentella, A. C. (1981). Language varieties among Puerto Ricans. In C. Ferguson & S. Heath (eds.), (pp. 215–38), *Language in the USA*. Cambridge UK: Cambridge University Press.

CHAPTER THREE

PLANNING FOR THE STANDARDS-BASED CLASSROOM

THIS CHAPTER WILL FEATURE

- Planning and managing instruction
- Considering standards in planning
- Planning strategies

YOU WILL EXAMINE

- Program or course planning
- Unit planning
- Daily lesson planning

INTRODUCTION: SETTING THE STAGE

In Chapter 2 we discussed several methods and approaches to foreign/second language teaching in classroom; however, not all are compatible with an interactive and standards-based approach. You will note that we were very careful in not recommending any one method or approach over another. We both agree that a wide repertoire will allow you to choose techniques that will serve all your students. In the same regard, learning to plan effectively is probably most readily achieved from a holistic approach. It might be argued that effective planning is one of the important keys to effective teaching. If this is true, what does it take to plan effectively?

Effective planning begins long before the teacher enters the classroom. A lesson plan should entail a thoughtfully devised description of goals, objectives, activities, outcomes, and assessments. The task of planning for teaching would be considerably simpler if our only concern was to identify the context to be learned by our students.

We have important decisions to make regarding basic content and general goals we will be working from (MacDonald, 1991).

Planning for an interactive standards-based second language classroom requires careful thinking and consideration. Learners in K–12 settings are well served when they are enabled to integrate knowledge of the academic content areas and their ability to build on their own existing knowledge. Planning also requires a clear articulation of the goals and objectives teachers are trying to achieve. Good planning and preparation requires that teachers know what materials and resources are available and how they can be used to create a positive learning experience for all students (Pelletier, 2000).

Research related to the effectiveness of language minority education has been documented in the importance of creating a classroom environment that promotes instructional strategies, including high cognitive complexity of lesson, an integrated and thematic curriculum, collaborative learning, and building upon the language-culture knowledge base that the student brings to the classroom (Au, 1993; Chamot, Dale, O'Malley, & Spanos, 1992; Cummins, 1996; Dalton & Sison, 1995; Garcia, 1991, 1994; Goldenberg, 1991; Henderson & Landesman, 1992; Rosebery, Warren, & Conant, 1992; Tharp & Gallimore, 1988; Thomas, 1994; Valdez Pierce, 1991; Warren & Rosebery, 1995). This consideration also benefits language majority students as it opens their worlds to perspectives and values they may not otherwise have opportunities to explore.

Eugene Garcia summarizes this research by emphasizing that an outstanding key to students' success is an interactive, student-centered learning context. This builds on the language and culture of the home:

- Any curriculum, including one for diverse children, must address all categories of learning goals (cognitive and academic, advanced as well as basic).

- The more linguistically and culturally diverse the children, the more closely teachers must relate academic content to a child's own environment and experience.

- The more diverse the children, the more integrated the curriculum should be. That is, multiple content areas (e.g., math, science, social studies) and language learning activities should be centered around a single theme. Children should have opportunities to study a topic in depth and to apply a variety of skills acquired in home, community, and school contexts.

- The more diverse the children, the greater the need for active rather than passive endeavors, particularly informal social activities such as group projects, in which students are allowed flexibility in their participation with the teacher and other students.

- The more diverse the children, the more important it is to offer them opportunities to apply what they are learning in a meaningful context. Curriculum can be made meaningful in a number of creative ways. Science and math skills can be effectively applied, for example, through hands-on, interactive activities that allow students to explore issues of significance in their lives. (Garcia, 1994, p. 275)

In order to plan effectively, a teacher must have a relatively broad view of the teaching–learning process as well as knowledge of the subject matter one is preparing.

THINK, PAIR, SHARE

Before you begin reading this chapter, complete the following with a partner.

1. Before reading, here is what I know about task and standards-based planning:

   _____

   _____

2. Before reading, here is what I learned from my partner:

   _____

   _____

Subject matter and content need to be organized and sequenced in such a way that students are provided the best possible chance of attaining learner goals and objectives. Therefore, effective planning requires that the teacher fully understand the learning goals and can predetermine learning foci, lesson sequencing, activities and projects, as well as teaching methods and strategies that will be most appropriate.

PLANNING AND MANAGING INTERACTIVE INSTRUCTION

Lesson planning is critical to both a student's and a teacher's success. For maximum learning to occur, planning must produce lessons that enable students to make connections between their own knowledge and experiences, and the new information being taught (Rummelhart, 1995). It is essential to plan lessons, which make learning "real world" for students. When this occurs content is more meaningful and students are able to make real-life connections to materials and activities introduced in the classroom.

The research literature written over the last several years is a very clear indicator that supports involving the learner more actively in the learning process (Kagan, 1989; Lee & VanPatten, 1995; Scarcella & Oxford, 1992). Therefore, in an interactive classroom, teachers must provide activities that allow students to actively use the language. This involves planning lessons that provide optimal opportunities for students to be active participants.

For beginning and preservice teachers, planning can be one of the more daunting tasks of teaching. Planning can seem endless. Try to begin thinking about planning in such a way that you will divide it into three different levels: **course** or **program planning, unit planning,** and **daily lesson planning.** These three types of planning have a different purpose and each covers a different period of time. See Figure 3.1 for information on long-range and short-term planning. We will first concentrate on course or program planning.

---

1. LONG-RANGE PLANS—YEARLY PLANNING

Purpose:
How were plans created?
What constraints exist with the plans?
   City/school system/community
   School or state curriculum guides
   Department
   Theoretical principles
   Beliefs
   Values
   Incoming and continuing learner interests/abilities/backgrounds
   Funding
What does the plan look like?

---

2. LONG-RANGE PLANS—QUARTERLY PLANNING (MAY BE ORGANIZED BY MARKING TERM)

Purpose:
How were plans created?
What guides the plans?
   City/school system
   School or state curriculum guides
   Department
What does the plan look like?
Short-term planning includes units, weekly plans, and daily lessons. It supports the goals of the long-term plans and puts into action these goals on a daily basis. Interview your cooperating teacher, department chair, or other teachers in the building to discover how they organize their short-term planning.

---

3. SHORT-TERM PLANS—UNIT PLANNING

Units may be organized around themes or subject areas. Some units are interdisciplinary and use a variety of knowledge content areas. Units have a beginning and an end.

- Review examples of "model" units from your school of education. How are they organized?
- Ask your cooperating teacher (or other teachers) to share units she has completed. What do you notice?

FIGURE 3.1   Long-Range and Short-Term Planning

4. SHORT-TERM PLANS—WEEKLY PLAN-BOOK PLANNING

Teachers commonly complete weekly plans in a plan book distributed by the school system. These books are often available in office supply stores, and you may want to purchase one to document the lesson plan you will be teaching during the week.

Another option is to copy from your teacher's plan book. Make multiple copies and place them in a three-ring binder to use as your own plan book. This will give you a complete documentation of all lessons you have taught.

How is your cooperating teacher's plan book organized?

Is it color coded? Could it be?

How will you organize your plan book?

5. SHORT-TERM PLANS—DAILY LESSON PLANNING

Daily lesson plans stem from long-range planning and short-term planning goals.

Does your cooperating teacher ever have a need for a daily plan?

How did he do his daily plans when he was student teaching?

What is the value to the daily plan in the scheme of long- and short-term planning?

FIGURE 3.1 (*continued*)

REFLECT AND RESPOND

1. What are some of the major considerations involved in the planning process?

   _____

   _____

2. Using Garcia's list on p. 84, what are three ways to include students' cultural and linguistic background in planning interactive lessons?

   _____

   _____

3. Look at Chapter 4 on Assessment and describe the connection between assessment and planning.

   _____

   _____

NATIONAL, STATE, AND LOCAL STANDARDS DOCUMENTS

National Standards	State Framework	District Curriculum	Lesson/Unit Plan
Goals	Goals for Instruction	Local Goals for Instruction	Specific Objectives for Learning
Standards	Standards Content Unit types Structure of content	Content Unit Specifics Suggested units and sequence Methods Resources	Content Lesson Specifics Unit topics and lessons Procedures Teaching/Learning Resources for unit lessons
Sample Progress Indicators	Recommended Assessment procedures	Specific Assessment techniques	Specific objectives and assessments

Source: Standards for Foreign Language Learning, 1996.

COURSE AND PROGRAM PLANNING

Course and program planning often include subject matter elements, learning goals, and teaching methods. This type of planning takes place in accordance with an entire year or semester. Planning frequently resembles a broad outline.

    I. Central goals and purposes of the course or program
      A. Local standards
      B. State standards
      C. Local stakeholders: colleagues at school, parents, students, administrators, principals, and school boards
    II. Course content—what is to be taught
      A. Organizing principles—learner-centered, topics relate to real world
      B. Sequencing—logical progression from familiar to unfamiliar
      C. Resources—in the community, school and classroom—human, time, space, technology, books, money
   III. Assessment
      A. Course and program evaluation
      B. Teacher self-assessment
      C. Student

Most states have an adopted framework to which you can connect your yearlong planning. State frameworks are either content or performance-based in design. The chart that follows shows the interrelatedness of national standards, state frameworks, district curriculum and lesson/unit plans.

METHODS/APPROACHES AND PROGRAM MODELS

	ELEMENTARY IMMERSION	BEGINNING/ INTERMEDIATE FL	ADVANCED FL	ELEMENTARY ESL	SECONDARY BEGINNING ESL	ADVANCED ESL
BEHAVIORIST METHODS						
Grammar-translation		x	x			x
Direct Method	x	x	x	x	x	x
Audiolingual Method	x	x	x		x	x
RATIONALIST METHODS						
Cognitive Anti-Method	x	x		x	x	
Cognitive-Code Method	x	x		x	x	
FUNCTIONAL APPROACHES						
Cognitive Academic Language Learning Approach (CALLA)	x			x	x	x
Communicative Language Teaching	x	x	x	x	x	x
Total Physical Response	x	x	x	x	x	x
Total Physical Response Storytelling	x	x	x	x	x	x
The Natural Approach	x	x	x	x	x	x
HUMANISTIC APPROACHES						
Community Language Learning		x	x		x	x
Silent Way		x	x		x	x
Suggestopedia		x	x		x	x
Rassias Method		x	x		x	x

Planning is greatly influenced by the particular program model in which you are teaching. You must also consider appropriate methods and approaches when determining how you will teach. The chart on the previous page demonstrates Methods and Approaches and Program Models in Second Language teaching.

In the context of understanding the terminology currently being used in curriculum development, Shrum & Glisan (2000, p. 49) define *goal, objective,* and *framework* as:

Goal: an aim or purpose of instruction, often stated in broad terms, as in the five goal areas of the SFLL; for example, "to gain knowledge of another culture"

Objective: what the learner will be able to do with the language as a result of instruction, defined in terms of observable behavior; for example, "The learner will be able to invite a friend to go to a social event"; sometimes the term **outcome** is used to refer to an objective

Framework: state document that describes goals and standards to be met by language programs

There are numerous program models in second language education. Wherever you find yourself teaching in the United States, you will most likely experience one or several of the models listed here.

PROGRAM MODELS

bilingual immersion education—Academic instruction given in both first and second languages for grades K–12

90–10 model—Referred to as early total immersion in Canada. Ninety percent of academic instruction is in the second language. Ten percent of academic instruction is in the first language.

50—50 model—Referred to as partial immersion in Canada. Academic instruction is half a day in each language.

developmental bilingual education—Academic instruction half a day in each language for grades K–5 or 6. This used to be referred to as Maintenance Bilingual Education or Late Exit Bilingual Education.

English as a Second Language (ESL) or English to Speakers of Other Languages (ESOL)—All academic instruction is in English.

ESL content or sheltered instruction—ESL content classes are usually self-contained at the elementary level for one or two years, with a gradual shift to moving students to their age-appropriate grade level classes. Secondary students attend classes taught by teachers with dual certification in ESL and a content area subject.

ESL pull out—Students are taken out of the grade level classroom for English language instruction according to grade level and language need. This is the most expensive of all program models in bilingual/ESL education because it requires hiring extra resource teachers who are trained in second language acquisition (Chambers & Parrish, 1992; Crawford, 1997). In the United States, ESL pullout is the most implemented and the least effective model (Thomas & Collier, 1997).

immersion—Students attend specially designed content-area classes taught in the target language. Teachers are usually certified in both the content area and the target language.

inclusion—The ESL teacher and classroom teacher plan and teach together in the grade level classroom.

mainstreaming—Once the ESL teacher determines that ESL students are proficient to move to all-English classes, the transition is made to content-centered courses.

monitoring—The ESL teacher monitors classroom progress of students who are close to exiting the ESL program as well as those students whose language needs are addressed in programs other than ESL.

sheltered English—This is a specialized form of an immersion program. Students coming from varying native language backgrounds are taught by a teacher with a background in both subject-matter and ESL pedagogy. Students usually have a regular ESL class as part of the curriculum.

submersion—Students are "submerged" in regular content-area classes with no special second language instruction. Research indicates that students do not do well in this model and some schools elect to use a pullout model program to assist students.

transitional bilingual education—Academic instruction half a day in each language with gradual transition to all second language instruction in approximately two to three years.

two-way bilingual education—Language majority and language minority students are taught together in the same bilingual class.

Sample Schools Representing Program Models for English Language Learners

Inter-American School.   This is a public school serving a population of limited English proficient (LEP) students in Chicago, grades prekindergarten to grade eight. Founded as a preschool in 1975, this school was created as a bilingual preschool—one in which children and their languages and cultures would be regarded and respected. Today this is a citywide magnet school. The students attending are 70 percent Hispanic, 13 percent African American, and 17 percent white. The goal of the program is bilingualism and biliteracy for all students, including native speakers of English.

A large segment of the school's curriculum is integrated across the disciplines and built around themes that reflect the history, culture, and traditions of the students. Therefore, there is a great deal of emphasis placed on the study of the Americas and Africa, especially how African history and culture have influenced the Americas.

Hanshaw Middle School.   Hanshaw is a middle school located in Modesto, California. It has a population of students grades six through eight—56 percent Hispanic, 26 percent white, 11 percent Asian, and 5 percent African American. Hanshaw teachers make curriculum design decisions based on the following principle: every lesson or skill must be relevant to the students' lives. Planning instruction focuses on helping students know the "why" of an answer. Most importantly, teachers build on students' own experiences in thematic instruction. Themes unify instruction across science, math, language arts, and social studies, incorporating topics from the California curriculum frameworks.

Foreign Language Program Models

There are three program models for early foreign language education: **FLES, FLEX,** and immersion. Foreign Language in the Elementary School (FLES) is a sequential, articulate program in which the goal is to teach the four skills—listening, speaking, reading, and writing. The number of contact minutes varies from school to school.

Foreign Language Exploratory or Experience (FLEX) programs are scheduled such that they take place over a given period of time, occurring from six to nine weeks or a semester. The goal for students in FLEX programs is to learn *about* the language. Culture is usually strongly emphasized and communication is not a goal.

Immersion programs provide students the opportunity to learn content subjects in the target language, usually at the elementary levels. This may range from a designated segment of the day (partial immersion) to a full day (total immersion). The goal of immersion programs is to provide extended learning opportunities in which the student can develop a certain level of language proficiency while learning subject content.

Texts and materials for FLES and FLEX programs are often teacher generated. Summer workshops and staff development throughout the school year are offered in many school districts as a means of providing teachers with materials, ideas, and collaborative networking. Textbook analysis and selection for ESL, bilingual, and foreign language programs is much more established and regulated by state and/or districts' boards of education.

THE ROLE OF TEXTBOOKS AND OTHER MATERIALS IN PLANNING FOR CONTENT-BASED INSTRUCTION

Textbooks are useful for planning in that they are usually written in such a way that they provide an organizing framework for curricula. Additionally, most textbooks include activities, additional resources, and certain types of multimedia. These may include audiotapes, video tapes, CD-ROMs, and Internet resources. Be very careful not to rely exclusively upon a single textbook, however. Remember that in working with second language learners, you will want to provide such a wide array of instructional materials that it is literally impossible for one textbook to satisfy all your needs and those of your students.

Textbook Analysis and Selection

Once determinations have been made about course or program planning, consideration must be given to resources: texts and textbook(s) selection. We carefully distinguish here between **texts** as those forms of print media represented in Chapter 5. *Textbook* is defined as one type of text such as a book used in an educational curriculum. Teachers should not limit themselves to a single textbook. We strongly encourage you to consider multiple textbooks from which you pick and choose those segments that fit your course or program objectives. Once you allow yourself the freedom to use multiple sources, you will find that you are much more likely to satisfy all of your requirements and ultimately you will not feel restricted and confined to one single textbook. The same is true for selecting appropriate texts. Using authentic text materials will not only provide avenues to connect your students to the target language and culture but it also affords the teacher multiple opportunities to bring real-world aspects into the classroom. Galloway defines **authentic texts** as "those written for oral communications produced *by* members of a language and culture group *for* members of the same language and culture group" (Galloway, 1998, p. 133). Authentic written materials should also be presented, if possible, in their original form to allow students to use nonlinguistic cues to interpret meaning (Grellet, 1981).

Textbook analysis and selection is a process that in many school districts takes place every four to seven years. Therefore, teachers should be discerning consumers when selecting textbooks since they will be using these books for a designated time frame. Textbook adoption committees are usually selected at both the state and local levels. Teachers, administrators, and curriculum developers all take part in this process. Textbook fairs are often held during which time the representatives from the various book companies present their "latest and greatest."

The following is a list of questions *second/foreign language* teachers may want to consider in analyzing and selecting textbooks:

Is the textbook visually appealing?

Does the book incorporate appropriate cultural information about the target language?

Is the textbook free of biases: cultural, gender, or racial?

How is the book organized for my goals and learners' interests?

How do my activities go beyond including the three communicative modes, e.g., **interpersonal, presentational,** and **interpretive?**

Do the textbook activities allow creation of language, knowledge, and negotiation of meaning?

How does the textbook incorporate interactive activities for diverse learning styles?

How are the following presented: e.g., language diversity, literacy, listening?

How is a focus on language forms integrated into the activities, e.g., discourse, genres, vocabulary, grammar, phonology, morphology?

How are the activities sequenced?

How are the national standards implemented throughout the book?

How is technology integrated in the text?

Does the book offer ideas for alternative forms of assessment?

Is the textbook teacher or student-centered? Does it combine both equally?

How does the textbook align with your state and local standards?

Does the book provide accommodations for learners who are
       heritage language learners (foreign language)?
       gifted?
       physically or emotionally challenged?

Does the book provide authentic written texts?

THE NATURE AND ROLE
OF CULTURE IN PLANNING

In Chapter 2, we discussed the importance of providing instructional strategies and assessment practices that reflect the cultural, linguistic, and cognitive diversity of your students. The diversity of learners, both racial/ethnic and cognitive, will continue to play a role in impacting curriculum and planning. The changing ethnic texture of the U.S. population has major implications for all of the nation's institutions, including schools, colleges, universities, and the work force (Banks, 1998). Students of color will make up about 46 percent of the nation's student population by 2020 (Pallas et al., p. 19). Most teachers now in the classroom or in teacher education programs are likely to have students from diverse ethnic, cultural, and racial groups in their classrooms during their careers. This is true for both inner-city and suburban teachers (Banks). So how then are the backgrounds, experiences, and individualities of these learners represented, acknowledged, even celebrated in the classroom? How does a teacher begin to consider and embrace the multitude of diversity when planning the program/course, unit, or daily lesson?

First, let us consider the national standards—both TESOL ESL and for foreign language. By definition, the ESL national standards were designed to address learners who represent racial, ethnic, linguistic, and cultural diverse backgrounds.

Next, take a close look at the ACTFL Standards (see www.actfl.org) and determine if they are written with consideration for students representing an array of diverse backgrounds, i.e., racial, ethnic, linguistic, and cultural. You might ask yourself how decisions are made when national standards are written and then begin to focus on the impact for planning lessons.

After examining the standards for both ESL and foreign language, teachers must approach planning in such a way that they are: a) meeting national, state, and local standards; and b) providing a curriculum that is inclusive of all learners. See the sample lesson plans on the book's website at (www.ablongman.com/hallhaley1e). This teacher incorporates national, state, and local standards in a unit on the Civil War.

After you have become familiar with national, state, and local standards, you must look at your curriculum and determine how to plan for a unit.

UNIT PLANNING

One key element in unit planning is to provide achievable and measurable unit objectives based on a standards-based curriculum. Teachers must know what the program goals are and how the levels they teach fit into long-range and short-term goals. Additionally, teachers must provide a sequence of instruction that will acknowledge student's prior language learning experiences and the expectations of the next level of instruction.

Assessment

When planning for assessment it will be helpful to understand and be capable of using various types of assessments for evaluating how students learn, what they know and are able to do. In Chapter 4 we discuss in greater detail current trends in assessment practices. For planning purposes, it is important to understand that assessment is an ongoing process, which includes formative and summative measures that may be formal or informal. Assessments may include observation, teacher-made tests, student self-assessment, peer assessment, standardized tests, portfolios of student work, performance-based tasks, or projects.

PLANNING FOR DIVERSE LEARNER NEEDS

Considerations for diverse learner needs will be discussed in greater detail in Chapter 8. For the purposes of this chapter we will address accommodating the needs of diverse learners as it relates to planning. First, we will address culturally and linguistically diverse exceptional students, and then we will describe the Individual Education Plan for special needs students.

Culturally and Linguistically Diverse Exceptional Students (CLiDES) is a term defined quite broadly. "Culturally and linguistically diverse" describes persons from a variety of cultural/racial/ethnic backgrounds for whom English is not a first language. For the purposes of this chapter the term "exceptional" will be used for abilities ranging from gifted to physical, emotional, or learning disabilities.

Teachers planning for classes that are culturally and linguistically diverse have the challenge of determining whether a specific student behavior is the result of cultural differences or evidence of a learning or behavior problem. Teachers need to be especially sensitive to the possibility that what at first appears to be a learning or behavior problem may actually be a difference in the beliefs or customs of the student. Therefore, when planning we suggest that you include a wide array of activities that cover students' learning styles. Note on the sample lesson plan templates in Figures 3.3 and 3.4 there is a section on Reflection, which focuses the teacher's attention to the need for accommodating *visual, auditory*, and *kinesthetic learners*. Similarly, we will further this discussion of planning in Chapter 8, which will cover an interactive approach for working with diverse learners.

Federal law, the Individuals with Disabilities Education Act (1999), requires detailed, written instructional plans for students with special needs. The **Individual Education Plan (IEP)** is jointly prepared by the teacher, student, parent, someone who has recently evaluated the child, and usually the building principal or a special education teacher. The IEP is a legal and binding document which must be strictly followed. Be certain that you carefully read all of the **accommodations** requirements and ask questions when in doubt. Accommodations may include: a) preferential seating for hearing or visual disabilities, b) longer wait-time for responses to questions, c) exemption from timed activities, including quizzes or tests.

PLANNING ACROSS PROFICIENCY LEVELS— DIFFERENTIATED INSTRUCTION

In addition to acknowledging that planning must include a recognition of diverse learners, as educators we must also recognize that students learn at different speeds and that they differ widely in their ability to think abstractly or understand complex

Teacher_____ School_____
Grade(s)_____ Level(s)_____ Class Description_____

PLANNING PHASE
Performance Objectives
1.
2.
3.

Lesson Outline:
Content:_____
National/State/Local Standards:_____

TEACHING PHASE
(1) Setting The Stage (Preparation)
Warm-up Activity:_____
Language Goals: (Vocabulary/Structure/Communicative Language/Functional Language)
_____

(2) Providing Input (Presentation)
Activities:
a.
b.
c.

Four Skills
Listening Activity:_____
Speaking Activity:_____
Reading Activity:_____
Writing Activity: _____

(3) Guided Participation (Practice)
a.
b.
c.

(4) Evaluation

(5) Extension/Expansion

Methods/Approaches/Strategies

_____

FIGURE 3.3   Sample Lesson Plan Template—English as a Second Language

Other Activities:
Follow-up:

Assessment:

Homework:

Technology:

Materials:

Closure:

REFLECTION PHASE
Efforts to Accommodate:

  Visual learners_____

  Auditory learners_____

  Tactile learners_____

  Specials needs learners_____

What worked well?_____

What didn't work well?_____

What will you do differently as a result of this plan?_____

How might this lesson be improved?_____

One important thing I learned was_____

FIGURE 3.3   (*continued*)

Cycle of Planning for Inquiry or Problem Posing

Identify issues
of interest

Evaluate:
Process,
outcome

Decide
next
steps

Develop
ways of
representing
issue

Act on
plan and
document
results

Analyze issue:
Describe, define.
personalize,
address larger

Create a solution: Gather
resources, evaluate options,
plan, decide on audience to
present to

In each phase of the cycle, language and literacy components are determined by the activity: oral communication, written communication, strategies for communication and learning, socio-cultural awareness, specific content, thinking processes and value formation.

FIGURE 3.3   (*continued*)

Teacher_____ School_____

Grade(s)_____ Language(s)_____ Level(s)_____

Date_____ Number of Students _____ Time_____

PLANNING PHASE
Performance/Task-based Objectives

1.

2.

3.

National/State/Local Standards:_____

TEACHING PHASE
(1) Preparation
Lesson Outline

Warm-up Activity:_____

Theme or Topic:_____

Vocabulary:_____

Verb(s):_____

Grammatical structure(s):_____

Cultural perspectives:_____

Listening/Reading/Viewing selection(s):_____

(2) Presentation and (3) Practice
Three Modes:

Interpersonal Activities:_____

Presentational Activities:_____

Interpretive Activities:_____

Methods/Approaches/Strategies:

_____

(4) Evaluation

(5) Expansion/Extension

FIGURE 3.4   Sample Lesson Plan—Secondary Level Second/Foreign Languages
Created by Dr. Marjorie Hall Haley, George Mason University (2001)

Other Activities:
Follow-up:

Assessment:

Homework:

Technology:

Materials:

Closure:

REFLECTION PHASE
Efforts to Accommodate:

   Visual learners_____

   Auditory learners_____

   Kinesthetic learners_____

   Specials needs learners (disabled and/or gifted)_____

   Heritage/Native speakers_____

What worked well?_____

What didn't work well?_____

What will you do differently as a result of this plan?_____

How might this lesson be improved?_____

One important thing I learned was_____

FIGURE 3.4 (*continued*)

ideas. This is more challenging when we consider the range of proficiency levels that you will encounter in an ESL or bilingual classroom. How can you be expected to plan for reaching *all* students? Can you teach to the standards and still differentiate?

"There's absolutely no contradiction between excellent standards-based instruction and excellent differentiated standards-based instruction," states Carol Ann Tomlinson (1999), author of several books on differentiated instruction.

There are three aspects of differentiating:

> *content*—refers to concepts, principles, and skills that teachers want students to learn
> *process*—refers to the activities that help students make sense of, and come to own, the ideas and skills being taught
> *products*—refers to culminating projects that allow students to demonstrate and extend what they have learned

Planning for differentiating instruction while meeting national, state, and local standards *is* possible. It takes careful thought and deliberation. As a beginner teacher, you will probably want to seek advice from a mentor or senior teacher if you start to feel a bit overwhelmed. Remember, what is most important is that you approach every class and every individual student as separate and unique. Get to know your students—their backgrounds, interests, and experiences. Take your students where they are and work with them to reach their full potential.

DAILY LESSON PLANNING

In this section we will guide you through the construction of a daily lesson plan, using the template provided in Figure 3.3.

PLANNING AND CONTENT-BASED INSTRUCTION

Planning Phase

In the Planning Phase you will want to identify a) performance objectives, b) content of the lesson, and c) national, state, and local standards. Planning for content-based instruction in either a ESL or foreign class requires the teacher to have knowledge of not only the subject matter but also the national, state, and local standards. Go back to Chapter 2, Table 2.1 and reread the content-based lesson plan the teacher created using CALLA. Notice how the teacher aligned the lesson plan with national TESOL ESL K–12 Standards.

Chamot and O'Malley offer the following as guidelines for planning and teaching content:

GUIDELINES FOR TEACHING CONTENT (CHAMOT & O'MALLEY, 1994)
- Provide hands-on and cooperative experiences.
- Start by linking the lesson topic to students' prior knowledge.

- Teach and have students use technical vocabulary appropriate to the content subject.
- Address different student learning styles: use visual, auditory, and kinesthetic means.
- Follow a general overview of the lesson or unit with new information in chunks; include active practice.
- Show students how to ask and answer higher-level questions about content.
- Monitor students' comprehension on an ongoing basis.
- Teach students how to "know when they don't know"—and what action to take.
- Show students how to use graphic organizers to identify prior knowledge, prepare study guides, and restructure prior knowledge.
- Provide books, articles, and other resources on content topic; teach students how to use them.
- Provide explicit instruction in learning strategies for understanding, remembering, and using content. (p. 37)

All instruction however, cannot be planned. You will encounter those times when an event happens and your students will want to discuss it, right then and there. It may be a significant world event, or a student has relatives visiting from his or her home country and wants to share a cultural experience. These are sometimes referred to as **teachable moments.** Rather than ignore or put off the student, temporarily put your plan aside and regard this as a potential learning experience.

Identifying Objectives

Identifying objectives can be simplified by answering just four questions:

1. What do you want your students to know?
2. What do you want your students to be able to do?
3. How can you assess their growth to guide your instruction, help them see their progress, and provide their parents and the community with useful information to support your efforts?
4. What measurements would help you compare your students' achievements with other students at similar levels in your school, district, or state?

These four questions can guide teaching and learning. Typically, objectives are designed in conjunction with school, district, state, and/or national standards. However there may also be points at which contradictions or conflicts occur. Resolving these points requires consulting with stakeholders to map out which points are significant to change and why.

Go to Chapter 2 and reread the teacher's lesson plan on p. 68. Notice how the objectives are stated. An objective for a high school advanced ESL class might be, "Students will locate information appropriate to an assignment in text or reference materials."

Teaching Phase

Once objectives have been identified and goals set, the next step in planning is to decide on an instructional sequence. This is where you create your Teaching Phase.

Setting the stage—This occurs at the beginning of every class period and focuses student attention on the topic, prompting students to access existing knowledge about the topic and the lesson. Example: The teacher brings in thematically related props (e.g., clothing, foods, stuffed animals) and identifies and describes each.

Providing input—This consists of the presentation of the target language vocabulary, grammar, or content (e.g., cultural information). Input is presented orally by the teacher, with visual support in the form of pictures, gestures, and/or written language. Example: The teacher uses visuals or props presented in Setting the Stage to introduce new vocabulary, grammar, or content.

Guided participation—This provides students with specific tasks in which students usually work together in pairs or small groups. Example: In pairs, Partner A describes a picture that Partner B draws; partners later switch roles.

Extension—This requires students to participate in a culminating activity in which much, if not all, the lesson's target vocabulary, grammar, and content are used. Example: Each student must interview a classmate and elicit information needed to be able to fill out the table, chart, paragraph, or questionnaire provided by the teacher.

Methods/Approaches/Strategies—You select the combination of methods and approaches that will be most appropriate to meet your objectives and to accommodate your students.

Other activities—In this section of your plan you create a follow-up activity, assessment (formative or summative), homework (where appropriate), what technology you will use, necessary materials, and how you will bring closure to the lesson.

Reflection Phase

Becoming a reflective practitioner should be a goal that you set for yourself. Not only does it entail knowledge gain but it will enhance your perspectives on teaching and learning. This knowledge growth will then affect your classroom practice. This is the section of your plan where you go back and reflect on what happened during the lesson. Start by asking yourself if you accommodated *all* learners. Then reflect on: a) what worked well, b) what didn't work well, c) what you will do differently, d) how the plan can be improved, and d) one important thing you learned.

Note how this differs dramatically from the type of planning for inquiry or problem posing in the Appendix. The sharing of power to determine the course design is explicit in the inquiry driven language and literacy class. The instructor needs to be familiar with the process but not necessarily with the outcome, as these will differ as the students enter or continue in the program. A plan such as this offers more heterogeneity of learning experiences and sharing of the assessment responsibilities with the students. A conscientious effort on the part of both teacher and learners to document what has been accomplished and in what manner occurs in this type of planning. At the same time this type of lesson provides for opportunities authentic needs-related language use (various purposes, types) critical thinking processes in different roles and grouping of students (discovery, identification, analysis, creativity, evaluation, etc.), and value formation (cultural awareness and social responsibility). The challenge in these types of plans is to ensure that the breadth and depth of the inquiry continue growing in conceptual and linguistic complexity and do not become too redundant in replicating discoveries or learning in earlier inquiries.

The following represent Omaggio Hadley's (2001) guidelines for planning lessons for a foreign language classroom:

GUIDELINES FOR PLANNING LESSONS
1. Develop a plan that is contextualized and encourages students to use the language actively to explore a particular theme.
2. Plan activities that will help students reach functional objectives.
3. Plan a variety of activities to accommodate learner differences.
4. Plan activities that are appropriate to the proficiency level of your students.
5. For each lesson that you plan, prepare a brief outline of what you intend to do during the class period.
6. Evaluate your plan after the class is over.
7. Over the course of the semester, plan lessons to include the full range of course goals. (Omaggio Hadley, 2001)

Other Considerations in Daily Planning

Time.   As a beginning teacher you may be quite surprised to discover that the lesson you taught at the beginning of the day may fail miserably in the afternoon. (Ask any veteran teacher!) The time of the day will to some degree impact your ability to effectively carry out your lesson plan. What are some factors that influence this? Students at the very beginning of the day may need a little more energizing, e.g., you may want to plan more interactive openers/warm-up activities to get your students started. You may see a change in your students' performance after lunch. The phenomenon may also occur at the end of the day when students may be feeling tired and just want the day to be over. How might instruction in block scheduling, after-school programs, and club life differ from daily planning? How might culminating activities in each semester build up school and community awareness and appreciation of your students' growing communicative abilities?

Place.   Given the growing numbers of students annually enrolling in pre-K–12 schools, often there are not enough rooms for every teacher. When this occurs teachers must share rooms, requiring one teacher to be a "floater." Usually a "floating" teacher carries all his/her materials on a cart. Careful planning for this teacher is critical since it's not always possible to go back and retrieve a forgotten item. However, if you are fortunate enough to have your own room, your planning should take into

WHAT ARE MY THOUGHTS?

You may choose to self-evaluate by writing your thoughts on the lesson plan or attaching this form to each plan.

1. Did the students learn from my lesson? Were they actively engaged? How do I know?
2. For what reasons did I depart from my lesson plan? Why? What alternative considerations could I have taken in this departure?
3. What do I think was the most effective part of the lesson? For which group of the students? How would more students benefit?
4. Were the materials/visuals/aids appropriate? Why? Why not?
5. What would I change/keep the same the next time I do this lesson?
6. What do I see as my teaching strengths?
7. What areas would I like to have my cooperating teacher/community leaders/ students assist me in reaching?
8. What other professional help is available regionally, nationally?

FIGURE 3.5   ACTion #7B—Student Teacher Reflective Guide

Modified from *Strategies for Successful Student Teaching. A Comprehensive Guide* by Carol Marra Pelletier, p. 63. Copyright 2000, 1995 by Allyn & Bacon.

consideration how seats are arranged, students' ability to see the boards clearly, where the computer(s) is/are located, and how you strategically place equipment such as overhead projector, TV/VCR. You should decide where you will place print materials and how you will use your bulletin boards for interactive activities. These must all be taken into consideration when planning for instruction.

Locating Other Resources.   A single textbook cannot meet the needs of every student. Therefore, you will need to supplement your curricula with additional resources. When you plan you will want to consider what other resources and materials to use. With the increasing popularity of information technology, more information than ever on effective planning is available for teachers. We suggest you use multiple texts as resources, including the Internet, magazines, newspapers, films, CD-ROMs, videos, student-generated items, e.g., things discovered, developed, or researched, among others, such as student generated/developed/found/discovered/researched materials, into your objectives for lessons. These can be included as part of your lesson objectives. This allows you to select those segments which are of particular importance to you and your students.

The Lesson Plan Format

While there is no one single best lesson plan format, we recommend that you consider various examples. Of the templates we have provided in Figures 3.3 and 3.4, first notice that these templates provide an organized, logical way of putting on paper your approach to standards-based planning. As a beginning teacher you will want to design lesson plans with this degree of specificity and detail. Later, as you become more experienced at planning, you will be able to modify this to a much shorter version. Figure 3.5 is an example of a reflective guide for student teachers who may want to keep a journal or log of their lesson planning and teaching experiences.

PLANNING AND ALTERNATIVE
SCHEDULING FORMATS

Teachers today find themselves being asked to assume more and more responsibility in accommodating the numerous needs of students and to radically change their teaching styles to include Block Scheduling, implement the standards, and utilize modern technology. For some, this is a source of major conflict and concern. The old way was just fine. For others, change is exciting and invigorating and the realm of creative and successful possibilities is endless.

Block Scheduling is based on the preference for in-depth instruction and extended learning sequences. Data is gradually being collected comparing learning outcomes and teacher and student reactions. Is Block Scheduling a trend? Will we move away from this and on to something else in a few years? The answers to those questions lie in how teachers meet the challenge and succeed in this longer time frame.

Block Scheduling may offer a potential solution to: classes too large, insufficient time for labs, too many failures, too little individualized instruction, few team-teaching opportunities, too short class, lunch and planning periods, and too many dropouts.

Second language teachers may find the following benefits of Block Scheduling: a ninety-minute immersion greatly helps students, fewer interruptions during class, and less clerical work. Additionally, some teachers boast of having fewer total students each semester, and less paperwork and grading.

However, some concerns about Block Scheduling are continuity, content and methodology, and standardized tests. A traditional two-semester, fifty-minute course that meets 180 days provides 9,000 minutes of instruction, whereas a class that meets ninety minutes per day for ninety days offers 8,100 minutes of instruction.

Block Scheduling provides the following advantages for students: longer time frames, more remedial and advanced instruction, increased opportunity for success in four courses rather than six, enhanced quality and quantity of time each student spends with a teacher.

Descriptions and Types of Block Scheduling

The main principle underlying Block Scheduling is based on a preference for in-depth instruction and extended learning sessions. There are two frequently used models of Block Scheduling: the 4×4 model and the Rotating Block model.

The 4×4 model is also called the Straight Block or the 90/90 model. Students take four ninety-minute classes a day, five days a week, for an entire semester. When the second semester begins, students take four different ninety-minute classes a day, five days a week, for the remainder of the school year. Thus, students take a total of eight classes each year, which adds up to a total of thirty-two over the course of their high school education. (This is an increase from the normal twenty-four.)

THE 4 × 4 MODEL

Semester One

Course One: Social Studies (7:30–9:00)

Course Two: Algebra I (9:05–10:35)

Lunch: 10:40–11:10

Course Three: English (11:15–12:45)

Course Four: Gym (12:50–2:20)

Semester Two

Course Five: Geometry (7:30–9:00)

Course Six: History (9:05–10:35)

Lunch: 10:40–11:10

Course Seven: Biology (11:15–12:45)

Course Eight: Art (12:50–2:20)

The 4 × 4 block offers many positive outcomes such as:

- Students have fewer classes to concentrate on, hopefully leading to better performance
- Longer blocks of time for instruction
- Enhances the quality and quantity of time teacher spends with each student
- Sufficient time for lab classes and visits to language and computer labs
- Less "changing time" between classes during the day (four as compared to eight)
- Fewer preparations for teachers
- Greater opportunity for individualized instruction
- More opportunity for group work and cooperative learning activities
- Fewer class interruptions
- Greater ability to make connections, both within and between different areas of the curriculum
- Greater opportunity for team teaching

However, there are also some disadvantages that must be addressed when considering the 4 × 4 model. Some of these include:

- More time is needed to prepare for a ninety-minute class.
- Generally, less material can be covered in a semester-long class than in a year-long class.
- Lack of continuity exists between two course levels. For example, if a student takes French I in the fall and French II the following fall, there will have been an eight-month gap between the two courses.
- Teachers may be required to teach more than five graduation-credit classes a year, thus increasing their work load.
- It is incredibly difficult for a student to transfer in or out of a school on the 4 × 4 plan, due to its unique nature.
- It is difficult to prepare students for standardized tests (such as the AP exam, or college placements exams) since students cover less material and they may take the course in the fall and the standardized test in the spring.

Another popular model of Block Scheduling is the Rotating Block, also referred to as the Flexible Block, the A-B Block Schedule or the Eight-Block Schedule. With the Rotating Block model, students take four ninety-minute classes on one day, and then four different ninety-minute classes the next day. This schedule continues on a rotating basis throughout the entire school year. Thus, students are taking a total of 8 classes for the entire year, which adds up to thirty-two classes over the course of their high school education. A model, with sample classes is shown below:

THE ROTATING BLOCK MODEL

A Day	**B Day**
Course One: Social Studies (7:30–9:00)	Course Five: Music (7:30–9:00)
Course Two: Algebra (9:05–10:35)	Course Six: History (9:05–10:35)
Lunch: 10:40–11:10	Lunch: 10:40–11:10
Course Three: English (11:15–12:45)	Course Seven: Biology (11:15–12:45)
Course Four: Gym (12:50–2:20)	Course Eight: Art (12:50–2:20)

The Rotating Block Schedule has many positive attributes, some of which overlap those of the 4 × 4 schedule:

- Students have two days to complete their homework.
- This schedule provides students with more opportunities to learn. Under Rotating Block Scheduling, students sign up for eight classes instead of seven.
- Student have sufficient time for lab classes and visits to language and computer labs.
- Rotating Block Scheduling spreads teacher preps over two days and therefore provides more flexibility in scheduling.
- It allows time for diverse activities such as field trips, guest speakers, technology, and films.
- There is more opportunity for individualized instruction.
- Compared to everyday models, alternate day schedules mean that students have fewer classes, quizzes, tests, and homework assignments on any one day.
- There is more opportunity for group work and cooperative learning activities.
- Fewer class interruptions occur.
- Rotating Block Scheduling allows greater opportunity for team teaching.

Even though students now have the continuity of a course for an entire year (as opposed to the 4 × 4 block), there are problems to consider with the Rotating Block Schedule as well. One of the main concerns is that since teachers see a student only at most every other day, often times it takes a bit of review during class time for students to recall what was covered the day before. In this same vein, when there is a long weekend or holiday vacation, a lot of information can be forgotten and will need to be reviewed or retaught during the next class. Further, when students are absent, it is more difficult for them to make up the work (since it is essentially work for two classes that they need to make up), and when they return to class, it has been far too long without hearing the foreign language to be able to pick up right where they left off.

Teachers must consider the instructional issues. Many teachers voice concern that students will not be able to pay attention for the longer block scheduling periods. However, experience suggests that it is not the length of a particular class, but rather what takes place in that class that holds the students' attention. If teachers assume that an entire teacher-centered format of instruction is the best approach for block scheduling, consider this again! A variety of activities and careful planning will offer the best solution.

EFFECTIVE PLANNING AND TEACHING STRATEGIES

Teacher planning is paramount to the success of the implementation of Block Scheduling. A well-planned ninety-minute class has the potential to go by very quickly, whereas a poorly-planned class will feel more like day-long class. The main objective in planning is to provide a wide variety of activities—both teacher- and student-centered. Additionally, teachers must address their students' numerous learning styles and intelligences.

Work smarter, not harder. Have students take more responsibility for their learning. One way to do this is through cooperative learning, group, and paired activities. Engage students in activities in which they work together and the teacher becomes the facilitator. Additionally, teachers can use skits, improvisations, dramatizations, and role plays. Encourage students to participate and to become involved in the planning of activities for their class. Most importantly, provide variety in your planning efforts: time to read, write, listen, discuss, experience, experiment, analyze, compute, produce, and create.

It is possible that no major curriculum changes will be necessary, especially when using the alternate day schedule. However, a **pacing guide,** a long-term planning tool, is invaluable, as it provides tentative dates of completion, **benchmarks** of various chapters, topics, and projects. It helps teachers stay focused about where they should be at what time of the year (Canady & Rettig, 1996).

Teachers must be willing to try new ways of structuring a lesson. The following sample lesson plan divides the ninety-minute block into seven component parts:

SAMPLE LESSON PLAN
Homework and previously learned material review (10–15 minutes)
Oral paired activity (10 minutes)
Listening activity with teacher or student-directed questions (15 minutes)
Present new material (10–15 minutes)
Cooperative learning guided practice (10 minutes)
Listening/writing activity (10–15 minutes)
Reteach/closure/assign homework (10 minutes)

There are numerous variations to the above plan. No one approach is better than another. It is recommended that teachers experiment and try the format that best suits their individual schedule of classes and circumstances. It is also a good idea to try a variety of formats before settling on one. Depending on the needs of the teacher and students and structure of the material, a variety of outlines can be included in one's teaching repertoire.

THINK, PAIR, SHARE

After reading this chapter, complete the following activity with a partner.

1. What steps can teachers take to critically consider the alignment of their curriculum with a state framework, national standards, and their students' needs?

_____

_____

2. What characteristics will be most beneficial to you when analyzing or selecting texts and textbooks?

_____

_____

3. What components of communication do you still need to develop vocabulary, pronunciation, grammar, literacy, communication strategies, learning strategies?

_____

_____

Strategies for Teaching on Block Scheduling

Providing a variety of teaching strategies is essential to successful teaching on Block Scheduling. The following are some you may wish to consider.

Cooperative Learning Activities. Changing grouping structures (whole class, small group, pair, and individual assignments) is an excellent way to bring variety into a ninety-minute class. The trend towards more communicative language learning encourages students to work in small groups or pairs in interactive, situational language practice, which is better served in longer class periods.

Learning Centers. Another effective strategy that can be used with Block Scheduling is the use of learning stations/centers. These may be organized according to content or themes, preferred learning styles, or multiple intelligences. These are a great way to move the students around from one task to the next, while working in cooperative groups. Many objectives can be tailored to suit a particular station. Learning stations allow the teacher to divide the class into groups of four or five and designate work sites at various locations around the room. Each site is equipped with specific instructions, materials, and any necessary equipment, e.g., cassette recorder, computer, markers. Students are given specific time directions and the teacher facilitates instruction by moving around to each station, offering assistance where needed.

Simulations. Simulations offer students the opportunity to create a replica of a real-world situation. Students are provided opportunities to "immerse" themselves in the target language and culture.

SUMMARY

In this chapter we have attempted to provide you with ways to enhance your planning skills for interactive standards-based language instruction. This will make the planning phase of teaching more manageable and meaningful. Planning for the inclusion of cultural, linguistic, and cognitively diverse learners will better enable you to teach for reaching all learners. Moreover, connecting national standards, state frameworks, and local curriculum guides will ensure that you are preparing your students to succeed by meeting the challenges in mainstream classes throughout their educational experience. It is important to remember that planning is not teaching. Incorporating purposeful texts and textbook analysis and selection will prove extremely beneficial as you plan meaningful instructional activities and assessments.

EXERCISES AND ACTIVITIES

DISCUSS AND REFLECT

1. Discuss why Block Scheduling emerged and has been so popular.

2. Observe second/foreign language teachers teaching on Block Scheduling and on traditional scheduling. How are their lessons and activities different and/or similar?

3. Offer your suggestions on how you might use Block Scheduling most effectively.

ASK YOURSELF THESE QUESTIONS

1. Why is it important to reflect on the effectiveness of your planning?

2. What additional resources will you utilize in your planning efforts?

3. How do teachers plan for multilevel classes?

4. Which model of Block Scheduling is the most appealing?

ACTIVITIES

1. Talk with an experienced second/foreign language teacher and find out the pros and cons of Block Scheduling. Then talk to an elementary ESL teacher and discuss time frames and teaching.

2. Write three questions about Block Scheduling to ask students and three to ask teachers.

3. Write a lesson plan for a beginning foreign/second language class on Block Scheduling.

WHAT DO TEACHERS THINK?

The following excerpt describes an elementary ESL teacher's approaches to planning.

As an ESOL instructor at the elementary level, I have to balance twin objectives with my lesson plans. While developing my students' ability to comprehend and produce oral and written English, I need to coordinate with the classroom teachers as much as possible in order to support the students' mainstream academic goals. A successful lesson plan is one that reinforces my colleagues' lessons and strengthens the students' ability to grasp the content in English.

I coteach with another instructor. When brainstorming for a unit or theme, we sort potential activities according to the multiple intelligences they engage. This helps us tap into the students' varied intellectual strengths and keeps us from relying on a single intelligence mode.

Preplanning doesn't necessarily dictate what transpires during a given lesson. Some of my best planning resources are my students. As I was working on "color" vocabulary with a group of beginning ESOL students, Suany (age seven) started to sing "Blue bird, blue bird through my window" to herself in Spanish. Hearing her, I changed my plans on the spot. Suany and I taught her classmates the song in English, all the while pretending to be birds flying in and out of windows. At the lesson's end, the children filed out singing the song (and they had their colors down pat). Suany's spontaneous insight engaged her classmates' musical and rhythmic intelligence and our subsequent "flight" kinesthetically reinforced new vocabulary. This serendipitous turn of events reinforced my conviction that the best lesson plans are those that deliver and reinforce content through multiple channels.

Connie M. Thibeault, ESOL Teacher, Fairfax County Public Schools, Virginia

FIELD-BASED EXPERIENCE

Visit an elementary, middle, and high school second or foreign language teacher. Discuss his or her strategies for emergency or substitute lesson plans.

CASE STUDY

Frank Chapot is a second-year ESL teacher in a suburban public high school. He asks your advice about strategies to use for interactive standards-based planning. You invite him to a curriculum planning meeting. When the meeting begins the teachers discuss aligning their curriculum with local guides. Since Frank is new to this school district, he is unfamiliar with this kind of planning.

ACTIVITY: AFTER READING THE CASE STUDY, ANSWER THE FOLLOWING QUESTIONS AND THEN SHARE YOUR RESPONSES WITH A PARTNER.

1. How can the more experienced teachers in the department assist Frank?
2. What steps can Frank take to familiarize himself with standards-based planning?

ACTION RESEARCH

1. Create a lesson plan and try using it in a classroom. What worked? What didn't work? How will you follow up this lesson? What materials/resources were useful? What form of assessment will you use? Make revisions to the plan and then reteach the same lesson. What was different?

2. Interview teachers with three or more years experience. Ask them to share with you their ideas on effective planning strategies. Collect three to five of their lesson plans. Using the plans, which categories of the formats are useful to you for planning your own portfolio?

ADDITIONAL RESOURCES

National Association for Bilingual Education—*www.nabe.org*

National Association for Multicultural Education—*www.nameorg.org*

American Association of Applied Linguistics—*www.aaal.org*

Center for Applied Linguistics—*www.cal.org*

Teachers of English for Speakers of Other Languages—*www.tesol.org*

American Council on the Teaching of Foreign Languages—*www.actfl.org*

American Association of Teachers of French—*www.frenchteachers.org*

American Association of Teachers of German—*www.aatg.org*

American Association of Teachers of Spanish and Portuguese—*www.aatsp.org*

APPLICATION ACTIVITY

Arrange for an interview with the curriculum coordinators in at least two school districts. Discuss what efforts are made to insure that national, state, and local standards are met. Next meet with two teachers, one from each of the school districts. Determine what these teachers do in planning to provide various resources to supplement their texts or textbooks.

GLOSSARY OF TERMS

accommodations   steps taken to provide additional support to students. Example: directions read aloud, un-timed quizzes and/or test

authentic texts   those written for oral communications produced by members of a language and culture group for members of the same language and culture group (Galloway, 1998)

benchmarks   performance indicators based on learner's needs

course planning   may be considered long-range planning, e.g., for quarter, semester, or year

culturally and linguistically diverse exceptional students (CLiDES) describes persons from a variety of cultural/racial/ethnic backgrounds for whom English is not a first language; exceptional may mean having abilities ranging from gifted to physical, emotional, or learning disabilities.

daily lesson plan may be considered short-term; includes objectives, lesson outline, and reflection

foreign language in elementary schools (FLES) a sequential, articulate program in which the goal is to teach the four skills—listening, speaking, reading, and writing

foreign language experience/exploratory (FLEX) programs in which the goal is for students to learn *about* the language. Communication is not a goal.

framework state document that describes goals and standards to be met by language programs

goal an aim or purpose of instruction, often stated in broad terms, as in the five goal areas of the SFLL (Shrum & Glisan, 2000)

immersion programs provide students the opportunity to learn content subjects in the target language

individual education plan (IEP) a legal document that brings parents, teachers, and other school staff together to guide the delivery of special education supports and services for a student with a disability

interpersonal mode features active negotiation of meaning; all four skills of listening, speaking, reading, and writing can be involved

interpretive mode focuses on appropriate cultural interpretation of meanings in written and oral discourse; activities can include listening and viewing

objective what the learner will be able to do with the language as a result of instruction, defined in terms of observable behavior (Shrum & Glisan, 2000)

outcome sometimes used synonymously for objective

pacing guides curriculum presented by scope and sequence

presentational mode features formal, one-way communication to listeners or readers; speaking and/or writing skills are used

program planning includes goals, curriculum guides, state frameworks, and assessment plan

teachable moments opportunities for teaching certain topics that were not planned in advance

textbook one type of text, such as a book, used in an educational curriculum

texts forms of print media such as newspapers, magazines, and applications.

unit planning may be organized around themes or content areas. Some units may be interdisciplinary.

REFERENCES

Au, K. H. (1993). *Literacy instruction in multicultural settings.* Fort Worth, TX: Harcourt Brace Jovanovich.

Ballman, T. (1998). *From teacher-centered to learner-centered: Guidelines for sequencing and presenting the elements of a FL lesson. In The Coming of Age of the Profession: Issues and Emerging Ideas for the Teaching of Foreign Languages.* Boston: Heinle & Heinle.

Banks, J. A. (1998). The lives and values of researchers: Implications for educating citizens in a multicultural society. *Educational Researcher, 27*(7), 4–7.

Canady, R. L., & Rettig, M. D. (1996). *Teaching in the Block: Strategies for Engaging Active Learners.* Princeton, NJ: Eye on Education.

Chamot, A. U., Dale, M., O'Malley, J. M., & Spanos, G. A. (1992). Learning and problem solving strategies of ESL students. *Bilingual Research Journal, 16*(3–4), 1–34.

Chamot, A. U., & O'Malley, J. M. (1994). *The CALLA Handbook: Implementing the cognitive academic language learning approach.* Reading, MA: Addison-Wesley.

Chambers, J., Parrish, T. (1992). Meeting the challenge of diversity: An evaluation of programs for pupils with limited proficiency in English: Vol. 4. *Cost of programs and services for LEP students.* Berkeley, CA: BW Associates.

Crawford, J. (1997). *Best evidence: Research foundations of the bilingual education act.* Washington, DC: National Clearinghouse for Bilingual Education.

Cummins, J. (1996). *Negotiating identities: Education for empowerment in a diverse society.* Los Angeles, California Association for Bilingual Education.

Dalton, S., & Sison, J. (1995). *Enacting instructional conversation with Spanish-speaking students in middle school mathematics.* Santa Cruz, CA: National Center for Research on Cultural Diversity and Second Language Learning.

Galloway, V. (1998). Constructing cultural realities: "Facts" and frameworks of association. In J. Harper, M. Lively, & M. Williams (eds.) (pp. 129–140), *The coming of age of the profession.* Boston: Heinle & Heinle.

Garcia, E. E. (1991). *Education of linguistically and culturally diverse students: Effective instructional practices.* Santa Cruz, CA: National Center for Research on Cultural Diversity and Second Language Learning.

Garcia, E. E. (1994). *Understanding and meeting the challenge of student cultural diversity.* Boston: Houghton Mifflin.

Goldenberg, C. (1991). *Instructional conversations and their classroom application.* Santa Cruz, CA: National Center for Research on Cultural Diversity and Second Language Learning.

Grellet, F. (1981). *Developing reading skills.* Cambridge, UK: Cambridge University Press.

Hadley Omaggio, A. (2001). *Teaching Language In Context.* Boston: Heinle & Heinle.

Henderson, R. W., & Landesman, E. M. (1992). *Mathematics and middle school students of Mexican descent: The effects of thematically integrated instruction.* Santa Cruz, CA: National Center for Research of Cultural Diversity and Second Language Learning.

Kagan, S. (1989). *Cooperative Learning: Resources for Teachers.* San Juan Capistrano, CA: Resources for Teachers.

Lee, J., & VanPatten, B. (1995). *Making communicative language teaching happen.* New York: McGraw-Hill.

MacDonald, R. E. (1999). *A handbook of basic skills and strategies for beginning teachers: facing the challenge in today's schools.* White Plains, NY: Longman Addison and Wesley.

Moll, L. C. (1988). Educating Latino students. *Language Arts, 64,* 315–324.

Ovando, C. J. (1994). Change in school and community attitudes in an Athapaskan village. *Peabody Journal of Education, 69*(2), 43–59.

Pallas, A. M., and others (1989). The changing nature of the disadvantaged population: Dimensions and trends. *Educational Researcher, 18*(5), 16–22.

Panfil, K. (1995). Learning from one another: A collaborative study of a two-way bilingual program by insiders with multiple perspectives. *Dissertation Abstracts International, 56–10A, 3859.* (University Microfilms No. AAI96-06004).

Pelletier, C. M. (2000). *Strategies for successful student teaching: A comprehensive guide.* Boston: Allyn & Bacon.

Rivera, C., & Zehler, A. (1990). *Collaboration in teaching and learning: Findings from the innovative approaches research project.* Arlington, VA: Development Associates.

Rosebery, A. S., Warren, B., & Conant, F. R. (1992). *Appropriate scientific discourse: Findings from language minority classrooms.* Santa Cruz, CA: National Center for Research on Cultural Diversity and Second Language Learning.

Rummelhart, D. E. (1995). Toward an interactive model of reading. In R. B. Ruddell, M. R. Ruddell, & H. Singer (eds.), *Theoretical models and processes of reading.* Newark, DE: International Reading Association.

Scarcella, R., & Oxford, R. (1992). *The tapestry of language learning: The individual in the communicative classroom.* Boston: Heinle & Heinle.

Shrum, J., & Glisan, E. (2000). 2nd ed. *Teacher's handbook: Contextualized Language instruction.* Boston: Heinle & Heinle.

Tharp, R. G., & Gallimore, R. (1988). *Rousing minds to life: Teaching, learning, and schooling in social context.* Cambridge, UK: Cambridge University Press.

Thomas, W. P. (1994). *The cognitive academic language learning approach project for mathematics.* Fairfax, VA: Center for Bilingual/Multicultural/ESL Education, George Mason University.

Thomas, W. P., & Collier, V. P. (1997). *School effectiveness for language minority students.* Washington, DC: National Clearinghouse for Bilingual Education.

Tomlinson, C. (1999). Mapping a route toward differentiated instruction. *Educational Leadership.* V 57, n1, 12–16.

Valdez Pierce, L. (1991). *Effective schools for language minority students.* Washington, DC: Mid-Atlantic Equity Center.

Warren, B., & Rosebery, A. S. (1995). *"This question is just too, too easy!" Perspectives from the classroom on accountability in science.* Santa Cruz, CA: National Center for Research on Cultural Diversity and Second Language Learning.

CHAPTER FOUR

EVALUATING AND CREATING INTERACTIVE AND CONTENT-BASED ASSESSMENT

THIS CHAPTER WILL FEATURE

- Introduction to assessment
- Reasons for assessment
- Alternative assessment/performance-based tasks
- Focusing on interactive oral language assessment

YOU WILL EXAMINE

- Focusing on reading
- Focusing on writing assessment
- Student self-assessment
- Interactivity and technology-based assessment
- Understanding standardized tests

INTRODUCTION: SETTING THE STAGE

Planning before you enter the classroom was emphasized in Chapter 3. In addition to this necessary step, much of what actually gets learned in class occurs through interactions that arise moment-by-moment in the class. That is, through the daily decision making in your interactions with students in the class, community, and world, you affect students' development of proficiency and identities as learners. Therefore it is vital to ask how you can evaluate the progress students make through your planned activities by evaluating the content of your lessons, the instructional and learning processes, and student achievement. In our beginning chapter, we have advocated constructivist learning principles, which recognize that students will make sense of instruction in different and often conflicting ways; therefore, it is inevitable that students will proceed to learn to use a language at a different pace, with varying degrees of fluency, and with different levels of attainment. Nonetheless, instruction must vary in order to make possible a baseline of set expectations that students will be able to achieve. Within the heterogeneity of achievement levels, **progress indicators** need to be defined, demonstrated, and defensible for various stakeholders (e.g., students, parents, community members, and school administrators). To evaluate content, process, and products we must assess how students are interacting with each other, with the materials, and with our instruction in the particular time and place where we teach. As you will need some tools for assessing your students' progress, we'll present strategies to critically deal with school and classroom alternative assessments as well as institutional tests.

INTRODUCTION TO ASSESSMENT

When you think of **assessment,** what pops into your mind? Tests? Grades? This is what most people outside of the teaching profession probably see as the bulk of what assessment is. However, the term assessment refers to much more than tests and grades. Actually, the assessment of students and their achievements involves development of materials, processes, activities, and criteria to be used as tools for determining how well and how much learning is taking place. It also is an essential means of evaluating your planning and instruction as a teacher.

Assessment can be a challenge in an ESL environment, as all students begin at varied levels and have different personal histories of learning. Cultural norms and life experiences influence how students respond to instruction. Therefore, any classroom assessment used or created must enable students to express their understanding and knowledge development individually. This does not mean that each student necessarily needs a separate assessment tool. Instead, it means that as a teacher, it is your goal and charge to incorporate tools that will help all your students reach high levels of achievement while individualizing their paths to common objectives and basic learning goals.

More and more learners, as well as ESL foreign language learners, are becoming bilingual in classes that develop not only language but also interdisciplinary content and culture. For these students, language assessment will soon be intimately linked to learning through language. So in these contexts, valid and reliable **integrated assessments** are needed that relate to the students' goals and curricular expectations. Integrated assessments are thematically linked language and literacy practices that call on learners to build relevant skills across time to reach accomplished levels of language performances across genres in subjects in their curriculum.

While foreign language learning outside of content-based instruction or immersion focuses primarily on the linguistic elements of the language, for ESL learners "minimizing the English proficiency and maximizing the learning potential" (Faltis & Wolfe, 1999, p. 269) allows for ESL learners to achieve comprehension and understandings by legitimate peripheral participation in situated learning opportunities. (Lave & Wenger, 1991). Thus assessment procedures focus on how students take up

THINK, PAIR, SHARE

Before you begin reading this chapter, complete the following activity with a partner.

1. As you were learning another language, in what ways were you informally tested to demonstrate your ability to use the target language for learning subject matter?

    _____

    _____

2. After sharing with your partner, how did your experiences (tasks and tests) resemble the type of tests you faced interacting with other speakers of the target language?

    _____

    _____

3. How were these assessment events different from paper and pencil tests? Why?

    _____

    _____

4. How did you use the information from these assessments to further your learning?

    _____

    _____

5. As a language educator, how, when, and why is your performance evaluated?
    a. What counts as a "good" performance in your evaluation?

    _____

    _____

roles in classroom learning, make use of genres related to these roles, and make contributions that change the nature of the activity and its consequences.

Before deciding on how or when to assess students, you must first decide why you are assessing them. What is the purpose for this assessment? Placement, progress, and evaluation of instruction are the three most important areas for which you will use assessment. We will examine each of these and give specific strategies or examples.

ASSESSMENTS FOR SPECIFIC DECISION MAKING

Placement

While **evaluation** is often conceived of as placing values on information gathered in a program, assessments gather information about learners. No assessment is flawless; each

THINK, PAIR, SHARE (*continued*)

b. When are these evaluations conducted and for how long?

_____

_____

c. How valid and reliable is the manner of collecting information about your performance?

_____

_____

d. What level of participation do you have in terms of interpreting the information gathered?

_____

_____

e. How is the information going to be used?

_____

_____

6. Consider multiple means to demonstrate the quality of your instruction:
    a. What would you include/exclude in a portfolio for a job interview? and Why?

_____

_____

b. What would you include in a portfolio for a professional development plan?

_____

_____

method has its advantages and limitations. Nonetheless assessments are needed to gather information deemed helpful to make programmatic and instructional decisions. The quality and quantity of information that is necessary depends on who needs what type of information, when it is needed, and why.

Initially appropriate placement into a program of study is a concern. Most districts have clearly delineated standards for ESL placement. Some use section letters (e.g., A, B, B1, C) to put students in classes appropriate for their level of comprehension in the target, or L2, language. As ESL teachers, your role is to help in this process by contributing your evaluation of the students' abilities based on assessments you administer. Often the actual placement assessment tools will be standardized across the school district or county. These tools may include oral and written components that require the students to demonstrate reading, writing, speaking, listening, and interacting facility in the L2. However, once the student is placed in your class, any further assessment leading to a level change will come as a result of your work with him or her and your observational records and documentation of the student's progress.

For second language learners, future academic success depends on learners' ability to master another language at the same time they are expected to learn content areas at their grade level. Yet often, unless assessment of their range of understanding of content knowledge is conducted through their mother tongues, assessments are highly likely to underestimate their level of past learning (Valdes & Figueroa, 1996). Furthermore, since placement assessments are conducted through the second language, learners are limited to what they can express. Consequently, their second language ability masks how much past learning they can display, which may further underrepresent what students already know and what they are capable of achieving. When placed in instruction lower than their ability, students may quickly become disinterested, bored, and disruptive of their own and other students' learning. When placed into too high levels of challenge without adequate help, often students struggle, feel frustrated, and finally drop out. It is no wonder that given such conditions, second language and non-mainstream dialect speakers are overrepresented among those who leave formal schooling before graduating. Thus placement into a supportive curriculum is a significant pedagogical, ethical, and social consideration that affects not only progress in the classroom but achievement and future aspirations in educational institutions.

Your careful observation notes can be vital to detecting if the placement procedures have failed to capture the student's strengths in relation to your curriculum. If the student seems to be handling the instruction with extreme difficulty, take notes on what the student is capable of doing. This will help indicate the level of instruction needed. Then consult with the student and family to find out additional information that may be affecting the student's performances at school. With this additional information and consultation with other teachers and counselors, you can better identify more appropriate placement. Advocating for the student's correct placement can ensure that the student's learning is not disrupted and that he or she receives the needed help or additional services.

Progress

Monitoring progress and student achievement is the most common reason to use assessment. As the teacher, you are responsible for demonstrating the students' work and the changes in their abilities or learning periodically. This requires you to use multiple tools and means of collecting information about each student. In an ESL or Foreign Language environment, simple pencil-and-paper tests will not suffice. Instead, more sensitive measures of second language development are needed. Alternative means of assessment allow you to obtain a clear picture of the students' knowledge base and comprehension development in both language and content area studies.

Second language development is not linear but nonetheless is cumulative. Therefore, assessment practices for interdisciplinary or content-based instruction need to probe in complementary ways increasingly more complex performances requiring disciplinary knowledge and language skills. This means attention should be paid to creating a variety of formats for assessment, as well as increasing language and thinking demands across formats. In general, for learners initiating their language learning, assessment probing comprehension through more nonverbal formats would allow them to demonstrate their understanding (listening and reading) while still developing productive skills (speaking and writing) through measuring performances as indications of their understanding and by increasing demands for their production as they gain control of these skills.

An easy way of understanding this is, for example, a placement exam entirely in L2 for subjects such as math or science, which typically requires reading word problems or requires manipulation of symbolic representation of concepts ($H + H + O = H_2O$ = water). Word problems would most likely fail to capture what students already know about these subjects because it is possible that students could understand the science or math and not know to choose or mark the correct answer among the multiple choice answers or not know the English word *water*.

Progress assessment and its eventual evaluation normally require a graded outcome. Grades are difficult to assign to students at such varied levels of learning coming to a common environment in which state and district standards are imposed. The best way to handle this part of your responsibility is to keep in mind that each student must be judged on his or her individual skill development and the level of learning each student has achieved with regard to the standards in place.

Keeping a dated log with pages dedicated to each student, and columns identifying the language objectives, content objective, and strategies objectives will allow you to jot observations on a regular basis without becoming overwhelmed. There are also observation instruments that would permit you to focus on generic categories. See Additional Resources at the end of this chapter.

Fortunately, in many districts teachers are provided with the opportunity to support the grades assigned to each student with a brief narrative that can give more specific and directed information about each student's academic growth. This narrative can be derived as a result of evaluation of the assessments and observations you have collected throughout the academic year. It is clear that much of the assessment and evaluation process is hinged on your ability to develop, maintain, and review your records. Be an organized assessor!

Evaluation of Instruction

When provided in a timely fashion and conscientiously used, the results from our assessment and testing procedures could inform us 1) how well our assessment procedures and content match our instructional content and practices, and 2) where gaps exist in our enabling activities and instruction. This useful feedback could hold true for students as well. This **washback** clearly should be evident in modifications made by both teacher and students. Often when teacher and students do not share how the results should be used, the washback may not be evident.

In many cases, the intentions of the assessment designers are to place learners in environments to monitor how well learners make progress and achieve. However, if we make assessments to provide feedback for adjusting instruction, results from assessment can help teachers provide more tailored support to the student. From this information teachers can find different ways to introduce, reuse, and apply the language, concepts, and strategies that learners may be struggling to learn. Furthermore,

THINK, PAIR, SHARE

Consulting with teachers at your school, find out:

1. What evaluation questions are particular to your curricular program?
   _____
   _____

2. How do these questions and answers impact your classroom instructional planning?
   _____
   _____

3. What are issues that have been ignored in the past but are relevant to your instruction?
   _____
   _____

4. How is ESL students' participation in all aspects of school life evaluated to improve their chances of success? Include participation and roles in such things as school assemblies, after-school programs, student government, and sports.
   _____
   _____

the feedback can enable the teacher to provide greater challenges, allowing students to stretch beyond what they have already learned to deepen their understandings, further their abilities, and gain new skills.

All assessment should be in some way for the purpose of tailoring instruction to students. If you pay attention to the results of your assessment of students, you can make important decisions about the style of your instruction and about specific activities you employ in your classroom. The cycle of assessment becomes complete and most effective when it truly reflects change or adjustments in your instruction.

ALTERNATIVE ASSESSMENT

Language learning is affected by the goals, expectations, experiences, and motivations of the individual student but traditional paper-and-pencil tests assume that students' performances vary only in terms of the **constructs** being measured by testing. Also, aside from essay exams, multiple choice paper-and-pencil tests tend to seek a single right answer. The types of thinking evoked by these traditional assessments fail to challenge students to consider a variety of possible ways to solve complex problems in authentic contexts, where answers are rarely right or wrong. What has been further criticized is that standardized testing usually has high stakes for the learner, effectively labeling them in potentially devastating ways to the future learning of the student. As a consequence, schools and parents fall into spending much time to teach to standardized tests in order to raise scores. Graves (2002) states, "Enormous amounts of time that should be spent in teaching are stolen by the efforts to prepare for tests. Unfortunately, preparation for the tests means the students handle short-answer questions, read short paragraphs, and fill in bubbles for the correct answer." Furthermore, this type of testing often does not provide the feedback for improving learning or instruction.

As a response to these traditional testing methods, **alternative assessments** have been proposed to enable us to attend to differences in learners, address learning over a period of time, and include communicative performances in a variety of rhetorical types and genres such as project work, simulations, games, portfolio, and debates. Saville-Trioke's model of assessment captures the multifaceted aspects that assessment must necessary take into account: context of testing, the sociocultural background of the learner, language proficiency, academic achievement, personality factors, and instruction. Thus alternative assessments try to address learners' progress toward authentic language use in tasks that require interactions similar to those in the world outside of classrooms and schools.

In the past literature on assessment, authentic language is presented in two very distinct ways: 1) authentic to school and academic learning, and 2) authentic to the world outside schools, the community, and the workforce. The latter focus involves language learning for specific purposes, while the first accepts all that is part of schooling as "authentic." The emphasis on school-like language may explain why in many second and foreign language curricula dialects and language variation according to social class, gender, race, and ethnicity are not fully incorporated or valued. Rather a supposedly nondescript "standard" language is emphasized exclusively in language assessments, such as cloze tests for reading and essays. Performances on these indirect measures represent "reading comprehension" and "writing ability" for academic purposes and are judged on the basis of their appropriateness to the school setting. Cummins (2001) identifies the language of schooling as more abstract and context independent, requiring the learner to use language to learn in ways not found outside of schooling.

On the other hand, authentic-to-life assessments may be letter writing, reading a manual/recipe to complete a task, or related to handling a job or to work in our professions, e.g., writing reports, or reading and disputing bills. These performances may be judged by criteria developed with the communicative goal of the actual situation in mind. This differs greatly from other school tasks judged on standardized criteria. People in government, private and public institutions, professional organizations, and media share in influencing the shifting norms of acceptable language use.

Nonetheless both types of authentic assessments identify behaviors that must be displayed. The assumption of all assessment is that there are specified behaviors that will be measured. (You can't measure unless you know what you are measuring and how to measure it.) For this reason, there have been two conflicting approaches: holistic and discrete language use or behaviors.

Valette (1998) asserts that learners' control over performances begin with smaller chunks of language performance and are built progressively through to bigger, more complex performances that demonstrate proficiency and accuracy. She claims to measure this by student performances that indicate **"prochievement."** Valette feels that her five-step instructional model builds learner's proficiency (i.e., guided observation, guided analysis, guided practice, simulated performance, and performance). She stresses "not to engage students in step 4 (simulated performance) activities until they demonstrate at step 3 (guided practice) that they can pronounce the language so as to be understood by native speakers, and they have a reasonable control of the vocabulary and structures which the role-play activity will require" (p. 351). Thus proficiency-oriented assessments would need to determine whether a student were ready to move from one level to the next, building in a diagnostic purpose for assessment as well as an achievement purpose. Given her model of instruction, listening comprehension would need to be developed first, learning how language works, building skills through drills and practice before guided conversations and role play. Thus students would need to have assessments that measure how well they move step-by-step before the student finally is ready for real communication in an authentic situation.

When students make use of language for their own purposes or at least to express their own thinking, making choices about relevance of information and varying their organization of that information for different purposes, they are learning sometimes unarticulated and unconscious social and pragmatic norms for being members of a language community. Additionally, learners often do not perceive the assessment in the same ways that the assessment was intended. Holding this view, alternative assessments would include the learners' perspectives, examine how well students take up the roles in activities, and how well they communicate their learning through classroom language and literacy practices. These details help teachers see the tasks from the students' perspectives and serve to guide students to higher levels of learning. Evidence is gathered in this way, which identifies where assistance is needed.

Cushman (2000) identifies authentic performances as "what students can really do." However what students can do is contingent upon what values are being conveyed through schooling. The values are indicated in the curricular objectives against which their learning is later assessed, e.g., proficiency-based or language socialization. Students who are nonnative speakers are expected to meet the same objectives but may not be able to display their achievements in English if their proficiency is still developing. What assessments can be carried out to help learners demonstrate their progress in the language proficiency as they express their learning of the content, skills, thinking habits, and dispositions?

This is less difficult in classes where both L1 skills and academic skills are being cultivated. Content in these classes can be assessed using the primary language or both, thus reserving assessment of second language for a separate assessment. In cases where bilingual students lack confidence and understandably may want to avoid the use of their weaker language, it is often difficult to gather enough evidence of their use of the L2 for displaying their knowledge. It is important to understand that by testing in only one language (L2), we communicate the denial of importance of the

ESL student's own identity and culture (L1) and we limit what knowledge he or she can demonstrate.

So the issue becomes how to create tasks that require the use of the skill or skills that students need to practice in order to attain proficiency. Cushman states, "The best performances are authentic reflections of a student's development of thoughtful habits of mind; they honor and use that student's unique qualities rather than force them into a predetermined mold" (p. 24). Wiggins (1992) advocates building higher order thinking skills in both instruction and assessment. Because assessment must reflect what is needed to solve real problems, Wiggins argues for having assessments "worth practicing and mastering." O'Malley & Chamot (1994) identify an approach that combines assessing thinking skills with language learning skills and content learning. According to this approach, students will learn how to learn in an academic environment through L2 in ways that support learning important discipline-specific concepts and discourse.

Assessment activities and tasks need to be constructed so that comprehension of subject matter and thinking behaviors can be demonstrated directly through either oral or written communicative performances. Feedback to and from the students on their progress is vital to helping them take control of their learning.

How can this be done in realistic terms? Can all complex problems be carved up step by step and not lose the whole? If you answer "yes," the small pieces are treated as "enabling processes," as Chamot and O'Malley identify for practicing higher order thinking strategies. Foreign language performance-based assessments aim to be contextualized, authentic, task-based, and learner-centered. They attempt to do these by creating instructional and assessment scenarios that use specified stimuli, settings for interaction, and specific interrelated tasks for language use and take into account the learner's background. Feedback is provided on the linguistic forms students use as well as their use of specific genres.

An excellent example of performance-based assessments for proficiency has been developed by Minnesota's Center for Advanced Research on Language Acquisition (CARLA) and the Minnesota Articulation Project. These include speaking and writing assessments whose purpose is to measure achievement of specific objectives as in specific vocabulary and grammar related to preselected topics and functions taught in chapters or during semesters through simulations and role plays. A sample of their assessments in French, German, and Spanish and the criteria for judging these performances can be found at *http://carla/acad.umn.edu/MLPA.html*. These performances have been practiced by students throughout the curriculum and thus represent a close connection between assessment and instructional content and practice. Learners are expected thus to be familiar with the themes, functions, situations, and tasks that are common to both the curriculum and the assessments.

Another form of assessing proficiency through performances is less direct and uses more context reduced formats. **Integrative testing,** testing that calls upon multiple skills at one time in a particular task, and is characterized by discrete point testing through cloze tests, dictations, and vocabulary tests, is a less concrete and more abstract measure of reading. More recently, simulated proficiency interviews have been used for testing classroom oral performances. Research by studies correlating reading ability, vocabulary expansion, and amount of reading (Cummins, 1996; Elley, 1991; Postlethwaith & Ross, 1992) use level of vocabulary development as an indicator of reading level. Since these are artificial tasks constructed to tap an underlying trait and to provide information gathered economically from a vast number of students, they are expedient and may not at all resemble "authentic" tasks. Rather they involve what are presumed to be similar thinking processes, language and content knowledge, and behaviors that represent those in real-life behaviors.

INTEGRATED PERFORMANCE ASSESSMENTS

Integrated assessments are used in assessing complex performances that are required to carry out all major phases of real-life tasks. These assessments often have students draw upon materials, concepts, and knowledge from content areas to solve a problem, answer a research question, or create an innovation. The quantity, type, and degree of integration of assessments vary due to 1) how well the range of tasks is representative of, if not a replicate of, those involved in the significant real-life performances expected, 2) how coherent and continuous (dependent upon) each task is with each other, and 3) how well they lead to further learning. Integrated assessments are contextualized and may not easily be broken down into discrete tasks and generalized to other performances.

Therefore integrated assessments are often used for examining student performances in an entire learning event or project. Assessment from this perspective requires the student to be involved from the initiation to completion of an activity. Assessment takes into account the student's quality of participation and level of skill in planning, carrying out, and evaluating the activity. The format and the content of the scoring rubric are given to students prior to use of the rubric, which provides useful feedback to help learners focus on the significant quality indicators of their various performances. In the upcoming sections we'll examine particular integrated assessments that provide alternatives to discrete assessing of discrete items. In addition we'll present how to rate these assessments through creation of criteria or rubrics.

Components of Content-Based Interdisciplinary Language and Literacy Assessments

What are the components of performance?

As an alternative assessment to paper-and-pencil assessments, performance-based assessments measure holistically how well students are able to carry out selected activities. Performances may be carrying out traditional school tasks or authentic performances required in a workplace, e.g., conducting experiments as a scientist. For our purposes of learning in a content or interdisciplinary curriculum, performances would require being able to demonstrate ability to conduct inquiries, use representational systems (e.g., understand/read/ write/talk about charts, graphs, essays, reports, Web pages) to communicate with a variety of audiences (e.g., peers, teachers, counselors) to ask and answer questions, clarify, and to negotiate their participation with others in a task.

Procedural knowledge means students know "how to do X," and declarative knowledge means that students know the "important facts about X." In language learning, knowledge about language doesn't mean that one knows how to use that language. Similarly, knowing how to speak, read, and write in a language doesn't mean one can talk about the structure of the language.

For **content-based learning** and particularly in interdisciplinary learning consideration, both performances to demonstrate content and communicate learning processes and discoveries are needed. In other words, ESL students not only need to know about writing conventions in reports about their science investigations but also about using science concepts appropriately in their performing the science project. Performances that would be needed are measurements of language development in the genres of the subject discipline, the concepts, and the thought procedures, or habits of the mind. According to Faltis and Wolfe (1999), content matter refers to the day-to day topics, eg., American Revolution or disciplinary ways of thinking, "while subject matter refers to the larger field or discipline of study [history]" p. 278.

When instruction includes assessment as a way of determining the direction, content, and pace of instruction, it is called ongoing assessment through instruction. Lessons from a psycholinguistic perspective would suggest that all significant aspects of the lesson be identified in advance for assessment in clear terms understood by the student. This assumption is that there is a universal understanding that needs to be shared about the exam and that it can be conveyed by clarity of instructions of the assessment, objectivity in the scoring of the assessment, and in maintaining similar conditions for all students taking the assessment.

From a sociocultural perspective, how to assess in ways that help students learn requires an understanding of students in particular contexts and their ways of constructing understanding. A very simple example was pointed out by Sabuur, an ESL teacher in a middle school that recently started receiving students from Japan into its ESL inclusion program. In correcting Naoto's paper, a newly arrived 12-year-old student, Sabuur marked the wrong answers with a "✔" and returned the checklist to the student with a "4" prominently on the sheet. Naoto stared a long time at the sheet in disbelief. Though the rating scale was familiar to the other students who knew that "4" was the highest grade, for Naoto the low number indicated low performance and the "✔" signaled which of his answers were correct. He could not believe that he had answered so many incorrectly because he could *read* and *write* enough English to answer most of the questions, and he knew quite a bit about insects and their habitat. Because he could not *speak* well enough to be understood, Naoto became very quiet.

In Japan, answers were ticked off when they were correct, not incorrect. Throughout the rest of the class time, rather than being as engaged as usual in the subsequent lesson on the topic, Naoto was sullen and withdrawn. As Sabuur moved around the class to see the questions students were formulating for their inquiry, Naoto burst into tears. What was a simple KWL exercise turned into a scene of tremendous emotional upheaval. Sabuur took Naoto aside and, through the help of another Japanese student who translated for him, explained the grading system and the meaning of a "✔." Gradually the misunderstanding was removed and Naoto regained his lost identity as a "good" student. That day Sabuur learned a valuable lesson about feedback practices in another culture.

Not all teachers and students are as able to negotiate common understanding as readily as Naoto and Sabuur. While instructions about the assessment were clear and Naoto was able to perform to his best, the interpretation derived from the feedback was different. In understanding how assessment practices take place in other countries, we begin to see how culture influences a) the importance students give to such assessments, b) how the procedure and interpretations of the consequences may not be clear, and c) how "clarity" is a relative term requiring negotiation between students and assessors. Rather than having merely technically sound assessment instruments, teachers need to ensure that students have a meaningful role in shaping assessments and interpreting the results of their assessments. Conferencing with students with a helpful peer can be a significant way to involve students.

There are many different ways to use alternative assessment within an ESL classroom. The following sections focus on what tools can be used to assess students in the areas of oral language, written language, and reading.

ORAL LANGUAGE ASSESSMENT

Interviews

Interviews often are used as a tool for oral language assessment. Either teacher-conducted or guided with peer interaction, interviews can provide you with keen insight into a student's command of oral language. Specifically, they can show how a student takes in an interrogative statement and is able to function with the language to respond successfully with a comprehensible, appropriate answer. In a content-based learning environment, this method can also determine the student's ability to understand and use academic language. Since the interview is a result of the interaction between the interviewer and student, the interviewer needs to be adept at establishing rapport with and eliciting responses from the learner in order to get a representative and sufficient sample of what the learner can accomplish. Since interviews allow us the possibility to analyze a learner's communicative ability in conversation, students can take either the interviewer or interviewee role to demonstrate their ability to communicate.

Some criticism has been raised in defining proficiency as determined by interactions in interview situations or simulated interviews. Interviews are only one type of interaction given the actual demands of using language in a variety of interactional contexts, such as presentations, recitals, and speeches. For this reason, it is essential to assess all learners in an ESL setting with a variety of tools to best demonstrate their level of oral proficiency.

Retelling

Story **retelling** is a technique for measuring students' integrated comprehension (through reading, writing, listening, and speaking), which is related to actual literacy practices called upon in education and genres outside of schools (e.g., investigating, summarizing, reporting, and creative writing). Retelling a story calls on a learner's ability to display what was paid attention to, which requires not only listening but also involves oral production and reading comprehension being displayed and performed for authentic purposes—learning to act on his or her world and construct knowledge. It is also possible that the student's storytelling "grammar," i.e., way of relating a story, might not be the same as what the teacher expects as an oral text. Differences may cause the teacher to question if the student understood the story when the student's embellishments were added, or when linearity or relevance were not detected by the teacher. Again there is a need to specify the criteria of a "good" story and to practice using this "criteria" (Mitchell-Kernan, 1999). Some of the rubrics for reading may be culturally biased, e.g. "If children are not used to having books around them, they do not initiate reading by themselves." Unless the teacher is explicit about the criteria, the child may be negatively evaluated. Also interaction in storytelling needs to be monitored because being singled out for storytelling might produce anxiety, which initially would impact performances. Students who are more proficient could be used as role models and helpers to the others who are less proficient. Work that is interesting and relevant to the learners evokes the type of thinking necessary for high level thinking. A suggestion is to have stronger students provide modeling for other students and ensure that others gradually develop their proficiency by taking on this role. Story retelling could be practiced in small groups, then reenacted in a larger group, rotating the role of story reteller.

Anecdotal and Observational Records

For the purpose of oral language assessment, anecdotal and observational records can be the simplest way to document and review your students' progress. Each day in the classroom your impressions and observed changes in your students' oral proficiency function as extremely important assessment tools. **Anecdotal records** are short described encounters or experiences that your students may have during their learning. In these records you can take the additional step of making judgments or drawing some conclusions about a given situation. **Observational records** are less subjective and can serve to document exactly what you see, or in this case hear, a student say or do during learning. Both forms of assessment tools allow you to build a collection of information over time about each student without interfering or interrupting the natural interactive nature of classroom conversation. Then, when you need to evaluate the students' progress, you can review and consider your anecdotal and observational records to help depict the true nature of the learners' development.

Taking anecdotal or observational records can be as simple as writing notes in a notebook, or more creative, using adhesive labels printed with each student's name on them. When designing your assessment techniques and organizational style, be creative. Do what makes you most comfortable and functions best in your teaching environment. No matter what format your records take, be sure to keep up with them, as they will serve as dynamic assessment tools when analyzing student progress.

WRITTEN LANGUAGE ASSESSMENT

Portfolios

A **portfolio** can be defined as a student-created grouping of work that may highlight specific development of skills or knowledge over a time period. For K–12 students, working portfolios are used to gather ongoing work as well as completed work. **Showcase portfolios,** because they are focused, consist of chosen pieces that exemplify the many stages of skill growth experienced by each individual student. For this reason they can serve as a summative assessment for grading purposes or public exhibitions. **Assessment portfolios** are used to provide evidence of meeting criteria for quality either in formative stages or for summative measures of achievement.

When using portfolios as assessment tools, it is essential that you carefully plan how you want the portfolio to be designed. Will it be a full compilation of work, or will the student select specific examples based on given criteria? Showcase portfolios, which highlight certain qualities or skills, can serve as a summative assessment for grading purposes or exhibition. The number and range of entries need to be identified ahead of time, as well as the type of portfolio. In order to make portfolios effective assessment tools, they must accurately reflect the goals set for your students in the areas of language development and content. The portfolio could be the basis for oral as well as written assessment. Since students learn to discuss their work in portfolios, they reveal how they approach tasks, and identify how they see their work progressing and how they will take the next steps toward completion. Through these conversations students learn to demonstrate their ability to speak about their learning, revealing what they consider important and their strategies for improving their work. Furthermore they may receive feedback from their peers, parents, and instructors on what needs improvement. Their reasoning for accepting or rejecting these suggestions demonstrates the students' comprehension and ability to use academic language and higher order thinking. Throughout the portfolio review conversation with the teacher, interaction is highly individualized and focused on the student's particular strengths and weaknesses. Research supports the beneficial effects of dialogue around text comprehension and student writing (Wells, 1994; Pressley 1995; Beck & Kucan, 1997).

The standards for judging quality of the portfolios can be formulated together with the learners, gradually increasing demands in relation to their growing ability to attend to the tasks, control their performances, and become more skillful in their performances. Standards also can be imposed by curricular expectations explained in a rubric by the number of entries and range of qualities being assessed.

Because portfolios contain concrete examples over time of student work, self-assessment and future goals, they can be revisited and used as evidence to support a student's promotion or placement in a curriculum or individualized study plan. Given the benefits of technology, portable electronic portfolios can be used to compile, store, and retrieve video, photo, and sound files in addition to written documents. For this reason, the scope and depth of a portfolio are determined in accordance with the assessment purpose, span of time available, and who is conducting the assessment.

When many English language learners and their parents are first introduced to portfolios, the notion that students and their parents have a role in the assessment practice and that students must explicitly articulate their learning may not be familiar. Students and parents may need to be persuaded of the portfolio's value. Furthermore, learners may be uncomfortable discussing their levels of doubt, questions, thinking, and learning, as these traditionally have been indicators of not being good learners. For some students, talking about what they have learned is seen as "being boastful" and thus not easily entered into. Resistance to portfolios may well arise due to lack of familiarity with what is expected; therefore, instruction needs to include how portfolios will be used and for what purposes.

A science course at high school level planning for an ESL learner's portfolio may have entries that include the following:

SCIENCE CONCEPTS
Science practices with language and literacy:
-   -Asking questions
    -Selecting one question and making guesses about cause and effect (hypothesizing)
    -Looking for evidence: observation, writing notes and findings, and reading other sources
    -Finding and describing patterns
Student's self-analysis of selected work:
-   Oral work: group dialogues, presentations
    Written work at various stages: planning, first drafts, revised drafts
    Use of technology
    Responses to peer feedback
    Parental analysis and reflection

Portfolios help students develop the tools to become more effective learners by getting them to express their perspectives as well as getting them to take into consideration other perspectives. This is true because portfolios necessitate the involvement of the students' judgments throughout the learning process. Student involvement in the development of the portfolio, through piece selection, enables the learner to get to know his or her strengths and weaknesses. It also provides the opportunity for the students to take part in a **metacognitive** or self-assessing task. The value of the student involvement is that they can become more conscious learners by applying knowledge of themselves to improve their skills. Portfolios make assessment a cooperative, interactive process that allows for valuable learning to take place.

Rubrics

A **rubric** is broadly defined as an organized and well-defined document used to analyze and assess. In this case we discuss rubrics as tools for written language assessment; however, they can also be used for oral and reading assessment. Rubrics can be either holistic or analytic in nature. If you use a **holistic** rubric, you will assign one number as an evaluation of a student's work without breaking the project's requirements down into specific, separate categories. Conversely, **analytic scoring** requires you to make a judgment based on predetermined criteria for each aspect of a written project (e.g., mechanics, composition, expression). An analytic rubric allows you to give separate ratings for each defined skill within the writing.

Rubrics must constantly be upgraded and revised on the basis of student performance. What are considered "high" standards must be justifiable, essential, and realistic for the students. For children from diverse language groups the content of instruction should be as high as necessary for the child's level, yet accommodations must be made to allow the display of the content if L2 is being used. Furthermore, if one's rubrics have as an assumption that there are general or universal underlying traits, the rubric's ability to capture these traits will require research to be substantiated. If, on the other hand, the rubric is too limited to a particular task, its generalizability to other learning would require evidence. Thus rubrics need to be reviewed and evaluated as part of accommodations made to learners with special needs.

STEPS TO DESIGNING A RUBRIC

- ❏ Check your curriculum to see which performances should be taught.
- ❏ Identify which specific performance and content standards are targeted.

Conferencing

One simple and extremely useful assessment tool for writing in an ESL or FL environment is **conferencing.** By holding regular one-on-one meetings with each student in your class regarding his or her writing, you can more clearly see where the student stands developmentally and give each student the individualized support needed to augment learning. Conferencing allows you to help students visualize and set short-term and long-term writing goals. The follow-up that conferences provide enables you to see the specific areas of improvement or need in every student's work, and gives you the opportunity to make them more aware of how they can progress and enhance their skills. An additional benefit of this assessment method is that you can also teach a student how to look at another person's work and critically analyze it, opening the door for more peer conferencing and editing. One of the best parts of conferencing is the time you have to bring each student to a better understanding of his or her own learning style.

Dialogue Journals

Considering there are often time limitations in the classroom for oral communication, the practice of using written **dialogue journals** is an effective way for teachers to communicate with students to obtain a sense of their **affective levels** and the ease or difficulty of their ongoing understanding. Dialogue journals, written conversations between teacher and student, consist of communication on a daily or weekly basis in which students write about what they choose, and the teacher writes back regularly. Journals are a way that teachers can learn more about the students' backgrounds, interests, and needs.

As described by Berriz (2000), a variety of journals can be used to supplement classroom activities: (a) morning journals open the day with personal exchanges written freestyle, (b) math, science, and literature response journals provide students the opportunity to record main ideas, thoughts, and questions about content areas, and (c) end-of-the-day journals are academic oriented and involve group participation. In end-of-the-day journals, one student leads the class in a discussion generating three main ideas learned during the day, three other students write these in complete sentences on the board, and then students enter their summaries of learning in their end-of-the-day journals.

This one-to-one communication helps students to adjust to a new environment in a less threatening way because journals are in written format, which provides for more privacy. It also allows the teacher to view the particular language and literacy needs of each student. The teacher is more focused on content than on form; the purpose is to learn about topics that are important to the students such as family, school, or personal concerns. There is no preset form—students may write comments, descriptions, complaints, or arguments with supporting details—of course, the complexity of the writing depends on the level and proficiency of the L2 learner. The main emphasis is on the student's comfort with the subject matter and form of communication; the purpose is not for the teacher to overtly correct errors in writing but to serve as a model of correct English usage. The teacher tries to respond at a modified level slightly beyond the student's proficiency level so that the reading will be somewhat challenging. In addition, the teacher echoes what the student is saying and provides some personal exchange about him- or herself. Newly arrived nonliterate students can begin by drawing pictures with a few words beneath and later move on to dictating to a teacher or more proficient student until they are ready to write on their own. Journals link personal experiences and observations to academic learning and provide a safe place to communicate with the teacher.

READING ASSESSMENT

One of the most important people in any school environment is the reading specialist. As an ESL educator, you are responsible for guiding your students through the process of reading skill building, but keep in mind that the reading specialist in your school will have many ideas and materials to assist you in this endeavor. The following assessment methods are not only means of determining progress, but are also tools to make the learning and instruction more cohesive and interactive.

Running Records

Running records are a system used often with early readers to determine how students are making sense of texts. In a running record, the teacher follows a standard set of written symbols to note each miscue made by the reader. A miscue is a reflection of efforts by the reader to interpret texts ranging from insertion of particular words/sounds, omissions, repetitions, or corrections. In **miscue analysis,** a passage is selected at the level at which the learner is expected to comprehend. The student orally reads a passage while the assessor codes each miscue that occurs following the reading on a separate sheet. Then the learner recalls and retells what was read, and reflects on or self-evaluates the reading and retelling. When the reader's comprehension is confirmed, the teacher analyzes the miscues as they affect the student's meaning and retelling. From this analysis, the teacher can obtain an indication of the learner's thought organization, thinking, and strategies. Often this analysis captures the learner's struggles to master the language of the subject specific language as well as general language. This is a somewhat intensive assessment tool, but one which allows for very specific analysis of how the multiple systems of reading are understood by the learners after the reading is completed. Keeping good running records of each student will make evaluation of progress more directed at individual goals.

Creative Comprehension Exercises

When a student has limited proficiency in a language, it is a challenge to determine how well he or she understands the material read in a classroom. Also, keep in mind that one can have the phonetic skills to read seemingly well, but without the comprehension that is needed to truly grasp the information. Therefore, it is necessary to be creative with your reading comprehension assessment tools. Use **visual organizers** and drawing as a way for the students to express knowledge. For example, when dealing with a science book about the moon, create a template or have the students create drawings of the moon and, depending on linguistic ability, write or say what they understood from the text about the topic. Teach them to gather and demonstrate facts. For fictional work, use the parts of a story (i.e., setting, characters, problem, solution) in graphic organizers shaped to fit the text. Make the expression of comprehension a fun, interactive, and creative learning experience for your students. Allow them to work in cooperative groups and come up with individually designed formats for demonstrating their comprehension. You will surely be amazed at the interest and enthusiasm for participation that bringing students into the assessment process can yield.

Inquiry Challenges

One of the most important skills you can help your students develop is the use of **inquiry.** Inquiry or questioning is a tool that students can and must use to attain knowledge and ensure comprehension throughout their academic careers as well as in real-life situations. The ability to pose coherent questions with the use of academic language is a clear criterion upon which you can assess not only reading comprehension but also oral language proficiency.

Upon approaching any text, ask your students to come up with three questions to which they want answers after reading. Then, after reading the given text allow the students to answer their own questions and meet with peers to pose questions to them as well. Finally, as a group, with you as a guide, request that the students develop one final question to ask the group based on what they have learned from reading the selection. As the guide for this instructional/assessment activity, you will be able to see and evaluate each student's ability to inquire, express reading comprehension, and use academic language by themselves, with peers, and in group settings.

Self-Assessment

Including students in the evaluation process may be quite familiar to teachers who have had recent professional development. However, helping English language learners become self-directed requires their awareness of the value this has for learning, as well as instruction on how to self-assess in a meaningful and guided way. By doing this, you can make metacognition and self-assessment part of each learning activity.

Every **self-assessment** has a purpose. When choosing or creating a self-assessment tool, be sure to pay close attention to the instructional and developmental goals you are attempting to teach. Second language learners need self-assessment tools that reach out to their instructional levels and allow them the chance to express their experiences without the interference of comprehension issues. This means that your self-assessment tools should be **scaffolded,** or designed to use language, terms, and ideas that are clear, common, and easily understandable to your students. Provide your students with any words, definitions, or concepts that they will need to utilize and understand in order to complete the self-assessment task in a lucrative way that gives them insight into their own learning.

How can you design effective self-assessment tools? The most important characteristic of an assessment tool or activity is how well it enables students to build metacognitive competence. If the student does not find a task enabling, is it? This is where the assessment of enabling skills needs to be refined, modified, or eliminated. Student input is needed to find out if the assessment skills they are learning actually "enable" them to perform or to achieve authentic tasks or not. They themselves can indicate this by reflecting on the assessment or relating this information when asked by the teachers. "How am I doing and learning?", rather than a plea to the teacher for a good grade could be a habit that good learners adopt in reflecting on their learning. Self-assessment and action in directing one's own learning are important to future academic success and lifelong learning.

If not helping the student, the assessment as well as the instruction of these "enabling" skills need to be changed. The process of developing these skills must be one that takes into account the interaction of the learners within the learning process. Enabling tasks are those that are successful based on the teacher's awareness of the levels of cognitive development, language proficiency, and learning styles present in the classroom. If the teacher develops self-assessment materials congruent with these factors, the products, performances, and outcomes of the process will be more effective in informing instruction and improving individual learning. **Benchmarks** for further assessment can be made by observing and taking into account how well the students did within the time constraints and available resources.

Some common formats for self-assessment include checklists, yes or no questions, sentence completion, or oral expression of the students' own perspectives on their own learning. No matter the format chosen, self-assessment and the instruction of metacognitive skills must be a centerpiece for your ESL students. The result of a strong self-assessment-rich classroom is a more enabled, highly functioning group of learners whose knowledge can and will more easily be enhanced in future academic environments.

INTERACTIVE AND TECHNOLOGY BASED ASSESSMENT

Part of assessment is the instrument's interactiveness with the learners. In computer-delivered assessment (also known as CBT—computer-based testing), particularly diagnostic tests, **interactivity** means that the test displays items that adjust to the learners, gradually responding and probing the student's limits to determine the extent of difficulty and what level students can accomplish. Upon completing the controlled exercises students find out how much of the material they successfully completed, and at the end of the sequence their progress on mastering the objectives is listed. When interactive assessment is used as a running record of students' learning, the record provides a way of noting students' strategies and progress.

Another aspect of interactiveness becomes an important issue in assessing oral performances, particularly in group settings. Since speaking in a group allows us the possibility to analyze a learner's oral communicative ability, the assessor needs to be aware of the limitations of observation in classroom oral interactions. Other students may or may not allow ESL learners sufficient access to the conversational floor, through interrupting or cutting them off, not letting them speak, or not attending to them. Thus the assessor's interaction with the learner, other learners' interactions, and the instruments' interaction are important aspects that affect measuring learners' ability to demonstrate oral communication.

UNDERSTANDING STANDARDIZED TESTS

Because the push for accountability has embraced standardized testing, norm-referenced and criterion-referenced tests are in high demand. Those who construct **norm-referenced tests** select a sample of students from a general population to whom they administer a carefully determined number of test items constructed to distinguish different levels of test takers' performance. The results of analyzing and selecting only the items that best sort the test takers produce the norm and the version of the test that will be used with a wider population. From the analysis of the sample population's performances, a calculation called "standard error of measurement" is determined. That is, from a technical viewpoint, an admission that all measurement is flawed. For that reason, there is a calculation made to build a band around the student's score in which the true score is assumed to fluctuate. By identifying this band, test makers can determine a satisfactory degree of confidence in obtaining a score that is representative of a student's ability.

The assumption is that all test takers will perform to their best ability and that the scores represent the best estimate of their true scores. Furthermore it is assumed that students' performances are not related to gender, race, ethnicity, or class difference, but have a normal distribution and fit a normal curve. Another assumption is that the items are fair and unbiased, thus creating the image of an even playing field. Often these tests are machine scorable through a scanning program or computer, and objective, meaning there is only one correct answer admissible and it is consistently rated as such. Normed reference exams are set up not to test information taught, but rather to force scores into a normal curve based on the items in the test. The scores are reported to the school districts in terms of percentile, median, mean, and standard deviation.

If teachers want to help students do better on these types of tests, they would need to teach to the test. In the short term, the most benefits would be reaped by preparing students to learn how to take these tests well, eg., test-taking strategies for prior preparation and during test taking, such as getting good rest before the exam, being prepared to give their best effort, bringing a treat to snack on, reading directions carefully, using time efficiently by doing more of the easy items first, and reviewing answers before solving the items that are the hardest.

The next effective strategy is to help students resolve more of the items correctly in relation to the weight of each test section. However in the long term, once more teachers teach to the test and students achieve the correct answers, those items will be removed and replaced by items that may be more difficult.

The **criterion referenced tests** are distinguished from norm-referenced tests because they identify levels of performance that all students are expected to aim for. These tests then measure how well the student performances meet the experts' prescribed levels of performance. Scores are reported in terms of bands of achievement from unacceptable to highly accomplished performances. Statistically analyzed scores from students and standard errors of measurement are calculated as well.

Setting cutoffs for both of the standardized tests results from negotiation between stakeholders. However, passing or failing cutoffs are often more political than technical. State educational officials as well as testing companies can change their cutoff scores depending on how many people consistently fail or succeed. Some school districts use these tests as both placement and exit tests. Find out which tests are being used in your district, school, and program. How are students, teachers, parents, and administrators making use of the information provided?

Whichever form of standardized testing is used in your district, be sure that you seek any accommodations available to make your ESL students more comfortable in the often pressurized testing environment. Give your second language learners the tools they need to perform at their highest level of ability by teaching them the skills of approach. Instruct them to approach the exams as a way to show what they know and how well they can express it. Review examples and let them work in groups to get ideas for strategic guessing, elimination of wrong answers, and other uncomplicated strategies for test-taking. If they learn as an interactive group, with each student contributing ideas, they will become stronger learners, analyzers, and ultimately test takers.

REFLECT AND RESPOND

1. Considering limitations of "recipe" critical thinking: Can higher order thinking be practiced in a step-by-step fashion in finding answers to novel complex problems?

_____

_____

2. How well related are the tasks in step-by-step instruction? Are alternative steps or thinking being disregarded or devalued?

_____

_____

3. How can performance criteria escape from being subjective?

_____

_____

SUMMARY

Becoming at ease with evaluation, assessment, and testing is similar to becoming clearer about your own and your curriculum's expectations for helping students achieve excellence. In this chapter we have shown how characteristics and goals of your program necessarily will need to be congruent with your classroom assessment and testing practices. Where there is conflict there will be goals that are not shared and no means to accomplish them.

For administrators of ESOL programs, the selection, placement, and graduation of students, as well as the professional development and growth of teachers are vital for creating a healthy learning community. Evaluation of all vital aspects of our community is well warranted. As teachers, we have a responsibility to make changes in our instructional practices to reach and teach all students to prepare them to take on roles in a rapidly changing, ever further globally interconnected democratic society. Valid, reliable, fair, and manageable procedures and instruments are needed to handle these responsibilities in an equitable and ethical manner. Our purposes for using these instruments, as well as the impact of decisions to use these instruments themselves, require our attention and constant monitoring to see to what degree they are serving our decision-making needs and at what cost (e.g., financial, time, human resources, consequences on students' futures).

Assessments of student progress and achievement provide information not only about how well students are doing but also how well the curriculum is serving students. If the feedback loop between assessment and instruction is broken, sustained high levels of performance and achievement will be difficult for students, discouraging for teachers, and a loss for the community in not receiving graduates who are prepared to contribute.

Authentic performance assessments can be conducted as a part of the instructional sequence, at critical points to check progress on projects, portfolios, conferences, and at the end to demonstrate outcome in exhibitions, presentations, plays, and reports. (See Additional Resources at the end of the chapter for more sample assessment tools.) These instruments need to capture evidence of students' abilities to use first and second language and literacy to learn content matter, develop new knowledge, and communicate and use what they have learned. Strong assessment practices are integral parts of the instructional process. Without this essential link between instruction and student achievement, our ability to serve our learners would be greatly hindered. For this reason, it is essential to keep assessment as a major priority in our teaching and planning.

EXERCISES AND ACTIVITIES

WHAT DO TEACHERS THINK?

In an elementary partial immersion classroom, assessment can be tricky. It needs to conform to the many different learning levels that exist among my students. How do I choose one way to assess them? I can't. So, I am often seeking new alternative methods for assessment of the diverse learners in my class.

I have found that performance assessments, based on responses developed by the student, help to bridge the gap for many of my second language learners. This type of true-to-life assessment style allows me to see each individual student's strengths, weaknesses, and learning styles.

Role plays are one way that I have instituted performance assessment in my classroom. These activities, based on putting the student in a simulated situation that illustrates academic points, help the students learn to become decision makers as well as give them an opportunity to understand concepts in a way relevant to them. Performance assessment tools like role plays reflect real life and seem to be the most enjoyable for my students.

In the process of encouraging students to show me what they know and in order to make them comfortable with performance assessment styles, it is imperative to first teach students to question and inquire about things. This is an essential tool for them, yet is often a major challenge for me as an educator. Many of my students are uncomfortable questioning, or the linguistic variation in the classroom is so pronounced that it is necessary for me to find ways to arrange students into groups that are more conducive to them opening up and using their oral language.

Constructed responses as are also very useful to me as assessment tools. Although much of this type of assessment depends on written language usage, the focus is on how students develop their ideas, rather than just the reproduction of information. This allows for all students to express their understanding in different ways. The responses given to these activities can give me insight into how the student perceives the concepts and help me decide how to instruct them in a more effective way.

I feel that performance assessments have made my classroom a truly motivational environment. My students know that they will have more than one way and more than one opportunity to show me what they know and how they can use it. I find that they take away their own perceptions and understanding of the material and I hope that they can use what they learn in my classroom as a springboard for deepened and enhanced knowledge in the future.

Amanda Seewald, Elementary Partial Immersion Teacher, New Jersey

FIELD-BASED EXPERIENCES

Explore in your school:

1. What are the institutional reasons for placement of students in your classroom? Consider: discipline issues, compliance with legal statutes, inadequate space due to overcrowding, scheduling problems, scores from language tests or observations on language development, assessments of what students know about content or a combination of these and other factors.

2. Are there students who are misplaced due to not having been adequately or validly assessed (e.g., language and content assessments, measurements that appropriately measure what you expect them to learn versus knowledge issues)?

3. What evidence (of their thinking, of their performance or their language use) from assessment would help you demonstrate this?

4. Examine the placement, achievement, or exit criteria for students and compare these with the curricular goals. Are there curricular areas missing or over- or underrepresented? How are the assessments providing the appropriate information to guide teacher and students towards meeting the curricular goals?

   a. Visit an ESL classroom. Who seems engaged in actively learning? How and why? Take notes and try to draw on the students' strengths to help them develop more complex thinking

   b. Observe a group of students during ongoing assessment-through-instruction sessions. What are the children capable of doing with assistance? Which students are not receiving adequate assistance to reach the curricular performance goals? Explore what conditions could be changed, such as interactional processes or content, to help their performance and understanding? Observe and report what happens when these conditions and interactions are changed.

   c. Determine when and what type of standardized testing is scheduled for your school district. Diagnose your students to find out what preparation your students will need: familiarization with the formats? understanding of the content? practice under the same testing conditions? explanation of the purpose and importance of the test? anxiety management?

CASE STUDIES
EFL TESTING EXAMPLE BY JANEATH CASALLAS

Janeath is a highly regarded elementary school teacher in Bogota, Colombia, who faces daily challenges in teaching English through children's literature as a foreign language in a public school. The Colombian Ministry of Education has announced its intentions to promote bilingualism in English and Spanish, and at the same time has cut budgets for teacher development and salaries. Further, the Ministry has initiated a new English test that all students will be required to pass in order to graduate from high school. Janeath has just received the reports on her students' performance on the English exam. Predictably, without much practice in the language, the students do poorly with more than half of the twenty-seven students scoring two standard deviations below the mean. Many of these were unfamiliar with the testing procedures and complained after the exam. Of the remaining eleven students, three of the best students scored one standard deviation below the mean and another seven scored three standard deviations below the mean. Only one student, who recently returned from having lived in New York, scored one standard deviation from the mean. Since her class outperformed all other classes, she was asked to devise a teacher workshop on how to better prepare teachers and students for the exam.

First she gathered the scores reported in the summary provided to her principal and noted where the students did the best and where in each grade students were performing poorly. She asked each teacher to come prepared to share what the students felt about taking the exam and where they thought they did the best and where the students felt they performed poorly. Not too surprisingly in some areas, when compared to the actual test report, the students were accurate in identifying their challenges but made more errors in identifying the areas they performed well at. This indicated to Janeath that though the students were probably guessing the right answers, they may be using strategies that needed to be refined to select the correct answers. Also she discovered how students were reading the picture stimuli much differently than the test makers had expected. Items that caused the students confusion were those in which the students' thinking diverged from the test makers', where more than one correct answer appeared possible, and where students were expected to use their background knowledge though the item clearly referred to experiences beyond their lived experiences. Since each teacher would need to work with their tests in their own grade and there were several areas to work on, Janeath designed a workshop for each grade. She asked the teachers to examine the strategies their students appeared to be using in answering the questions, and then to prioritize these in terms of significance. For her grade level, Janeath and her colleagues had the students draw pictures and create stories that explained a sequence of actions. The students learned how the sequence could change by using coherence markers, ordinal adverbs, and first, second, and third as well as other sequencing markers. The students also learned to judge which story sequence made the most sense. In this way, Janeath helped them learn to weigh the possibilities of different story sequences and the language used to create the sequences.

By the end of the workshops, the teachers and students were familiar with the formats involved in the English test, had practiced the thinking and language necessary to answer the questions, and created their own tests to practice with their own stories. The students appeared more comfortable when sitting for the next series of tests at the end of the school year because they had practiced writing stories, guessing endings, describing characters, understanding cause and effect and using multiple perspectives on interpreting stories from different characters' points of view, summarizing, and critiquing stories.

Janeath's assessment of the exam's emphasis on narratives helped her organize better instruction about story development and preparation for the exam strategies. Validation would be needed to find out if their efforts paid off. Accordingly, Janeath will repeat the analysis of the test results with her colleagues to further understand how standardized testing can be addressed without derailing their literature-oriented EFL curriculum.

ACTION RESEARCH

Work with an experience teacher whom you respect to discuss the following instructional issues.

1. Diagnose the instruction for particular students and determine class instruction.

2. Set acceptable goals (check with respected teaching peers, professional organizations, students, and parents).

3. Schedule for revising their evaluation procedures: good tasks and why, poor items and why. Address both content of the assessment and the match between the interactions required by instruction versus those required in the assessments.

4. Improve specific feedback to help learners achieve higher performances: How did students respond? Did they understand the feedback? How did they use the feedback, what was not heeded and why?

ADDITIONAL RESOURCES

Checklist for evaluation of curricula / program

PROCESSES OF EVALUATION

_____ With the representative stakeholders, through consensus we have identified the overall the significant processes and outcomes for which teaching and learning will be encouraged.

_____ We have identified where the conflicts are between stakeholders and how we will address or reconcile these with our curricular assessments.

_____ We evaluate how well the conflicts are addressed and evaluate how well the accommodations that have been made actually benefit those for whom the accommodations were designed (additional time given to do the assessments, familiarize students with the processes and instruments, create alternative assessments).

PROCESSES OF INSTRUMENT EVALUATION/PROCESSES OF INSTRUCTIONAL EVALUATION/RESOURCE ADEQUACY AND APPROPRIATENESS

_____ We evaluate the quality of and our use of all types of materials, equipment, and resources to maximize our benefit without unnecessary duplication, and we identify where additional resources are needed.

_____ We evaluate our procedures for assessment and testing to determine whether these are valid (assess what we value in our instruction through the curriculum), reliable (provide us with consistent measures), ethical (do not have biases that affect the performances of one group over another), and practical (do not exceed our constraints on training personnel, time, space, and money) within our curriculum.

_____ We evaluate our procedures for assessment and testing to determine whether alternatives are needed to accurately depict the accomplishments of all our student and teacher population.

Tasks and Materials

Text features: language, discourse organization, and content
Task features: classification of task types and response demands
Context features: paralinguistic features of the text, level and nature of support, processing load

_____ We evaluate our procedures for obtaining additional resources and their distribution and benefits to all our student and teacher population.

_____ We evaluate the learning community to see if relationships and systems of communication between students, their parents, teachers, and administrators are functioning as a team for learning and growth.

PROCESSES OF EVALUATION ON HOW INFORMATION GENERATED IS USED:

_____ We evaluate how well the assessments we use provide us with sufficient and relevant information about the quality in accomplishing 1) our instructional values, 2) rate and quality of accomplishment of our goals through evaluation of admissions procedures, counseling, advancement procedures and reward systems, graduation requirements, and 3) preparation for the further directions in which our graduates embark.

_____ We use the information gathered in the evaluation to point us in directions to continue what is successful and to identify and address those issues that are problematic to the success of particular populations.

_____ We use the information gathered periodically across levels of the program to adjust the instructional help needed by diverse populations of learners to reach and surpass the standards' scope and sequence.

_____ All teachers, not just ESL or bilingual teachers, who instruct children whose mother tongue is not English receive the information gathered to plan the teaching and learning processes for these learners, taking into account first language, prior knowledge of content, vocabulary, assessment formats, test-taking skills, and cultural orientation of the tests.

_____ Publicly we use the information gathered to contrast how the teaching and learning processes and products are measured through multiple means, not solely through standardized tests.

_____ We use information on how well accommodations are working to inform an accountability team that includes teachers, counselors, social workers, and parents to address individual student profiles and develop a plan for improvement to meet the demands of our instructional practices in all content areas, build the students' language proficiency, and help in their adaptation to the school culture.

_____ We use information from our evaluation to identify and address issues related to assessing students' performance for planning professional development our teachers and administrators.

For each of the above, identify:

what instruments, criteria, and rubrics are used to evaluate.
who uses these instruments with whom.
where these instruments can be found.
when evaluation occurs.
how valid, reliable, ethical, and practical using the instrument is, given the information generated.

Criteria for rubrics for framing new student selection (for admissions into a program or for entering the next level of instruction)

1. What characteristics, behaviors, and performances would students need to demonstrate for indicating readiness to benefit from your program? For example, based on the success of past students in your curriculum and their feedback on their first year experiences, what were their
   a. level of language awareness, oral proficiency, and literacy?
   b. conceptual understanding of content and learning skills?
   c. collaborative social skills?
   d. complex, creative, and critical thinking skills?
   e. intercultural awareness and appreciation?

2. What are indicators of this characteristic or behavior?
   a. Direct: leadership, performances, projects, essays, narratives, poetry, after-school activities, awards
   b. Indirect: documented performances, grades, test scores
   c. What factors may have influenced or mitigated the development of these characteristics that can be addressed by facilitated learning in your program?

3. Which of the above indicators are most valid? reliable? ethical? practical? Why?

4. What unique characteristics does this student bring that your learning community can benefit from?

5. How is the student representative of the wider community's potential for future development?

Self-Assessment Checklist

Depending on the students' abilities, can be either in the target language or their first language.

> **DOES MY STUDENT SELF ASSESSMENT INCLUDE:**
> self-set benchmarks to communicate their interests, thinking, and understanding?
> reflection on learning to push their limits, and encourage deeper complex thinking?
> self-direction for next steps: to help them assess the quality of their decision making?
> evaluation of relevance to themselves, to help them articulate a connection?
> evaluation of social skills, to help them plan and improve their ability to negotiate with others?

End of Semester Assessment Procedure for Grading

_____ Students (and their parents) understand the objectives and are aware of how these are assessed.

_____ Students (and their parents) understand the consequences of the semester assessment.

_____ Students (and their parents) understand the format of the semester assessment.

_____ Assessment documents student performances in relation to the objectives, not in comparison to their peers.

_____ Assessment includes multiple representative samples of the significant performances over the course of study, across tasks, across modalities (oral and written), and content.

_____ Assessment includes how extra credit assignments or how students' strengths or contributions are demonstrated.

_____ Students' own self-assessment of the significant performances is included and considered in the grading.

_____ In feedback, congruencies and conflicts with student assessment provide commentary on meeting the objectives of the period being assessed and readiness for next level.

_____ The appropriate format for reporting grades is used.

Daily Assessment Procedure for Teachers

Objectives as connected to overall curricular content:

PURPOSE:
a. Diagnostic—to identify further help needed
b. Progress in learning—to identify what current struggles are
c. Achievement—to identify what has been learned
d. Other: _____

FOCUS AS ASSESSED RELATIVE TO PARTICULAR CURRICULAR CONTENT:
a. Global observation during task: _____
b. Specific feature of task: _____
c. Specific content: _____
d. Resource/strategy usage: _____
e. Collaborative/interactional skills: _____
f. Communication: _____
g. Evidence of complex thinking: _____
h. Other: _____

FORMAT RELATIVE TO WHAT I HAVE USED IN MY INSTRUCTIONAL PROCESSES WITH THE STUDENTS:
a. Checklist
b. Observations
c. Performances:
  • interviews, discussions, speeches, debates, brainstorming, demonstrations, surveys, essays
  • illustrating stories, concepts, flowcharts, Venn diagram, maps; creating stories, learning logs, experiments
  • research, problem-based inquiries, inventions, plays, poetry
d. Project
e. Portfolio entry
f. Other

Individual/small group students/whole class: _____
Amount of time needed: _____
Location and materials needed: _____
Feedback format for students/teachers: _____
Date sent by teacher: _____
Date received by student: _____

GLOBAL SUMMARY: WHAT STUDENT SUCCESSFULLY ACCOMPLISHED
What specific points can be improved (e.g., activity, task, language function, content, learning strategy, evidence of thinking, presentation)? _____
_____
_____

Points that student/parents need to address: _____

_____

_____

Deadline for their responses to feedback: _____

Consequences or decision to be made affecting student: _____

_____

_____

Feedback format for student/parents

_____

Date: _____   Student/Parents responses: _____

_____

_____

_____

Feedback format for school/district administrators

Date: _____   Administrator responses: _____

_____

_____

GLOSSARY OF TERMS

affective levels   how students feel and think about themselves, class content, and school community

alternative assessment   methods by which student knowledge and learning are examined without the use of standard paper-and-pencil tests.

analytic scoring   assigning separate scores in designated categories on a scoring rubric

anecdotal records   notes that are written in an informal manner, noting student progress from direct observation

assessment   process of developing materials and gathering information about how much learning is taking place

assessment portfolios   consists of products representing samples of the student's work

benchmarks   work that is used in defining exemplary performance on the levels of a scoring rubric

conferencing   used as an informal assessment to determine student progress

constructs   what is being measured

content-based learning   studies in the specific subject areas as opposed to basic language study

criterion-referenced   an individual's score is interpreted by comparing the score to professionally judged standards of performance

dialogue journals   students make entries in a notebook on topics of their choice, the teacher responds, being careful to model effective language usage

evaluation   the process of using information to make determinations about student placement, progress, or achievement

holistic scoring   assigning a single score based on specific criteria

inquiry   a close examination of student performance; can be formal or informal

integrated assessment   assessments that relate to students' goals and curricular expectations; are thematically linked language and literacy practices

integrative testing   testing language and content at the same time

interactivity   learners are actively engaged in language use

interviews   assessment method used to determine student oral proficiency level

metacognitive   self-appraisal and self-regulation processes used in learning, thinking, reasoning, and problem solving

miscue analysis   one type of reading assessment that gives information on reading strategies, decoding skills, and comprehension while students read aloud

norm-referenced   a test that shows how individual scores compare to scores of a well-defined reference or norm group of individuals

observational records   notes that are taken for the purpose of observing student performance

performance-based tasks   tasks that require students to create a response, construct a product, or demonstrate knowledge

portfolios   a collection of student work, showing progress in one or more areas

prochievement   an achievement test based on tasks constructed to build proficiency, e.g., students learn scenarios in class and then are interviewed to perform similar scenarios

progress indicators   evaluate content, process, and products that show how students are performing

retelling   assessment method in which student reads or listens to a text and then gives an oral summary of its contents to demonstrate comprehension

rubrics   a measurement scale that is used to evaluate student performance

running records   a form of miscue analysis in which teachers record in detail what students do as they read aloud

scaffolding   contextual supports for meaning during instruction or assessment

self-assessment   individual learner appraises his or her own work

showcase portfolios   consist of chosen pieces of work that exemplify the many stages of skill growth experienced by each individual student

visual organizers   also known as graphic organizers, provide a visual representation in the form of a map

washback   information or feedback that teachers receive about instruction as a result of assessment and evaluation

REFERENCES

Berriz, B.R. (2000). Raising childrens' cultural voices: Strategies for developing literacy in two languages. In Z.F. Beykont (Ed.). *Lifting every voice: Pedagogy and politics of bilingualism.* pp. 71–93. Boston, MA: Harvard Education Publishing Group.

Chamot, A. U., & O'Malley, J. M. (1994). *The CALLA handbook: Implementing the cognitive academic language learning approach.* Reading, MA: Addison-Wesley.

Cummins, J. (1996). E-Lective language learning: Design a computer-assisted text-based ESL/EFL learning system. *TESOL Journal, 10*(15), 41–46.

Cushman, K. (2000). "Everything We Do is for a Purpose, and We Get Something Out of It." A case study of Landmark High School, New York, NY. *Reinventing High School: Six Journeys of Change.* Boston: Jobs for the Future.

Elley, W. B. (1991). Acquiring literacy in a second language: The effect of book-based programs. *Language learning.* 41, 375–411.

Fairclough, N. (1989). *Language and power.* London: Longman.

Faltis, C., & Wolfe, P. (Eds.). (1999). *So much to say: Adolescents, bilingualism & ESL in the secondary school.* New York: Teachers College Press.

Graves, D. H. (2002). *When testing lowers standards, it becomes a threat not a tool.* Community Commentary, Monday, January 7, 2002, CELT list.

International Language Testing Association (ILTA) (2000). *Code of ethics for second/foreign language testing.* Hong Kong International Language Testing Association.

Joint Committee on Standards for Educational Evaluation (1981). *Standards for evaluation of educational programs, projects and materials.* New York: McGraw-Hill.

Kucan, L., & Beck, I.L. (1997). Thinking aloud and reading comprehension research: Inquiry and social interaction. *Review of Educational Research.* 67:271–299.

Lave, J., & Wenger, E. (1991). *Situated learning: Legitimate peripheral participation.* Cambridge, UK: Cambridge University Press.

Mitchell-Kernan, C. I. (1999). *Myths and Tradeoffs: The Role of Tests in Undergraduate Admissions.* Washington, D.C.: National Academy Press.

Postlethwaith, N. T., & Ross, K. N. (1992). *Effective Schools in Reading.* The Hague, Netherlands: IEA

Pressley, M., & Woloshyn, V. (1985). Cognitive strategy instruction that really improves children's academic performance. Cambridge, MA: Brookline Books

Spolsky, B. (1995). *Measured words: The development of objective language testing.* Oxford UK: Oxford University Press.

Valdes, G., & Figueroa, R. (1996). *Bilingualism and testing: A special case of bias.* Norwood, NJ: Ablex.

Valdez Pierce, L., & O'Malley, J. M. (1996). *Authentic assessment for English language learners.* Chicago: Addison-Wesley.

Valette, R. (1998). The five step performance-based model of oral proficiency. In A. Mollica (ed.) (pp. 349–358), *Teaching and learning languages.* Lewiston, NY: Soleil.

Wells, G. (1996). Using the tool-kit of discourse in the activity of learning and teaching. *Mind, Culture, and Activity.* 3(2), 74–101.

Wiggins, G. (1992). Creating tests worth taking. *Educational Leadership*, (26), 26–33.

CHAPTER FIVE

INTERACTIVE LISTENING AND READING

THIS CHAPTER WILL FEATURE

- Interactive listening and reading
- Reading versus literacy
- Reading and viewing as interactive processes
- Strategy-based reading instruction

YOU WILL EXAMINE

- Types of reading strategies and skills
- Critical literacy

INTRODUCTION: SETTING THE STAGE

(Note: In an effort to visually portray psycholinguistic and sociocultural viewpoints, we have used icons to direct your attention. ◆ = psycholinguistic ■ = sociocultural)

The emphasis today in foreign and second language classrooms focuses a great deal of emphasis on oral practice. This may be one reason for a marked decrease in students' reading ability. Second/foreign language teachers have moved further away from the traditional grammar/translation methodology to one that involves more student interaction for learning academic content and oral communication. This in part has been driven by the goal of reaching a certain level of proficiency as defined by the TESOL ESL National Standards (see www.tesol.org) and the American Council on the Teaching of Foreign Languages (ACTFL) National Standards in Foreign Language Education (see www.actfl.org). In the enthusiasm to foster oral communication skills, however, reading skills have been neglected in the foreign language beginning and intermediate levels (Swaffar, Arens, & Byrnes, 1991).

THINK, PAIR, SHARE

Before you begin reading this chapter, complete the following with a partner.

1. Listening means:

_____

2. Literacy means:

_____

3. Reading means:

_____

As you read and interact with this chapter look for ways to examine your own beliefs about reading, listening, and **viewing**. Think about your own assumptions and how they affect/will affect your approach to teaching these skills in a second/foreign language classroom. We encourage you to pay particular attention to the sections on *critical literacy* as this may be an area that adds a new dimension to your base of understanding. Finally, use the skills and strategies in the chapter to explore and plan meaningful instructional activities that will be of practical use in the classroom.

A CLOSER LOOK AT INTERACTIVE LISTENING AND READING IN CONTENT-BASED CLASSES

We feel that reading comprehension should be regarded as an interactive process. Interpreting written texts is complex by design in that it involves a simultaneous coordination of attention, perception, and memory. Included in this are comprehension operations of testing hypotheses, separating main ideas from details, deducing meaning, searching for cohesive elements, and contextual guessing. However, when students begin to read in a foreign or second language, there are often unconscious strategies that cause them to begin translating word by word (Clarke, 1980; Kern, 1989; Phillips, 1984).

For both the second and foreign language learner in K–12 settings, listening and written language development play an important role in later development of overall proficiency in a language, and immediately impact schooling. Being able to follow directions or being able to interpret written language are often used for assessing placement into a particular grade level. Often these "receptive" skills, i.e., listening and reading, lay the foundations for both accessing and building understanding in another language both in face-to-face encounters and in responding to written texts. This construction of understanding through listening and reading is far from receptive and requires the active engagement of the learner. We call this active engagement *interactive*.

Listening comprehension is more than attending to and accurately perceiving an auditory stimulus. It involves "making sense" of the auditory information and often comprehension requires learners to demonstrate their understanding in face-to-face encounters as well as non-face-to-face encounters (e.g., listening to radio, television, videos, audio and Web sources). In terms of language development and acquisition, listening comprehension develops when learners have been engaged in meaningful and comprehensible oral interactions. It emerges as learners make sense of the flow of speech in chunks or segments of meanings in a particular context, gradually increasing their attention to larger and larger chunks as memory permits. In such contexts listening generally precedes oral production.

◆ From a psycholinguistic perspective, listening has also been studied as skills and strategies. Typically, researchers ask learners to listen to tape-recorded narratives and to respond to a set of questions to which the learner must select "the most appropriate response" from a multiple choice group of response. Other tasks have been created to test comprehension through following instructions, e.g., following a map, using manipulatives, or drawing a figure.

■ From a sociocultural perspective, learners respond to and create interpretations based on how they recognize social contexts. Listening comprehension is seen as embedded in understanding how individuals in face-to-face encounters relate to each other, who they are (their identities), and what they are likely to expect and do next. For second and foreign language users, this process may mean learning different ways of demonstrating their listening comprehension than in their first language as they become socialized into practices of a different culture. For example, in elementary classes, in the United States it is common to hear routine phrases such as "All eyes on me and feet on the floor" as the instructor directs the children's attention and has children settle down. In middle schools, directing the children's attention may be achieved by the sound of a bell signaling the beginning of the class. In Japanese classrooms, during opening routines for lessons in response to "kiritsu," "rei" may only require a single utterance "hajimemasu" or "onegaishimasu" and a bow. Thus being able to demonstrate listening comprehension becomes a part of developing appropriate expectations of participation in ongoing cultural routines, both typical and novel.

In contrast to the limited research on second and foreign language listening comprehension, there has been a long history of research on learning how to read, which has produced conflicting theories. Street (1984, 1993) offers a framework that categorizes the ways in which past research studies have conceived of reading from a psycholinguistic, a sociocultural, and an ideological perspective. Through his framework we see how each perspective defines reading and the role language and interaction play.

◆ From a psycholinguistic perspective, reading is conceived as an autonomous mental process occurring in the heads of individuals. *Interpreting written texts is complex by design* in that it involves a simultaneous coordination of attention, perception, and memory. Included in this are comprehension operations of testing hypotheses, separating main ideas from details, deducing meaning, searching for cohesive elements, and contextual guessing. Most of these prescriptions for individual skills are aimed at beginning readers. However, when already literate students begin to read in a second/foreign language, they often recur to unconscious and less effective strategies of translating word by word (Clarke, 1980; Kern, 1989; Phillips, 1984). Generic skills and strategies extracted from those used by successful beginning learners have been identified. These generic skills and strategies in turn have become the targets for instructional practices to help others to learn.

■ From a sociocultural perspective, reading is but one of the cultural practices with written language that is interrelated with oral language practices and embedded in social relationships of power constitutive of culture. In other words, in becoming a literate member of a particular group, both oral and written uses of a language are interdependent, and have particular functions in particular contexts. Learning to be literate involves specific ways to use language: valuing, feeling, thinking and acting. (See Bell, 1997, for her autobiographical research on learning Chinese literacy.) Here learning to read means knowing how social purposes, audiences, and conventions of language usage help build one's membership in a particular community. Learning to use and read a dictionary is distinct from learning to judiciously use a dictionary to understand unknown words. Viewed from this perspective, each social practice calls on a literacy for that particular practice.

In the upcoming section, we will look at a wider notion of literacy that includes developing interactive listening and reading in the content-based class.

FOCUSING ON INTERPRETING ORAL COMMUNICATION—INTERACTIVE, CONTENT-BASED LISTENING COMPREHENSION

We probably begin to listen to the world around us even before we are born. Mothers-to-be often talk to the babies they are carrying, as well as play music that they believe might be soothing or inspiring. Regardless of the actual merit of these actions, the fact is that we are focusing on sound and its effect on people and other living things. How this sound is perceived, attended to, and interpreted by the listener, affects what is learned from the experience. In classrooms for second/foreign language learners, this orientation toward sound needs to be directed and guided by the teacher.

This section of the chapter will describe recent trends in research on the development of listening comprehension in second language acquisition, and offer suggestions based on how to interpret oral communication for classroom instruction. One trend focuses on strategy-instruction as it relates to **interactive listening** in a content-based classroom. The following are samples of media used in interactive listening and teaching how to interpret oral communication:

- CD-ROM
- Cassette
- Television
- Video
- Radio
- Computer
- Verbal discourse

It is important to understand that each of the media listed above may have a variety of genres. For instance, CDs might be an interactive video game, movie, or music used in teaching science or social studies. Cassettes could be personal collections of favorite music, tape-recorded books, radio broadcasts, speeches, or letters.

Answer the following questions:

1. How would you classify these media in terms of which of these require a verbal response and which are engaged in for personal enjoyment, extraction of particular information to use, or for interacting socially with others or privately?
2. After you categorize these, how would learners begin to control the quality, rate, and implication of the information?
3. Which require learning to ask for help in learning to control these elements?

Interactive Listening Comprehension Development in Content-Based Classes

Interactive listening plays an important role in language learning. Specifically, the effective use of **reception strategies** by listeners in interaction can both resolve immediate comprehension problems and facilitate long-term language learning (Vandergrift, 1997). Interactive listening, sometimes called **participatory listening** (Dunkel, 1991), is an important but sometimes overlooked aspect of interpreting oral communication (Vandergrift, 1997). When students are actively engaged in interactive listening, the listener must take a more rigorous role, either giving verbal or nonverbal feedback or requesting clarification. Teachers therefore must provide students with useful reception and coping strategies that facilitate and enhance their ability to control the flow (e.g., modify the speed, volume), negotiate the content, or define a purpose for listening. Awareness and use of appropriate reception strategies will allow language learners to negotiate meaning more efficiently and effectively and to potentially solicit additional comprehensible input (Vandergrift, 1997).

Labarca and Khanji (1986) found that courses that focus on strategic interaction as the primary methodology, rather than a listening-based methodology alone, result in a significantly better performance in conversation. It is clear that the importance of social interaction and negotiation of meaning between L2 learners and native speakers has strong evidence from longitudinal studies (Gass & Varonis, 1994; Long, 1996; Pica, 1994; Pica, 1996).

Rubin (1994) identifies five major factors that affect listening:

1. text characteristics
2. interlocutor characteristics
3. task characteristics
4. listener characteristics
5. process characteristics

Text characteristics refer to its "intrinsic cognitive difficulty" (Brown, 1995). In other words, what it is that makes it harder to understand one text than another. *Interlocutor characteristics* are typically such descriptors as racial/cultural/ethnic, gender, age, and linguistic background. *Task characteristics* describe what the listener will do and for what purpose. *Listener characteristics* are level of proficiency, cultural background, and cognitive abilities. *Process characteristics* describe *how* the listener takes in what is being heard. For instance, for some learners this may include listening just for key words and phrases. For others, it may mean listening to try to understand every word.

Diverse Learners

Before planning which avenue to explore to introduce listening activities, you should be aware of your students' diverse needs, i.e., multiple intelligences, and learning styles (discussed in Chapter 2). The musical cloze activity you will see later in the chapter is one example of an interactive listening activity in which you can accommodate a sensory preference learning style, e.g., auditory learners. Additionally, this type of activity works well for the musical/rhythmic intelligence.

Certain factors that affect development of listening skills must be addressed. Incorporating the use of listening strategies is an effective way to achieve this.

Listening strategies are classified as being **cognitive** or **metacognitive.** Rubin (1987) defines these strategies as follows:

> *Cognitive* strategies include clarification and verification, guessing and inductive inferencing, deductive reasoning, memorization with a focus on storage and retrieval, practice with focus on accuracy of usage, repetition rehearsal, experimentation, application of rules, imitation and attention to detail. *Metacognitive* strategies are employed to monitor, oversee, regulate, or self-direct the cognitive progress; they involve self-management, self-evaluation, and knowledge about cognitive processes.

Classroom Application

In a musical cloze, students listen to a song on a CD or cassette and are asked to fill in the missing words. The sample in Figure 5.1 uses the song "Over the River and Through the Woods," in which every ninth word has been omitted. This is a **pure cloze** since no word bank is given. A **modified cloze** activity does include the word bank, i.e., a list of the missing words would be highlighted at the bottom of the page.

This activity allows the teacher to utilize the cognitive strategies *guessing and inductive inferencing, deductive reasoning,* and *application of rules.* As students listen to the recording, they guess the missing words and make inferences about the upcoming words, while at the same time they are able to make application of certain rules. Metacognitive strategies used are *self-management* and *self-evaluation.* Students listen and follow at their pace and then self-evaluate to determine how many words they have correctly identified and written in the spaces.

A follow-up activity might be to have the students bring in a favorite song that they want to transcribe. Depending on their purpose, their needs will be different. What types of help will they need in listening? Consider the various purposes:

1. to learn to sing the lyrics
2. to understand the emotions of the singer in the video

Over the River and Through the Woods

Over the river and thru the wood,
To [grandfather's] house we go;
The horse knows the way
[To] carry the sleigh,
Thru the white and drifted [snow,] oh!
Over the river and thru the wood,
[Oh,] how the wind does blow!
It stings the [toes,]
And bites the nose,
As over the ground [we] go.

Over the river and thru the wood,
To [have] a first-rate play;
Oh, hear the bell [ring,]
"Ting-a-ling-ling!"
Hurrah for Thanksgiving Day-ay!
Over [the] river and thru the wood,
Trot fast my [dapple] gray!
Spring over the ground,
Like a hunting [hound!]
For this is Thanksgiving Day.

FIGURE 5.1   Sample of a Musical Cloze

3. to create dance steps to the lyrics
4. to compose a similar rap song

ADDITIONAL INTERACTIVE CONTENT-BASED LISTENING ACTIVITIES USING SONGS

1. Listen for rhyming words.
2. Listen for grammatical words (these may be difficult unless context is stressed).
3. Comprehension questions such as short answer or fill-in-the-blank.

Linking Assessment to Interactive Listening

To accommodate students' different learning styles and intelligences, assessment practices should include a variety of instruments and procedures. In linking assessment to interactive listening, remember that informal observations are equally as important as a formal listening activity. This may involve alternative forms of assessment (as discussed in Chapter 4), which can tap higher order thinking skills. Assessing listening comprehension may include:

1. oral report
2. outlines, webpages, maps, charts, T-lists
3. computer-assisted language activities and simulations
4. musical cloze

LITERACY

One of the simplest and most straightforward definitions of literacy is an ability to read and write in a language. Other definitions include the ability to encode and decode written symbols and to interpret events and experiences in a social and political context. According to Fishman (1989) literacy should be regarded from a broad perspective as "a phenomenon that requires local cultural validity and that may, therefore, take different forms, pursue different goals, be linked to different contextual and institutional supports from one speech to another and even from one speech network to another" (p. 25). As a classroom teacher we urge you to think about defining literacy in context. What is literate for a college student may be illiterate for an elementary school student.

Literacy Development as a Cultural Practice

How is literacy a part of a culture's "toolkit" for maintaining continuity of traditions and values while at the same time creating new ways of thinking and creatively transforming culture? We examine three perspectives: (1) reading as an autonomous skill, (2) reading and writing as cultural practices, and (3) reading and writing as a site of sociopolitical struggle. From the perspective of *reading as an autonomous skill*, you will explore skills and strategies for working with second/foreign language learners engaging in the reading process. From the perspective of *reading and writing as cultural practices*, you will examine how particular cultures use and value reading and writing. From the perspective of *reading and writing as a site of sociopolitical struggle*, you will read how literacy stratifies social groups in a culture and functions differently across social groups. These three perspectives have different pedagogical implications in developing literate second/foreign language learners.

Pedagogical Means of Developing Sound Literacy Practices

As a classroom teacher you will want to encourage the development of sound literacy practices. Quite simply this can be done by providing ongoing opportunities for reading, listening, and viewing in your classroom. You may want to create resource centers or learning stations where students can browse through a variety of written materials at different levels of difficulty. Take time and **read aloud** to your students for enjoyment and follow this by discussing what was read and encourage students to relate it to their own lives and previous experiences. This will integrate new into existing information. You might also use a **guided reading** activity in which a small group of students is guided through a reading text using various kinds of reading strategies.

Moving from Guided Reading to Independent Reading: Strategies and Skills Approach in Content-based Teaching

In the past, one approach to teaching reading was through **bottom-up** activities. This involved teaching symbols, grapheme/phoneme correspondences, syllables, and lexical recognition first. Comprehension would follow when all these parts were added together. Today's research on reading, however, suggests a combination of **top-down** (reader uses his or her own experiences to understand a text) and bottom-up, or **interactive reading,** because both skills are important and successful. Good readers interact with the text, calling upon their knowledge and experience to interpret the new information (Carrell 1983, 1985; Hudson, 1982; Johnson, 1982). They continue reading in an attempt to find another idea that will clarify the unknown section; they adopt a reading style to fit the purpose—quickly searching for a global idea, ferreting out specific facts, or slowly savoring descriptions (Grellet, 1981). Using the practices of fluent readers as a foundation, teachers now espouse a process approach for reading instruction (Rusciolelli, 1995), or as Hamp-Lyons (1985) terms it, "text-strategic approach," which emphasizes ideas and generalizations rather than isolated facts; it concentrates on meaning rather than on form; it attends to the discourse level rather than the sentence level. Translated into classroom methods, it means creating general expectations about the topic by activating background knowledge, using titles and illustrations to predict content, searching for main ideas, practicing various modes of reading, and guiding lexical guessing. (Rusciolelli). Comprehension exercises include summarizing and interpreting, and for optimal benefit a final task integrates or transfers the information beyond the text (Phillips, 1984).

Use the chart in Figure 5.2 to allow students to self-assess their feelings about reading. You may want to consider doing this type of assessment at designated intervals, place them in students' portfolios, and discuss the results with students and parents.

Clearly this text does not provide enough space to enumerate the various forms of written discourse. However, what follows is a nonexhaustive list of kinds of text your learners may encounter.

TYPES OF TEXTS

novels	telephone books	essays	magazines
short stories	signs	poems	dictionaries
textbooks	menus	labels	maps
handbooks	travel schedules	messages	tickets
notes	greeting cards	reports	recipes
newspapers	bills	postcards	directions
television listings	forms	telegrams	applications

APPLICATION ACTIVITY

For each type of reading, identify

(a) the audience the text is directed to,
(b) the purpose for which type text is used,

MY FEELINGS ABOUT READING

Name:_____   Date:_____

Directions: Mark an X in the box that describes how you feel about reading.

	YES	SOMETIMES	NEVER
1. I like to read.			
2. I like to read long books.			
3. I prefer to read short books.			
4. I can retell stories I've read.			
5. I have trouble with new words.			
6. I use other words to help me find the meaning of a new word.			
7. I like to write about what I've read.			
8. I look at the pictures for clues to the story.			
9. I like to guess what may happen in the story.			
10. I know that stories have a beginning, middle, and end.			

FIGURE 5.2   Student Reading Self-Assessment

(c) what type of language structures would be found, and

(d) what strategy learners might use to make sense of the text for the purposes you identify.

READING

Selecting and Accessing Authentic Texts

Selecting and accessing authentic texts can sometimes be very challenging, given the wide range of resources available. Authentic material used in the classroom not only contains limited and sometimes biased and incorrect cultural information, it also presents rather limited written language samples (Moore, 1999). According to Rings (1986), the most authentic language samples are the spontaneous, unrehearsed utterances of speakers in real-life contexts.

However, the value of using authentic texts in a second/foreign language classroom is paramount to students' being able to learn to negotiate meaning about the target language and culture. Galloway (1990) recommends the following criteria for selecting authentic texts:

- Topic should be accessible to the learner.
- Length of text should not be intimidating to beginning readers.

- Linguistic level should be slightly above the reader's own level (Krashen i + 1 theory) unless the tasks are closely structured to involve focused listening/reading.
- Clues to meaning should be abundant—e.g., contextual, verbal, pictorial, linguistic.

As students work with authentic texts they may find it difficult to comprehend everything they see and hear. Once careful attention has been given to the selection of authentic texts, teachers will want to provide students with strategies that can help them organize, synthesize, and relate new information to their existing knowledge. See Chapter 9 for suggested reading activities that use technology and other multimedia.

Reading Skills

Building reading skills through activities that interest the student, connect to real life, and are relaxed rather than structured drills foster self-initiated and self-directed literacy development (Soderbergh, 2000). There are at least four types of reading skills:

1. **Intensive reading** is reading for complete understanding of an entire text.
2. **Extensive reading** is rapid reading for main ideas of a large amount of text.
3. **Skimming** requires the reader to look for the main idea or the general gist of a passage.
4. **Scanning** is a quick overview of the text, looking for specific details or information. A readily recognizable example of scanning is using the telephone directory.

Bottom-up suggests that readers first recognize a variety of linguistic notations, i.e., syllables, letters, morphemes, words, phrases, discourse markers, grammatical cues, and use a type of information-sorting process for establishing an order to these notations (Goodman, 1967).

Top-down is a means of processing text in which we use our experiences to understand a passage. This may include a set of sub-skills which include identifying key ideas and guessing meaning through a process sometimes referred to as a "psycholinguistic guessing game" (Goodman, 1967).

One way to incorporate the reading skills listed above is by using a grouping activity called The "Take-Five Model", as shown in Figure 5.3. This activity is designed to allow students to practice reading skills and strategies. The model is named this because of its five daily components: Get Ready, Read, Reread, Respond, and React. All students read the same text at varying proficiency levels. A teacher planning sheet that accompanies the Take-Five Model is shown in Figure 5.4.

INTERACTIONS WITH LITERACY

When learners have meaningful and challenging experiences with written communication, they develop not only an appreciation of the power of texts, but an understanding of how they too can create powerful texts. Instilling in learners how to deconstruct texts to get at meaning is a powerful way to introduce them to cultural ways of interpreting and creating texts.

CONTENT-BASED AREAS: MATH, SCIENCE, SOCIAL STUDIES, ENGLISH LANGUAGE ARTS

Get Ready (Whole Class)

Review previous work

Activate schemata

Develop vocabulary

Make predictions

Question

Anticipation guide

Graphic organizer

Survey text

Read (Various levels)

Read with a focus

Main idea

Reread (Various levels)

Learning logs

Skim

Complete graphic organizers

K–W–L

Respond (Various groupings)

Learning logs

Response journals

React (Whole class, Groups, or Pairs)

Share responses

Teacher or peer-led discussions

FIGURE 5.3 The Take-Five Model

Adapted from Wood, McCormack, Lapp, & Flood (1997)

A very important notion about texts is that they serve particular purposes as mentioned earlier and require different types of interpretation to make sense of them. In countries where there is "environmental print," announcements, posters, and signs are highly visible, and children grow up seeing adults pay attention to these messages and taking action. Eventually children come to understand that these events of contact with print codes not only influence information but attitudes and values that adults interpret and take action on. Children learn to imitate reading behavior, such as understanding the direction in which symbols are displayed, which sounds they represent, how to orient themselves to printed materials, and how to interact with print. As they gain further experiences with varied types of contact and purposes, they may even start

Teacher Planning Sheet

Title: _____

Chapter/Pages: _____   Date: _____

Get Ready

_____ Review

_____ Activate schemata

_____ Vocabulary

_____ Predict

Read

_____Read aloud   _____ Silent   _____ Pairs   _____ Other

Reread

_____ Set new purpose: _____

_____ Read aloud   _____ Silent   _____ Pairs   _____ Other

Respond

_____ Oral prompt:

_____ Whole class   _____ Groups   _____ Pairs

_____ Written prompt:

_____ Whole class   _____ Groups   _____ Pairs

React—Share Written Responses

_____ Whole class   _____ Groups   _____ Pairs   _____ Other

FIGURE 5.4   Teacher Planning Sheet for the Take-Five Model

Adapted from Wood, McCormack, Lapp, & Flood (1997)

to recognize these signs and learn to interpret to them. Generally these texts are classified into genres that change over time, not all of which may be equally valued or used by all members of the community. For example, comic book reading in some social groups is not considered an important practice. For others it is.

Use the list in Figure 5.5 as an inventory to determine your students' ongoing literacy development.

READING VERSUS LITERACY

■ Literacy from a Sociocultural View

Every social group has ways of thinking, behaving, and doing. These ways are dynamic and changing and are made up of language as well as constructed by language. Learning how to engage with written texts varies according to these social groups and cultures, As Heath (1983) points out, our prior experiences with text affect our expecta-

1. What parts of the text would you like to reread to a friend? Why?
2. What character did you most/least identify with? Why?
3. How did the author convince you of this character's personality? What might be the author's reason to create this character?
4. How important was this character to the entire plot?
5. What literary techniques/devices did the author use to build the plot, (e.g., sequence of events, narration, perspective, setting, imagery, metaphors, analogies, personification, dialogue, diary entry, genres, suspense?
6. Which techniques would you like to use in your story?
7. Rewrite the story from another character's perspective. Use as many of the author's techniques as you wish to create your story.
8. Read someone else's story. What did you like? What make his or her story effective or not?
9. Which audiences would appreciate your story? Why?
10. What illustrations should accompany your story? Why?
11. Write an advertisement for your story: What are the most important points about the story's appeal?
12. Choose fonts to feature certain information over others. Describe your decision process.
13. What genre does this story belong to? Why?
14. How would you classify this plot?
15. As you respond to each other's story, tell the writer what parts most affected you and why.
16. Listen to/read the responses to your story. Which points did the audience understand about your story? Which ones were not noticed? Why? How will you consider this feedback to improve your story's impact?
17. Rewrite your story using the feedback you think will help you tell your story and gain the effect you desired. Revise your advertisement, illustrations, layout, and fonts accordingly.
18. Note the changes between the first version and the second version. What did you pay most attention to and why?

FIGURE 5.5   Inventory for Reading for Enjoyment and Creative Story/Novel Writing

tions of texts and how to use them. Without prior experiences, building connections to literacy are most effective when students are given responsibility and opportunity to control and contribute to meanings of the texts they listen to and read.

Literacy research shows that making connections to the lives of students and their backgrounds and helping them to reexamine these connections in considering other's perspectives leads to conceptual change and students learning to learn. As teachers we should try and move students from the known to the unknown and provide opportunities for the individual learner to constructs his/her own meaning. **Whole language** is an approach predicated upon the notion that the true meaning of literacy is meaning-making. Whole language involves collaboration, sharing, and interaction. This approach is based on the following beliefs:

- That literacy learning involves all four language skills—listening, speaking, reading, and writing
- That language learning should be meaningful, purposeful, and relevant
- That literacy occurs with texts and writing

REFLECT AND RESPOND

1. What kinds of written texts (genres) are used for learning in your language classroom (e.g., syllabary/alphabet flash cards, posters, games, lists, rules, diaries, logs, letters, postcards, advertisements, reports, labels, essays, newspapers, comics, novel, plays)? (For emerging ESL literacy, see research in Morroco by Blanton, [1998]; for adolescents see research on middle school literacy events by Lewis [2001].)

   _____

   _____

   _____

2. What types of practices (kinds of listening and reading) are required for students to engage meaningfully with these texts and what types of participation in these practices? (See Luke & Freebody [1997]; Floriani [1994]; Freebody, Luke & Gilbert [1991].)

   _____

   _____

   _____

3. In which of the following listening stances do you want your students to gain skill: active audience for author's chair; paired/collaborative listening and note-taking; peer-led group discussion; teacher-led group discussions? (Freebody, Luke, & Gilbert, 1991).

   _____

   _____

   _____

4. What norms are you going to use? (Street, 1993; Heath, 1983; Pappas & Zeker, 2001)

   _____

   _____

   _____

5. How will you support their participation in these roles, allowing for emergence of language over time, individual variation in rate, adjustment and readjustment of language until learners become more conventional users, focusing on language being used purposefully to achieve some end meaning, to continue to present challenges? E.g., allow for learner selection of book to read, allow for drawing to show understanding, allow for learner to ask for spelling, allow for students to note differences and similarities between stories.

   _____

   _____

   _____

- That written language has a unique system that is somewhat different from oral language
- That language is learned in a social context
- That language learning is a social process
- That language is modeled by a teacher or more capable peer

Critical Literacy

In a Black township outside Johannesburg teenagers take part in a multilingual storytelling project building with local oral traditions and contemporary mass media to contest the political realities of post-Apartheid South Africa. In rural India, Urvashi Sahni describes how primary school children appropriate the written symbol system to imagine and compose different and optimistic futures. These are two examples of *critical literacy*. Critical literacy sets out to read backward from texts to the contexts of their social construction (i.e., economies of text production), and to write forward from texts to their social use, interpretation and analysis (i.e., economies of text use). Teachers start with what their students know and then ask them to review the text (phrase by phrase), screen (image by image), and realia (piece by piece) in an effort to see *how* they are constructed and how they might be constructed differently (Luke, 2000).

Comber (1999) describes characteristics of critical literacy as:

- engaging with local realities
- mobilizing students' knowledge and practices
- researching and analyzing language practices and their effects
- designing texts with political and social intent and real-world effects

Sharing the power to collaboratively define the literacy experience with students helps learners see themselves as capable of making changes through their own creation of identities as thinkers and actors in their classroom and communities (Oyler, 1996; Pappas & Zecker).

Socially Responsive Critical Literacy Interaction

Use the following two questions to determine your socially responsive approach to critical literacy interaction as afforded by critical literacy.

1. What relationships between the reader and written text do you want to cultivate?
   a. Reader-resistant/oppositional stance to messages by author
   b. Author's perspective as seen through character, plot, language use, etc.

2. What are some of the potential meanings that can be derived from the text?
   a. For whom is the text written?
   b. Why?
   c. How do we know?
   d. How might it be rewritten?

Reading, Listening, and the National Standards

The ESL Standards describe the language skills necessary for social and academic purposes. The standards specify the language competencies English Speakers of Other Languages (ESOL) students in elementary and secondary schools need to become fully proficient in English, to have unrestricted access to grade-appropriate instruction in challenging academic subjects, and ultimately to lead rich and productive lives (ESL Standards, 2001).

Development of the ESL Standards was influenced by the national standards of English language arts and foreign language. These three language standards share an emphasis on the importance of (ESL Standards, 2001):

1. language as communication
2. language learning through meaningful and significant use
3. the individual and societal value of bi- and multilingualism
4. the role of ESOL students' native languages in their English language and general academic development
5. cultural, social, ad cognitive processes in language and academic development
6. assessment that respects language and cultural diversity.

Listening and Reading Strategy Instruction

Research clearly points to the advantages of explicit reading-strategy instruction. Barnett (1988) and Kern (1989), in separate studies to determine the benefit of reading strategy instruction, reported mixed results. Students who received training made considerable gains in comprehension, but they did not score significantly higher than those students with no instruction. Kern determined that those students who benefited most from the training were weaker readers. He posits that middle and high ability readers may have already transferred effective skills to second language reading. Hosenfeld (1984) used word-guessing techniques with individual students and found that their problem-solving behavior upon encountering an unknown word improved. Hamp-Lyons compared a traditional and a "test-strategic" approach with positive results for the latter.

Listening and reading comprehension involve both cognitive and social processes. Listening an reading are active cognitive processes that require an interplay between various types of knowledge (Shrum & Glisan, 2000 p. 121). Listeners and readers draw upon four types of competencies as they attempt to comprehend an oral or a written message:

1. *grammatical competence:* knowledge or morphology, syntax, vocabulary, and mechanics
2. *sociolinguistic competence:* knowing what is expected socially and culturally by native speakers of the target language
3. *discourse competence:* the ability to use cohesive devices such as pronouns, conjunctions, and transitional phrases to link meaning across sentences, as well as the ability to recognize how coherence is used to maintain the message's unity.
4. *strategic competence:* the ability to use a number of guessing strategies to compensate for missing knowledge (Canale & Swain, 1980)

NOW VIEW THE VIDEO CLIP OF TEACHERS USING READING AND LISTENING ACTIVITIES

Activity for viewing the video clip:

1. Identify the reading and listening skills demonstrated in the video clip.

   _____

   _____

2. What assumptions did the teacher make about his/her students when selecting this activity? How was this beneficial?

   _____

   _____

3. Describe an alternative way to approach teaching this lesson.

   _____

   _____

Reading skills and strategies run the gamut from such traditionally recognized reading behaviors as skimming and scanning, to rereading, contextual guessing or skipping unknown words, tolerating ambiguity, making predictions, confirming or disconfirming inferences, and using cognates to comprehend, to more recently recognized strategies such as activating background and knowledge or schemata (Zvetina, 1987) and recognizing text structure (Block, 1986; Carrell, 1985, 1992; Carrell, Pharis, & Liberto, 1989).

H. Douglas Brown (2001) offers the following as principles for designing interactive reading techniques:

- In an interactive curriculum, make sure that you don't overlook the importance of specific instruction in reading skills
- Use techniques that are intrinsically motivating
- Balance authenticity and readability in choosing texts
- Encourage the development of reading strategies
- Include both bottom-up and top-down techniques
- Follow the SQ3R sequence (see glossary)
- Subdivide your techniques into prereading, during-reading, and after-reading phases
- Build in some evaluative aspect to your techniques

In exploratory, descriptive investigations with small numbers of individual learners using think-aloud techniques, studies have identified relations between certain types of reading strategies and successful and unsuccessful foreign or second language reading (Carrell, Gajdusek, & Wise, 1998). In Hosenfeld's 1977 study of U.S. high school

PIZZA!

Listen carefully to the following telephone conversation between Marisol and Presto Pizza employee, Steve.

You will hear the conversation twice. Steve had trouble hearing some of Marisol's words . . . answer the questions on the next page with a partner, and see if you can help Steve!!!!

Steve: Hello, this is Steve at Presto Pizza; how may I help you tonight?

Marisol: Yes, I would like to place an order, please.

Steve: Would this be for pick-up or delivery?

Marisol: I would like them to bring it to me, so, _____, please.

Steve: And what is your name?

Marisol: My name is Marisol Roja.

Steve: Just to confirm, do you live on 2300 Green Street, Apartment 12?

Marisol: Yes, that's right.

Steve: And what would you like to order tonight, Ms. Roja?

Marisol: I would like a large pizza.

Steve: What toppings would you care for on your pizza?

Marisol: Well, I really like _____, _____, and pepperoni, but my friend Asra is a vegetarian, so that won't work! Tonight you better make it just plain cheese because I don't like many vegetables like she does.

Steve: Do you want the crust to be thick or thin?

Marisol: I definitely want _____ crust for my pizza.

Steve: Would you care for anything else, ma'am?

Marisol: Sure! I would really like some _____ to drink with the pizza!

Steve: Okay, your total is $16.85. It should be ready in about half an hour.

Marisol: Thank you soooo much!!! I'm getting hungry already!   Good night.

    and answer these questions aloud with a partner.

Is Marisol going to pick up her pizza, or will someone bring it to her (delivery)?

Did Marisol want thick or thin crust for her pizza?

Did Marisol order anything else with her pizza? If so, what?

Which toppings (things you put on the pizza) does Marisol usually like on her pizza?

Why does she order a pizza with only cheese on it?

What is a VEGETARIAN? Do you know one?

Marisol has a ten dollar bill ($10), a twenty dollar bill ($20), and a fifty dollar bill ($50). Which one will she use to pay for her order (Don't forget she needs to add a tip!)?

Source: Bawden, A. (2003). *Pizza!* Unpublished work, George Mason University.

students reading in a foreign language (French, German, or Spanish) but thinking aloud in English, her example of a "successful" French reader did the following things: (1) kept the meaning of the passage in mind during reading, (2) read in what she termed "broad phrases," (3) skipped words viewed as unimportant to total phrase meaning, and (4) had a positive self-concept as a reader. By contrast, Hosenfeld's "unsuccessful" French reader: (1) lost the meaning of sentences as soon as they were decoded, (2) read in short phrases, (3) seldom skipped words as unimportant and viewed words as equal in their contribution to total phrase meaning, and (4) had a negative self-concept as a reader.

READING AND VIEWING AS INTERACTIVE PROCESSES

Reading and viewing are highly interactive processes and both can be treated accordingly in today's classrooms. First, consider the sound and visual social orientation that dominate today's school-age population. Classroom teachers are competing for students' attention. We are often amazed at how students quickly memorize the lyrics to rap or other pop culture songs but have difficulty remembering to do their homework. Second, think about those forms of print media which are most appealing to today's learners—aesthetically appealing, lively, and animated. Viewing often includes these attributes. Viewing as a process includes videos, movies, television programs, interactive multimedia, computer games, and plays. Using video provides a unique way of bringing the target cultures into the classroom and making learning more meaningful and stimulating (Shrum & Glisan, 2000). Swaffar and Vlatten (1997) recommended that viewing should be silent at first. During this time students can look for possible messages and cultural nuances suggested by the visual images. Afterward, once they are exposed to the sound, they can determine whether their visual comprehension matched their auditory. They engage in comprehension tasks and use the new information they learn through the viewing as the basis for discussion, role playing, and creative writing (Swaffar & Vlatten).

Integrating Listening and Reading Skills

Integrating listening and reading skills can be accomplished when you focus on selecting materials that allow for interaction with the texts. Structure and sequence your lessons in such a way that students are exposed to listening and reading activities which address their interests, level of comprehension, and cultural backgrounds. Most importantly, make certain that students understand the purpose for which they are being asked to listen and/or read. Denise McCarthy (1994) offers the following

GENERAL GUIDELINES FOR PREPARING LISTENING/READING ACTIVITIES:
1. Choose short, lively stories that can be finished in a few class periods and summarize that story before and after each segment.
2. Prepare a good audiotape of the story, read by someone who can give it life. Offer skills practice that can be transferred to the reading experience.
3. Challenge students to identify vocabulary through context.
4. Create classroom activities that motivate them to listen and read for pleasure.

REFLECT AND RESPOND

1. Why should listening and reading be interactively taught?

_____

_____

2. How are listening and reading skills similar? How are they different?

_____

_____

3. What specific strategies can be used for teaching listening and reading?

_____

_____

INTERACTIVE, CONTENT-BASED LISTENING AND READING ACTIVITIES

1. *Index Card Match: Social Studies*—Students are given index cards on which some are written answers and on others questions about the US government. One student begins by reading their card and everyone listens to see if they have the card that matches. This continues until all matches are made.

2. *Group Review: Science*—Students are divided into small groups to discuss the ecosystem. Each student writes down a statement. Students pass the papers in a circle. On a neighbor's paper, a student asks one question about the statement.

Assessing Interactive Listening and Reading

Teachers can assess interactive listening and reading using such things as rubrics (see Reading Response Log, Figure 5.6) to Musical Cloze (see Figure 5.1). Other assessment activities might include story retelling, journals, debates, portfolios, and a cooperative learning project. Chapter 4 covered in greater detail more specific information on ways to plan for effectively assessing interactive listening and reading.

STRATEGY-BASED READING INSTRUCTION

Reading Strategies

Noteworthy contributions to understanding the teaching of reading is the foreign and second language reading research which focuses on reading strategies. Reading strategies are of interest not only for what they reveal about the ways readers manage interactions with written text but also for how the use of strategies is related to effective

Directions: Have students work in pairs or in groups to complete the log. Students should share their responses within groups and then with the entire class.

Name _____ Class _____

Date	Key Concepts	New Vocabulary	Questions I have

FIGURE 5.6   Reading Response Log—Content-Based Science: Photosynthesis

reading comprehension (Carrell, Gajdusek, & Wise). Reading strategies help students engage with the text and monitor their comprehension. Students need to have a wide range of strategies from which to select those that are most appropriate for them.

The term *strategies* is used deliberately, rather than the more traditional term *skills*, to refer to actions that readers select and control to achieve desired goals or objectives (Paris, Lipson, & Wixson, 1983; van Dijk & Kintsch, 1983). Although there

REFLECT AND RESPOND

1. What reading and listening strategies, skills, or techniques were used by your second/foreign language teachers at the elementary, secondary, or college level?

   _____

   _____

2. Were those reading and listening strategies, skills, or techniques content-based and/or interactive? If yes, in what ways?

   _____

   _____

3. Were those reading and listening strategies, skills, or techniques effective? If yes, why? If no, why not?

   _____

   _____

is no clear agreement (cf. Paris, Wasik, & Turner, 1991) on the deliberate aspect of using strategies. Wellman (1988), on the one hand, says: "To be a strategy, the means must be employed deliberately, with some awareness, in order to produce or influence the goal" (p. 5); and on the other hand, Pressley, Forrest-Pressley and Elliot-Faust (1988) say: "It is now recognized that strategy functioning at its best occurs without deliberation. It is more reflexive than voluntary" (p. 102). Overall, the emphasis with the term *strategies* is on *deliberative actions*.

TYPES OF READING STRATEGIES IN SECOND LANGUAGE LEARNING
PREREADING STRATEGIES
Skim the text for general ideas.
Read the introduction and conclusion.
Do semantic mapping.

DURING-READING STRATEGIES
Predict the main idea of each paragraph.
Skip unknown words; guess meaning from context.
Draw pictures to demonstrate what reader understood.

AFTER-READING STRATEGIES
Retell what you think the author has said.
Relate the text to your own experience.
Respond to the text.

Directions for using Anticipation Guide: Have students read the title of the reading selection and skim the words in bold. Then in pairs or groups students should complete the grid.

History of the Aztecs in Mexico

The **Aztecs** were a wandering Native American tribe who traveled to **Mexico** sometime in the 13th century. **Religion** was an important part of their lives. They established a **civilization** that included temples, pyramids, and cities. In the early 1500s, the Aztecs had **accumulated** enormous wealth. The **empire** continued to grow for generations. The Aztec capital, **Tenochtitlan,** was a most beautiful city that served as the center of Mesoamerican civilization.

M = My opinion   + = Agree
G = Group opinion   x = Disagree
A = Author's opinion

M	G	A	What do you believe?
			1. The Aztecs were Native Americans.
			2. The Aztecs came to Mexico to find a new religion.
			3. Tenochtitlan was the Aztec capital.
			4. The Aztecs built great temples and pyramids.

FIGURE 5.7   Sample Anticipation Guide

READING RESPONSE LOGS

The teacher provides students with questions based on comprehension of the text. Students may work in groups or individually for this activity.

ANTICIPATION GUIDES

Anticipation guides are used to generate prereading and postreading discussion. They usually consist of three to six statements about an upcoming topic that students are asked to react to by deciding whether they agree or disagree and why. Anticipation guides can be used as a tool for students to share their own views with other members of their group. Students are afforded the opportunity to defend or explain their own views while listening to similar or different views of their peers (See Figure 5.7).

LITERACY SCAFFOLDS

Reading and writing activities that give teacher or peer assistance in order for the student to be able to fully participate in ongoing classroom procedures. An example is an **interactive dialogue journal** in which both teacher and student carry on a written conversation.

SEMANTIC MAPPING

Illustrating the major points of a text using some sort of visual representation. Mapping allows the reader to explore central issues in the text and focus on what is of personal significance to the individual reader. Students are encouraged to use both pictures and words. Mapping fosters a greater comprehension of the text because it "forces readers to consider the structure of the [text] as a

Directions for using semantic mapping:

Semantic mapping can be used with several of the types of texts listed on page 158. Have students use these to look for central concepts in math, science, social studies, or English Language Arts and to focus on what is of personal significance to him/her as an individual reader. Examples might be to ask students what they know about plants, seeds, animals (science), shapes, patterns, formulas (math), ancient culture, law, geographic regions (social studies), sentence formation, noun/adjective agreement, verb tense (English language arts).

Table X-Semantic Mapping

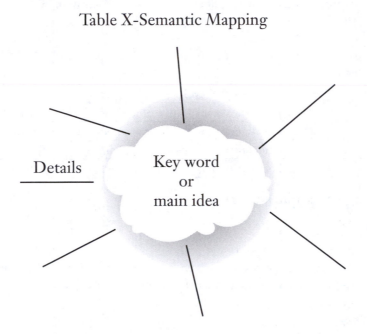

FIGURE 5.8 Semantic Mapping

framework for its content. To make a successful map, readers need to reread, revising original assumptions and coming to new understandings" (Thomas & Wilson, 1993) (See Figure 5.8).

SQ3R—A PROCESS USED FOR APPROACHING A TEXT:
1. *Survey*—Skim the text for main ideas.
2. *Question*—Ask questions about what one hopes to get from the text.
3. *Read*—Read the text while looking for answers to previously generated questions.
4. *Recite*—Say aloud or write the important points of the text.
5. *Review*—Review the importance and relevance of what has been read.

Advance Organizers
Advance organizers provide ways to activate relevant background knowledge to facilitate learning and retention of new material (Lee, 1986; Omaggio, 1993).

THINK ALOUD

Students are encouraged to use oral language for guessing, predicting, or discussing text.

READ ALOUD

It is important to read aloud to students at all grade levels K–12. Choose texts about which your students will have some prior knowledge and for which you will be able to offer assistance in their comprehension.

MORNING MESSAGE

The teacher previews the day's activities for students by writing them on the board; while saying the words, the teacher models the organizational/mnemonic function of the text.

LANGUAGE EXPERIENCE APPROACH

An approach based on students' dictations that can be used with learners, preschool through adult. Students create their own material for reading. One successful way of using this is to use students' personal experiences as the foundation for discussion. Then the teacher writes down the experiences and the students can recopy or illustrate as a story. Students dictate stories or ideas as a whole class. As they dictate the words, the teacher writes them on the board or chart paper, asking students to read the words back as the teacher points to them.

ECHO READING

The teacher reads a sentence and the students repeat or echo the sentence. It allows the teacher to discover the level of syntax of individual students.

GUIDED READING

A small group of students is guided by the teacher through a reading text that is at the students' instructional reading level. The text should be challenging and therefore the teacher guides students with appropriate reading strategies that will enable them to comprehend the text.

SILENT SUSTAINED READING

Everybody in the school reads at the same time every day. Usually everybody reads for a half hour and students are allowed to select whatever appropriate material interests them.

The national ESL Standards for Pre-K–12 Students (TESOL, 1997) acknowledge the importance of learning strategies for English Language Learners (ELLs). One standard for each of the three goals (1. to use English in social settings, 2. to use English to achieve academically in all content areas, and 3. to use English in socially and culturally appropriate ways) demonstrates strategy-based instruction, as follows:

Goal 1, Standard 3: Students will use learning strategies to extend their communicative competence.

Goal 2, Standard 3: Students will use appropriate learning strategies to construct and apply their academic knowledge.

Goal 3, Standard 3: Students will use appropriate learning strategies to extend their sociolinguistic and sociocultural competence.

Whatever strategies are emphasized, learned, and used, it is generally agreed that they should be taught through explicit instruction, careful modeling, and **scaffolding** (Echevarria, Vogt, & Short 2000), This is sometimes referred to as **sheltered English experience.**

You will also want to self-reflect and determine if you are meeting the needs of your students. The following is adapted from a checklist for Effective Practice with English Learners (Freeman & Freeman, 1999):

1. Is the curriculum organized around "big" questions?
2. Are students involved in authentic reading and listening experiences?
3. Is there an attempt to draw on students' background knowledge and interests? are students given choices?
4. Is the content meaningful? Does it serve a purpose for the learners?
5. Do students have opportunities to work collaboratively?
6. Do students read and write as well as speak and listen during their learning experiences?
7. Are students' primary languages and cultures valued, supported, and developed?
8. Am I reaching *all* students? Are students involved in activities that build their self-esteem and provide them with opportunities to succeed?

APPLICATION ACTIVITY

1. Select a short text, preferably content-based. The language of the text should not be too easy or too difficult for your students.
2. Decide which issues/ideas in the text are controversial, especially those for which students may have misconceptions.
3. Prepare five to eight short, declarative statements on each identified issue or concept that reflect how your students might think. The will be the Anticipation Guide.
4. Try not to create statements taken exclusively from the facts in the text. (See the sample Anticipation Guide in Figure 5.7.)

Anticipation Guides activate prior knowledge and can be used to challenge misconceptions. They encourage predicting and help you determine a purpose for reading. Most importantly, Anticipation Guides can be used to motivate students to read.

Integrating Technology with Listening and Reading

Listening and reading activities should be extended to include the integration of technology. The World Wide Web offers both listening and reading resources for every level reader. However, as the teacher you must ensure that students are given clear objectives and goals when using multimedia so as to avoid their getting lost in what can be very frustrating and defeating.

READING ASSESSMENTS

Reading assessments can take place before, during, and after the reading activity. You can begin to look for signs of reading proficiency by focusing on students' phonemic knowledge at the primary grades, background knowledge at grades three and four, and strategy knowledge at the upper levels (Willson & Rupley, 1997). Then you can use your students' strengths to approach and build those areas of difficulty. Assessment should be summative (Did my instruction work?) and formative (What do we do next?).

The following are several examples of various types of reading assessments:

- *Checklist*—a simple checklist given to students to self-assess or peer assess
- *Conference notes*—teacher takes detailed notes following a student/parent conference. A copy should be given to the student and parent.
- *Observations*—an informal way to assess students on an ongoing basis
- *Interviews*—these can take place between student and teacher or between peers
- *Exit slip*—students are given one or two questions at the end of class. "What worked well for you today?" "What is *not* working well for you?"
- *Admit slip*—students are given one or two sentences to complete as they arrive in class. "I like reading because . . ." "I don't like reading because . . ."
- *Dialogue journal*—this is a way to nonverbally communicate with your students and get to know them beyond their classroom texts.

Assessing Reading Using an Informal Reading Inventory

Informal Reading Inventories (IRSs) can provide you with a way to learn more in-depth information about your students' reading processes. These are commercially available instruments usually published in a spiral notebook. They include a set of reading passages of gradually increasing difficulty, usually kindergarten through sixth grade level or beyond. IRIs are usually administered one-on-one.

Samples of commercial Informal Reading Inventories include:

1. This inventory can be used with students through grade twelve. It includes an interest and attitude interview.

   Flynt, E. S., & Cooter, R. B. (1995). *Flynt-Cooter Reading Inventory for the Classroom*, (2d ed.). Gorsuch Scarisbrick: Scottsdale, AZ.

2. This inventory includes upper-level and content-specific spelling inventories with diagnostic information on the type of orthographic knowledge that a reader is using to process a word.

   Bear, D. R., Invernizzi, M., Templeton, S., & Johnston, F. (2000). *Words Their Way*. Columbus, OH: Merrill Publishers.

3. CARI is most useful for teachers who want to construct a quick comprehension assessment on a selection of the course textbook in order to determine if certain readers might struggle with the text.

   Vacca, R., & Vacca J. (1999). *Content Area Reading Inventory (CARI)*. New York, NY: Harper Collins.

Reading Levels

If you decide to use Informal Reading Inventories, you will find simple formulas to determine whether a student is reading a particular text at one of three levels: *Independent*, *Instructional*, or *Frustration*. These formulas take into account word recognition and comprehension. The IRI will indicate the number or percentage or word recognition errors or miscues that identify Independent, Instructional, and Frustration levels.

Independent reading level indicates an easy text for the reader. The reader requires little or no help. Comprehension is determined by having the student retell the text or answer comprehension questions. Students read with approximately 98 percent word recognition accuracy and 90 percent comprehension.

Instructional reading level is obvious when students are able to read classroom materials at their instructional level with the teacher's assistance. For instance, you may create a study guide to help students focus on main ideas and key concepts for their reading on the rain forest. Students' word recognition is approximately 95 percent accurate and comprehension is about 70 percent.

Frustration reading level is visibly noticeable for those students having great difficulty with world recognition and comprehension. Students are below 90 percent word recognition and at or below 70 percent in comprehension.

The relationships between strategies and comprehension are not simple and straightforward; use of certain reading strategies does not always lead to successful reading comprehension, while use of other strategies does not always result in unsuccessful reading comprehension (Carrel, Gajdusek & Wise). Research reported by Anderson (1991) shows that there are no simple correlations or one-to-one relationships between particular strategies and successful reading comprehension. Anderson concludes from his studies that successful second language reading comprehension is "not simply a matter of knowing what strategy to use, but the reader must also know how to use it successfully and [to] orchestrate its use with other strategies. It is not sufficient to know about strategies, but a reader must also be able to apply them strategically" (p. 19).

Figure 5.10 includes a reading passage for an intermediate ESL secondary Science class. Use the text and complete the following exercise:

PREREADING
1. Skim the text for general ideas and then list two

_____

_____

DURING-READING
2. Make a list of the words you skipped. Can you guess their meaning from context?

_____

_____

NOW VIEW THE VIDEO CLIP OF TEACHERS USING VARIOUS READING STRATEGIES

Activity for viewing the video clip:

1. What types of texts listed on page 158 were used in the video clip?

   _____

   _____

2. Identify the type of reading strategies used.

   _____

   _____

3. What steps were taken to make these *interactive* reading activities?

   _____

   _____

Rainforests

It is estimated that rainforests cover two percent of the Earth's surface – that's six percent of the land mass. Over half the plant and animal species live in rainforests. Rainforests are home to about half of the five to ten million plant and animal species on the globe. Tropical rainforests can be defined by two factors: location (in the tropics) and the amount of rainfall they receive. Many foods we eat today originated in rainforests: avocado, banana, cayenne pepper, cola, and ginger, to name a few.

Tropical rainforests are the Earth's oldest living ecosystems. There are fossils from the forests of Southeast Asia that have existed in their present form for seventy to one hundred million years. Unfortunately, rainforests are being destroyed at an alarming rate. Some scientists believe that at least fifty million acres a year are lost.

FIGURE 5.10   Sample Reading Selection

AFTER-READING

3. Retell what you think the author has said.

   _____

   _____

THINK, PAIR, SHARE

After reading this chapter, complete the following activity with a partner.

1. After reading, here is what I learned about interactive listening, reading, and viewing.

   _____

   _____

2. After reading, this is what I learned from the chapter and these are some of the more important things I want to remember.

   _____

   _____

SUMMARY

In this chapter we have examined interactive listening and reading by exploring *strategy-based reading, reading and listening as interpretive skills,* and *reading and viewing as interactive processes.* Additionally, we have included types of reading strategies and skills and interspersed critical literacy and its relevance to today's second/foreign language classroom teaching. It is important to remember that students must be encouraged to read and this is often accomplished by the text selection—our classrooms should be print-rich environments. Also, it is critical to remember students' array of cultural background and levels of comprehension. As a classroom teacher you must be willing to provide cognitive and motivational strategies for your students to use. Effective teachers model and demonstrate these strategies. They provide opportunities for construction of meaning from texts and variety of skills and strategies to use before, during, and after reading. Ineffective teachers focus on isolated instruction that focuses on repeated practice with worksheets.

EXERCISES AND ACTIVITIES
DISCUSS AND REFLECT

1. As a second/foreign language learner, what were your experiences with listening and reading?

2. What skills or strategies did you use that you think might be helpful for your students?

3. What are some things to consider when selecting listening and reading activities?

ASK YOURSELF THESE QUESTIONS

1. What are some things that you can do to assist students in the comprehension of what they read?

2. How do a student's schemata impact on his/her ability to learn what you teach?

3. What kinds of things do or will you do to prepare students for listening, reading, and viewing?

WHAT DO TEACHERS THINK?

The use of technology (computers, video equipment, etc.), authentic texts, student questionnaires/surveys, and a variety of meaningful interactive instructional techniques will help engage learners and keep them on task. Use of gestures, facial expressions, pictures, realia, and whatever visual or media that will get the topic or point across is instrumental to successful reading and listening. The presentation of important concepts should incorporate brainstorming, think aloud sessions in the native and target language through KWLs, graphs, T-lists, charts, semantic webs and concept maps. Teachers should not only model how to solve problems and ask questions for clarification, but also implement mini-lesson on learning strategies, such as finding key words and summarizing information.

Implementation of cooperative learning activities, group projects, and hand-on activities will give students a reason to use academic language for functional purposes. Asking students what they already know, or having them pool their resources in a brainstorming session, will help them define the limits of the topic and relate it to previously acquired knowledge or experiences. Students' prior knowledge and experience influence how he/she approaches new material.

Sally Atkins, ESL and Spanish Teacher at Osbourn High School in Manassas, Virginia

FIELD-BASED EXPERIENCES

Arrange to visit three foreign or second language classes with three different teachers. Observe how each teacher approaches reading and listening. What skills and strategies do the teachers use? Are their classrooms print-rich environments? Describe a few of their reading and listening activities. What evidence do you need to characterize their approach to literacy? What instructional skills and strategies do they use? How are their students engaged in the lesson? How do they provide appropriate help?

CASE STUDY
CARLA WILLOUGHBY

As a young, inspired, first-year teacher I have lived through my first nightmare! I stood in front of my 9th grade beginner level ESL Science class and in a monotone voice read a passage out loud from our text to a room full of vacant minds with faces that glared back in apathy. This was my reading lesson that backfired. Big time!

It was the custom with this particular high school text to read short passages. These readings offer snippets of background information about science topics that relate to students' everyday lives. In my first class period, I had two of the students share reading the text in a read-aloud. Afterwards, I asked directed questions about the text and nearly all of the students stared at me as if they hadn't even realized we had actually been reading something.

Fortunately, my new understanding of the reading process has helped me to understand what went wrong with this approach to teaching reading. Or perhaps I should say that this understanding has opened my eyes to see what I *didn't* plan for that day; a mistake founded in my own ignorance of the reading process. You see, for someone who had never previously looked at the reading process through a metacognitive lens, I just took for granted that all my students used the same reading strategies and skills as I did. Little did I know how complex were the building blocks of my own reading comprehension. I could not understand how my students were unable to process the new information, which to me appeared straightforward and simple.

Activity: *After reading the Case Study, answer the following questions then share your responses with a partner.*

1. What are some considerations for making this lesson more effective?

2. What reading and/or listening skills or strategies can this teacher use to improve this lesson?

3. How could Carla find out what students already know about this reading?

4. How could Carla use visuals, semantic maps, or games to prepare students for what they don't know in the lesson?

5. How could Carla assess students' ongoing comprehension?

ACTION RESEARCH

◆ A Psycholinguistic Approach

Consider the following as an action research project:
Select a second/foreign language student who is experiencing difficulty (a less accomplished reader). Try several of the reading skills and strategies mentioned in this chapter with the student. Keep daily charts of his/her progress over a designated period of time. At the end of the pre-selected time, interview the student to determine what changes, if any, had taken place.

■ A Sociocultural Approach

While the learner is engaged in a project, note what listening or reading tasks the learner can accomplish without aid. Note those that still remain difficult. At the beginning identify what types of scaffolding the learner needs to accomplish the task. At the end of the project, what new listening or reading tasks can the learner accomplish without help? What areas still remain to be learned?

ADDITIONAL RESOURCES

Adult ESL Literacy—Adjunct ERIC Clearinghouse for Adult ESL Literacy Education (202) 429-9292 or via e-mail at: *ncle@cal.org*

International Reading Association (IRA)—P.O. Box 8139, Newark, DE 19714-8139 or visit their home page: *http://www.gsh.org/ira*

APPLICATION ACTIVITIES

1. Create a semantic map (graphic organizer) that summarizes the major ideas presented in this chapter. Which ones are new to you? Which will you follow?
2. Ask your students or classmates to identify reading and listening strategies or skills which they have used successfully. Have them describe the strategy/skill, how to use it, and how they know it works.

GLOSSARY OF TERMS

advance organizers ways to activate relevant background knowledge to facilitate learning and retention of new material

after-reading strategy retell what you think the author has said, relate the text to your own experience, and respond to the text

anticipation guides used to generate prereading and postreading discussion.

bottom-up suggest that readers first recognize a variety of linguistic notations and use a type of information-sorting type of process for sorting out an order to these notations

cognitive characterized by what one knows

during-reading strategy predicting the main idea of each paragraph, skipping unknown words, guessing meaning from context, drawing pictures to demonstrate what reader understood

echo reading the teacher reads a sentence and the students repeat or echo the sentence

extensive reading rapid reading for main ideas of a large amount of text

guided reading students in a small group are guided by the teacher through reading a text that is at the students' reading level

intensive reading reading for complete understanding of an entire text

interactive dialogue journal an example of a literacy scaffold. Teacher and student carry on a written conversation

interactive listening listening that actively engages the listener in tasks that relute to what is being heard, e.g., responding or reacting

interactive reading a combination of bottom-up and top-down reading skills

language experience approach based on students' dictations, teacher writes words on board on paper and then asks students to read the words back as they are pointed to

literacy scaffolds   reading and writing activities that give teacher or peer assistance in order for the student to be able to fully participate in ongoing classroom procedures

metacognitive   self-management and self-evaluation about what one knows

modified cloze   a written text with every *n*th word omitted. Missing words are given in a word bank somewhere on the page.

morning message   teacher provides the day's activities for students by writing them on the board and then models the text for the students

participatory listening   students actively engage in interactive listening

prereading strategy   skimming for general ideas, reading the introduction and conclusion, semantic mapping

pure cloze   a written text with every *n*th word omitted. Missing words are *not* given in a word bank listed somewhere on the page

read aloud   traditionally used with young children. Involves reading texts out loud

reading response logs   the teacher provides students with questions based on comprehension on the text

reception strategies   include Global reprise, Continuation signal, Lexical reprise, Fragment reprise, Lexical gap, Positional reprise, Hypothesis testing, and Forward inference (see Vandergrift, 1997)

scaffolding   providing support and assistance to help learners in the use of academic language through interactive learning activities

scanning   a quick overview of the text, looking for specific details or information

semantic mapping   illustrates the major points of a text using some sort of visual representation

sheltered English experience   all subject matter is taught in English. Content is organized in order to promote second language acquisition

silent sustained reading   everyone in the school reads at the same time every day

skimming   requires the reader to look for the main idea or the general gist of a passage

SQ3R   a process for approaching a text: S = survey the text for main ideas. Q = ask questions about what one hopes to get from the text. 3R = read, recite, review.

think aloud   students are encouraged to use oral language for guessing, predicting, or discussing text

top-down   a means of processing text in which we use our experiences to understand a passage

viewing   a process using media such as video, TV, computer, etc.

whole language   learner-centered, literature-based approach to language teaching

REFERENCES

Anderson, N. J. (1991). Individual differences in strategy use in second language reading and testing. *Modern Language Journal 75*, 460–742.

Barnett, M. A. (1988). Reading through context: How real and perceived strategy use affects L2 comprehension. *Modern Language Journal, 72*, 150–162.

Bell, J. (1997). Literacy, culture and identity. New York: Peter Lang.

Blanton, L. L. (1998). *Varied voices. On language and literacy learning*. Boston: Heinle & Heinle.

Block, E. (1986). The comprehension strategies of second language readers. *TESOL Quarterly, 20*, 463–494.

Brown, H. D. (2001). *Teaching by principles: An interactive approach to language pedagogy*. White Plains, NY: Longman.

Canale, M., & Swain, M. (1980). Theoretical bases of communicative approaches to second language teaching and testing. *Applied Linguistics, 1*, 1–47.

Carrell, P. L. (1983). Evidence of formal schema in second language comprehension. *Language Learning, 34*(2), 87–112.

Carrell, P. L. (1985). Facilitating ESL reading by teaching text structure. *TESOL Quarterly, 19*, 727–752.

Carrell, P. L., Wise, T., & Gajdusek, L., (1998). Metarecognition and EFL/ESL Reading. *Instructional Science, 26* (1–2), 97–111.

Carrell, P. L., Pharis, B. G., & Liberto, J. C. (1989). Metacognitive strategy training for ESL reading. *TESOL Quarterly, 23,* 647–678.

Chamot, A. U., & O'Malley, J. M. 1994. *The Calla handbook: Implementing the cognitive academic language learning approach.* Reading, MA: Addison-Wesley.

Clarke, D., & Nations, I. S. P. (1980). Guessing the meanings of words from context: strategy and techniques. *System, 8,* 211–20.

Comber, B. (1999). Critical literacies: Negotiating powerful and pleasurable curricula—How do we foster critical literacy through English language arts? Featured Speaker Presentation to the National Council of Teachers of English 89th Annual Convention, Denver, CO, November 18–21.

Dunkel, P. A. (1991) Computerized testing of non-participatory L2 listening comprehension proficiency: An ESL prototype development effort. *Modern Language Journal, 75,* 64–73.

Echevarria, J., Vogt, M., Short, D. (2000). *Making content comprehensible for English language learners.* Needham Heights, MA: Allyn & Bacon.

Freeman, D., & Freeman, D. (Dec/Jan, 1999). Effective practice with English learners. *TESOL Matters.*

Fishman, J. (1989). Non-English language ethnic community schools in the USA: Instruments of more than literacy and less than literacy. In E. Z. Sonino (ed.) (pp. 25–33), *Literacy in school and society: Multidisciplinary perspectives.* New York: Plenum Press.

Floriani, A. (1994). Negotiating what counts: Roles and relationships, texts and contexts, content and meaning. *Linguistics and Education, 5,* 241–274.

Freebody, P., Luke, A., & Gilbert, P. (1991). Reading positions and practices in the classroom. *Curriculum Inquiry, 21,* 436–457.

Galloway, V. (1992). Toward a cultural reading of authentic texts. In H. Byrnes (Ed.), *Languages for a multicultural world in transition.* Northeast Conference Reports (pp. 87–121). Lincolnwood, IL: NTC/Contemporary Publishing Group.

Gass, S., & Varonis, E. (1994). Input, interaction, and second language production. *Studies in Language Acquisition, 16,* 283–302.

Goodman, K. S. (1967). Reading: A psycholinguistic guessing game. *Journal of the Reading Specialist 6,* 126–135.

Grellet, F. (1981). *Developing reading skills.* Cambridge UK: Cambridge University Press.

Hamp-Lyons, L. (1985). Two approaches to teaching reading: A classroom-based study. *Reading in a Foreign Language, 3,* 363–373.

Health, S. B. (1983), *Ways with words: Language, life, and work in communities and classroom.* Cambridge, UK: Cambridge University Press

Hosenfeld, C. (1977). A preliminary investigation of the reading strategies of successful and nonsuccessful second language learners. *System, 5,* 110–23.

Hosenfeld, C. (1984). Case studies of ninth grade readers. In J. Charles Alderson and A. H. Urquhart (eds.), (pp. 231–49), *Reading in a Foreign Language,* London: Longman.

Hudson, T. (1982). The effects of induced schemata on the "short-circuit" in L2 reading: Non-decoding factors in L2 reading performance. *Language Learning, 32*(1), 1–31.

Johnson, P. (1982). Effects on reading comprehension of language complexity and cultural background of a text. *TESOL Quarterly, 15,* 169–181.

Johnson, P. (1982). Effects on reading comprehension of building background knowledge. *TESOL Quarterly, 16,* 503–516.

Kern, R. G. (1989). Second language reading strategy instruction: Its effects on comprehension and word inference ability. *Modern Language Journal, 73,* 135–149.

Krashen, S. (1982.) *Principles and practice in second language acquisition.* Oxford, England: Pergamon Press.

Krashen, S. (1984.) *Writing: Research, theory and application.* Oxford, England: Pergamon Press.

Labarca, A., & Khanji, R. (1986). Beginning French–Interactants' Communication Strategies. 19p Reports–Research/Technical. AW:ED249798.

Lee, J. F. (1986). Background knowledge and L2 reading. *Modern Language Journal, 70,* 351–54.

Lewis, C. (2001). *Literary practices as social acts. Power, status and cultural norms.* Mahwah, NJ.: Lawrence Erlbaum.

Long, M., (1996). SLA research and options in syllabus design. Presentation to CREAL colloquium, University of Ottawa, Canada. October.

Luke, A. (1991). Literacies as social practices. *English Education, 23*, 131–147.

Luke, A. (2000). Critical literacy in Australia, *Journal of Adolescent and Adult Literacy, 43*.

Luke, A., & Freebody, P. (1997). The social practices of reading. In. S. Muspratt, A.

Luke, A. & P. Freebody (eds.) (pp. 185–225), *Constructing critical literacies* Cresskill, N.J.: Hampton.

McCarthy, D. (1994). (Winter) Integrated listening and reading skills. *TESOL Journal*. P. 37.

Moore, Z. (1999). Technology and teaching culture in the L2 classroom: An introduction. *Journal of Educational Computing Research, 20* (1), 1–10.

Omaggio, A. C. (1993). *Language teaching in context. Proficiency oriented instruction.* Boston: Heinle & Heinle.

Oxford, R. (1996). *Language learning strategies around the world: Cross-cultural perspectives.* Manoa, HI: University of Hawaii Press.

Oyler, C. (1996). *Making room for student. Sharing teacher authority in Room 104.* New York: Teachers College Press.

Pappas, C., & Zecker, L. Barro (Eds). (2001). *Transforming literacy curriculum genres. Working with teacher researchers in urban classrooms.* Mahwah, NJ.: Lawrence Erlbaum.

Paris, S. G., Lipson, M. Y., & Wixson, K. K. (1983). Becoming a strategic reader. *Contemporary Educational Psychology, 8*, 293–316.

Paris, S. G., Wasik, B. A., & Turner, J. C. (1991). The development of strategic readers. In R. Barr, M. L. Kamil, P. B. Mosenthal, & P. D. Pearson (eds.) (pp. 609–40), *Handbook of Reading Research*, Vol. II. New York: Longman.

Phillips, J. K. (1984). Practical implications of recent research in reading. *Foreign Language Annals, 17*, 285–295.

Pica, T. (1991). Classroom interaction, negotiation, and comprehension: Redefining relationships. *System, 19*, 437–452.

Pica, T. (1994). Research on negotiation: What does it reveal about second-language learning conditions, processes, and outcomes? *Language Learning, 44*, 493–527.

Pica, T., Young, R., & Daughty, C. (1987). The impact of interaction on comprehension. *TESOL Quarterly, 21*, 737–758.

Pica, T., Lincoln-Porter, F., Paninos, D., & Linnell, J. (1996). Language learners' interaction: How does it address the input, output, and feedback of L2 learners? *TESOL Quarterly, 30*, 59–84.

Pressley, M., Forrest-Pressley, D., & Elliott-Faust, D. (1988). What is strategy instructional enrichment and how to study it: Illustrations from research on children's prose memory and comprehension. In F. Weiner & M. Perlmutter (eds.) (pp. 101–130), *Memory Development: Universal Changes and Individual Differences.* Hillsdale, NJ: Lawrence Erlbaum.

Rings, L. (1986). Authentic language and authentic conversational texts. *Foreign Language Annals, 19* (3), 203–208.

Rubin, J. (1987). Learner Strategies: Theoretical assumptions. Research history and typology. In A. Wenden & J. Rubin (Eds.). *Learner Strategies in Language Learning.* Cambridge: Prentice-Hall.

Rubin, J. (1994). A review of second language listening comprehension research. *Modern Language Journal, 78*, 199–221.

Rusciolelli, J. (1995). Student responses to reading strategies instruction. *Foreign Language Annals, 28*, 262–73.

Scarcella, R. C., & Oxford, R. L. (1992). *The tapestry of language learning.* Boston: Heinle & Heinle.

Shrum, J., & Glisan, E. (2000). *Teacher's handbook: Contextualized language instruction.* Boston: Heinle & Heinle.

Soderbergh, R. (2000). Reading and writing as language acquisition from the first year of life. A Research Symposium on High Standards in Reading for Students from Diverse Language Groups: Research, Practice & Policy. Washington D.C.: Office of Bilingual Education and Minority Languages Affairs, U.S. Dept of Education.

Street, B. (1984). *Literacy in theory and practice.* Cambridge, UK: Cambridge University Press.

Street, B. (Ed.) (1993). *Cross-cultural approaches to literacy.* Cambridge, UK: Cambridge University Press.

Street, B. (1999). New literacies in theory and practice: What are the implications for language and education? *Linguistics and Education, 10*(1), 1–24.

Swaffar, J., Arens, K., & Byrnes, H. (1991). *Reading for meaning.* Englewood Cliffs, NJ: Prentice Hall.

Swaffar, J., & Vlatten, A. (1997). A sequential model for video viewing in the foreign langugage curriculum. *The Modern Language Journal, 81*, 175–188.

Thomas, S. K., & Wilson, M. (1993). Idiosyncratic interpretations: negotiating meaning in expository prose. *English Journal*, January, 58–64.

Vandergrift, L. (1997). The Cinderella of communication strategies: Reception strategies in interactive listening. *The Modern Langugae Journal*, *81*, 494–505.

van Dijk, T. A., & Kintsch, W. (1983). *Strategies of Discourse Comprehension*. New York: Academic Press.

Wilson, V. L., & Rupley, W. H. (1997). A structural equation model for reading comprehension based on background, phonemic, and strategy knowledge. *Scientific Studies of Reading*, *1* (1), 45–63.

Wood, K. D., McCormack, R. L., Lapp, D., & Flood, J. (1997). Improving young adolescent literacy through collaborative learning. *Middle School Journal*, *28*, 26–34.

Zvetina, M. (1987). From research to pedagogy: What do L2 reading studies suggest? *Foreign Language Annals*, *20*, 233–238.

■ ■ ■ ■ ■

CHAPTER SIX

FOREGROUNDING ORAL COMMUNICATION

THIS CHAPTER WILL FEATURE

- an examination of communicative diversity
- an examination of theories of oral communicative development
- implications from research for the language classroom
- focusing on oral communication in content-based language learning

YOU WILL EXAMINE

- oral communication development—language socialization in society and language classrooms
- simultaneous first and second oral development
- developing oral communication in sequential language acquisition: subtractive contexts
- second language acquisition research
- differences between oral language development in second and foreign language

INTRODUCTION: SETTING THE STAGE

The most challenging and also the most rewarding aspects for many second and foreign language learners are to have their own utterances convey their intentions and be understood by their audiences. When the second language that they are learning represents their interior worlds, they begin to feel that they can do something with this "other" language. In other words, they feel that the language is "working" for them, allowing them to take action. Being an agent of their own words in another language begins to create their identity as a user of that language. On learner preference surveys perhaps for this reason many learners claim their goal is "to learn how to speak the language" and that they want to focus on this moreso than on any other aspect of communication.

However when learners identify speaking as their goal, they may not fully understand under what conditions they can develop this ability nor what they would need to do to become fluent, let alone become accurate in communicating in another language. In a setting where the second language is used in schooling, bilingual education experts have estimated that it takes a child from three to five years to develop basic interpersonal communication and on average five to seven years to develop academic level language (Thomas & Collier, 2001; Cummins, 2000). Results such as these are obtained by second language learners who are in a supportive bilingual learning environment and have meaningful relationships with those who communicate in the target languages. We'll discuss how developing oral fluency and proficiency in a foreign language proves much more elusive and challenging.

Also in this chapter you will learn how second language learners and foreign language learners may become familiar with only a few varieties of the target language because all language communities have diversity and vary according to such social factors as race, class, gender, and age. Understanding the social nuances of language use may help learners become better equipped to communicate where such diversity is a given. Indeed, even native speakers do not have access to all varieties in their native language and yet given our multicultural and global reality, those that recognize this fact are learning to expand their repertoires. Far more complexity in learning to interact with language diversity exists than research has been able to elucidate. Nonetheless, we will examine how much we know and how much there is still to find out.

FOREGROUNDING ORAL COMMUNICATION

Speaking perhaps has been the most theorized in second language and foreign language literatures from both psycholinguistic and sociocultural perspectives. For many second language learners, overall proficiency in speaking necessarily involves listening comprehension, but oral development usually lags behind listening comprehension. For foreign language learners, speaking is generally "pushed" through instructional approaches and methods that attempt to have learners, if only temporarily, orally reproduce some aspect of the language. For example, in the methods introduced in chapter 2, in the audiolingual method the repeated pronunciation of a sound, word, or phrase was highly valued in the classrooms using this method despite the fact that these words failed to convey the learners' own intentions. Nor did these repeated utterances appear immediately controllable by the student or relevant to students' lives outside of class. In fact, such pushed output often helped the learner to seem further incompetent when interacting because the output did not relate directly to the demands of the communication in interactions with speakers of the language. To be more orally productive, learners would need to be more capable of responding in a relevant and socially appropriate manner to the communication of others. Nonetheless in this method, as well as in others, "good" learners complied with the instructor's drills and produced, if only temporarily, the strange sounds they were taught to imitate. Some eventually did learn to utter the correct phrase at an appropriate opportunity but often could not understand the native speaker's responses to their utterances. Fewer persisted to higher levels to achieve a better command. But many others claim to have studied a language without learning to use it for any purpose for their needs and many came to accept these conditions and processes as normal for language learning. Why does this occur?

From a sociocultural perspective, learners begin interpreting their language learning experiences in the classroom according to the beliefs, processes, and products of their activity. According to Halliday (1993, p. 93), "When children learn language, they are not simply engaging in one kind of learning; rather, they are learning the foundations of learning." The culture of the classroom and the teacher and learner relationships therein create norms for learning language. In other words, learners become socialized to learning language. Language is one social system of signs that helps to construct reality and one's identity as a member of a group. When taught in this manner, foreign language learners interpret the classroom experience as signifying what it means to learn a language. Thus, this experience shapes their beliefs about language, learning processes, and knowledge built through their activity.

The particular classroom and the teacher and learner relationships therein become one source for shaping the accepted norms for learning language. Typically, as the traditional foreign language lesson emphasized grammatical accuracy at the expense of the development of fluency and proficiency, many students believed that accuracy was most important and making errors was to be avoided. Traditionally this belief was illustrated in the classroom by teachers' grading learners on accuracy through exercises that required filling in verb paradigm charts, memorizing dialogues, and in practicing by filling in blanks in sentences (i.e., cloze exercises). However, in the last twenty years, with developments coming from classroom-based research on communication by bilingual, second, and foreign language learners, more insights into the acquisition and learning processes have shaped our instruction. The further development of instructional programs and techniques provide the potential for having more learners achieve bilingualism, biliteracy, and multiculturalism through classroom experiences. As well, educational reform policies have extended the length of time for learning languages in such programs as elementary dual language and immersion programs, content-based language instruction, and public bilingual Montessori programs (Farmer, 1998).

In our text, learning a second/foreign language will mean being able to use the language for learning content and being able to demonstrate that learning through projects performance-based assessments, to use strategies to overcome limited proficiency and learning, and to learn about the learner's culture through the experiences of learning about others in authentic settings. For learning foreign languages, note the components of the Communication, Connections, Cultures, and Communities standards in the *National Standards for Foreign Language Learning* at www.actfl.org. For English as a Second Language learners, consult with the TESOL standards at www.tesol.org.

REFLECT AND RESPOND

1. Our prior experiences with language learning shape what we come to expect as normal and natural. What oral communication tasks were used in the classroom when you initiated your study of another language? How did these tasks affect your oral language development?

   _____

   _____

2. In early stages of oral communication development in a second/foreign language, learners tend to use what they already know from their first language, borrowing words, sounds, gestures, and spelling. What aspects of your primary language did you use to communicate orally with speakers of your second/foreign languages?

   _____

   _____

3. Being able to communicate orally in another language means that we have had opportunities to express our ideas and support for making our intentions clearer. What outside of classroom experiences could have been connected to your classroom learning that could have helped you become more orally proficient?

   _____

   _____

SIMULTANEOUS FIRST AND SECOND ORAL DEVELOPMENT

What should teachers know about students' backgrounds for preparing them to study another language? If we examine first and second language development in oral communication with children acquiring a first and second language simultaneously prior to schooling, their cognitive development, and metalinguistic development often out pace monolingual children. Bilingual children raised in an environment supportive of their bilingualism develop flexibility with **metalinguistic** concepts (e.g., learning to talk about language with terms such as "language", "sound", "word", etc) and **cultural norms** for the use of two languages earlier than monolingual children (Gonzalez, 1995; Cummins, 1978, 2000; Bialystock & Cummins, 1991; Peal & Lambert, 1962; Valdes & Figueroa, 1995). As members of a community negogiate community norms, the prescribed norms are not completely evident in actual practice. Nonetheless, over time learners engage in conversations, provide and obtain information, express feelings and emotions, and exchange opinions according to appropriate norms learned in their families and communities. They also learn which topics are public versus private and how to talk about these. Norms for interpreting discourse also help shape learners' expectations about what is being "meant" though often not openly stated verbally. These include understanding and determining when to remain silent, how to indicate they are attending to the speaker (**backchanneling**), and deciding when to use a range of **kinesic** and gestural possibilities.

In order to further develop their membership at home and in their communities, students learn to map the signification systems in their new languages at school and at home. They learn to interpret and use **body language** (posture, use of space, eye movement and contact, facial movement, and physical contact and distance), **prosody** (tone, fillers, pauses, stress, speed, pitch, and loudness), and **gestural** modes (gestural cues that also are an indicator of attitude and feelings and a significant part of face-to-face communication). Gestural cues are a major indicator of attitude and feelings and a significant part of face-to-face communication. Also they learn how to manage their interactions with others by using hesitations, pauses, repetitions, and **gambits** to gain time to speak, maintain, or compete for their turns at talk. Even though they are not fully accurate in their first language use, they learn to engage others in talk, build coherence in exchanging ideas with others in a joint construction of dialogue.

Through time the variability of performances with others helps them recognize the range of diversity in their community as well as in those who are outsiders. As they gain these performative and interactive skills, they associate with and gain further practice with the discourses in their community's way of using these languages and literacies (Kelly & Green, 1998). Sometimes these communities in the United States become users of hybrids of both languages, forming such varieties known as Calo in Spanish and Creole in French. (See Bergen, 1990, for examples from Spanish.) Sometimes they maintain their separate natures, maintained in religious institutions such as in the Catholic church's former use of Latin, in the Islamic religion's use of Arabic, or in Jewish temples' use of Hebrew.

As you can see, people learn to use oral language interacting across different domains of their social life: personal, public, educational, and later occupational. Opportunities to interact successfully orally and aurally within these domains help learners to participate meaningfully. In the classroom, these domains intersect and interact when teachers draw on learners' background knowledge to extend learners' oral performances. In school, the teachers' expectation of oral practices may inadvertently conflict with students' ways of speaking. In addition, teachers' expectations may conflict with the students' level of preparedness to handle the demands of spontaneous oral communication requiring listening comprehension, thinking, and oral expression. Having an understanding of the larger oral practices that students engage in over time and meaningful rehearsal using these oral practices assist learners in moving from a preverbal stage toward using productive chunks of language to answering questions, and later, full oral participation in the larger practices.

Additionally teachers will need to attend to how they manage their oral interactions for potential conflicts with the students' previous schooling or home experiences (Scollon & Scollon, 1995). These may include modeling unfamiliar oral language responses, allowing for more wait time between eliciting a student response, and allocating turns more equitably. Eventually, these interventions should allow students to take over and actively demonstrate their own creative contributions by leading or carrying out new oral performances with peers (Wells & Chang-Wells, 1992). To achieve this, teachers will need to scaffold their instruction for a hetergeneous cultural group of students with heterogeneous oral language development.

School is among the first public institutions that communities offer to educate and socialize children through language study and practices. Therefore continuity between home and school is a vital concern to encourage early second language learners' progress in oral language development, which interacts with their literacy development and future academic success. According to Cocking (1994), it is difficult to understand the precise source of continuities and discontinuities that may occur. However various discontinuities have been identified such as: (1) developmental factors that have been assumed to be universals in contrast to culture-specific patterns across different groups of bilingual and monolingual children (Bialystock, 1991; Bialystock & Cummins, 1991; Diaz, 1985; Diaz & Klinger, 1991; Diaz & Padilla, 1985; Hakuta, 1986; Markman & Hutchinson, 1984; McLaughlin, 1990). (2) patterns and value in oral interactions and (3) uses of and interactions with literacy. Acknowledging these discontinuities at school as a major obstacle to success for learners whose primary language is English, concerned educators have called for more culturally inclusive and relevant pedagogy both in ESL and mainstream classes that receive English language learners.

In foreign language learning, the continuity has been largely framed around gaining community and family support for the study of another language and curricular articulation; hence not so tied to helping students bridge their home cultures with the classroom and school culture. Nonetheless, both community support and continuity with classroom experiences are vital to the success of learners. But how can families and schools support each others' efforts in a second language? Let's turn first to examining oral language development.

DEVELOPING ORAL COMMUNICATION IN SEQUENTIAL LANGUAGE ACQUISITION

Schools with second language or immersion programs receive children who are **emerging bilinguals** as well as children who are monolingual in a language other than English. To fully support subsequent bilingualism, not only is communicative language necessary but further literacy is critical. Learning language to learn subject matter is crucial to academic success. Therefore early language development with literacy as a goal involves oral practices supporting the children's meaningful use of printed material. Typical classroom routines for enculturating students to pay attention to language use in enjoyable ways at the same time they learn how to interpret and use language are: question and answering routines, sharing time with books, storytelling, illustrating their own stories and sharing their illustrations, creating games, reciting poems or singing (Maley, 1987) and dramatization of stories (Gaudart, 1990; Scarcella & Crookall, 1990; Scarcella, 1987).

Children move from these oral forms to integrating their own written language in logs or self-authored books, which later become meaningful reading for them. In addition, they learn to play with language to shape it to make their meanings understandable to audiences. In a sense, they come to own the language because they have written themselves into these practices. In another sense, they have created identities as users of the language. Practices with print, which help students build their oral abilities for relevant authentic tasks, prepare them to think and use language for learning.

To bring second and foreign language users to such a high level of accomplishment, engagement in relevant and sustained oral language practices is necessary. Learners who are regularly excluded, either intentionally or unintentionally, from shaping their ideas into language for a particular audience are effectively denied entry into practices that affect their social, emotional, and intellectual growth. Children who exclude themselves or resist participating in oral practices in the second or foreign language are removing themselves from cultivating their membership and ownership of that targeted language and culture. Teachers and students can reproduce inequities if turns at talking are not shared or if the privilege of talking excludes certain learners (Grundy, 1997). Caring teachers and peers can help reduce resistance if their classroom ways of talking are evaluated to see if everyone has an opportunity to speak and be heard. Understanding the causes for a student's resistance and avoidance is important to changing classroom dynamics that may be oppressive. Additionally, because not everyone will want to lose his or her accent, accuracy in phonological development will require the learner's own desire, attention, and persistence over time.

Efforts from the learner are needed as well. As simultaneous learners of two languages, children gradually develop the pronunciation of those with whom they interact who use these languages. However, they do not just mimic this language but actively build their own understanding through their daily meaningful experiences with members of their community.

Subsequent language learners face influence from their first language. From psycholinguistic research, this is referred to as *interference* from the first language. Interference can be thought of as the first language's negative transfer onto the second language. To overcome these unwanted influences on the second language's sound system (**phonology**), there is a need to recognize that not all differences are significant nor can all be addressed at once. In fact, according to psycholinguistic research there is a developmental order. However research has not identified that order for each language for every learner. In fact, each learner may progress through the similar stages but at different paces for the various levels of oral production from particular sounds or combinations (phonological,) to rise and pitch (intonation and stress—prosodic), to types of oral performances for various audiences (e.g., speeches, jokes, sermons, conversations) (**genre**). **Paralinguistic** aspects that accompany oral speech, such as voice quality, gestures, volume, posture, and eye gaze are all nonlinguistic aspects of oral communication and have yet to be researched for second language learner's developmental accuracy or rate of achievement across languages.

Much of what we know about the oral developmental sequence for second language is from learners of English as a second language and is based on the studies of their acquisition of phonemes, morphemes, syntax, and more recently pragmatics and discourse. Further, much of what we know about learners in a foreign language class comes from studying university or professionals (adult learners) of a language.

For learning culturally relevant use of oral language (e.g., the culture in language for deciding what kinds of communication, with whom, when, where, and how communication can take place) both **pragmatic** and **discoursal levels** present challenges to the learner becoming a subsequent bilingual. While much sociolinguistic research has been carried out cross-culturally focusing on particular **speech acts** (e.g., requesting, apologizing, praising), little has been carried out on how the learner 1) acquires skill in taking up particular **stances,** such as expressing friendliness or distances, politeness or rudeness; 2) distinguishes between public versus private speech, or between irony or humor; or 3) learns to express and interpret emotions through culturally appropriate oral practices. Wierzbicka (1999) has initiated promising research that attempts to identify how emotions are communicated across languages. To date, very little research has addressed the socioemotional development of bilingual children across second language programs (Dewaele & Pavlenko, 2002).

LANGUAGE AS A RESOURCE

As learners draw on their first **language as a resource** in learning another language's practice, research on their varied ways of using language will be important. To date very few K–12 classroom research studies in foreign languages have been conducted to examine in a multilingual and multicultural environment how learners' gender, social class, ethnicity, and race play a role in their oral communicative development. Nonetheless there continues to be vibrant activity in research in native and second language settings where these issues are being identified as affecting ways of self-presentation, vocabulary use, and types of discourses learned (Malone, 1997; Dewaele & Pavlenko, 2002; Orellana, 1995, 1994; Ehrlich, 1997; Willett, 1995; Ochs, 1992; Rampton, 1991). Through primarily using **discourse and conversational analysis** of talk in everyday life, a vast new source of information is being created that can serve language educators. This interactional sociolinguistic and anthropological linguistic research demonstrates how language is used as social action. It moves away from seeing language forms as having a one-to-one correspondence with meaning. That is, typically in a language class learners study vocabulary, phrases, and conversations with definite meanings attached to the provided utterances, and definitions. This can be seen in the turn-by-turn responsiveness between participants in talk. Teachers who use analyses of these moments of student engagement can monitor how their oral interactions in the classroom privilege certain members of the class and types of talk. The consequences that talk has for these learners are social, academic, and cognitive. The social outcomes affect their engagement and investment in learning, their identity, and status among their peers in class and with the teacher.

The academic consequences of talk shape the learner's construction of personalized understanding of concepts and use of those understandings in school. The cognitive outcomes affect how new information is related to past knowledge and how it affects generalizations to current and future language and content learning. This research highlights how several aspects of teachers' oral interactions need to be monitored— distribution of turns in a lesson, recognition of students' contributions, and sanctioning individuals' behaviors of one group of students moreso than others.

Another very important contribution from interactional sociolinguistic and anthropological linguistic research is that notions of such influences as contexts, role, status, politeness are created in and through interactions. That is, the context is not just the physical surroundings, time, and place of the interaction, but rather what each participant brings to bear in the interaction as evidenced through his or her talk. For example, through the talk a **participation structure** can be created by a teacher signaling the start of a class with a mere "OK." She controls who can talk by merely calling a student's name. The utterance of "ok" introduces a change in the context from informal activity to a formal lesson: beginning a new **frame** is created in which there are positions for students and herself, where the teacher takes position as authority and creates the position for students to be subordinate in this participation structure. Students who speak out of turn are often perceived as challenging her authority to control, and she may respond by allowing or disallowing them permission by a variety of comments or by merely uttering loudly "OK" and calling their names. The same utterance of "OK" and students' names hence is both a nomination to speak and prohibition from speaking.

Students who follow her lead are perceived as collaborating in maintaining the frame of the lesson, and her position as an authority by recognition and remaining silent. Within the same interaction, the *participation structure* can change. The teacher can signal that she is trying to build solidarity with students by, among other ways, using their language to align her with them or by sharing with them the authority to determine turn-taking and the lesson. Hence while they are still in the same physical setting and time frame, the participants in this interaction change positions relative to each other.

We can see changes in power, control, and status through a close analysis of students' talk in their interactions by examining how they say what they say, when they say it and to whom, with what consequences, and how certain meanings are sanctioned or not. Changes in the emotional tone of an event, miscommunications, or noncommunication occur by not merely choosing the incorrect grammar or vocabulary, but through the negotiations between participants' interpretations of what is happening, i.e., communicative interactions affect their relationships (Goodwin & Duranti, 1992). Elbissi (2003) outlined the effective ways that a teacher can help children become powerful constructors of knowledge, allowing them to share how their experiences connect to the texts studied in class.

Several important concepts from this research can help teachers prepare learners to engage in social action through language and understand how communication varies across cultures. For teachers in elementary grades, oral instructions about daily routines can be encoded into graphic representations of the schedule and labeled. When students are given the role of daily monitor, taking turns to orally read these graphics or labels, they take on public stances of leadership. Teachers can also use students' interests to change the schedule, having students vote on which activities to accomplish in which sequence.

For middle and high school students, a teacher can use simulations, including a combination of activities such as discussion, dramatization, observations, and reflection. Learners can try out interactions, view, and analyze videotaped scenes from their own experiences in school or from television, movies, or commercials. They can analyze the participant structures about who can participate and how. A focus on language use can help the learners identify the different cultural **interactional frames,** how they begin, build or collapse, and end. By trying out different endings, they can learn to anticipate and use strategies to control the oral communication to negotiate their intentions. Learners can identify how speakers use strategies in taking **positions** through the interactions and how the learners see these positions affect their relationships of distance or solidarity. They can then look to see how *voice* can change to legitimize status positions. For example, what does sounding like an authority mean? What options exist and which ones are higher and less privileged, and what positionings may benefit whom and why? For example, taking a lower status position in a conversation makes a display as less powerful but may be strategic for accomplishing a particular goal.

There are other invisible yet palpable features of culture in communication—those elements that reveal attitude, emotions, and dispositions. Body language, eye gaze, and paralinguistic elements such as volume, intonation, and prosody in oral communication play a major role in face-to-face communication as they color the learners' utterances with emotional tones. Because we use our knowledge about culture to distinguish between a loud voice as anger or excitement, eye gaze as respectful or suspicious, posture as defiant or obedient, at times teachers and English language learners misinterpret these cues or are unaware that they are communicating divergent messages through these cues.

As all these concepts of interactional frame, participation structure, positioning, use of paralinguistic elements occur in daily social interactions, beginning second language learners may need help in recognizing these social mores. Intermediate and advanced learners may need help expanding their repertoires to find and create options beyond what they have experienced. Foreign language learners without experiential learning either through simulations, study abroad, or immersion may need overt instruction in recognizing and then using these aspects of language as action. This is a major challenge because many textbook conversations are built to highlight grammatical features rather than to highlight managing these social interactions.

Unless their education has been disrupted by poverty, war, or immigration, older-school-aged learners who are being introduced to another language for the first time in the middle and high school grades generally draw upon their personal history of learning in schools. They bring these personal and educational histories with them, which may include varying levels of knowledge about language and how it works, of literacy and how pleasurable or not it is, and perceptions about school and their future. Immigrants, refugees, and displaced or homeless learners must also deal with traumas and loss of comforts of home and culture, which may further affect their ability initially to give much attention to language learning and school achievement, particularly when family life and support are disrupted. Age, native language ability, previous level of education, learning styles, degree of motivation, and incorporation into target groups play a major role in learners being able to draw upon resources from their prior language learning and schooling in learning a language in a classroom.

CLASSROOM LANGUAGE LEARNING

Research on classroom language learning has either tried to globally encompass this complex environment and interaction that influence learning a language or has tried to reduce its complexity and control isolated features. In the latter case, researchers have tried to predict the role of isolated features and to generalize their effect on the language learning pace, progress, or achievement. For this reason we will cite from both types of research studies, as they define "language learning" differently and have different assumptions about the learner (Harley, Cummins, Swain, & Allen,1990).

From sociolinguistic research, we know that our attitudes towards speakers of a language influence our use of language, and our use of language influences who accepts us into their group. Sometimes this is mostly invisible because we assume as natural and logical such conventions as knowing how to respond to people (Gee, 1992; Heath, 1984). This implicit appropriation of "what's out there" in the **discourse** makes it difficult to see the assumptions and values underlying our use of language which evolve as our range of experiences and relationships with others and institutions constantly expand.

Any one individual experiences only a fraction of what diversity actually exists even in the same community, as these experiences depend on their exposure to social and regional varieties of language use that differ according to race, gender, social class, and ethnicity. At other times we deliberately pattern ourselves by imitating language used by people who influence us. By examining with our students the ways people communicate with each other, we can uncover cues to the values they have: how they see the world, and most of all, how they see themselves. Teachers who utilize this fact can find evidence of the social bases of second language learning in the types of language that their students begin to use spontaneously. It will be important to help students recognize the social contexts in which such language is considered appropriate and to help them find alternative expressions for use with audiences in different contexts. The social theories on human development and activity introduced in chapter 1 provided an understanding of the powerful role contextualized language use plays in developing concepts from our lived experiences. Dialogic communication can help clear up students' misconceptions about language learning that may hinder their progress and persistence in language study.

SUBTRACTIVE BILINGUALISM

Prior to this section, supportive conditions and processes for becoming bilingual have been presented. While one hopes as a language teacher to create the ideal environment that may be supportive of learners becoming bilinguals, often there are obstacles that prevent learners from achieving this goal. Some factors are due to external societal and institutional factors that influence what happens in schools. Others are interactional factors that evolve from student/student or teacher/student encounters (Valdes, 2001).

Since not all segments of society are equally represented among the decision makers affecting learning or teaching, a hierarchy of influences responds to the social hierarchy of the decision makers. Power differentials and their influence on instruction directly affect what is viewed as possible and achievable. For example, often children whose mother tongue is not English or the standard variety of English are expected to give up their first language and learn English only. Rather than viewing their ability to use their native tongue and literacy as assets, the focus is placed on their lack of English, which is seen as a "deficit" (Flores, Tefft-Cousin, & Diaz, 1991).

THINK, PAIR, SHARE

Answer the following questions with a partner.

1. What developmental features in communication do you notice (or anticipate) when children are learning a second language? Mention both oral and nonverbal features.

   _____

   _____

2. How might middle and high schools students beginning their foreign language study become more motivated to build oral communication fluency?

   _____

   _____

3. How can we better prepare learners to participate successfully in face-to-face interaction with native speakers from a wide range of social and cultural backgrounds? What kinds of activities would foster collaboration between English language learners and students in the mainstream classes?

   _____

   _____

Education from this perspective is called **subtractive bilingualism** because oppressive practices contribute to discount the learners' development in one language, their self-esteem, and their potential to use what they know. This practice also creates a false assumption that one must give up a language to learn another rather than recognizing that strong literacy in one language helps build strong literacy in the second.

In contrast, children whose mother tongue is English are expected to get a sprinkling of another language through Foreign Language in the Elementary School (FLES) programs or Exploratory Language programs at the middle school but not enough to learn the other language. Both the subtractive bilingual situation and the sprinkling of foreign language instruction contribute to maintaining monolingualism and to not fully taking advantage of each learner's potential to use prior knowledge in a way to encourage and value becoming bilingual.

SECOND LANGUAGE ACQUISITION RESEARCH

From the psycholinguistic research, which attempts to provide generalized explanations and predictions about the mental process of groups of learners' acquisition of language, several variables have been identified that play important roles in influencing the learning of another language. These include the native language, language universals, interaction, output, and instruction. Several theories, or models, and hypotheses have been offered to account for parts of the learner's process in using input in the second language to promote acquisition. These include input and output theories and hypotheses.

Input hypothesis was first introduced by Krashen, providing a basic universal explanation for a language acquisition process. In this theory, a learner's emotions and attitudes set up an affective filter that may impede or allow the learner to interact with language stimuli. If this language is at a level slightly within the learner's grasp of understanding, then the stimuli can become comprehensible input that would permit the learner to acquire the language at a subconscious level, much like first language acquisition. Krashen used the notation $i + 1$ as shorthand for comprehensible input. In this theory, acquisition was distinct from learning because it credited the learner's subconscious processes for permitting the ability to communicate.

Many researchers subsequently challenged the notion that comprehension played such a singularly important role. In the ensuing twenty years, researchers contributed to modifying Krashen's input hypothesis by identifying the important role that learners using the language plays in stimulating acquisition. Along these lines, Long (1983) proposed a hypothesis that took into account the need for comprehensible input, conversational interactions to make input comprehensible, and comprehensible output to push students beyond semantic processing to syntactic processing. This has come to be the foundation for what is considered the interactionist account of language acquisition.

The **interactional hypothesis** predicts language acquisition as a result of learners' active communicative efforts to understand and be understood. When learners are stretched through their interactions to modify their language use beyond the word level, they begin to develop complex language at the syntax level.

What kinds of input and interactions would promote language acquisition? Subsequent research found that native speakers accommodated their language when speaking to those they perceived as nonnative speakers. That is, sympathetic native speakers used a simplified form of talk called "foreigner talk" to respond in a comprehensible manner and provided input that could not have served the learner's acquisition. Findings from research in the classroom found that when learners made their language more comprehensible to peers in group work where unique information was held by each person, their modifications stimulated acquisition (Doughty & Pica, 1986). The evidence from later studies also suggests that comprehension alone may not provide sufficient and consistent input for learners to acquire the language, thus giving rise to examine types of learners' involvement in interactions and the role of direct instruction study of certain aspects of language.

The **output hypothesis** was formulated by Swain (1985) who studied sixth-grade French learners in an immersion setting. The immersion students understood French yet did not reach proficient oral levels in grammar, discourse, and sociolinguistic measures. Swain noted that learners' attempts to produce language might have a more significant role in pushing acquisition forward. Rather than merely serving as more input, the successive attempts at output were viewed as a way for learners to test hypotheses about the target language and progressively produce more accurate, coherent, and conventionalized language.

THINK, PAIR, SHARE

Answer the following questions with a partner.

1. From both sociocultural research and the psycholinguistic research, learners are seen as active in their learning of a second language. Being merely exposed to the second language is insufficient for learning how to use the language. Consider what kinds of conditions in your school might marginalize English language learners from their active participation in school life. How can these issues be addressed by all teachers in the school?

   _____

   _____

2. What kinds of activities would encourage learners to use their L2 or feedback in their next oral performances? Draw on involving peers and school and community members.

   _____

   _____

Classroom-Based Research on Oral Communication Development

Further research on feedback indicates that particular types of corrective feedback helped learners produce more accurate target language forms. Corrective feedback helped learners acquire particular word formations rules in French but did not have much effect on the learners generalizing to new items (Carroll, Roberge, & Swain, 1992). In classes for English learners, research has shown that despite its availability, not all feedback is attended to and productively used by the learners. Factors that need to be considered are: quantity, complexity and timing of the feedback, and learners' recognition of the usefulness or need for feedback in accomplishing the particular communication either in the moment of interaction or for later use in similar conditions. Corrective feedback is helpful when compared to modeling, particularly when students are lead to make hypothesis and then induced to make errors, following up with corrective feedback (Herron & Tomasello, 1992; Herron, 1991). For teachers this suggests that learners have a major role in responding to second language input and feedback before it can become helpful to their proficiency. Their active attention to and use of reconstructed L2 information can be helpful for their susbsequent learning.

Input Theories

The research that evolved to examine what kinds of learning in classroom settings can best facilitate acquisition are called **learnability theories.** These theories tried to identify stages in learner development and types of tasks and interactions. **Processability theory** predicts that the sequence in which the learner can process speech is determined by the sequence in which learners develop processing prerequisites needed to handle the language's components. This theory makes predictions that the learner's working memory will need time to process each grammatical structure. If these structures are complex, then the learner will proceed through stages of development in processing. The theory has implications that learners can only be taught a structure when learners can manage its processing demands.

Gass and Selinker (2001) offer an integrated view of second language acquisition process that explains five stages in a learner's process in which learners notice input because of its frequency, their affective connections to the input, and the input's connection to prior knowledge. Learners attend to this type of input because they engage in processes of comparison or contrast. Additionally, as they comprehend this input at a number of different levels, they can associate it with a purpose that could be for long-term integrated learning.

Output Theories

During the process of acquisition, the development of learners proceed through stages of **interlanguage,** which gradually can develop into full nativelike proficiency. It is during this development that fluency emerges first, and accuracy later. Intonation with regard to pitch differentiates items in information structure of discourse and boundary tones. English and Germanic languages use pitch to set the focus or important information of the phrase. High pitch is associated with foregrounding new or contrasting information in relation to either previous discourse or contextual knowledge. Lower-pitched tones, often of the function words, signals information that is given or predictable in the discourse. Not having any pitch, a flat intonation, reduces the discourse indicated by cues. Pitch is also used to signal the intention to continue or relinquish turns in conversations. Yet pitch control in English and many European languages is one of the features of language that indicates the emotional stance of the speaker in relation to the topic and or persons with whom the speaker is engaging. In Chinese, pitch control also indicates lexical and morphological differences.

Psycholinguistic research also acknowledges individual differences in the acquisition process. Psychological factors that signal individual differences and unique patterns found in specific children have been identified in the research by Harley, Cummins, Swain, and Allen, 1990. Further research in this direction focused on learning variation that identified how learners may have varied preferences in learning, or **learning styles** (cognitive), that help them process, store, and retrieve information. These vary according to the learner's understanding of the task demands, background knowledge of the task, and conditions of learning (time, space, noise, alone or with others, and light levels). Learning styles are also affected by such traits as affective levels, modes of processing information (e.g., haptic/kinetic, auditory, visual, and verbal), and types of cognition (e.g., analytic-linear, associative).

For language teachers this natural variation in how people learn will require multiple types of activities to encourage learners to learn both in their preferred or familiar ways of learning, as well as to add ways of learning when they are not taught in their preferred style. Instruction would not only need to identify what oral performances are expected but also how to cope with the social and linguistic demands to accomplish these communicative tasks.

Inventories to characterize and label learners have been invented that are specific to language learning (Ehrman, 1998; Oxford, 1991; Chamot & Omalley, 1990). As a result, research has identified learning strategies that "good" language learners use and strategies to deal with communicative demands in second and foreign language settings (Wendon & Rubin, 1987; Wenden, 1991). In terms of oral communication, several of the characteristics of "good" learners are:

1. Find their own way to make use of the language
2. Are creative and experiment with the language
3. Create opportunties to use the language inside and outside of the class
4. Learn to tolerate uncertainty and to try to get the gist of what is being said without understanding every word
5. Make errors work for them
6. Transfer knowledge of their primary language to help them in the second
7. Let their knowledge of the context help them comprehend
8. Learn from making good guesses about meaning
9. Learn chunks as wholes and formalized routines to sound proficient
10. Manage to use their production to keep interactions going
11. Learn to differentiate their language according to the audience and formality

As well, research on areas of human intelligence has identified types of strengths that learners may have that have gone unrecognized as intelligences. (see Chapter 3.) From this research on **multiple intelligences,** specific application to language learning has recently been undertaken to examine the role of these intelligences in the language acquisition. (Hall Haley, 2001; Thomas, 1999).

Instructional Challenges

As was pointed out earlier, foreign language teachers often have to manufacture conditions for learners to feel a need to engage in communication using the target language. For ESL learners the need to communicate in the target language is much more urgent and felt inside and outside of their bilingual or ESL classroom. Yet both groups of learners are expected to build on what is already known, to challenge their previous thinking, and become members of another language community.

TWO PERSPECTIVES: FLUENCY AND PROFICIENCY VERSUS IDENTITY AND AGENCY

A basic level of accomplishment that many learners desire is to understand native speakers and be able to be understood by native speakers. More advanced learners would want to also influence and act upon the world through oral communication. As attention to communication and learning in the classroom has grown, it has spawned

REFLECT AND RESPOND

1. What challenges have you faced in developing your skill in oral communication in your target language? (In which levels are you more confident and capable: gestural/kinetic, phonological, prosodic, rhetorical/genre, discourse?)

_____

_____

2. If we allow for skill-level differences within our classrooms due to students progressing at different rates, what oral communicative practice routines and projects will we choose that will help socialize learners and promote community-building within the classroom? What theories support your positions?

_____

_____

3. Examine your language program or curriculum to see where and when you can introduce the practices listed in #2 to be aligned with your understanding of stages of learners' oral communicative development.

_____

_____

research on the social construction of knowledge, language as discourse, and social practices. These areas are examined for connections between language forms, cognitive processes, and discourses.

In our field, *fluency, accuracy* and *proficiency* are all terms constructed to indicate linguistic levels of communicative accomplishment, with a normative goal of reaching a model similar to an idealized educated native speaker. Other educators have questioned using the native-speaker-as-model goal because this has a tendency to replicate hierarchies of power that subjugate the learner in ways similar to the hierarchy of colonies to imperialist nations. Instead, a variety of transformative approaches are proposed to build learner identities and agency using the target language. Let us examine what these two directions have to contribute.

Planned Oral Communication

Let us consider now changing from spontaneous communication and looking to planned communication. **Monologic communication** (communication in which the speaker has an audience but the interaction is more limited), such as reading aloud to others, speeches and lectures, planning, and rehearsals play a bigger role than they would in face-to-face encounters. Students can use their limited attentional resources to focus on planning first, practice phrasing, and voicing their prepared written communications. Using graphic

REFLECT AND RESPOND

There are several activities in a typical lesson plan in which unplanned oral communication is needed: brainstorming, predicting before reading activities, shadowing a video character's speech, explaining a story map, peers asking questions of the author, author answering questions from peers, explaining own thinking in problem solving, to name a few.

1. Discuss what kinds of language would be used and what kinds of interactional demands students would face in each.

Oral Communication	Kinds of Language *Example:* lexical, sentence/phrase prosodic features narrative combined and coordinated discourses	Interactional Demands *Examples:* Monitoring what has been said, bidding for turn, turn-taking, turn-giving, maintaining turn, taking notes, coordinating visuals with talk	Examples
Brainstorming in whole class			
Predicting before reading activities in pairs			
Shadowing a favorite video character's speech individually			
Explaining a story map to the teacher			
Peers asking questions of the author			
Author answering questions from peers			
Explaining own thinking in problem solving			
Debate			

2. How would you scaffold students' oral production in each?

_____

_____

3. What strategies would you want students to use in each?

_____

_____

4. Explain which seems to be most difficult/easy to accomplish.

_____

_____

organizers, learners can decide what content to include and how to organize it into a narrative structure. Their next phases could build in coherence and cohesion through expressions that tie their ideas together to produce the effects they are aiming for. As they finish their planned oral communication, learners can devote attention to performance issues such as volume, enunciation, phrasing, gesturing, and pace. In this cycle of activity, learners attend to communicating to an audience for a purpose. To create a supportive community, students in the audience can be taught to praise, comment on what impressed them, and give suggestions.

In the next phase, they may draw on their observations of interactions and listening, and/or draw on their abilities to guess/brainstorm important features of the discourse in which they will take part. What do they think is happening there? Who speaks to whom about what and why? How do they want the audience to respond? How does the communication affect the audience? How do they know? Which cues are linguistic and which are nonlinguistic? For younger students this may mean using graphics to guide a storytelling narrative. An easy way to see how this works is to obtain or have students draw stick puppets or comic strips to represent an issue or concern they want to narrate to their classmates, families, or communities. Their story line could be developed after the instructor models a story that is read and enacted for the whole class. The story could be based on:

- a funny thing that they noticed.
- a place/person they have visited that is special to them.
- an activity that they would like to do for their neighborhood. Students would need to decide to whom they would tell this story.

Riggenbach's (1991) study of fluency reports that the features of fluency defy quantification and general characterization. Instead she supports a more holistic and qualitative approach to identify learners' strengths and weaknesses and allow them to use these points to monitor their progress.

To develop fluency and later more accuracy, from a psycholinguistic perspective, learners need to develop an awareness of what it takes to engage in negotiations in a particular setting with particular interactions with interlocutors through developing hypotheses testing, and later building automatization for faster and less dysfluent oral communication (Towell, Hawkins, & Bazergui, 1996). The type of negotiations that are engaged in must allow for generating cognitive processes similar to those needed in negotiations outside of the classroom in order for the classroom learning to be usefully applied. In other words, the underlying cognitive processes of the interaction and negotiation need to be comparable between what is asked in the classroom and what is asked in natural settings. This will allow learners to develop strategies that will enhance developing those cognitive processes.

In her study comparing students studying French abroad with students who had not, Freed (2000) was able to discern which features native speakers, both professionals and nonprofessionals, used to perceive distinctions between these two groups of students who had similar levels of motivation, anxiety, and/or aptitude. The open-ended ratings given by the nonprofessionals tended to include comments on their sense of students' levels of confidence with the language and students' comfort in speaking. This group of raters valued the students' strength of voice and more monotonous tone. The group of professional raters tended to emphasize linguistic complexity, grammatical structure, and ease of interaction and vivacious tone of voice. The ratings of both professional and nonprofessional native speakers favored the students who studied abroad and descriptors used by both groups included: "lack of hesitation," "richness of vocabulary," "articulate," "faster rate of speech," "accent," and judged the studied-abroad group as being more highly motivated and having greater potential for improvement. Surprisingly, the two student groups' performances on the Modern Language Aptitude Test (MLAT) were significantly different but in favor of the students who had not studied abroad. Freed interprets this result as being consist with past findings (Freed, 1990; Goodman, Freed, & McMannus, 1990) that indicate that the MLAT does not seem to predict success in oral skills.

Finally, overall global ratings between the two groups of students in gain scores on ratings prior to departure and ratings upon return did not show statistical significance between the groups until the advanced students were removed from the sample. This suggests that advanced students in both groups were more alike than the beginning students. For the initially less fluent group, the students who had gone abroad were found to be different from those who had not.

While Freed's study confirms that fluency ratings are subjective, she also identifies what raters seem to notice: the particular dysfluencies of learners that are less systematic than native speakers' dysfluencies. Among the traditional features of fluency, those who studied aboard spoke more, were faster, and had less silent pauses and fewer dysfluencies related to isolated sounds. More revealing for acquisition processes is the finding that those in the studied-abroad group had a "tendency to attempt linguistic expression[s] that . . . . not work; they reformulate their speech, producing more false starts than is evidenced in the speech of those who have never been abroad." Their processes of development still needed more time to achieve accuracy, but they gained fluency that must have been also a function of their confidence to engage as language users.

The studies on fluency have implication for instruction in that confidence can be built by learners who persist in the communication and who have success at negotiating meaning.

CASE STUDY: ORAL LANGUAGE DEVELOPMENT IN AN INTERDISCIPLINARY LESSON FROM ELEMENTARY FOREIGN LANGUAGE CLASSROOM

Huihong Bao

Amherst Chinese Summer Camp

Recently we started a free summer camp for elementary school children in grades one through four to learn Chinese. We opened our camp for ten days and ran it for two and a half hours each day from 10:00 A.M.–12:30 P.M. We designed the program and the admissions forms and created the publicity campaign: flyers and newspaper announcement. We also recruited from the local schools and the neighborhood closest to our campsite.

REFLECT AND RESPOND

- Refer back to the information you provided in the chart at the beginning of this chapter. Given that you are aware of the varieties of language use that can be learned, and given your learners' purposes for language use in your school and community, what **range of oral communication practice** do you want to incorporate in your curriculum?
- Given one example of a particular genre of oral communication (e.g., telephone call, friendly conversation, interview, speech), how you would introduce students to both socially defined conventions and creative practice which would
  - help them identify social contexts: ranges and types?
  - introduce participation structures in the talk, and relationships to people in those contexts as evidenced by talk: enemity/amity, distance/solidarity, commitment/indifference?
  - guide them through a logical sequence of acts in the frame?
  - provide opportunities for learners' own choices in those contexts to go with/against the flow, withdraw/engage?
  - help them deal with conflicts in interpretation?
  - help them reflect on their choices of positioning in expressing meaningful/relevant communication?
  - help them reflect on the oral interactions' consequences on thinking, membership, and building across differences?

I designed oral activities for children to engage in songs, poems, and stories that were typical of children's genres in China. I planned to teach a new song every day and review all songs at the midpoint. I also planned to have games that incorporated physical activities that required counting, jumping, running, and lots of singing. To guarantee parental support, I invited them from the first day to participate in our activities. Not all would stay but I was determined to involve them too. I also had members of the community, one Chinese-speaking and the other French-speaking, assist with the activities. I had plenty of help to manage the activities with the children.

To prepare the literacy objective of my classes, which was just to familiarize the children with the writing system and actually write a few characters for a postcard/greeting, I created large posters for each of the songs I wanted to teach. I asked my son to draw pictures to illustrate the objects named in the songs. Then all the posters decorated the wall. My posters made the walls a sea of print and pictures, which would take my students to another literacy.

When the camp was in session, I tried to establish a stable routine in Chinese that the students would get used to participating in. Our daily activities started with a morning greeting to begin the lesson, then in moving between lessons we sang songs. We lined up for going to the bathroom, distributed and received snacks, expressed gratitude to the children whose parents contributed the snacks, and ended the day with a song.

At the end of the camp, we had a final performance in which the children had to perform as a group to model the activity, and to teach their parents one of their favorites. The children were able to sing some of the songs alone, others required help. But the parents were impressed at how much the children were able to follow the rou-

REFLECT AND RESPOND (*Continued*)

1. Speeches, plays, poems, presentations, and storytelling are all planned oral activities that can be mediated through activities to write and read aloud texts. Students can plan what they will say, revise, and edit what they will say. Later they will need to practice delivery in terms of how they will say it. These performances require different demands for public speaking. What skills are needed that are related to producing quality or effective performances? Think of aspects such as credibility, accuracy of information, argumentation, style, and patterns of emphasis. Nonverbal aspects of the performance are also important gestural, posture, pausing, and intonation needed in addition to reading and writing.

Performance	Audience response desired	Features of talk: narrative structure, patterns of emphasis or omission, genre, argumentation forms, figures of speech / Nonverbal aspects	Effectiveness: credibility, accuracy of information
Speeches	Persuade / Move emotionally		
Plays	Identify with character, or author's theme		
Poems	Appreciation of imagery		
Presentations	Introduce new information		
Telling short stories	Appreciation of narrative		

3. What strategies would you want students to use in each as audience, and later as author?

_____

_____

4. How would you scaffold students' oral production in each?

_____

_____

tines, songs, and games. A few even commented how their children were using their Chinese greetings outside of the class with others in the community. One parent marveled at how her son wrote Chinese characters much better than he did English letters. Another parent even wrote a thank you card in Chinese letters for each of the helpers and me.

In reflecting on my goals for oral development of the children during the intensive summer camp, I realized that I had tried to push the children's oral production of Chinese during class time. The constant repetition lasted only during class time but many had no one to use Chinese with outside of class. At most they could spontaneously sing one or two of the songs we had taught and say greetings. Since I lead most of the oral communication in Chinese, the students did not have many opportunities to take roles to initiate any conversations or learn oral routines that they could use with others. Instead the children learned to perform songs, recite poetry, and play games in Chinese. In order for them to develop their own voices in Chinese, I think I will have to create more roles for them to lead rather than follow. Perhaps having each child share a game with my help in translating major ideas in Chinese could build a class treasure chest of activities.

Fluency Building: Error Correction

In a fluency/proficiency directed program, concern is directed at pushing the learners' acquisitional processes through interlanguage development. This is accomplished by providing correction to only those features that can be reasonably be managed at the learners' level of proficiency. For fluency to develop, students need to be in positions to use language spontaneously, thus allowing for the process of **creative construction** (learners' novel constructions from overgeneralization as they acquire another language). Research by Wennerstrom (2000) supports helping learners to focus on **clause level** output or **productive chunks** (Chafe, 1987; Pawley & Syder, 2000). She used a fluency rating from the standardized test, SPEAK,[1] to analyze two specific aspects of intonation. The first intonation is a pitch generally used to differentiate between known and unknown items in the information structure of the discourse, and the second is the pitch to signal the end of a conversational turn. By examining these two features in a nonnative English speaker's conversation with a native speaker, she could see the effect on the native speaker's responses. The degree to which the nonnative speaker can use these two features is assumed to be an indicator of fluency. Wennerstrom found that the "ability to speak phrasally rather than word-by-word, focusing on the main idea of each utterance in a coherent manner and collaborating in the turn-taking process" lead to the perception of fluent speech by native-speaker interlocutors.

In terms of errors, according to Brumfit (2000), "Correction should have either no place or a very minor place in fluency work, for it normally distracts from the message or may be perceived as rude" (p. 69). For example, if students are learning to narrate an event in the past in Spanish or French, they have several tenses to

---

[1] This is used in many universities in the United States as a means to measure international students' communication in English prior to their employment as instructors.

choose from depending on the aspect of the event that they are foregrounding or backgrounding. These choices also require morphological changes in verb forms. Rather than correct every error, the initial correction may take into consideration the overall purpose and effect on the audience of the narrative and overall use of regular verb conjugations in the narrative. As the learner makes subsequent revisions, and as instruction to the class progresses, more accuracy can be expected. According to the learnability hypothesis, in allowing for a learner to receive only the amount of correction that he or she can attend to and manage, the learner's avoidance of using difficult forms has a chance to give way to taking risks with language use, thus aiding the instructor to see how the learner gradually internalizes the linguistic conventions being taught: genre, audience engagement, prosody, grammar, and pronunciation. Timing and amount of correction for each learner may be different.

In contrast, for foreign language learning, Faerch and Kasper (1986) argue that in order for input to be used by the learner in the acquisition process of linguistic features to move beyond communicative intake and achieve an integration of the input as learning, attention must be drawn to formal features rather than allowing for overall comprehension of meanings. If the duration of communicative interactions is too short, either because they are too infrequent or too short, the learner cannot analyze the input so that it can be stored in memory and retrieved later. Thus the input will not have a role in acquisition. Therefore the instructor needs to become very familiar with his or her students to tailor the relevant error correction to the learner. One way to manage such correction is by allowing students to participate in self-assessments that move them to greater awareness of their own strengths and weaknesses. Checklists that have the features that move between the general and specific targeted features of oral communication, function particularly well when students are taught to work collaboratively in pairs to assess each other. Teachers and learners could construct their own checklists to use. During a course, items could be added or removed according to the progress of the learner. These lists in turn could serve as evidence to document the progress for grading purposes.

Another viewpoint in the early literature on error correction presented the problem of **fossilization,** primarily the persistent use of incorrect grammatical structures in speech when insufficient linguistic support is provided to the learner (Higgs & Clifford, 1982.) This concern seems to be the major impetus for many foreign language classes to turn to discrete skills, building step-by-step exercises with each skill needed to accomplish an integration of all skills, followed by reinforcement with homework on the same skill. Unfortunately, this approach does not inoculate the student from making the same grammatical error even when the material is retaught. The assumption that any complex performance can be disassembled into discrete skills misses the important point that the development of an internalized grammatical system does not follow a linear path. Nor does the sum of all parts of the grammatical system equal what is needed to understand their interworkings or even use the language in particular communicative events. Montero-Velez (1986) shows how oral language development and literacy are linked. Furthermore, the learners' beliefs and responses to a particular error may be caused by numerous factors, from avoiding any opportunity to use complex forms, to overmonitoring, or to resisting focusing attention to details perceived to be unimportant or impossible to attend to.

Other feedback strategies are needed to tailor the feedback to the type of learner's oral performance and adjusted to the learner's readiness for the feedback, level of confidence, and interest and attitudes toward feedback. For example, typically in a lesson memorization, comprehension, and application activities are integrated. During a memorization phase, students may be engaged in oral games that help them list and recognize information gathered from a aural source, CD, tape, or video. Feedback on accuracy of grammatical forms and vocabulary or may be built into playing a game. In an ecology lesson on researching their target-language community's resources, a game incorporating question formation in English, "21 questions," could be played with all reasonable questions accepted. In the comprehension phase, the same grammatical forms may be potentially used in an interview in which students ask and answer each others' questions with their best guesses (hypotheses) as answers. Feedback at this level could focus on the accuracy of the question forms used, ignoring those in the answers. The questions would then be used in the application stage to determine which of the answers seemed true, false, or unknown. From this point on, students would attempt to find confirmation, contradiction, or clarification to the questions they chose. Feedback could then concentrate on helping students use strategies to carry out the process and focus on the accuracy of the content.

IDENTITY AND AGENCY BUILDING: MOVING FROM WHOLE TO PART

If we conceive of oral communication as a tool with which learners gain access to membership, knowledge, values, and ways of thinking, then it is not something that they can possess; rather it is afforded by their social relationships and experiences using it (Kohonen, Jaatinen, Kaikkonen, & Lehtovaara, 2001). In this sense it is not acquired, but rather appropriated gradually as learners create their identities in the new language. As they exercise their agency, either individually or collectively, dealing with the constraints of power relationships in a particular culture, they are able to gain independence. The oral communication needed may well include dealing with emotions and ethical relationships with uncertainties or dilemmas in the learner's reality. In this vein, the types of oral instruction would be integrated into a larger picture of activity in which personal meaning of the students can be voiced and in which they become self-actualized through communication.

Genre Is Greater Than its Parts

Because it is much easier to understand communication in a particular context, projects that encourage learners to observe and collect information about the language community they wish to learn, help them formulate their questions or guesses about the culture and language (Kawakami & Dudoit, 2000). Two ways that are often used in critical language learning are known as **consciousness raising** and **problem posing.** To initiate a connection to the students' levels of awareness about a target language and community, students are guided to express what they currently know about the other and the manner of thinking about the "other," which serves to initiate their learning the language of the other. In particular, projects that involve students affectively and cognitive in problem solving and that are related to subject matter in other classes would easily satisfy a "big picture" requirement for a holistic project. Activities to help learners work to make common plans and to present the project orally, visually, kinesthetically, and acoustically would be helpful in getting learners to start using their textbooks as resources, but not as replacements for the language.

Tasks and activities that would help students succeed with their projects might include:

- moving from identifying their interests and questions.
- planning the stages and naming these as parts of their project.
- collecting information and representing their projects to different audiences.

Throughout this process the students learn how to express both their current ideas and the knowledge they are constructing. Oral communication in the target language serves them throughout the process of completing projects dealing with difficulties in locating resources and resolving other problems which undoubtedly will also occur. A cycle of learning how to focus on the variety of ways language is used can be rehearsed and captured using tape recorders as a way of storing each day's oral logs. It serves both as a listening exercise for the following day and a review of what has occurred. Written practice could also be integrated for note taking and subsequently these notes become reading practice in much the same capacity as the tapes served the learners.

Teacher's Feedback

In contrast to the attention paid to errors in accuracy-directed instruction, feedback is given here to apprentice the learner. By modeling language, thinking, and interaction appropriate to responses to the whole event and including focus on language forms, the learner gains greater control over the larger performance. Therefore the language use in the classroom, including the teacher's own use of language in giving instructions, directions, and coping strategies when students' utterances are not intelligible, are in effect models of negotiation of meaning through communication. Richards and Lockhart (1996) focus on linguistic elements of **teacher talk,** which is the type of modifications teachers use to be comprehended by their students. Repetition of instructions, speaking at a slower rate, pausing, changing pronunciation, and modifying vocabulary, grammar, or discourse are among the strategies used in teacher talk. Richards and Lockhart identify these as potential areas where "teachers may develop a variety of teacher talk which would not sound natural outside of the classroom" (p. 184). In this sense, both the demands for language natural to the classroom and natural to outside the class need to be balanced. This is extremely important in considering the type of feedback to provide students as they gain control of their oral performances. Types of teacher talk that can respectfully scaffold students' oral communication include modeling, restating, and clarifying students' utterances. These can also be taught to students as a way of actively listening to each other. Furthermore, teacher or peer questioning, probing, and eliciting further comments from the speaker can encourage further elaboration. Recent research has shown how teacher's talk that models values and ways of thinking are appropriated by learners to guide their own peer interactions.

For example, if self-presentations were being practiced, the teacher's feedback would ask for more information about areas that were not included or unclear to draw the learner into a dialogic conversation to improve the recitation. The goal of such feedback is to extend the learner's first attempt, draw their attention to areas that could be improved, and provide additional resources to consult in order to manage a higher level or better level once revised. Through this type of feedback given to students, they learn to be appreciative audiences and learn to provide useful feedback to each other. The feedback provides support for learners by extending their utterances until the learner can carry on alone, scaffolding the learners' utterances.

An Example of Instructional Practices: English as a Foreign language

The following tasks were inspired by Tim Murphy's (2000) presentation of his conversation course for English as a Foreign Language learners in Japan that was reported at the annual meeting of the American Association for Applied Linguistics, in Vancouver. Tim used Vygotskian concepts of **scaffolded interaction** and Bhaktinian notions of **appropriation** to structure tasks that would help his students gradually appropriate English prosody and develop interactional conversational ability. Though these learner-centered tasks have been modified from his initial tasks, they still are based on several key concepts that draw on sociocultural concepts of development.

The following series of inquiry tasks can be used at any level of proficiency. As an ongoing ungraded assignment for building expectations of conversations, learners are asked to take advantage of opportunities to search outside of the classroom for target language listening opportunities. Students are asked to guess the relationship of the conversation partners and take mental notes by listening to the conversation or write them down as soon as possible. Students bring back their listening notes and report on who they saw, where, when, and what they heard. They then discuss what evidence they have for their guesses.

On the next level of listening, students are asked to **shadow** a conversation between native speakers. This could be a videotaped movie, CD, or conversations overheard in the subway. Since these are not extended discourses, they are asked to handle only what they can attend to. In addition to what they notice about the speakers' setting (time and place), in this task learners are asked to focus on either mimicking or modifying the intonation patterns of the last segments they hear of in the turns. For example, if they heard "I was walking on the beach and saw a starfish in the sand," the learner could either copy the intonation or change it according to the type of practice they needed:

a. rising intonation at end of sentence to practice asking questions—*a starfish in the sand?*

b. changing the stress pattern to create contrastive emphasis and demonstrate shock or surprise—a STARFISH in the sand

Note that these tasks take into account developmental factors, allowing students to move from imitation, attending to nonverbal or verbal cues. Helping students develop greater persistence and providing practices through tasks that are controlled by the learner, allows learners to receive help to become engaged interlocutors dealing with active listening and interactive speaking. Students are given chances to get closer to handling social interactions through native levels of speech, while developing sense of the structure of conversations through a variety of styles, and an understanding of who can talk to whom, how, and why. And most importantly, their own **interlanguage** and identity as users of language are stressed. In this way, teachers may cultivate a classroom culture where risks at communication are encouraged and supported despite learners' initial low levels of fluency and proficiency.

For beginning learners, through hands-on learning and cooperative grouping we can build oral interactions that help learners develop content knowledge, communication skill, and positive identities as learners.

Building in Complexity: Shifting between Fluency and Accuracy

To support each child's oral development, there will be a need to provide a balanced perspective on fluency and accuracy throughout a lesson. For the teacher, getting to know the student's strengths will allow instruction that helps gradually move from silent participation with comprehension, to production of chunks of oral language, to more complex oral exchanges and presentations. For the English language learner, getting to know other students and the teacher may reduce the discomfort of not being able to make sense in another language and may provide the support for taking risks during oral communication. For this reason, lessons that help build learner confidence in fluency need to foreground activities for negotiating meaning and gradually shift to foregrounding accuracy by focusing on forms of expression.

Icebreakers are mini-lessons that allow students to use an oral routine or expression with their classmates under low risk conditions. They are used for various reasons:

- To introduce or get to know each other
- To review previous material
- To preview new material
- To introduce new material inductively or deductively

DIFFERENCES BETWEEN SECOND AND FOREIGN LANGUAGE LEARNERS

Social and Academic Consequences of Sounding Like the "Other"

While research in second and foreign language face similar challenges to help students become bilingual, foreign language learners do not experience the same level of challenges to their identity that second language learners do in social and academic

REFLECT AND RESPOND

1. Icebreaker activities are designed to help learners get to know each other and interact using their second language in classroom settings. What are the potential benefits of carrying these out on a regular basis using concepts from content versus unrelated warm-up oral games? Are there any drawbacks?

   _____

   _____

2. Given that learners cannot attend to feedback on all features of their oral production, what would you do to determine when you will help students focus on accuracy in their intonation or pronunciation?

   _____

   _____

settings. When using a language that is different from their target peers, second language learners understand that this may have consequences that reduce their acceptance by peers, particularly when their primary language is stigmatized by the mainstream. Under hostile conditions, when this threatens their affiliations with their valued membership in a culturally distinct heritage group, students may resist learning another language (Spack, 1997; Valdes, 2001). Mantle-Bromley (1994) faced unexpected cultural challenges when her middle school students held attitudes that potentially could have thwarted their efforts to learn another language and to develop an appreciation for cultural difference. As this study suggests, that not only are there direct academic consequences and possible discontinuation in their language studies, but more serious societal costs—continued monolingualism, intolerance, and bigotry.

Discontinuities in Schooling

Given the current lack of articulation between public institutions before implementation of national standards, few foreign language learners have had continuity between their language studies beginning from elementary, middle and high school, through university. Many are "repeat" beginners, with histories of little-to-moderate development and less than enthusiastic expectations to survive, much less succeed. Often this lack of success becomes one of the reasons to claim that they cannot learn a particular language and thus instigates their dropping out of one and into another language course, a bit hopeful, but perhaps realistically jaded by the prior experience. Or they choose to opt out of all language courses by taking substitute courses such as computer science or computer languages. For every failure we face consequences that deepen the possibility of entrenched monolingualism, sentiments of antibilingualism, growing elite bilingualism, and cultural imperialism.

In the case of some ESL learners whose prior academic learning or language learning is not recognized or valued by U.S. schools, there is little hope of continuity in their studies unless the schooling practices here allow them to demonstrate their capacity to learn as well as to demonstrate what they have learned. Frequently, heritage language learners and recent immigrants face constraints that impede their development of bilingualism and academic learning in math, science, and social studies (Short, 1993; Minicucci, 1996). Often in prior language studies, traditional memorization of grammar has been more pervasive than the current demands for application and performance. Many heritage language learners have had little formal study of their own language. Further, these students may face a stiff penalty for academic success if they take on cultural practices that threaten these affiliations with home and community cultures—they may feel alienated in both settings. At the same time they face a penalty for failure—limited or no access to higher education, which in turn limits status or upper-economically-oriented careers.

Both groups may face discontinuities that constrain them affectively, fostering attitudes about the impossibility of becoming a user of another language. Whether or not the belief is that it is too hard to learn to communicate orally in another language, or that discrimination is inevitable because for not being able to speak without an accent (Lippi Green, 1997), these beliefs and attitudes undermine attempts to help learners develop into socially responsible Five Cs : confident, critical, competent, and crosscultural communicators. For students learning under these conditions the ESL classroom and school become sites of struggle.

GOING BEYOND THE NATIONAL STANDARDS

Throughout this book we have considered the existing National Standards for TESOL profession and the profession of Teachers of Foreign Language in identifying the types of research studies that are supportive and instruction activities that implement techniques to try out. The challenging task still remains to tailor these to meeting the needs of your learners.

If we consider the foreign language communication standard, in relation to a focus on oral communication, three modes are identified: presentational, interpersonal, and interpretive. In the following paragraphs, we introduce you to **critical language awareness** which will provide you with several ways you can go beyond the current standards and adjust your activities to your learners.

Critical language awareness is an innovation that began in Britain and over the past twelve years has been introduced in the United States. Labercane, Griffith, and Feurerverger (1995) describe this innovation's goal to build up learners' awareness of the significant role language plays in social life and in particular in school life. In teaching language awareness, students learn to understand the roles of politics and culture as they are carried out in daily communication in their communities (Morgan, 1995–96). As an illustration, while you can comply with the technical details of the standards for communication in foreign languages by including the three modes (presentational, interpersonal, and interpretative) in your overall activities, you can naturally surpass these by

REFLECT AND RESPOND

1. Bilingual learners often are involved in mediating the English communication of their parents in situations that monolingual peers do not (Delgado-Gaitan, 1999). In these roles, they are called upon to translate for their parents or family members. Often children must navigate between two cultural norms for communication in the adult world. As a result, they can develop skill through crossing norms back and forth in both languages and addressing adults with respect. Brainstorm what types of projects could be developed to build upon their bilingual experiences and introduce higher levels of awareness of language use on social relationships in both languages. Consider the places where students take on these roles and how the knowledge gained can be built upon through subject matter in the curriculum.

   _____

   _____

2. Of the projects you have brainstormed, which can help students re-create and extend their oral language into multimedia or written products useful for their parents or community service organizations needing bilingual materials?

   _____

   _____

3. Discuss how you would prepare scaffolding for both English and the primary languages of the learners to collaborate with community outreach workers or teaching aides in your school.

   _____

   _____

4. Despite the use of authentic vernacular varieties of English inside and outside of schools by teachers, administrators, and students alike, there is still a stigma attached to their use in classrooms. Brainstorm ways in which these vernaculars could serve as a helpful bridge toward learning standard English forms.

   _____

   _____

ensuring that the majority of your communicative activities in class relate to the learners' backgrounds and areas of interest and by creating space in the curriculum to allow them to draw connections between what they are doing in the class to the wider social world. You would be helping learners build an interpersonal connection when they communicate their feelings, opinions, and beliefs to their groups or whole class. By having them draw on their lived experiences to contrast or compare how the communicative practices of their communities and the target language communities are similar or different, you would be contextualizing the *Standards for Foreign Language Learning's* standards for Comparisons and Cultures. Evidence of this occurs when learners can

REFLECT AND RESPOND

1. Examine the following assessment rubric, Language Proficiency: Oral Language Development. In what ways would it need to be adapted to your students for fostering planned oral communication in the classroom?

   - discourse level fluency (makes presentations to peers in small groups, to whole class, to other audiences)
   - critical language awareness (uses language to affect audiences in desired ways and culturally accepted ways)
   - identity and agency (expresses own voice and uses language for own intentions and purposes)
   - phrase and word level accuracy (uses a range of language and displays content knowledge)

LANGUAGE PROFICIENCY: ORAL LANGUAGE DEVELOPMENT

Interview Assessment Scale

9. *Expert speaker.* Speaks with authority on a variety of topics. Can initiate, expand and develop a theme.

8. *Very good non-native speaker.* Maintains effectively own part of a discussion. Initiates, maintains and elaborates as necessary. Reveals humour where needed and responds to attitudinal tones.

7. *Good speaker.* Presents case clearly and logically and can develop the dialogue coherently and constructively. Rather less flexible and fluent than Band 8 performer but can respond to main changes of tone or topic. Some hesitation and repetition due to a measure of language restriction but interacts effectively.

6. *Competent speaker.* Is able to maintain theme of dialogue, to follow topic switches and to use and appreciate main attitude markers. Stumbles and hesitates at times but is reasonably fluent otherwise. Some errors and inappropriate language use but these will not impede exchange of views. Shows some independence in discussion with ability to initiate.

5. *Modest speaker.* Although gist of dialogue is relevant and can be basically understood, there are noticeable deficiencies in mastery of language patterns and style. Needs to ask for repetition or clarification and similarly to be asked for them. Lacks flexibility and initiative. The interviewer often has to speak rather deliberately. Can cope but not with great style or interest.

4. *Marginal speaker.* Can maintain dialogue but in a rather passive manner, rarely taking initiative or guiding the discussion. Has difficulty in following English at normal speed; lacks fluency and probably accuracy in speaking. The dialogue is therefore neither easy nor flowing. Nevertheless, gives the impression that he is in touch with the gist of the dialogue even if not wholly master of it. Marked L1 accent.

3. *Extremely limited speaker.* Dialogue is a drawn-out affair punctuated with hesitations and misunderstandings. Only catches part of normal speech and unable to produce continuous and accurate discourse. Basic merit is just hanging on to discussion gist, without making major contribution it.

2. *Intermittent speaker.* No working facility; occasional, sporadic communication.

1. *Non-speaker.* Not able to understand and/or speak.

Baker, D. (1989). *Language Testing: A Critical Survey and Practical Guide.* London: Edward

REFLECT AND RESPOND (*continued*)

2. Review the one of the following assessments. What information is provided about learners by using this assessment? How would you use the information to inform your instructional decision making about oral communication?

_____

_____

COMMUNICATION SKILLS INVENTORY FOR BILINGUAL CHILDREN*

Bilingual Oral Language Development

Child's Name: Observer:
Birthdate: Position:
Child's First Language: Date:
Child's Second Language:

LESSON:

COMMUNICATIVE BEHAVIOR	FIRST LANGUAGE	SECOND LANGUAGE
1. Comments on own actions	1.	1.
2. Comments on other's actions	2.	2.
3. Describes experiences accurately	3.	3.
4. Describes events sequentially	4.	4.
5. Attends to the speaker	5.	5.
6. Follows directions	6.	6.
7. Initiates interactions	7.	7.
8. Takes turns during conversation	8.	8.
9. Maintains topic	9.	9.
10. Answers questions	10.	10.
11. Requests attention	11.	11.
12. Requests information	12.	12.
13. Requests action	13.	13.
14. Requests clarification	14.	14.
15. Requests needs	15.	15.
16. Requests feelings	16.	16.
17. Describes plans	17.	17.
18. Supports viewpoints	18.	18.
19. Describes solutions	19.	19.
20. Expresses imagination	20.	20.

Modified from L. J. Mattes and D. R. Omark, 1984. *Speech and Language Assessment for the Bilingual Handicappe*

REFLECT AND RESPOND

1. What collaborative learning and oral practice would help learners prepare to talk about each of the phases described in the following lesson example?

    _____

    _____

2. What themes from content and their community could be used to generate discussion?

    _____

    _____

3. What assessment strategies would you use in each phase?

    _____

    _____

LESSON EXAMPLE

In a high school history content standards, students are asked to engage in the following genres of oral communication:

Descriptive phase (talking about information in the text)

Personal interpretative phase (relating what was learned to own experiences and feelings)

Critical analysis phase (drawing broader inferences about author's intentions, audience and claims by looking at language ues, structure of the text, images, metaphors, etc.)

Creative action phase (applying what they learned to real situations) articulate culturally embedded practices for communication from their own experiences learning the language. Students' construction of this knowledge allows them to develop confidence in their ability to interpret the communicative scene–e.g., nonverbal, is not said in context, with whom and how, expectations, scripts of power relationships, image maintenance. Their engagement also allows them to build their own scripts/texts for the present and potentially the future. Across time, undoubtedly, they would be enabled as users of the language to not only technically communicate in the target language, but also take creative action armed with the culture's semiotic tools to do so.

In U.S. schools, we can be responsive to all learners' needs by engaging them in our communication and learning in ways that will prepare them for the challenges posed inside the classroom and outside in the wider community. These challenges can foment new ways of disciplinary and interdisciplinary thinking and varied oral communication. By including the learners' communities, our classroom communicative practices will always be dynamic and changing. We can also encourage through our classroom processes, attention to democratic consciousness and community development through critical language awareness. In these ways, learners participate in oral practices that have potential for transforming their current realities.

SUMMARY

This chapter has provided a fresh look at oral communication development in second language and foreign language classrooms by stressing that learners develop when they genuinely have something to say that is relevant and meaningful to them and when the consequences of learning language enable them to put their thoughts into action in their classrooms, schools, and communities. The classroom and school conditions need to be examined to allow and support learners' development in various roles using oral communication with a diverse audience. Learning through language and learning language to communicate occurs both at a conscious level and an unconscious level. Language socialization occurs through participation structures, cultural frames for understanding, and structuring talk, feedback, and revision processes. These social processes affect what kinds of oral communication are taught, and how learners develop expressing their ideas and feelings in a classroom. Supportive environments are needed to provide students with safe opportunities and help them communicate in their second or foreign languages. This highlights how talk between teachers and students, and students and students, in the classroom influence learners' second language oral development from the primary language strengths. Psycholinguistic research emphasizes the learner's need to be actively making sense of a manageable amount of linguistic input. Yet not all learners will progress at the same pace given their differences in learning and interacting. This comprehension activity often precedes being able to orally communicate. Additionally, focused attention on particular aspects of the oral language can help learners build automaticity. Mistakes are evidence of the processes that learners are developing to learn a language.

Oral communicative skills do not develop in a single day. Listening comprehension usually outpaces oral development. Learners need to engage with supportive and interactive audiences over time, and have authentic purposes for that interaction in order to see how their language skills affect their lives.

Becoming better at oral activities depends on factors both internal and external to learners. When learners are actively engaging in recursive and creatively repetitive oral activities that are structured in the socialization of the class they can develop higher levels of oral and listening skills in dealing with varied audiences, various participation structures in class, and learning conventions used in disciplinary-based oral practices. The teacher's choices of oral activities need to balance building fluency in overall participation as well as accuracy specific to discrete structures or forms of spontaneous and planned oral communication. Peer oral feedback to students who read their writing aloud provides learners with reading, writing, and listening and speaking opportunities that help them learn to use language to collaborate and build up their comprehension. This type of oral communication involves their decision making in providing helpful feedback, and in listening and writing critically. Oral inquiry into the communities that students want to join similarly offers opportunities to ask, listen, report, read, and write about their experiences.

In many second language classes this authentic oral communication is accomplished by linking to interdisciplinary content themes but can be expanded into areas of inquiry needed by the community. For foreign language classrooms, rather than disjointed activities to create interaction, having a thematic interdisciplinary organized project would allow for intrinsic language demands to spring from these academic pursuits, which in turn would require communication with users of the target language and preparation for these encounters.

Speaking practices conform to cultural assumptions and conventions that pose challenges to second and foreign language learners—from values of what is good, to how to express logical connections, to building coherence, developing voice, and addressing an audience. Learning about these assumptions and conventions, and honing skills to organize information and structure arguments to develop one's own voice in another's language requires more than following models. It requires both critical and creative practice over time, with varied audiences and communities.

Focusing on diversity in the oral and writing practices in both target and learners' language communities can help students and teachers become more aware of the social groups whose oral practices are a part of all communities and which ones are currently valued. This inclusion in the oral development of students has the potential for raising learners' awareness of how their language choices position them in different contexts and yet allow for them to critically expand their repertoires in both languages. Student and teacher reflection on how to encourage antibias and discriminatory oral practices could help reduce stereotyping and prejudiced assessment of nonnative speakers or speakers of other speech varieties based on their accents or vocabulary. Research by Mantle-Bromley and Miller (1991) with learners of Spanish attests to the necessity and effectiveness of cultural sensitivity activities in creating more positive attitudes for these learners.

From selective review of research presented here, teachers can see the complexity of learning to speak due to the integrated levels of communicative performance that must be managed. Nonetheless, several concepts are important to make use of in our practice. First, an understanding that the classroom must provide space for learners to use language to communicate their ideas and to negotiate meaning in both face-to-face spontaneous communication and in planned oral discourse for learning and displaying knowledge. Learning to use oral communication is not a neutral task of information transfer from one person to another, but rather it is important social work to relate to others and to create identities in a social context. Second, learners risk committing errors at many levels in oral expression, from phonological to discourse; therefore, students need time for oral participation in order to develop fluency and even more time to develop accuracy. Opportunities in the classroom need to be created to promote oral fluency where learners can gradually manages more complex oral genres. For learners to be motivated to use these opportunities, their own needs, interests, and background knowledge need to be central to their communication. Learners need to feel their peer and teachers' support. Collaborative learning in dyads or small groups, where membership is valued and where each individual is seen as a resource, will promote respectful and safe contexts for taking a risk. Since there is great diversity in any one person's perspective, carefully monitoring social relationships and understanding how knowledge is created through language use, we can encourage English language learners to persist and fully develop their learning potentials.

EXERCISES AND ACTIVITIES
DISCUSS AND REFLECT

1. Consider the differences between *dialogue memorization* versus speaking in *face-to-face* encounters with sympathetic interlocutors:

    How are the demands placed on the learner's oral participation different in relation to pressure on memory, relevance to unfolding context, importance of negotiating understanding (managing the other's understanding of one's purpose and image), meaningfulness, urgency for communication, accuracy of language forms/structures? Fill in the chart on the next page:

2. What strategies can be taught to students to learn how to handle face-to-face interactions in the target language?

    Coping with composing your message while searching for the words
    Managing interaction
    Paraphrasing
    Monitor own positioning and interpret other's positioning- affective tone emotional or attitude towards matters talked about.

3. Recurrent oral social routines in the classroom build up repetitive practices that appear to be acquired by the students who engage in them without overt attention paid to these routines. These socialization and enculturation processes can be a powerful way of shaping students' identities and aiding students to subconsciously

ACTIVITIES IN ORAL PERFORMANCE	DIALOGUE MEMORIZATION	FACE-TO-FACE COMMUNICATION
1. Prior to this performance, students prepare by:		
2. The student interlocutors must orally:		
3. This is meaningful pedagogical practice because:		
4. During this, students orally:		
5. The interlocutors feel this is relevant because:		
6. The level of urgency to communicate is:		
7. The degree of focus on linguistic accuracy (phonological, morphological. syntactic, pragmatic, discoursal) is:		
8. Other features:		

learn about appropriate language usage and social values. How might you use these practices to scaffold students' thinking and oral development in a math or art lesson?

4. Stories, poems, rhymes, myths, and songs introduce oral practices that exist in every language community but are not known in all social groups due to age, gender, class, ethnicity, race, and other diversity. How might students' backgrounds be utilized to examine the diversity that exists in their communities and share, compare, and contrast these with the target language community's diversity? Using the target language orally, how might instructors encourage students to change this situation and to have other communities learn about their rich oral traditions? How might students use their writing abilities to document these oral practices?

WHAT DO TEACHERS THINK?

Amy Graf, a twenty-plus-year veteran teacher in the Dennis Yarmouth School District, was puzzled by something she had been noticing over the years. The songs, poems, and riddles that she had been including into her lessons seemed to be the things the students most remembered at the end of the year and often many years later. She asked, "How does music, rhyme, and movement make learning more memorable?" How might her question be answered and explained?

FIELD-BASED EXPERIENCES

1. Get permission from your immediate supervisor to videotape and study your own class. Monitor student participation in your lesson. What types of oral communicative participation do you engage in? What is allowed for the students? How do these types of communication lead to content and language acquisition as active learners? Who engages in this and to what degree? Who is left out? How might the students who were left out or not highly engaged be more engaged? (Check affective levels, relevance, and meaningfulness of your lesson. What kind of identity as learners can be formed here?)

2. Throughout the next month or marking period, have students keep "Pronunciation Diaries" in which words or phrases are categorized into "easy" and "difficult" to pronounce, remember, or understand. First have learners create a mind map of related meanings around their word. Then have the learners create a phrase that is meaningful to them. Periodically check their diaries to incorporate their phrases into your lesson. At the end of the semester have students revisit their maps and indicate which are no longer a problem and the strategy that helped them remember their phrase. Compile these for next year's or the next group of learners. Note which ones still remain difficult. Do they have any characteristics in common? Can you devise a learning strategy that can help other students?

ACTION RESEARCH

1. Find out your students' attitudes toward speakers of a target community versus the business community's attitudes and efforts to target these communities for consumer markets. You may want to consider such oral messages from radio advertisements and television commercials produced by major companies to analyze their use of language visual effects, and imagery. What can be done to build relationships and improve attitudes between the target language community and your students?

2. Ask heritage language speakers to participate in group interviews to understand their individual history of oral communication development: To what degree do they maintain their use of oral language with family, friends, and institutions? What obstacles have been overcome to improve their communicative abilities? Are there any patterns that the students want to change?

3. Document target language community support/resources that could help learners in oral language development: interviews, songs, stories. How can learners contribute to increasing these resources? Consider using Internet resources as well as low technology, e.g., mail projects..

ADDITIONAL RESOURCES

Text Resources

Brinton, D., Snow, M. A., & Wesche, M. B. (1989). *Content-based second language instruction.* New York: Harper & Row.

Cameron, D. (2001). *Working with spoken discourse.* Thousand Oaks, CA: Sage.

Celce-Murcia, M. (2000). *Discourse and context in language teaching. A guide for language teachers.* New York: Cambridge University Press.

Chamot, A. U., O'Malley, J. M. (1994). *The CALLA handbook: Implementing the Cognitive Academic Language Learning Approach.* Reading, MA: Addison Wesley.

Clark, R., et. al (1990). Critical language awareness, Part I: A critical review of three current approaches to language awareness. *Language & Education: An International Journal,* 4(4), 249–60.

Cullen, B. (1998). Music and song in discussion. *The Internet TESL Journal. http://www.aitech.ac.jp/ ~iteslj/Techniques/Cullen-Music.html.*

Ehrlich, S. (1997) Gender as social practice: Implications for second language acquisition. *Studies in Second Language Acquisition, 19,* 421–46.

Evans, L. S. (1990). Storytelling and oral language development in ESL classrooms. *TESOL Newsletter, 24*(5): 3, 16, 18, 30. Oct.

Farmer, M. (1998). Creating Montessori bilingual programs. Spotlight: Montessori—Multilingual, multicultural. *Montessori Life,* Vol. 10, 2, 22–5, Spring.

Fillmore, C. J. (1979). On fluency. In Charles Fillmore, Daniel Kempler, & William S-Y. Wang (Eds) pp. 85–101, *Individual differences in language ability and language behaviour,* New York: Academic Press.

Gaudart, H. (1990). Using drama techniques in language teaching. In A. Sarinee (Ed.), *Language teaching methodology for the nineties, Anthology Series, 24.* 230–249

Maley, A. (1987). Poetry and song as effective language learning activities. In W. M. Rivers (Ed.) (pp. 93–109), *Interactive language teaching*. New York: Cambridge University Press.

Mohan, B. (1986). *Language & content*. Reading MA: Addison-Wesley.

Richards, J. (1996). Songs in language learning. *TESOL Quarterly 3*(2), 161–74.

Scarcella, R., & Crookall, D. 1990. Simulation/gaming and language acquisition. In D. Crookall & R. Oxford (Eds.) (pp. 223–30), *Simulation, gaming and language learning*. New York: Newbury House.

Shier, J. H. (1990). Integrating the arts in the second/foreign language curriculum: Fusing the affective and the cognitive. *Foreign Language Annals, 23*(4), 301–14.

Short, D. (1994). Expanding middle school horizons: Integrating language, culture, and social studies. *TESOL Quarterly, 28*(3), 581–609.

Towell, R. J. (1989). An analysis of the oral language development of British undergraduate learners of French. *Dissertation Abstracts International, 49*(8), 2135A–2136A. Feb.

Yang, Y. (1999). Practicing pronunciation through proverbs. *The Internet TESL Journal. http://www.aitech.ac.jp/~iteslj/Lessons/Yang-Proverbs.html*.

A TEMPLATE FOR LESSON PLANS

Interactive Activities: identity and agency, and fluency and proficiency

a. Potential activities
1. Plan an inquiry into a recent event that affected the school community or greater community
2. Create a play based on the composite oral history of the ELLs' families (interviews turned into drama or narrated art exhibition)
3. Establish an audiotape or CD library of learners' favorite fables, jokes, songs, etc., with sing-along booklet.

b. Disciplinary and interdisciplinary oral practices
1. Brainstorm what is known
2. Categorize
3. Select and give explanation as to why
4. Plan and report what will be explored
5. Tell what was done/learned/discovered
6. Tell what could be done next time
7. Use language to provide helpful feedback

c. Scaffolding and feedback versus correction by instructor, peers, or learner
1. Determine what is important to attend to when, where, how
2. Plan oral interaction versus in progress oral interaction
3. Assess what to focus on after interaction and make suggestions for improving
4. Document next step/focus
5. Review/reenact second attempt at #c.1

d. Monitoring and documenting: Progress toward greater control of students' oral development
1. Assess where greatest difficulty lies
2. Plan what can be done
3. Monitor what is done

4. Reassess efforts and difficulty
5. Assess how groups work fairly
6. Make suggestions to improve

e. Assessment of oral language development (see TESOL, ACTFL guidelines for proficiency and performance standards) and cautious assessment of disciplinary understandings

GLOSSARY OF TERMS

appropriation   sociocultural term for the stage at which one's learning of cultural tools and practices is used to serve one's own purposes

body language   corporal movements that are interpreted as significant in revealing a person's disposition in communication

conversational analysis   a research tradition that examines the social basis of talk through analysis of natural language use

cultural norms   the implicit and explicit boundaries of acceptable behavior within a culture

dialogic   a Bakhtinian notion that through dialogue with peers and instructor, learners play an active role in developing a personal understanding of learning; the nature of collaborative talk where learners consider different points of view and have the power to make decisions

discourse analysis   interpretivist research that analyzes how patterns of language use in both oral and written texts reveal how people understand their real-world contexts

discoursal levels   levels of meaning making components of discourse, involving at the broadest level sociocultural knowledge about participation and interaction, pragmatic skills for interpreting and creating contexts through language, and at the micro level, linguistic elements of prosody, syntax, morphology, phonology, and vocabulary

gesture   a form of face-to-face nonverbal communication that involves the use of body movements, head nods, winks, pointing, etc., to signal meaning to an interlocutor

interference   a psycholinguistic term for the negative influence of the primary language on the learning of the second language

interlanguage   psycholinguistic term for a second language development stage in which a student's features of language use are approximating, yet still are distant from, "native" models

kinesic   the study of bodily and gestural communication

"language as a resource"   a sociocultural orientation that views every language embodying more than linguistic values, in fact being essential for access to cultural resources of historically created knowledge, ways of knowing and being

language socialization   a process by which members of a social group become competent participants in the group's ways of interpreting communicative interactions

metalinguistic   describes language used to talk about language, e.g., word, grammar, sound.

paralinguistic   features of oral language that reveal a user's disposition; includes such things as stress, tone and pitch

pragmatics   study of what speakers mean and how hearers interpret meaning; "how language can be used to do things and mean things in real world situations" (Cameron, p. 68)

phonology   the study of sound patterns in a language

prosody   suprasegmental elements of language that cue how an utterance is to be interpreted e.g., the rise and fall, stress, and rhythm of voice

scaffolded interaction   assistance to a novice provided by a more skillful partner to enable the novice to reach a more complex performance without the more skillful person taking it over. E.g., In terms of teacher talk, such actions as adding clarifying statements to learner's statements and checking with the learner to see if this were what was intended; expanding what the learner intended; voicing or connecting the logic of one student's statements with another.

speech acts   a class of utterances that when uttered constitute a social action, e.g., greetings, joking, apologizing

REFERENCES

Bao, H. (2001). Chinese Summer Camp. University of Massachusetts. Amherst. Unpublished Manuscript.

Bergen, J. (Ed.) (1990). *Spanish in the United States: Sociolinguistic issues.* Washington, D.C.: Georgetown University Press.

Boal, A. (1992). *Games for actors and non-actors.* London: Routledge.

Bialystock, E., & Cummins, J. (1991). Language, cognition, and education of bilingual children. In E. Bialystock (Ed.), *Language processing in bilingual children* (pp. 222–232). Cambridge: Cambridge University Press.

Brumfit, C. (2000). Accuracy & fluency. In H. Riggenbach (Ed.). *Perspectives on fluency.* (pp. 61-73). Ann Arbor: University of Michigan Press.

Canale, M. (1983). From communicative competence to communicative language pedagogy. In J. C. Richards and R. Schmidt (Eds.). *Language and communication, 2–25.* New York: Longman.

Carroll, S., Roberge, Y., & Swain, M. (1992). The role of feedback in adult secing language acquisition, error correction and morphological generalizations. *Applied Psycholinguistics,* 13(2), 173–198.

Chafe, W. (1987). Cognitive constraints on information flow. In R. Tomlin (Ed.). (pp. 21–51) *Coherence and grounding in discourse.* Philadelphia: John Benjamins.

Cummins, J. (2000). *Language, power and pedagogy. Bilingual children in the crossfire.* Clevedon, UK: Multilingual Matters.

Dewaele, J-M., & Pavlenko, A. (2002). *Language Learning,* (June) 52, (2), 263–322.

Diaz, R. (1985). *The intellectual power of bilingualism in Second Language Learning by Young Children.* Sacramento, CA: Advisory Committee for Child Development Program.

Diaz, R., & Klinger, C. (1991). Towards an explanatory model of the interaction between bilingualism and cognitive development. In E. Bialystok (Ed.). *Language processing in bilingual children.* Cambridge: Cambridge University Press.

Diaz, R., & Padilla, K. (1985). *The self-regulatory speech of bilingual preschoolers.* Paper presented at the 1985 meetings of the Society for Research in Child Development. Toronto, Canada.

Ehrman, M. (1998). *Interpersonal dynamics in second language education: A visible and invisible classroom.* Thousand Oaks, CA: Sage

ElBissi, J. (2003). *Ms. Casey, I have a text-to-self connection.* Paper presented at the Ethnographic and Qualitative Research in Education. Duquesne University, Pittsburgh, PA.

Faerch, C., & Kasper, G. (1983). *Strategies in interlanguage communication.* New York: Longman.

Faerch, C., & Kasper, G. (1986). The role of comprehension in second langage learning. *Applied Linguistics,* 7, 257–274.

Farmer, M. (1998). Creating Montessori bilingual programs. Spotlight: Montessori—Multilingual, multicultural. *Montessori Life,* 10, (2) 22–25.

Flores, B., Tefft Cousin, P., & Diaz, E. (1991). Transforming deficit myths about learning, language, and culture. *Language Arts.* 68, 369–379.

Flowerdew, J. (Ed.). Long, Michael H. (pref.). Richards, Jack C. (pref.). (1994). *Academic listening: Research perspectives.* Cambridge, Eng: Cambridge University Press.

Freed, B. (2000). Is fluency in the eyes (and ears) of the beholder? In H. Riggenbach (Ed.). *Perspectives on fluency.* (pp. 243–265). Ann Arbor, MI: University of Michigan Press.

Gass, S., & Varonis, E. (1985). Variation in native speaker speech modification to non-native speakers. *Studies in Second language Acquisition,* 7 (1): 37–57.

Gaudart, H. (1990). Using drama techniques in language teaching. In A. Sarinee (Ed) *Language teaching methodology for the nineties, Anthology Series.* 24, 230–249.

Gee, J. (1992). *The social mind: Language ideology and social practice.* New York: Bergin and Garvey.

Gonzalez, V. (1995). *Cognition, culture, and language in bilingual children: Conceptual and semantic development.* Bethesda, MD: Austin & Winfield.

Goodwin, C., & Duranti, A. (Eds.). (1992). *Rethinking context.* Cambridge: Cambridge University Press.

Hall Maley, M. (2001). Understanding learning-centered instruction from the perspective of multiple intelligences. *Foreign Language Annals,* 34(4), 355–67.

Halliday, M.A.K. (1994). *An introduction to functional grammar.* London: Edward Arnold.

Harley, B., Cummins, J., Swain, M., & Allen, P. (1990). The nature of language proficiency. In B. Harley, P., Allen, J. Cummins, & M. Swain (Eds.), *The development of second language proficiency* (pp. 7-25). Cambridge: Cambridge University Press.

Heath, S.B. (1983). *Ways with words.* Cambridge: Cambridge University Press.

Herron, C. (1991). The garden path strategy in the foreign language classroom. *French Review, 64,* 966–977.

Herron, C. & Tomasello, M. (1992). Acquiring grammatical structures by guided induction. *French Review,* 65, 708–718.

Hruska, B. (2000). *Bilingualism, gender, and friendship: Constructing second language learners in an English dominant kindergarten.* Paper presented at the annual meeting of the American Association of Applied Linguistics. Vancouver.

Kaplan, R., & Baldauf Jr., R. B. (1997). Language planning. From practice to theory. *Multilingual Matters No. 115.*

Kawakami, A. J. & Dudoit, W. (2000) Ua Ao Hawai'i/Hawai'i is enlightened: Ownership in a Hawaiian language immersion classroom. *Language Arts,* 77, 384–391.

Kelly, G., & Green, J. (1998). The social nature of knowing: Toward a sociocultural perspective on conceptual change and knowledge consruction. In B. Guzzetti & C. Hynd (Eds.) *Perspectives on conceptual change: Multiple ways to understand knowing and learning in a complex world.* (pp. 145–181). Mahwah, NJ: Lawrence Erlbaum.

Kohonen, V., Jaatinen, R., Kaikkonen, P., & Lehto-vaara, J. (2001). *Experiential learning in foreign language education.* New York: Longman.

Labercane, G., Griffith, B., & Feurerverger, G. (1995). Critical language awareness: Implications for classrooms in a Canadian context. Eric Documents 414378.

Lippi Green, R. (1997). *English with an accent. Language, ideology, and discrimination in the United States.* New York: Routledge.

Malone, M. (1997). *Worlds of talk. The presentation of self in everyday conversation.* Cambridge, England: Polity Press.

Mantle-Bromley, C., & Miller, R.B. (1991). Effect of multicultural lessons on attitudes of students of Spanish. *Modern Language Journal,* 75 (4), 418–25.

Mantle-Bromley, C. (1994). Students' misconceptions and cultural stereotypes in foreign language classes. *Middle School Journal,* 26 (1), 42–47.

Mantle-Bromley, C. (1995). Positive attitudes and realistic beliefs: Links to proficiency. *Modern Language Journal.* 79 (3), 372–86.

Markman, E.M., & Hutchinson, J. E. (1984). Children sensitivity to constraints on word meaning: Taxonomic versus thematic relations. *Cognitive Pyschology,* 16, 1–27.

Mendelsohn, D. (1991-92). Instruments for feedback in oral communication. *TESOL Journal,* 1 (2), 25–30.

McLaughlin, B. (1990). The relationship between first and second languages: Language proficiency and language aptitude. In B. Harley, P. Allen, J. Cummins, & M. Swain (Eds.), *The development of second language proficiency* (pp. 158–174). Cambridge: Cambridge University Press.

Morgan, B. (1995-96). Promoting and assessing critical language awareness. *TESOL Journal,* 5 (2), 10–14.

Morgan, W. (1997). *Critical literacy in the classroom: The art of the possible.* New York: Routledge.

Murphy, T., & Alber, J. L. (1985). A pop song register: The motherese of adolescents as affective foreigner talk. *TESOL Quarterly,* 19(4), 793–795.

Montero-Velez, A. M. (1986). Relationship of preschool literacy to oral language development among Spanish-English: Spanish pronunciation. *Dissertation Abstracts International.* 47 (1): 166A–167A. Ann Arbor, MI.

Ochs, E. (1992). Indexing gender. In C. Goodwin, and Duranti, A.(Eds.). *Rethinking context.* (pp. 335–356). Cambridge: Cambridge University Press.

Orellana, M. F. (1994). Appropriating the Voice of the Superheroes: Three Preschoolers' Bilingual Language Uses in Play. *Early Childhood Research Quarterly,* 9 (2), 171–194.

Orellana, M. F. (1995). Literacy as a Gendered Social Practice: Tasks, Texts, Talk, and Take-Up. *Reading Research Quarterly,* 30 (4), 674–708.

Oxford, R. (1993). Individual Differences among Your Students: Why a Single Method Can't Work. *Journal of Intensive English Studies,* 7, 27–42.

Pavlenko, A., & Jarvis, S. (2002). Bidirectional Transfer. *Applied Linguistics,* 23 (2), 190–214.

Pawley, A., & Syder, F. (2000). The one-clause-at-a-time hypothesis. In H. Riggenbach (Ed.). *Perspectives on fluency.* (pp. 163–199). Ann Arbor, MI: University of Michigan Press.

Riggenbach, H. (2000). *Perspectives on fluency.* Ann Arbor, MI: University of Michigan Press

Riggenbach, H. (1991). Toward an understanding of fluency. A microanalysis of non-native speaker conversations. *Discourse Processes,* 14, 423–41.

Scarcella, R. (1978). Socio-drama for social interaction. *TESOL Quarterly,* 12, 41–46.

Scarcella, R., & Crookall, D. 1990. Simulation/gaming and language acquisition. In D. Crookall & R. Oxford (Eds.). *Simulation, gaming and language learning.* (pp. 223–230). New York: Newbury House.

Scollon, R., & Scollon, S. (1995). *Intercultural communication.* Oxford: Blackwell.

Spack, R. (1997). The acquisition of academic literacy in a second language: A longitudinal case study. *Written Communication*, 14 (1), 3–62.

Thomas, W., & Collier, V. (1997).Two languages are better than one. *Educational Leadership*, 55 (4), 23–26.

Towell, R., Hawkins, R., & Bazergui, N. (1996). The development of fluency in advanced learners of French. *Applied Linguistics* 17 (1), 84–119.

Tuyay, S., Jennings, L., & Dixon, C. (1995). Classroom discourse and opportunities to learn: An ethnographic study of knowledge construction in a bilingual third grade classroom. *Discourse Processes*, 19, 75–110.

Valdes, G., & Figueroa, R. (1995). *Bilingualism & testing: A special case of bias*. Ablex Publishing.

Wells, G. & Chang-Wells, G. L. (1992). *Constructing knowledge together: Classrooms as centers of inquiry & literacy*. Portsmouth, NH: Heinemann.

Wendon, A., & Rubin, J. (Eds.) (1987). *Learner Strategies in Language Learning*. New Jersey: Prentice-Hall.

Wennerstrom, A. (2000). The role of intonation in second language fluency. In H. Riggenbach (Ed.). *Perspectives on fluency*. pp. 102–127. Ann Arbor, MI: University of Michigan Press.

Wierzbicka, A. (1999). *Emotions across languages and cultures. Diversity and universals*. Cambridge: Cambridge University Press.

FOREGROUNDING WRITTEN COMMUNICATION

THIS CHAPTER WILL FEATURE

- Research on writing
  - as a skill
  - as a process
  - as an interactionally accomplished cultural practice
  - as power

YOU WILL EXAMINE

- understanding emerging literacy
- purposes for writing
- interactive writing in content-based classes
- teaching of interactive second language writing
- integrating technology and writing
- writing and the standards
- working with diverse learners
- writing assessment

INTRODUCTION: SETTING THE STAGE

In the previous chapter, both oral communication between teachers and students, as well as the oral communication between students, play a major role in furthering students' social, cultural, and cognitive development in schools through building their second language proficiency. As we shall see later, oral interactions are also important in the learner's development of writing for different audiences.

Gradually through schooling, writing becomes the principal means by which learners display their knowledge and competence in many academic subjects. When

THINK, PAIR, SHARE

Before you begin reading this chapter, complete the following with a partner.

1. Consider your day today. What types of writing did you engage in? Which were harder to do than others?

   _____

   _____

2. What tools did you use?

   _____

   _____

3. What types of help did you receive or look for?

   _____

   _____

4. Try to remember the first time you learned how to do each type of writing. What helped you improve, enabling you to reach the level you currently have attained?

   _____

   _____

learners successfully use their orality for literate behaviors, they become considered "educated." It is no wonder that learning to write is one of the most highly valued outcomes of education. However, as highly valued as it is, writing is one of the last communicative modalities for learners to develop control over, even for many children whose first language is English.

In this chapter we will present a selection of research studies that shed light on what we currently know about learning to write in school and the processes that developing second language writers engage in to become authors. These studies can be grouped into four research orientations that examine writing as product, as a process, as interaction, and as power.

TEACHING INTERACTIVE SECOND LANGUAGE WRITING IN CONTENT-BASED CLASSES

Extensive practice with writing can be provided for only in long-term curricular planning. This means teachers' writing practices need to introduce the full range of writing that students face for learning across the curriculum. A range of writing types and tasks is necessary, together with opportunities to receive feedback through the processes of composing and revising within extensive practice (Grabe, 2001). Bartolome (1998) argues that without learning the conventions of academic discourses, second language learners will be excluded from further educational opportunities.

Each discipline tends to encourage the use of writing in specific ways. In science, writing activities include maintaining logs to document scientific methods of inquiry: formulating questions, making hypotheses, following procedures for measurement, and documenting observations. To represent findings, a variety of formats is used, such as graphs, charts, slides, transparencies, and posters. Oral and written reports then narrate the procedures for a wider audience. For a more public audience, the "messiness" of the process is tidied up to present a linear text. Typically these reports provide detail on questions, type, and quantity of materials used, the hypothesis, procedures for collecting and analyzing data, and explanations of the findings. In history, students are called upon to recount events through summaries and to draw lessons from past events through comparisons, contrasts, and evaluation. In math, students are called upon to explain their reasoning or processes in solving a problem.

WRITING AND THE STANDARDS: DIFFERENCES BETWEEN FOREIGN AND SECOND LANGUAGE

Typically in the United States, students begin studying a foreign language after they have developed basic literacy in English. In fact, many schools have used reading scores as a gate-keeping device to allow only those who are strong in English language arts to be admitted into their limited number of available foreign language courses. In beginning foreign language classrooms, writing is often used for practicing grammar exercises, spelling dictations, and at best, short descriptive paragraphs. Usually as the learners advance into higher levels, they are introduced to essays and reports written in the foreign language.

Though the National Standards for Foreign Language have raised the bar for demonstrating ability to understand and produce written communication, the focus is primarily on producing certain functional texts, such as phone messages, posters and letters. Here we can see the emphasis more on text production than on learning through written language use.

Depending on the type of dual immersion and immersion programs (full, partial, late), similar writing expectations for both languages may exist. In some programs, depending on the language, the curriculum may not require as full a range of writing in the foreign language as is required in English as a second language (ESL) classes.

In contrast, ESL standards specify functional tasks in writing for each span of grades across three dimensions: social language, academic content, and culturally appropriate ways.

In these standards, functional uses of writing for learning content is a prominent goal.

INTEGRATING TECHNOLOGY AND WRITING

Computer technology affords a variety of tools that can be helpful resources for developing writing. These can be divided into such categories as tools, resources, and interactions. Under the tool category, word processing packages, complete with spelling and grammar check, thesauri, dictionaries, graphics and sound files, and presentational tools are available on both PC and Mac platforms in many schools and public libraries. As well, the Internet provides access to electronic sources of searchable data banks on different content areas, books, music, graphics, photos, and animation and movie files. Teachers who make use of these tools as students work through their processes of writing recognize that extra time is needed to help students (and themselves) who have limited access to computers become familiar with the features of this technology. Because *point and click* technology has made using applications easier, it obliges the user to develop ready comprehension or to recognize an icon and click on it. Knowledge about how one word processing package works can be used as an approximate model for making use of other word processing and electronic sources. Exceptions that are particular to different packages can be noted along the way. Often students who use computers at home will immediately offer what they know and how similar or different their applications are. This provides a great chance to share tricks for using related applications.

Even on a limited technology budget, where limited or no access to the Internet is available, and limited access to computers is the norm, word processing packages can serve in a number of useful ways. Many features that are straightforward and do not need discussion may be necessary to explain for students just starting to use computers: starting the program, opening, typing, deleting, highlighting, cutting, pasting, undoing changes, printing, saving, and closing a file. In addition, one of the first tools that can be easily used is the drawing and table creation tools available in most word processing packages. With this tool, webs, charts, tables, and graphs can be easily created as templates for students or by students. These can be stored on each computer, diskette, or zip disk, or printed for each student. Since word processing packages come equipped with templates for outlining, writing letters, and creating presentations, these can be used to have students notice conventions in writing in these genres as well as become familiar with using the technology. However some of the features may be used in ways that may not seem so readily apparent.

A feature that is helpful in the revisions stages of writing is the *find* feature. When they are asked to check if they have overused an expression or if they tend to make mistakes with a particular word or phrase, the find feature can help them quickly check for all instances of use. This step in the self-revision process puts them in control of making decisions about the need for repetition, elimination, substitution, or variation. Similar to the corpus linguistic researchers, students can find out the patterns they use and then attempt to vary their language use. Also, spelling and grammar features can be turned off to allow students to test their editing abilities. In this way they may be encouraged to print their drafts, read them to writing partners, and then make changes before turning on the helping devices. Whether or not these helping devices are used to check their editing, students still need to decide what to change and how to change their writing. These decisions can be tracked from version to version by using the tracking feature or by having students maintain logs. Students will soon discover that the computer's suggestions may not always be correct for capturing what they want to convey. Teachers can use these moments to discuss with students their strategies for thoughtfully using the helping tools provided by each software package.

As computer technology provides faster and more reliable access to the Internet, a wider range of resources is potentially accessible. Using the World Wide Web will familiarize students with sources that they will need to judge as reliable, credible, or accurate. Students can be asked to generate their initial ideas about what indicates reliability, credibility and accuracy. Their discussion could also include which sites are forbidden to access and why. Writing activities that involve the Web as a resource would include writing descriptors for such tasks as using search engines, taking notes, and learning how to cite references. Prior to beginning a search, teachers can draw semantic webs to help English language learners find many ways to express the same concept and help narrow the search with specific descriptors or key concepts from their content areas. For example, in studying the relationship of climate to patterns of human life (geography), students could generate as many words related to climate as may help them focus on the topic they are interested in. Semantic maps visually extend students' vocabulary in groupings that are easier to remember. As a class activity, after searching for their topic, students could generate a list of valuable sites that provide resources in each of their content areas.

There are several text-based virtual environments that are accessible via the World Wide Web. Three are interactive in real time (synchronous): chatrooms, MOOs, and MUDs. (See more information in chapter 9.) Delayed writing in asynchronous communication occurs through participation in threaded discussion groups (listservs), e-mail exchanges, and bulletin board postings. Each type of interaction places different demands on the learner's writing. Synchronous communication, such as carried out in MOOS, requires the use of descriptions as a way of creating sensory experiences. Students would need to create a persona, greet everyone, and introduce and describe themselves and their actions while dialoging in writing with others in the same environment. Because this communication depends on rapid keyboarding skill, rapid reading comprehension, and fast-paced responsive dialogue, it is challenging even for the most proficient writer. English language learners can participate by "lurking" before deciding how they will participate. By lurking—that is, entering into the environment and just reading the messages—students can learn how to participate and determine with whom and when they want to interact. In asynchronous communication, English Language Learners have more time to compose their written responses after several drafts. Both forms of writing introduce learners to different social contexts that have rules of participation and conventions for communicating. These learning experiences lend themselves to discussion in which students compare face-to-face conversational rituals with those in the virtual worlds and other written texts. The contrasts help learners build a sense of the range of options that exists between oral and written communication.

One of the major contributions technology has to offer second language learners is the possibility to interact and collaborate with distant partners in a variety of asynchronous projects. Sayers (1993) helped create a multiple-site distance learning community with students collecting cultural artifacts and sharing them with Web partners. This exchange project brought immigrant children in contact with peers in countries they had left. They shared critical collaborative inquiry on proverbs, folktales, and even jokes. These international exchanges utilized the bilingual students' abilities in both languages. They were the cultural brokers for the ESL classes at their schools and for the classes in their former home country. Because they knew both languages, they could interpret messages that monolinguals in both countries had written. This interaction helped them to value their linguistic resources, reach beyond their abilities to use each language, and refine their communication with both audiences.

THINK, PAIR, SHARE

1. What might be some types of writing that are required using synchronous versus asynchronous communication on the Internet? Chatrooms versus sent mail? In which type of written communication would your students be able to participate meaningfully? Why?

_____

_____

2. Since the language in written messages in e-mail exchanges can vary in register and tone through the use of vernacular and standard varieties of English, what activities to code these varieties could help your students develop the ability to analyze words or phrases and determine appropriate use? Consider creating a logbook of equivalent expressions, a wall chart of expressions and their definitions and use, etc. Share your ideas with a colleague.

_____

_____

In a project that united both community and school contexts using computers, Vasquez (2002) reports on an after-school project using the students' own hybrid language practices to help them expand their writing and thinking. The project, La Clase Mágica, used interactive communication by computer to link community members, elementary students, and university students in fun and educational activities. The activities were cognitive-based lessons that permitted students' use of both English and Spanish languages to develop problem-solving skills. Adults and children, and eventually parents of the children, became involved in developing their computer skills and writing abilities. As a result of their involvement, parents and students took on greater leadership roles to maintain and improve the project. This project exemplifies how new technologies of literacy can be used to improve community resources and create reciprocity in learning across institutions and distance.

INTERACTIVE WRITING INSTRUCTION

When creating an encouraging environment that allows writers to express their ideas and develop them more fully, you cannot expect uniform performances across all learners. Rather, you need to build in levels of support as the learners can control more and more of their writing. Flecha (2000) identifies seven principles that can facilitate learning through dialogue with students: egalitarian dialogue, cultural intelligence, transformation, instrumental dimension, creating meaning, solidarity, and equality of difference. These principles encourage emerging writers to take writing seriously. The following types of interactive writing activities are dialogic and address the TESOL standards to use English for social, academic, and culturally appropriate language.

One instructional activity is the "author's chair," where students read their own writing and as authors listen to comments from an audience of their peers. The audience members need guidance to comment on the aspects of the author's writing they liked best and why. The audience also provides suggestions for improvement.

Another form of interactive writing is carried out through collaborative peer talk or "chats." These activities encourage students to work in pairs to ask open-ended questions of each others' texts: what might happen, how the events might be connected, and how they might end. Students consider what characters might be like, do, etc. In this way, students help each other elaborate and build extended texts.

Interactional journals/logs also provide opportunities for students to gain fluency and develop proficiency through writing with the instructor or peers. Collaborative written feedback or dialogic interactions have the potential of affecting the direction of students' subsequent revisions. In this way, writers begin to monitor the communicative quality of their texts to satisfy their reading audiences. In the process, they learn to structure their writing in logical ways to make their texts reader friendly. As well, they need to learn various styles of argumentation to build the relationship between their ideas and supporting details. Learners' decisions about the purpose of their writing determine what demands they need to face for effective argumentation. To be effective and interesting, a wider range of lexical choice and rhetorical strategies to involve the audience are needed. Teachers can help students take on "word" studies by teaching them to make use of tools (e.g., dictionaries, thesaurus) to expand their range of vocabulary and through their reading interesting texts. Students' linguistic accuracy increases through building greater complexity in their writing.

As students engage in the interactive activities, they can develop dialogic thinking, which guides their own writing through self-talk. In a sense, this is talk that helps learners elaborate on topics to compose. Questions could include: What do I want to know about this topic to answer questions—who, what, where, why? Additional questions can be added as the learner develops ability to attend to greater detail.

With the above interactive writing instruction, students take into account their purposes in communicating with audiences that are present in their local context. As they gain experiences interacting with these audiences, they grow in their linguistic ability and develop resources to address audiences that are distant.

At different times learners will need specific strategies to start writing, revising, and editing their writing. In the following sections, you will find several options that can help at particular points in the writing process.

Prewriting Strategies for Getting Started

Sometimes the beginning is the biggest hurdle. Staring at a blank page doesn't make writing appear. So help writers get started by trying one of the following:

1. Prompted writing: chaining ideas for stories, a what if . . . , tell what might happen when . . . , think of what would happen if. . . . This technique is great for generating hypotheses in science experiments or changing events in history to predict how

these changes would impact us today. This also works well to problem-solve issues that affect the students' lives in their communities, by envisioning a possible future.

2. Listing: a way to record ideas generated as students brainstorm (written down by teacher or peers); students subsequently group these ideas to decide which theme they will write about.

3. Dialoguing: using a picture that depicts a problematic situation or current event (a code); students dialogue in pairs about the picture. This is an icebreaker for developing ideas and works well in science, math, and social studies.

4. Clustering: mapping connections between ideas (cause–effect, problem–solution, etc.) This is an icebreaker for organizing or linking events in history, health, or science.

5. Cubing: using a paper folded into six sections and having students write quick notes in each of the six sections about the 1) description, 2) comparison, 3) associations, 4) analysis, 5) application, and 6) advantage/disadvantages. This technique helps learners write what they know and later research what most interests them. The starter works particularly well with topics in geography, history, and health.

6. Freewriting: allows the learner to start writing on a topic over a sustained period of time without lifting the pen or pencil from the paper. Later this is examined to generate ideas that are shaped into a graphic organizer or outline and are subsequently refined. This is an icebreaker for developing writing fluency.

Writers Workshop

When students compose in a workshop, your support of their different phases will need to be tailored to their developing areas of writing. Keep in mind that everyone works at a different pace, so it is important to consider the whole picture and be systematic in supporting their writing. Consider including the following items for peer feedback and a self-check list.

INTERACTING WITH PEERS' DRAFT ESSAYS
1. Gathering information
   a. primary sources: interviews, surveys, observations
   b. secondary sources: other texts, books, Web pages on this topic
2. Judging quality of information
   a. Add/remove information to define theme
   b. New/old contrast
   c. Reliable/untrustworthy
3. Organization
   a. Logic in organization: beginning, support, and conclusion
   b. Cohesion within sections: topicalization
   c. Coherence across sections
4. Making choices
   a. word craft: using words that work
   b. images and metaphors
   c. involving the audience

EDITING CHECKLISTS (WORD CHOICE, GRAMMAR, SPELLING, PUNCTUATION, CAPITALIZATION)
1. Personalization of areas that learner needs use in proofreading
2. Style sheet for citation
3. Checksheet of essential steps of the tasks or products that meet the assignment instructions
4. Tools used to check writing: dictionary, thesaurus, spell checker, own spelling list

Writing Conferences

One of the most effective ways teachers can help students develop their authority as writers is to engage them in conversations as writers. Teachers' writing conferences with individual students using a written text that the student has produced have been found to make significant contributions to helping students fine-tune their sense of audience and make revisions to their texts (Goldstein & Conrad, 1990). Students need to have access to resources and instruction on how to use the resources (e.g., how to borrow from text, how to use word processing applications on the computer, evaluation criteria). What revision options, strategies, or self-monitoring of changes do you want to encourage at each phase of writing?

Consider the following questions.

QUESTIONS
Prewriting
What ideas are you considering as your main question or theme?
How did you generate these ideas?
Where can you find more information about these ideas?
How will you record your information?
To whom do you want to address this writing?
Why?

Organizing
Tell me about the purpose of your writing.
How did you relate your ideas to your purpose?
Which ideas don't fit? Why?
Which ideas are important?
Where do these ideas come from? (own experience, texts, discussions, interviews, Web pages?)
Which are you going to use and why?
In what order are you going to use these ideas?

Drafting
Have you identified a purpose and audience?
How is the beginning related to the purpose?
How do the supporting sections reach the purpose?
How does the writing end?

Revising
How did your peers respond?
Which parts appealed to them?

Which parts did they not understand?

How will you change your writing? your language choices—metaphors, images, sounds, and your content? Did you use your own ideas and experience? What parts will you expand? Why? What parts will you eliminate? Why?

How will you reorganize?

How will you use additional resources available: another perspective, another source of information?

What next steps will you take?

Revising as Audience/Reader

How was your response helpful to the author?

Did you offer an opinion (agree or disagree)?

How did the author's use of language affect you (phrasing and voice)?

Did you recognize the way the author organized his/her writing? (perspective, progression of ideas, presentation of content)

Did you recognize strategies used by the author that were effective?

MAKING SUGGESTIONS FOR REVISION

How is it for appropriate content and relevance to topic?

Is there expression of perspective and voice?

Are there linguistic strategies to involve and affect audience?

FINAL PRODUCT

Did you write a summary of the changes made through the drafting stages?

Did you identify strategies of writing that you handled well?

Did you identify aspects of writing that still cause you concern?

Did you check mechanics: spelling, capitalization, punctuation, etc.?

Did you include the final revision?

Writing Assessments

Portfolio assessment is perhaps the most widely used classroom assessment for writing. In the assessment section of this text, you will find additional types of assessments to use. Remember that writing selected for inclusion in a portfolio may vary according to your purpose. If the purpose is to document progress (formative), you are looking for the student's evidence of making better revisions and editing decisions that result in improvement. The student's ability to note changes and plan strategies for subsequent changes is important. The following elements will help you monitor that progress:

CHECKLIST OF CONTENTS TO INCLUDE

peers' assessment

self-assessment: own spelling lists, story webs, checklist for discourse level and surface level features, resources used

number of drafts

reflection on changes in each draft

plans for finalizing writing

If the portfolio is being used as a showcase portfolio (summative), the students could be asked to select their best writing (one to three texts) and explain what they feel particularly proud of in their writing. As well, students could identify the areas of their writing that they are still learning to control and what strategies they are using. Through the experience of presenting their writing, students become aware of not only the elements that are important, but also show how they can control the processes. By revealing this knowledge about writing and their own learning, students help teachers identify where to intervene and provide support: in clarifying what the task requires, such as more effective procedures for writing, or additional sources for the student to consider to shape his/her perspective. Also, the particular areas of difficulty for each learner can be identified and addressed with specific instruction. This may be an appropriate time to note the learner's development of language awareness (in understanding discourse, semantic and syntactic, and mechanics).

Using the portfolio process allows learners to participate fully in the evaluation of their writing. Through this guided participation, they can emerge as confident writers.

Teaching Diverse Learners

Because literacy is a cultural practice, emerging literate kindergarteners who speak languages other than English at home face numerous challenges in becoming literate in English. Often beginning learners participate in activities that may not make much sense immediately. They must learn how schooling places value on certain explicit writing practices. An example of an oral practice commonly found in North American school settings is one in which students learn to say the names of letters in English classrooms as a step toward learning both reading and writing. That is, teachers use this metalanguage of letter names as a way to teach letter recognition. In Western languages, letters have names; however, in languages like Japanese and Korean, that use syllabaries, symbols represent syllables or morphophonemes. There are no names for the individual syllables. Only the sound is represented. In learning to write in English as a second language, this means that children must figure out the systematic correspondences between letters, the letters' names, and the sounds they represent. The sound of the name of the letter *d*, for example, does not represent the sound represented by the letter in words spelled with it (which is why words that employ the same sound as the name require a vowel be added, as in *decoy* or *diaspora*). For other children whose primary languages use Roman alphabetic letters, and who come with print awareness from their languages, the names of the letters in English may be confused with what they have already learned. For example *e* in English sounds like *i* in Spanish. When teachers ask children to write and spell their names, they may know how to do so in their primary language, but not be able to "spell" in English. Children who have had experience writing from right to left in their primary language will need to learn directionality of English, left to right, top to bottom. While there is no catalogue of culturally diverse practices with written texts and the difficulties these may present, what matters here is the perspective of recognizing that each child's past experiences with print create knowledge that may show up as they begin writing in their second language. Teachers who are able to recognize this knowledge as a resource can learn much about what students already know. By building on students' knowledge through participation and explicit guidance through writing activities, learners can develop the ability to interpret and use written language to convey their own intentions.

Older children who have been successful in their past schooling experiences can more readily show evidence of their knowledge in all areas of written communication. At the discourse level, their past experiences may affect their decisions about what topics can be written about or not, how to organize their ideas, and how to use rhetorical devices, lexical collocation, and mechanics. Learners who have strong first language literacy have the possibility of transferring what they know to learning second language writing (Fu, 1995). While they may be errors for English speakers, these are actually indications of competing resources that the student is learning to sort out and use (Johns, 1990, 1992; Ventola & Mauranen, 1996).

Older students who have had limited or no prior schooling or who have had unsuccessful writing experiences may feel that they simply cannot read or write (Franklin, 1999; Guerra, 1998). Their past experiences may have convinced them that writing is not a worthwhile activity because they may have had experiences that made writing irrelevant and meaningless, such as copying information from chalkboards. It will be important for these learners to see how knowing how to write impacts their lives now and in the future. As learners progress, other issues emerge, such as plagiarism. As many second language learners do not share the same cultural orientations to text, even plagiarism may not be seen as anything more significant than copying from a more authoritative source rather than the more serious "stealing" of intellectual property (Scollon, 1995; Fox, 1994). Appropriate "borrowing from other texts" is a writing practice that students will also need to learn.

For the above reasons, when teachers orient students to literate behaviors in the second language, the influences of prior literacies, and differences in cultural values and purposes of writing need careful attention. If recognized in learners' texts, the mismatches in literacies can become points for discussion. Students with these resources can build upon them to develop awareness and understanding of how each language works in written texts and the cultural practices for creating and using these texts.

(Note: In an effort to visually portray psycholinguistic and sociocultural viewpoints, we have used icons to direct your attention. ◆ = psycholinguistic ■ = sociocultural)

RESEARCH ON WRITING

The field of second language writing does not have a comprehensive theory of the writing processes to be able to make predictions about writing development (Grabe, B., 2001). Unlike the theories in second language acquisition, second language writing research has focused on pragmatic issues in building models of teaching and learning how to write. Contrastive rhetorical research has focused on identifying the composing processes that second language learners used by analyzing the second language learner's texts for lexical and syntactic and rhetorical characteristics. As the field moved from behaviorist to constructivist theories of learning, ◆ psycholinguistic research in writing began to examine the cognitive processing needed to create texts. With an understanding of the writer's processing involved, research could manipulate various conditions to find out how learners learn to produce effective texts. ■. Sociocultural research has concentrated on interactional aspects of writing that influence how writers understand the nature and purposes of writing and how they construct knowledge, social relationships, and their identities through learning to write. Critical literacy research has studied the ways in which learners use their writing to question the taken-for-granted understandings that are communicated through texts and to take action in their context using writing in their own interests. Without a unified theory of writing, each research area has provided its own definition of "good" writing either from perspectives that focus on product, process, or interaction, and more recently, power relations.

Writing as *Product*

Similar to research on speaking, from the 1970s and well into the '80s, much of the research on second language writing investigated primarily syntactic features of texts produced by second language writers. These studies tried to make claims about writing based on learners' errors in structuring these texts. Early models of good writing from research lead teachers to focus on production of exemplar texts from a composition and rhetorical perspective, primarily focusing on learners' argumentation styles in ESL (North, 1987). During this period of research, implications for teaching writing stressed controlled composition, or bottom-up progression, from sentence level skill building spanning from syntax to mechanics of punctuation, capitalization, and spelling. Thus instructional goals established for learners sought to have them produce written texts: sentences, paragraphs, and essays that were error-free.

The typical pattern of instruction devoted time to writing different types of complete sentences. Grammatical skills were taught to repair incomplete sentences. From this, paragraph skills were practiced using a prototypical theme sentence with five supporting sentences. Instruction about writing paragraphs often divided them according to their rhetorical functions, such as descriptive, how to, comparison and contrast, and persuasive.

The next stage moved to longer academic writing, such as reports and essays. At this point, instruction on organizing information introduced outlining skills to show a relationship between the major headings and supporting details. As the students produced longer texts, they practiced revising skills to monitor vocabulary choice, coherence, and cohesion between their sentences. In this approach, perspective, genre, and style, were added later as topics in a writing course. Instruction on editing skills were often recycled throughout the production of each text to ensure that learners checked writing for accuracy in using grammar and mechanics of punctuation, spelling, and capitalization.

Contrastive rhetoric studies try to identify differences in composition choices between ESL writers' texts and native English speakers' texts. In an early study, Kaplan (1966) explained that differences in organizational aspects of composition were due to differences in logic from one culture to another. As evidence, Kaplan contrasted the linearity of text structure in English writing with the circularity in argumentation used by Asian students, the parallelism through coordination of ideas used by Semitic language students, and the extraneous elaboration by Romance and Russian students. While he tied these differences in rhetorical structure to cultural differences, he was severely criticized for having made these generalizations from only one type of writing and attempting to label types of thinking of a whole population. Nonetheless his study was among the first to identify culture as a reason for differences in students' production of texts in English. Much later in a university setting, Bliss (2001) noticed that ESL learners met with success in writing descriptive texts in English, such as in creative writing and report writing (summaries, abstracts, lab reports, essays, etc.). However, when called upon to inform or persuade, multilingual students "have serious difficulties." Bliss states that learners fail to meet expectations that they should structure an assertive claim and substantiate it logically with sufficient evidence. Again, cultural differences in determining what is logical, connected evidence is identified as the problem. Bliss claims that students need to be able to use chronological, psychological, and rhetorical structures for academic English.

The trend of analyzing texts to specify elements of written language continues in corpus linguistic research, where computers are used to compile and analyze large databases (corpus) of texts (Biber, 1995). Researchers calculate the frequency of grammatical features, vocabulary, and idioms in the corpus and patterns of their co-occurrence (the way features combine to configure a text). By computerized analysis of a vast number of texts (corpus), a particular genre's characteristic patterns can be identified. This means that the usage of grammatical elements, such as nouns, distributive adjectives, phrasal verbs, and prepositions, can be more accurately described and taught based on empirical evidence from current texts. In addition, the most common meaning or their definitions can be taught in relation to the particular genre.

This type of research recently has been used to analyze elementary and middle school texts. One study, Reppen (1994), examined the changes that occur in children's written texts as their language proficiency increases between third and sixth grades. Reppen built a small corpus consisting of typical elementary books and types of writing that students produce from third through sixth grades. These texts were marked and tagged for their grammatical features, such as use of passive voice, pronouns, distributive adjectives, and nouns. Using factor analysis, she found five factors of linguistic features that co-occurred that she could use as a model of elementary school texts. The model identifies linguistic features in texts that distinguished between more oral-like writing ("on-line communication," as she calls it) and more written-like language use (which she calls "edited").

One example of a more oral-like feature is the use of "And" at the beginning of sentences. Examples of more written-like features include the use of dependent clauses and adverbial phrases. Her sample English essays were written by two groups of students, native English speakers and native Navajo speakers. Reppen demonstrated how the Navajo native speakers' use of more edited writing developed in similar ways to English native speakers despite their having started at different levels of proficiency. As both groups of students matured in age and grade levels, they also learned to distinguish the differences between the genres of description, narration, and explanation. Both groups increased in their use of edited language, and lexically elaborated language between third grade and sixth grade. However, the Navajo children made the largest gains, initially producing half as much written text in the third grade as the native speakers, to later producing in the sixth grade roughly the equivalent amount of text.

These are tentative conclusions because they represent each group's average production and there was wide variation in each group. Larger studies are needed to confirm whether these findings are generalizable. The trend in these studies indicates that texts written by English as a second language learners show similar characteristics of development in distinguishing between oral and written genres when compared to texts produced by native speakers of English age-peers.

This type of research commonly focuses only on the texts produced by learners. As more textual features of written texts do become identified by this research, we still know little to account for the different processes that learners use to produce these texts (from picture prompted writing, peer discussion, or group generated). Nor do we know the diverse contexts in which learners construct these texts: how much experience learners had in generating these texts and what they attended to while writing these texts. Also using research implications from this line of study is somewhat problematic for teaching writing. There are many ways that the range of quality and depth of content in students' writing could have been influenced from factors beyond their prompted writing, such as their background knowledge of the topic types of materials they read and their past experiences writing within time constraints. If the most significant aspect of writing were to have learners reproduce the genres they were taught, learners could learn to produce grammatically flawless, clearly well-organized texts. Yet texts are still written that are inaccurate in content and that have inappropriate discourse for different audiences. Textual analysis alone does not provide enough information to guide instruction.

Writing as *Process*

Within the psycholinguistic research literature, studies that attempt to identify writing stages and the corresponding mental processes have been conducted. A goal of these studies has been to create a model of the language production and cognitive processing demands that different types of writing place on the learner. In this research, there is an assumption that the individual writer must balance these demands to produce any particular text. In early research analyzing the complexity of the writing tasks, Bereiter and Scardamalia (1987) experimented with levels of task complexity and information complexity. They identified at least two different processes: composing (knowledge telling) and processing (knowledge transforming) demands on the learners. These would vary according to the purpose of the writing and complexity of the messages. In the following, tasks fit into a hierarchy of difficulty, proceeding from least complex to more complex writing: copying, listing, recounting, summarizing, synthesizing, critiquing, persuading, interpreting, creating new texts. At each stage, progressively more complex thinking and use of language is required.

Since this research is limited, trends in findings rather than generalizations have been identified. Even though the cognitive processing model creates a hierarchy of complexity, it cannot predict how learners can or cannot manage these complexities. Research on bilingual children's writing demonstrated how they drew on both primary

INFORMATION COMPLEXITY	TASK COMPLEXITY	COMPOSING	PROCESSING
Form and combine letters, learn to space letters and words, learn directionality of writing	Copying requires eye–hand motor coordination	not composing	Controlling mechanical production
Use single words	To list	Stating knowledge	Retrieving and recognizing words
Identify and extract important concepts from content	To paraphrase, to demonstrate understanding, to remember, and summarize simply	Composing short notes with minimum fluency in expressing own ideas	Recounting events
Determine primary from secondary sources	To learn, problem solve, summarize complexly, synthesize	Composing extended notes; Composing and transforming from multiple sources	Judging, selecting, and integrating
Assess credibility, quality, accuracy	To critique, persuade, interpret	Privileging perspectives and using evidence selectively but appropriately	Reorganizing information
Use techniques to produce desired effects on the audience	To create an aesthetic experience to entertain	Composing in new ways; figurative levels of composing	Violating composing norms in effective ways

Source: Based on B. Grabe, 2001 p. 50

language and second language knowledge to construct meaning (Edelsky, 1982). Because processing complexity can be increased or decreased by factors not involved with actual writing, such as time allowed to complete the activity, by supportive mediation with the learner in context of writing, or by using the technologies to produce writing, e.g., pen/computer), text complexity or cognitive difficulty alone cannot explain differences in writing proficiency.

Perhaps for these reasons, there has been more narrowed effort to research processing involved in the most ubiquitous writing found in academic settings, the narrative essay, and less on other genres such as note taking, logs, and creative writing. When learners are asked to compose "text responsive" writing, they are required to draw on a particular reading text to generate their compositions. In this way, students are judged by how well they can take information from texts and interpret this information in their own words for use to meet writing tasks. By restricting the range of information to a shared reading text that writers have, researchers can probe the degree to which learners have linguistic proficiency to respond in a register that resembles more text-like or more oral-like communication. As well, this type of writing is an indicator of the learners' varied ability to compose complex texts at the levels of discourse, syntax, and semantics. The features in their writing then can be used to distinguish between different levels of learners' writing development. Interactionist second language theory predicts that learners who engage in using the second language in the uppermost range of their interlanguage ability (negotiated pushed output), gain more proficiency in the second language to express their ideas in their own words.

Another area of research on learners' composing processes examines how the learner processes generate narrative essays. Through interviews, direct observations, questionnaires, and surveys, learners are queried on their processes. One line of research uses a technique of students narrating aloud how they compose their texts (talk-aloud protocols), as students move from prewriting to drafting to revising. In each phase, this information is used to reveal learners' use of strategies. In the planning stages, more proficient second language learners plan at the discourse level, while less proficient plan at almost exclusively the lexical level. In the composing stages, learners with lower ESL proficiency have difficulty transferring their ideas into the second language. The primary language becomes used when sufficient L2 proficiency is lacking. At the revision stage, it has been found that less expert writers attend to sentence level and word level revisions while more expert writers make changes at organizational, rhetorical, and discourse levels. Also, the wider the range of strategies that the learner had in his or her primary language, the more the learner could transfer to L2 writing. Finally, less proficient ESL writers draw on information from readings much moreso than less proficient ESL writers. Second language writing processes are affected by proficiency in the second language. However, writing strategies shape conscious second language knowledge (Krapels, 1990).

While this type of research involves the learner, criticism has been leveled because of the heavy dependence on what second language writers say rather than on how their cognitive processing may actually occur. Nonetheless, research, while indirect, is still considered the closest way of finding out about cognitive processing outside of intrusive surgery.

Recently the relationship between the development of phonological awareness and the development of writing has been researched to determine whether this is a prerequisite for reading and writing or an outcome of reading and writing. Vernon and Ferreiro (1999) researched whether children's ability to segment words into phonemes (phonological awareness) is a prerequisite for learning how to read and write. Their study shows that phonological awareness is not an either/or phenomenon, but that it develops across levels and that this development is related to children's writing development. Children's ability to benefit from systematic phonics instruction depends on their level of writing development. Their study offers an important implication for education. By encouraging children to write in kindergarten and first grade, spoken words become noticed and analyzed. In this way, as writing develops so too does phonological awareness.

Writing instruction during the '70s and '80s paralleled the research interest in processing, by breaking down the activity of composing into discrete processes. Similar to the product approach, the process approach assumes that good writing develops from the individual's application of skills. The skills that were identified were not sentence level, but rather skills in procedures to: 1) generate ideas, 2) structure these ideas, 3) produce a draft, 4) revise, and 5) evaluate the process. Unlike the structural approach of grammar skill building, the process approach was focused on the learner's practicing writing a variety of text types through these universal processes. One of the basic assumptions was that by participating in recursive processes of writing, learners would develop ability to produce these types of texts, without explicit instruction. When process instruction alone failed to account for improvements in writing, current practice now incorporates both processes and explicit teaching of rhetorical structures, genres, grammar, and mechanics.

Writing as Interactionally Accomplished Cultural Practice

Second language researchers who conduct qualitative studies have documented how learners develop writing in learning communities inside and outside of schools. In general, many of these studies present learning to write from the perspective of specific learners where oral and written language use is involved in literacy events in homes and their community, and later how this may conflict with their school's notions of literacy (Martin-Jones, 2000).

Specific literacy events are described to demonstrate how these writing experiences are shaped by learners' interactions with peers and with instructors (Zamel, 1990; Johns, 1992). These studies take place in particular classrooms where learners take on writer/reader responsibilities through journaling (Blanton, 2000). This means that learners begin to see themselves as writers and read texts as writers. Through these experiences, writers learn to vary their writing according to audience and purpose. There is no prescriptive formula derived from these studies. Rather they reveal how teachers who support students' active inquiry by helping them use their past learning, access and understand textual resources to build their knowledge. The process of learners' developing identities as authors in early language learning stages shows development of awareness of sound/symbol correspondence through drawings, borrowings from primary language literacy, visual images, and invented spellings.

Children's authorship of oral stories, as well as their oral and written retellings of stories that they have heard, reveal their social worlds, their development of narrative structures, and sense of audience. Through these retellings, children integrate the language of their families, texts that they have encountered, and experiences with language (Gallas, 1992; Dyson, 1997). Children's ability to assist family and community members in complex literacy events such as filling out job applications or visiting a doctor demonstrates their wealth of experiences (Vasquez, Pease-Alvarez, & Shannon, 1994). When their ways of talking are respected, they can move from oral interactions in the second language to writing in the second language. When these oral experiences become a bridge to writing, emerging literate learners can build up fluency and linguistic resources to use in their writing.

Teachers who engage students in different types of writing for learning topics that matter to them help students develop their own **voice** through interaction with their audiences and reflection on their writing. Additional textual resources may come from shared experiences in the class, communities, or books read aloud in class. Teachers' oral interactions using vocabulary from these sources and focus on a text's organization guides students to understand elements in narratives and build "story grammars." Students learn different ways to describe characters and settings, build a chain of events that make sense as a plot, and create endings. Through successful interactions students learn to take on the roles of confident writers and develop strategies to manage their writing. When these are lacking, students devise coping strategies (Leki, 1995). Teachers who reflect on their own questions while writing, can help model ways that students can think about their writing. Talking through these struggles further prepares emerging writers to think of texts as a product of the dynamics of composing and revisioning.

In order to socialize students to literate environments so that they can begin to use reading and writing purposefully and thus become aware of the importance of reading and writing, teachers create **print rich environment** classrooms where activities take place to invite learners to use a variety of written resources. This helps children gain a sense of the values and purposefulness of written communication. In daily activities by using lists, charts, mapping of ideas, graphs, etc., children gradually become aware of how to understand and use these texts in their local environment. Through this experience, students to learn to interpret and represent their knowledge through different extended written forms such as poems, stories, and reports. Teachers who ask students to write about their discoveries or questions in daily logs help learners develop fluency in expressing their own ideas (Hayes, Bahruth, & Kessler, 1998). With dialogue journals, a journal that allows for risk-free conversations between two parties, with the teacher, with peers in the classroom, or through Internet partnerships, students look forward to responding to the genuine need to tell more or explain. They learn to write about their own experiences and build appropriate syntactic structures, expression, and vocabulary into their own messages (Gutiérrez, Baquedano-Lopez, Alvarez, & Chu, 1999).

At the high school level, discussions to build knowledge can in fact exclude ESL students' participation in discussions. Duff (2001) describes how ESL students in Canadian mainstream social studies lessons became marginalized from class participation due to not sharing knowledge about popular culture of their mainstream peers. In their current events discussions, mainstream students' talk about issues raised in social studies were intertwined with references to texts from popular culture, cartoons, movies, and television programs. This **intertextuality** in the discussions permitted only mainstream students to use nonacademic and academic texts. The nonacademic worlds of the ESL students were not included, nor was the discussion made comprehensible. In effect they were prevented from participating. Because discussion in social studies classes is designed to build knowledge about topics, often the knowledge created is later called upon for writing essays. When discussions do not build shared knowledge, students face obstacles when writing to use that knowledge.

How can teachers interact with their students in ways to promote students' authority and confidence in writing? For personal writing, fluency in expression is a goal. Therefore, in responding to journal entries, encouraging students to write takes priority over correctness. Teachers model ways of using language by responding to the learner's messages and by restating or spelling words that learners have incorrectly used or misstated. Encouraging students to check with peers or dictionaries, as well as using their own primary language, helps students gain confidence as writers. Hayes, Bahruth, and Kessler show how this approach helped learners get into the routine of writing and develop longer, more connected and accurate texts. Typically beginning writers are fearful of making mistakes and avoid writing. For this reason, in order to build fluency, learners need time to develop with encouragement and resources to improve.

Other research examining the social nature of writing examines how teachers' feedback affects students' written texts. The textual relationship between teacher-written commentary and student revision reveals how they mutually shape each other. In other words, as the teacher-as-audience member responds to a student/author's writing, this allows the student/author to build expectations of satisfying the reader. Depending on the teacher's choice of focus in areas of writing, learners could be made to focus on only one type of feedback. As well, depending on the systematicity and quality of the feedback, learners could be nurtured. In an early study, Zamel (1985) found that ESL teachers' feedback focused primarily on students' syntax, and that their comments were unsystematic. Because subsequent studies that tried to identify the relationship between teacher feedback and learners' revision focused on inconsistent units of revisions, there are no generalizations from these studies (Goldstein, 2001). However, while it might be wishful thinking to assume that writers make revisions based solely on the feedback given by a single interactant, the revision process is too complex to be attributed to one source of feedback (Ferris, 1997). Revision processes more plausibly are affected also by numerous factors, including time constraints, familiarity with the writing tasks, and expectations for quality of writing. The research from this field has been criticized for its lack of generalizability given the limited number of participants that are generally reported. Nonetheless the very rich portraits of second language learners provide insights that statistical analysis cannot currently address.

Writing as *Power*

Particularly in the 1980s and '90s a new focus for research emerged called **critical literacy.** This orientation to writing as *power* is one that examines how power circulates through use of written discourse. Gee (1993) calls this literacy research "socially perceptive literacy" because it exposes how the use of language features serves particular social interests or ideologies. Teachers who implement critical literacy encourage learners to conduct inquiries that require the creation of new knowledge about an issue that is meaningful to them. Through this research process, learners are guided to speculate about and question how texts are produced and interpreted, as well as to think about their local conditions of interpretation. This means learners become writers through reading, talking about, and observing their realities and lived experiences. Research on how this is accomplished has been carried out in second language and recently in foreign language settings. Luke, O'Brien, and Comber (2001) describe how high school learners collected written texts in the community

REFLECT AND RESPOND

1. In building a literate community in your second language classroom, newcomers will need orientation in terms they can understand, with explicit information about what you are doing and explanations for why. Review the instructions in writing assignments you have given to your students or witnessed during field experience. Do you have any assumptions about these assignments that need to be made explicit to students? What revisions would you make and why?

_____

_____

2. To connect important concepts from content areas to your students' lives and encourage the types of writing that are required, you may find certain topics taboo, or not considered appropriate to write about. How would you accommodate students who feel this way? Or if you would not accommodate them, why wouldn't you?

_____

_____

through catalogues, advertisements, newspapers, and letters. In small groups, students were asked:

1. Try to classify texts (requests from charities or causes, public information leaflets, professional reading material)
2. When you have worked out five or six broad types of text, try to identify the following:
   a. Who produces them (e.g., public bodies, commercial enterprises, local authorities)?
   b. For whom are they produced (i.e., who are the consumers or the expected readers of the materials)?
   c. Why has the text been produced?
   d. Is this text of interest or relevance to you? Why or why not?
   e. Choose one text from each category that particularly appeals to you, either because of its style or content. Discuss your opinion with other members of your group.

(From Wallace, 1992, p. 66, as cited in Luke et al., 2001)

The purpose of this activity is to involve students in speculating on the production of these texts, who generated them, and for what audiences. Students were also asked to interpret the political and economic consequences and to connect these to their own discourse resources and cultural experiences. In this way students develop a sense of text as "institutionally located and motivated social strategy" (p. 116). The next steps were carried out by examining texts closely for how certain patterns of words are used to represent the topic, clustering of adjectives and nouns, who did the actions (agency), how moods (e.g., affirmative, imperative, interrogative, exclamatory) put the reader in a particular position in relation to the author. In other words, authors use language to construct a particular view of the social world, and readers can question that social world by examining what is portrayed as natural or not, what is new information or assumed to be known, etc. Luke identifies the next step as leading to some action "with and/or against the text" (p. 117). Students are encouraged to use their newly created knowledge about texts in ways that help them learn further. This could be envisioned as reaching a wider public with their results by creating a Web page, book, newspaper, or even by writing and performing a play.

Critical literacy has been used effectively with second language learners in grades as early as kindergarten (Vasquez; O'Brien) through adulthood (Auerbach, 1992). In critical literacy classrooms, teachers do not have a checklist of activities and worksheets for students to follow nor do students just reproduce model rhetorical texts. Instead, students learn to take a variety of stances in relation to the text, interpreting the text from multiple positions: oppositional, sympathetic, skeptical, etc. By looking at how writing is a representation of the author's interests to influence a particular audience, students try to identity that audience by asking "Who is included?" and "Who is omitted?" Similar to language detectives, they formulate hypotheses and look to find evidence to support or reject their ideas.

Starting at the discourse level, learners try to find patterns of language use across the whole text that reveal the author's intentions. Then they closely examine particular instances to see what techniques and rhetorical devices were used. Does the text allow for alternative ideas or is it **epideictic**? What type of imagery is used? How does it build up across the text? In following through, students then practice reconstructing texts they have analyzed. However, they change the beginning or ending of the text, or modify an unspoken presumption or value judgement by using the same devices they have identified as having been employed by the original author. They may reconstruct texts by using the devices to change the endings or beginnings to dialogue with the author. Other students may write a rebuttal or play to talk back to the author. The point here is to search for and discover how certain rhetorical devices work in the target language and then to practice employing those same devices in one's own writing.

Peers read their written texts and their audiences respond to these by commenting on parts that particularly moved them. Learners ask questions of each other's work to clarify what was meant, and to offer suggestions for improvement. Students, as authors, then decide which directions they will take. Through participation in these practices, learners come to understand their roles as readers/writers. They "write" themselves and "reread" themselves in the world. More importantly, through this writing process students learn to interrogate and create texts for their own interests, becoming critical readers and critical writers. In this way, ESL students' communication develops beyond the TESOL standards for everyday social interactions, for academic purposes, and culturally appropriate ways. Students become capable of transforming the ways texts represent reality and can challenge the omission or absence of topics and voices that are not included in them.

ASK YOURSELF THESE QUESTIONS

1. In what ways have you used critical literacy in your life to make literacy work in your interests?
2. In some ways, writing from the perspective of critical literacy can be seen as a focus on the linguistic elements in texts just as earlier instruction focused on rhetorical structure and grammatical features of texts. What similarities/differences do you see?
3. Critical literacy helps learners become socialized to literacy in ways that are similar to the perspective on writing as an interactionally accomplished cultural practice. What characteristics of writers and readers would develop in each type of instruction?

INTEGRATED APPROACH

To set up a model for explaining under what conditions writing in L2 develops, Grabe adapts the factors that (Spolsky,1989) had previously identified for general second language acquisition and uses them for writing:

- knowing the language
- knowing how to use the language (communicative competence)
- human learner
- individual abilities and preferences
- the social context
- attitudes and motivation
- opportunities for learning and practice
- formal instructional contexts
- processing factors
- cultural variability
- content and topical knowledge
- discourse, genre, and register knowledge (specific to writing)

Source: Grabe, 2001, p. 53

Grabe recognizes that each one of these influences how second language learners write. The level of knowledge about the language and proficiency in a second language influences the quality of writing. The individual learner and his or her abilities and preferences will affect how he or she learns and what he or she writes. The social context in placing demands on the learner to use conventions to relate as readers and writers, as well as how they include or exclude these learners, will affect learners' attitudes and motivations to learn to write. The opportunities that are provided and the learner's ability to engage in these practices in both formal and informal contexts in turn affect the ability of the learner to address audiences in these contexts. Constraints of time, complexity of the writing, and availability of resources to use obviously can influence learning to write as well. The last two items are particularly relevant to learning to write in schools. To be able to write effectively in any classroom, students need to be able to draw on previous knowledge about the content and topical knowledge that they learn through reading discussion and writing, as well as the knowledge of relevant discourse, genre, and register features that are used in these content areas. In the following section, we discuss the significant role of writing in academic success and beyond writing functions in schools.

PURPOSES FOR WRITING

Writing in schools serves many purposes that are personal, social, and academic. For instance, writing for oneself could be used as a tool for learning in several ways. While we listen and watch, or while we read, we take notes to capture what we consider important to remember. Here writing serves as a heuristic for storing information in our memory. When we write our questions or expectations before reading a text, this prepares us for reading for specific information. Writing after reading can serve to capture our thoughts, concerns, and feelings about what we have read. Often this is called **expressive writing.** After we write, we can look at these notes as objects which enable us to "loop back," permitting us to change either our expression and/or our thinking. Writing can also be a medium to communicate with various audiences, distant and near, for personal, social, and academic purposes. **Transactional** writing is the type of academic writing that expresses what we have learned about to explain, inform, instruct, or persuade an audience. In this way writing and reading are closely related to helping us learn, think and act.

Members of a community engage in written communication in predictable ways. Therefore, not everything that is important in writing is explicitly explained; rather, much of its meaning becomes part of is based on use of and interpretation of conventions. Genre and **register,** or tone of communication, are two conventions shaped by cultural practice and cannot be fully described by a list of all of their elements. Rather, these conventions are entailed by their configurations of content, vocabulary, register, and genre. So if someone begins a story, "Once upon a time," it evokes a fable-like frame for what is to follow without communicating explicit information about time or place. Part of learning to write in academic settings is learning how each discipline makes use of particular conventions to create and display knowledge in written form. In fact, often when these conventions are not followed, gatekeepers may discount the information as untrustworthy and the writer as incompetent. Thus, the use of conventions can signal having content knowledge.

Conventions exist but do not remain the same across time. New conventions are constantly being created. Across time an individual uses conventions, and changes occur that dynamically push and shape the boundaries of acceptability. Evidence of this can be found in literary or art movements or periods that distinguish themselves from past conventions, e.g., modernists, postmodernists, etc. Other evidence can be found in electronic written communication in chatrooms, e-mail, and Web pages, where users are expected to follow conventions specific to electronic communication called

REFLECT AND RESPOND

1. In addition to cultural difference in literacy practices, you may find that learners perform better when given a variety of ways to generate their ideas for writing, organizing, and revising their texts. Which of the following practices do you think would be helpful to a visual learner (V), an auditory learner (A), a kinesthetic learner (K), and a learner with Attention Deficit Hyperactivity Disorder (ADHD)? Mark your answers and then check your responses with a cooperating teacher.

   a. Having students listen to a story and map the main points with supporting points on a web.

   _____

   b. Creating a chaining story with teacher as scribe at the chalk board, each child contributing a sentence after "It all started with a bang! . . ."

   _____

   c. In a math word problem, manipulating objects in a division problem for which the learner needs to write an explanation as her answer.

   _____

   d. Prior to a science experiment, having students draw arrows between elements that they predict will combine and explain their predictions to a partner before writing down the one they believe is most accurate.

   _____

   e. Before writing an essay, talking in pairs about similarities and differences between two graphs on population growth.

   _____

2. As you become familiar with your students through their writing, try to keep a running record of what you are learning about their home cultures and literacy activities. This record can serve as a valuable resource for building your multicultural awareness. Reflect on and examine your own cultural identity and values in relation to your observations. Consult with members from these communities to clarify your observations and answer concerns and questions. The lessons you learn can also be shared with other teachers in your district who are teaching similar students.

"netiquette." Often e-mail and chat rooms create a middle ground between oral language and written language where punctuation and capitalization reveal emotions and tone. A new set of punctuation has emerged called *emoticons*. These indicate a range of feelings: happiness :-) ☺ sarcasm ^^), surprise !**! sadness :-(or ☹, etc. Capitalization

THINK, PAIR, SHARE

1. What might be some types of writing that are required using synchronous versus asynchronous communication on the Internet? Chatrooms versus sent mail? In which type of written communication would your students be able to participate meaningfully? Why?

_____

_____

2. Since the language in written messages in e-mail exchanges can vary in register and tone through the use of vernacular and standard varieties of English, what activities to code these varieties could help you develop your students' ability to analyze words or phrases and determine appropriate use? Consider creating a logbook of equivalent expressions, a wall chart of expressions and their definitions and use, etc. Share your ideas with a colleague.

_____

_____

STUDENT WRITING CONFERENCE SELF-ASSESSMENT

Name: _____ Date: _____

Directions: Mark an X in the box that describes how you feel about writing.

	YES	SOMETIMES	NEVER
1. I know what I want to write about.			
2. I use my experiences and what I know in my writing.			
3. I use different ways to help me start thinking about what I want to compose.			
4. I prefer to visualize my ideas with pictures, drawings, or outlines.			
5. I try to use new words from my lessons in my writing.			
6. I ask my friends and family to make suggestions.			
7. I decide what is important to include or eliminate.			
8. I like to choose different ways to use language to express my ideas and feelings.			
9. I check to see if my ideas are accurate.			
10. I check to see if my language use is appropriate and effective.			

APPLICATION ACTIVITY

1. Go back to the Types of Texts on p. 16 and prioritize these texts in terms of what your students will be engaged in this year. Which tasks will take the longest time to accomplish? Recycle that activity at various times during the year to get a sense of how students make progress.
2. Knowing that learning to write is a complex social, cultural, and cognitive activity, take stock of the areas you tend to assess with your students. How is your assessment determined by the needs of the learner? How do you provide systematic help for each phase of the learner's development for content learning? The following list of issues is provided for your consideration:

A. Overall Composing—Crafting a Personal Perspective
   1. Purpose—What are the learner's intentions?
   2. Audience—With whom is the learner trying to communicate?
   3. Message—How does the learner's content fulfill intentions?
   4. Genre—How does the learner show familiarity with the conventions for this type of writing?
   5. Cohesion—How is this built between sections of the text?
   6. Coherence—How does this occur across the entire text?
   7. Assessment—How well does the learner reflect on (1) effectiveness of the language choices made: metaphors, images, appeals to the reader, (2) identity as writer, (3) sufficiency of resources available to the writer, (4) adequacy of strategies used by the learner for the writing?
B. Elements for Varying Language Choices
   1. Presenting knowledge and ideas (specific content concepts and vocabulary)
   2. Arrangement/Ordering: a) chronology, b) spatially c) degree of importance, d)psychologically (engage reader through surprise= reader's attention is drawn through logically arranged ideas), e) rhetorically
   3. Indirectness/Politeness, Explicitness/Implicitness
   4. Interpersonal (own ideas, voice, expressions, etc)
      Ideational (beliefs, concerns, argument, and supporting evidence),
      Textual transaction (representing ideas and connecting these through psychological and rhetorical ordering)
   5. Genres: "precis," summary, abstract, lab report, essay exam, correspondence, note taking
   6. Rhetorical styles: descriptive narratives, reports to inform, essays to persuade
   7. Cohesion elements: subordination (background information that is not necessary to the agent/verb relationship), coordination and superordination
   8. Coherence devices: connecting through transitions to bridge facts or events mentioned, connecting ideas/claims and evidence, explanations
   9. Assessment: students reflect on (1) what language choices are being made, (2) for what reasons, (3) choosing other possible strategies

of an entire sentence can be used to "shout" and emphasize in angry tones or just to emphasize a single word. (See Resources for more on netiquette.)

Constructing a Web page also uses new conventions for combining images, sound, animation, and texts. Writers also need to consider how to include information on different parts of the screen (panels, drop-down, or pop-up menus) and hyperlinks to other pages with additional information. As well, the hypertext writer determines how different sets of texts will relate to each other or what kinds of links to other texts are relevant. Rather than linear development of genre, a more associative notion of hybrid text writing has emerged, combining diverse genres: newspaper, advertisement, essay, popular songs, and videos. Indeed, writing hypertexts seems similar to constructing a spider's web of meaning, with multimodal texts (oral and written) that are juxtaposed to provoke allusions on multiple levels.

This section has explained the multiple purposes that writing serves. In doing so we see that the other modalities of speaking, listening, and reading are important in learning to write. Reading and writing are integrated and support each other when writing is used as preparation for reading or comprehension. Oral activities and graphics when used together provide resources for students when they compose. Writing to serve one's own needs for memory or reflection on past activity can shape future action. Also important to keep in mind, members of a community follow as well as create conventions of writing to serve their purposes. Let's examine how particular disciplines encourage the use of certain writing conventions.

EXERCISES AND ACTIVITIES
DISCUSS AND REFLECT

1. To build a print-rich classroom, ask your students to bring in written texts or oral recordings from their home languages to start a multilingual library in your own classroom. As each text is brought in, have students create index cards on which they write: 1) bibliographic information: the title, author, place, and date of the publication, publisher; 2) their guesses about for whom the text is written and why. As you build in time for free reading, have students who chose to read the text jot down their guesses and their evidence. Periodically, group students who have read the text review the comments and decide whose guesses seem more accurate and why. In their authors' journals, students can reflect on the types of language use for writing to different audiences. These can then be used as a resource when students write similar types of texts. As well, these index cards begin to teach students about appropriate citation, a textual borrowing practice.

2. Writing in any language provides challenges even when you write in your first tongue. Aside from the linguistic challenges, writing may also produce a change in cultural viewpoints. When you write in a second language, what is acceptable, relevant, specific, and logical is culturally constructed by communities of that language. If you want to find out how second language learners might feel when they are crossing literacies, try this exercise. Find an advertisement in another language. With the help of a literate member of that language, find out:

   a. What is the ad's purpose? Do you consider this topic appropriate to be used in ads?
   b. To whom is the ad written? Who is excluded?
   c. How does the author use language, images, and color to try to persuade you?
   d. What are the differences between how the author's message affects you versus the community member literate in that language?
   e. How might you use what you just learned to help your students learn to interpret and produce texts they encounter?

INTERACTIVE PEER ASSESSMENT OF WRITING

Name: _____

PARTNER: _____

Date: _____

Directions: After listening to or reading your partner's text, talk to your partner and together write an example in each of the boxes.

MY PARTNER'S TEXT	QUESTIONS/COMMENTS I HAVE
1. Used this strategy to start writing:	
2. Decided the topic by.	
3. Collected additional information from these sources:	
4. Organized ideas by:	
5. Tries to use new words or phrases from our lessons:	
6. Taught me:	
7. Could be improved by:	
8. Was effective in getting me interested because:	
9. Was accurate because:	
10. Used language appropriately because:	

SUMMARY

In this chapter, we have shown how four directions in writing research have contributed valuable information to inform classroom writing instruction. Composition/rhetorical research on writing has revealed the growing linguistic and content complexity in learners' texts from the word level to sentence level, and to discourse level development. As the learner gains second language oral proficiency, writing helps the learner build second language knowledge and develops from using this knowledge in more conventional written texts. The psycholinguistic research on learners' production of written texts and their cognitive processes for text production reveal that balancing both global discourse decisions as well as sentence level grammar and lexical decisions are needed to produce second language writing. Students whose strategies concentrate on one level of decision making, will have difficulty in producing effective texts. Sociocultural research has yielded insights on how learners are apprenticed into learning communities (by teachers, peers, and family) to take on roles to produce and interpret culturally relevant texts. By building continuity of learning between

REFLECT AND RESPOND

1. Imagine that you've tried all the instructional strategies that you are aware of and a particular student's writing still shows little development or the student shows limited awareness of his or her own writing. What can you do? Think of three things that you might consider changing in your lessons to help this student.

   _____

   _____

2. Share your ideas with one of your partners. What had you not considered?

   _____

   _____

3. Select the options that you feel most comfortable with and try these with the student. What seems to work?

   _____

   _____

their learners' family, community, and school contexts, teachers can help learners use writing (through stages of inquiry, publishing, and presenting) to access wider sources of information. The critical literacy studies demonstrate that students who understand how language in texts works to structure social relationships, learn to use these textual elements to address societal inequities and serve both their interests and their communities' interests. Writing instruction can profit from these research studies, taking into account the need to include writing practice with a variety of texts to help learners build more proficient language use. As well, instruction in writing that incorporates writers' culturally diverse funds of knowledge helps learners build meaningful personal connections and their identities as confident writers. These social and cultural considerations are critical to sustaining learners' investment in learning to write and writing to learn.

Since school is where many second language learners begin learning to write in their first and second languages, becoming successful in the cultural practices for use of writing to learn is significant. Academic expectations for how writers should communicate are often the result of disciplinary practices and conventions for constructing knowledge and representing it. Therefore instruction in writing needs to prepare learners to identify their audience and take up audience-responsive writing for different purposes. Orientations to the second language literate behaviors are often necessary when children have prior knowledge of literacies in languages other than English. Older second language learners with prior accomplishments from schooling experiences in their native language use what they have learned not only at the word and sentence level, but more importantly at the discourse level of writing in perceiving purposes and values of written communication.

From understanding past research contributions, teachers can appreciate how learners are balancing a number of tasks linguistically, cognitively, socially, and culturally. These areas are intermingled when students learn through a number of types of written genres and registers. Instruction that orients second language learners to writing includes:

- identifying a meaningful and clear purpose for writing to a particular audience.
- brainstorming exercises to give learners a chance to generate content from their own life experiences.
- organizing principles to demonstrate the variety of ways to structure texts and their impact on the reader.
- revision processes that help the learner review their purpose, audience, and expression through lexical choice, syntactic variety, and metaphorical and technical language use.
- having resources available for students to extend what they know or confirm their understandings.
- opportunities to learn how to control mechanical aspects and conventions.
- opportunities to contribute their new knowledge to reach diverse audiences affected by this knowledge.

These steps necessarily involve speaking, listening, and reading, in addition to writing. Seen this way, writing is not an end in and of itself. Instructional practices such as group brainstorming, logs, dialogue journals, conferencing, writers workshop, and author's chair call upon writers to talk about their texts, listen to others' responses to their writing, and use resources and make decisions about revising their writing. Even while beginning learners are developing morphological and syntactic accuracy, they can draw upon their sense of social protocols in their contextualized classroom communication through daily use of address terms and formulae for politeness. Daily writing in a dialogue journal helps learners develop fluency in expressing their concerns while at the same time gives teachers a window to look into learners' worlds and a chance to be responsive to their individual concerns. Prewriting activities help learners generate ideas to consider. When given the opportunities to draw on their own lives to make connections to content areas, second language learners can participate and build upon what they know to learn the conventions of writing. Using graphic organizers helps learners visualize connections that they can later attempt to communicate through writing. Making semantic maps extends their comprehension and use of content vocabulary. Instructional practices such as conferencing, writers/presenters workshop, and author's chair call upon writers to talk about their texts and gain practice developing their voice. By listening to peer responses, student writers benefit from the variety of ways others express sympathetic and critical readings of their messages. Through revision with peers and teacher conferences, students further build their ability to talk about their thinking. This talk about thinking then can guide attention to details in their writing and self-monitoring. Later, as they read their writing aloud to peers, reading and peer questions

THINK, PAIR, SHARE

After reading this chapter, complete the following activity with a partner.

1. Identify a concept about writing that you did not know before this reading.

_____

_____

2. Tell what you found helpful/difficult about writing.

_____

_____

3. Select topics that you would like to try or find out more about.

_____

_____

4. What additional aspects would you now consider in teaching your students to write?

_____

_____

scaffold future writing. This practice serves to also prepare them to participate in writer's workshops and author's chair to gain access to suggestions for useful revisions to their writing. Providing sufficient time for writing for particular audiences helps students value the revision process as an important step in writing.

When learners are guided through inquiries that they themselves plan, carry out, and evaluate, writing serves the multiple purposes for which it is authentically needed in each stage. Writing to learn, writing to read, writing to think, writing to start writing, and writing to communicate knowledge and feelings with particular audiences are part of the myriad purposes that students learn when they are engaged in schooling. Furthermore when learners see how their writing can make a difference in accumulating knowledge to change their social realities, they can reap the benefits of using a cultural tool that is highly valued.

WHAT DO TEACHERS THINK?

Denise Marie Greenberg, a fourth grade teacher who participated in the Springfield Learning Community Collaborative, wrote about her experiences joining her students in writing. She noticed how much more they became invested in their own writing when they also saw her writing. She shared her writing with them and their writing became less confusing. Denise also noticed that that they wrote longer and more edited writing by using dictionaries, thesauri, and encyclopedia. But one thing that really impressed Denise occurred when she introduced "group chats," sharing your writing with a group.

"In the beginning I initiated group chats, but in the end two of the members used this writing tool more than anyone. Katie was a bilingual member of the group. When she came to me in September she could speak English, but she could not read or write it. Her first pieces were always in Spanish. When she wrote to me in her journal, she also used Spanish. Gradually she began to feel comfortable taking risks, and she began to try out her English. Her first attempts were almost unintelligible, but she kept trying and I kept praising. Soon she turned to another student in the group for help. Kendall was also bilingual, but in the opposite way. She could speak Spanish, but she could not read or write. She was completely fluent in English. Katie formed a bond with Kendall during writing time. Whenever she could not remember a translation for a word, she would ask Kendall. She also turned to her to proofread her story. Katie progressed more than any other writer this year due to this open atmosphere. In April she wrote a two-page story about her trip to Boston. It was written completely in English. In May, she was our "Author of the Month." She read her fictional story "The Mermaid and the Bear" at the school's Authors' Party. . . . I am proud to say that Katie is now truly a bilingual child." (Brooke, Vanzant, Greenberg, Hudak, 1997)

FIELD-BASED EXPERIENCES

1. To construct meaningful writing lessons for the students, teachers get to know the educational histories and interests of their students. In particular, what past experiences do the learners have with written language in their primary language? What local knowledge do students have that can be used in content based inquiries, e.g., areas in which parents or relatives can share their particular expertise? Have students help map out these funds of knowledge that class members have in their families. Use a family tree to map out what each member of the family is good at doing. Make connections from these areas of knowledge to the content that is in your curriculum.

2. What oral language practices are used in the students' communities, e.g., folktales, poems, songs, proverbs? Formulate activities that could gather these into written genres to share with wider audiences.

3. Access to the Internet allows for students to reach distant audiences. In telexchange projects, several distant classes can jointly explore topics of mutual interest across the globe (Sayers & Cummins, 1999) and make use of both primary and second language to learn. What writing requirements in the content areas would offer you the possibility of involving your students in surveying, interviewing, or exploring a concept that interests them? Find out what projects have been carried out in your district and how these can benefit your students.

4. What types of non-English texts could be translated into English by your students to help others in the school or community learn about their cultures and

homelands? What content-related information about the contributions and accomplishments from their communities can be gathered and featured at school in exhibits, demonstrations, or assemblies? How could writing activities figure in these events?

CASE STUDY
SECONDARY ESL

This is an authentic example of using a sociocultural approach to learning, particularly language and literacy in all modalities to take a stance. The geology instructor originally used this for her students at the university level, yet we have modified it for ESL and foreign language learners in K–12. As you can see, a focus on language is necessary, but also integrated are science, government, legal, economic, justice, and social knowledge to deal with a conflict. They provide students with a vision of where they might potentially work (as lawyers, as expert scientists, as team members, etc.) and use knowledge as they construct the language use needed for these areas.

"Using a Mock Trial to Develop Scientific Literacy in Introductory Geology"

Amy L. Rhodes, Department of Geology, Smith College, Northampton, MA.

In 1999 and 2000, students in an introductory, environmental geology course (65 students) conducted a mock trial that examined evidence related to an actual legal case presented in the story "A Civil Action," by Jonathan Harr. This book recounts the lawsuit brought by eight families from Woburn, MA, who charged that two industrial companies illegally dumped trichloroethlene and other industrial waste, which subsequently entered the groundwater, contaminated two municipal water supply wells, and caused their children to contract leukemia. A civil action provided a framework for teaching basic geologic principles that relate to groundwater movement, human water supply, and connections between industrial contamination and health problems.

Students worked in "expert teams" hired by one of the opposing sides of the law case, Anne Anderson et al. vs. W. R. Grace & Co. and Beatrice Foods, Inc., and were subpoenaed to testify as expert witnesses. The groups collected scientific data from the literature, technical reports, newspaper stories, and Internet in subjects of groundwater geology, contaminant chemistry, medicine, and statistics. Collaboratively, each group developed an argument, which they testified and defended orally in front of a judge (a retired lawyer) and a jury during a three-hour trial. Groups of attorneys (students from the class) worked with expert teams to develop questions for testimonies and cross-examinations. In lieu of witness depositions, each team distributed a list of witnesses, a summary of intended testimony and copies of references, kept on reserve at the library. This allowed opposing sides to prepare for cross-examinations. Following the trial, each student authored an individually-written argument supported by her group's research, and provided a written analysis of the argument, based on how her group's testimony fared during cross-examination. The mock-trial provided a format for oral debate and research of scientific concepts. It facilitated teaching how to develop and defend ideas and to understand the limitations of scientific data in and out of the courtroom.

www.northeastgsa.org
In press. Geological Society of America Process
Boston 2001
www.geosociety.org

Activity: After reading the case study, answer the following questions and then share your responses with a partner.

1. What are potential social, political, or ecological issues that affect your community that students' views could help resolve? What areas might the students consider interesting enough to want to influence? Which content areas would be needed to address or resolve this issue? What types of written language practice would they need to accomplish their plan (e.g., concept maps, permission or invitation letters, summaries, graphs, oral presentations)? What resources would they need to find out additional information (e.g., content area teachers, experts, texts, tools)? Given your school calendar time constraints, what deadlines would need to be followed to produce the expected stages of writing and investigation?

2. For your assessment of the above project, map out what you would consider satisfactory progress in the written process and products at each stage of the project—from initiating the inquiry, to collecting and using resources, to analyzing and interpreting information, to drafting reports, to revision, rehearsal and presentation of their findings. What are the essential elements?

ACTION RESEARCH

Consider one of the following action research projects:

1. Gather samples of kindergarteners' initial writing. What evidence do their writings reveal about their knowledge of creating written texts? Identify discourse features (their orientation to text, type of genre organization, register, content vocabulary, and concepts). Then respond to the surface level: grammar, mechanics of spelling, punctuation, capitalization, spacing, etc. Create a log for each student that will help you keep track of their emerging knowledge in these areas and leave space for other learning that may be surprising or unexpected. Give a copy of the areas you will be documenting to the students for their portfolios. You can represent each category with colorful icons, e.g., orientation to text could be a pen poised on paper, genre organization could be a spider's web, register could be two hands clapping, content could be represented by tools used in class for each content area, a scale for math, a magnifying lens for science. This will help you and the learner discuss indicators of progress in writing conferences and help determine lessons for whole class instruction. Your logs and the student's portfolio will help you determine what level of progress has been made and what to consider in determining a corresponding grade.

2. Select a student in your class who is facing difficulty in writing. Which assignments cause difficulty and what patterns of language use constitute evidence of difficulty? In

these same assignments, what patterns of language use indicate the learner's strengths? What learning style seems to be represented? In a conference with the learner, find out what the learner notices about his or her own difficulty and strengths in the assignments. How were the instructions understood and followed? To what degree did the learner know the steps to complete the assignment? Is more time needed? What types of help were needed and used? Did the student have any interests or concerns about the assignment? Did the student know how to improve his or her writing on these assignments? Share what you noticed in the writing, beginning with the strengths. Without taking over the decision making, use this information to offer options of specific strategies for next steps. The learner can plan to use a limited number of strategies in the next assignment. Monitor how the learner takes control of the writing processes and how the writing changes. Share what you have learned about your struggling writer with your fellow teachers to get other suggestions about how to help the learner.

3. Together with a content area teacher, identify the types of writing that students need to accomplish during the year. On a chart define the particular features of language that are involved in this type of writing and the specific concepts that are being learned in this content area. Use this information to conference with teams of ESL learners to find out where the concepts from their content intersect with their lives. Allow each team to brainstorm possible projects to explore the themes in the school, families, or communities. Decide on how the learning will be documented; for example, though individual or group journal entries on daily progress, midterm reports, final oral presentations, final written presentations. What technologies will learners need to carry out their inquiries? Build in time to orient students to lab equipment, computer applications, Internet and library resources as well as for the writing necessary to collect this information: note-taking, citation of sources, interview questions and protocol, etc. What progress do your students make in both classes? How well do students learn in both classes? What parts of your collaboration with the content area teacher need to improve?

ADDITIONAL RESOURCES

Text Resources

Cummins, J., & Sayers, D. (1997). *Brave new schools: Challenging cultural illiteracy through global learning networks.* New York: St. Martin's Press.

Freeman, Y., & Freeman, D. (1997). *Teaching reading and writing in Spanish in a bilingual classroom.* Portsmouth, NH: Heinemann.

Hyun, E. (1998). *Making sense of developmentally and culturally appropriate practice (DCAP) in early childhood education.* New York: Peter Lang.

Peitzman, F., & Gadda, G. (1994). *With different eyes: Insights into teaching language minority students across the disciplines.* Reading, MA: Addison Wesley.

Scott, V. M. (1996). *Rethinking foreign language writing.* Boston: Heinle and Heinle.

Wilhelm, J., & Edmiston, B. (1998). *Imagining to learn: Inquiry, ethics, and integration through drama.* Portsmouth, NH: Heinemann.

Electronic Resources

Foreign language list for elementary school teachers: *Nandu@caltalk.cal.org*

Journal of Second Language Writing: http://www.jslw.org

Second language lists: International EFL/ESL student discussion lists

Spanish language teachers and students: *http://www.nueva-tierra.com*

http:/www.Latrobe.edu.au and click on "teaching and learning"

Classroom Connect: http://www.quest.classroom.com

Epal.com *http://www.epals.com/*

Intercultural E-mail Classroom Connections Web page: www.teaching.com/IECC/home.cfm

Learnz 2001: http://socialstudies.unitecnology.ac.nz/ourplace/

Information on netiquette: http://users.rcn.com/mobius.ma.ultranet/Roadmap/map07.html

Discourse Features

The following are several features of discourse that writers use to engage a reader. This list is not exhaustive. Rather, it selects a few of the most commonly used features in each phase of the composition.

PHASE:	
Introducing the topic	Orienting devices
	1. Rhetorical question
	2. Explicit identification of a problem, controversy, or claim
	3. Quotation, joke, anecdote related to the topic
	4. Definition of the words or concepts in title
	5. Competing opinions on an issue
	6. Outlining past work on the topic
	7. Explaining the author's own interest
Developing the paragraph	1. Define an issue in the topic sentence by elaborating on its components or characteristics
	2. Build contrasting points to the issues in the topic sentence
	3. Provide examples that support the topic sentence
	4. Provide statements that qualify or restrict the meanings of the topic sentence
Building cohesion	1. Selective repetition of words, images, metaphors

2. Temporal

3. Spatial

4. Chronological

5. Reference: pronoun use, demonstrative adjectives, etc.

6. Transitional phrases

7. Maintaining sentence structures that support the topic, e.g., topicalization

Concluding

1. Brief restatement of main points

2. Connecting back to introduction with a twist made possible by the information presented

3. Closing with a quote that captures main feelings evoked by the information presented

4. Call to action that reader can take in response to the information presented

1. Create a list of the types of writing presented in this text. Which type of writing was the easiest for you? What was the most difficult? What strategies have you used to carry out these difficult writings? What has been effective for you?

With which of the types of writing identified above do your students might have difficulty? What type of support will you build into your lesson?

FIGURE 7.1

GLOSSARY OF TERMS

appropriation   process by which an individual gains ability to manage his/her own activity and learn. This occurs because of active participation in social interaction in particular contexts.

argumentation structure   a variety of ways "to make a point" by use of models, dissociation (hierarchical ordering of concepts and disengagement, etc.), and stylistic devices such as analogy, personification and metaphor

critical language awareness   an approach that helps learners understand how language encodes power relationships through linguistic structures and vocabulary choices

critical literacy   an approach to understanding that all texts as political and that represent particular interests/perspectives

critical studies   a field of research into culture, communication, social sciences, and humanities that sees all human activity as political and constructed by discourses that maintain ideological positions. Julia Kristeva, Edward Hall, Roland Barthes, Judith Butler, Michel Foucault, and Jacques Derrida are several of the prominent scholars who have made contributions in this area.

discourse features   all the devices and cues that activate a particular interpretation or understanding of a text. For example, hearing the introduction "Ladies and Gentlemen" allows you to quickly infer that you are listening to a public announcer because you remember past instances of public announcers.

epideictic rhetoric   has four characteristics: 1) assumes audience agrees with the speaker, 2) makes use of patterns and arguments familiar to the audience, 3) aims to reinforce and emphasize shared values rather than to stimulate critical thinking and deliberation, 4) succeeds when the audience comes to admire the presentation (Warnick, 2002)

errors   produced by misapplication of rules when knowledge or skill or both are not yet fully developed

expressive writing   writing after reading in an effort to capture thoughts, concerns, and feelings about what was read

gatekeepers   members of a group that take on the role of deciding who is allowed into the group or who is excluded

intertexuality   the presence of a variety of sources of knowledge in a text

invented spellings   learner's use of own sound/symbol representation, often from primary language if learner is literate in primary language; is a sign that learner is starting to develop sound/symbol correspondences. Later this develops into more conventionalized spelling.

language socialization   how your participation in recurrent communication in everyday life helps you become a member of the community using that language by sharing ways of interpreting and constructing

literacy event   events using oral or written communication to share or build knowledge, problem solve, or use cultural tools, e.g., sharing time and activities at home or in institutions, moments where teaching and learning take place to transmit or transform knowledge

local knowledge   knowledge created from learners' experiences with others in their communities

mistakes   produced by performances that are not fully attended to, i.e., learners can correct these if given time to revise

narrative structures   ways in which texts are structured

print-rich environment   classrooms where a variety of written texts are available for use

reader responsive prose   written text that has sufficient details and structure to convey author's intended message

register   level of formality, politeness, etc., to be considered appropriate for a particular audience

rhetorical devices   ways language is used to produce an effect on audience (to distance, create interest, solidarity, etc.); Aristotle identified three types of rhetoric: deliberative (advise for future), judicial (to consider the past), and epideictic (ceremonial).

scribing   writing down what someone else says as a record of the event

style   the overall pattern of semiotic features in a text

transactional writing   language that is used to inform, persuade, convince, etc.; contrast and compare to interpersonal language

voice   the ability of the learner to use written language to evoke communicatively a notion of self

---

REFERENCES

Auerbach, E. (1992). *Making meaning. Making change.* Washington, DC. Educational Resource Information Center, Center for Applied Linguistics.

Bartolomé, L. (1998). *The misteaching of academic discourses: The politics of language in the classroom.* Boulder, CO: Westview Press.

Bereiter, C., & Scardamalia, M. (1987). *The Psychology of Written Composition.* Hillsdale, NJ: Erlbaum.

Biber, D. (1995). *Dimensions of register variation: Across-linguistic comparison.* Cambridge: Cambridge University Press.

Biber, D., Reppen, R., & Conrad, S. (1998). *Corpus linguistics: Investigating language structure.* Cambridge: Cambridge University Press.

Blanton, L. L. (2002). Seeing the invisible: Situating L2 literacy in Child-teacher interaction. *Journal of Second Language Writing, 11*(4), 295–310.

Blanton, L. L. (1987). Reshaping ESL students' perceptions of writing. *ELT Journal, 41*(2), 112–118.

Bliss, A. (2001). Rhetorical structures for multilingual and multicultural students. In C. Gilliam Panetta (Ed.) (pp. 15–30), *Contrastive rhetoric revisited and redefined.* Mahwah, NJ: Lawrence Erlbaum.

Brooke, E. Vanzant, T., Greenberg, D., & Hudak, K. (1997). *Exploring Changes in Instruction. Teacher Research Reports from the Springfield Learning Community Collaborative.* Dr. J. Willett & Dr. J. Solsken, Co-Principal Investigators, University of Massachusetts, Amherst: School of Education.

Cole, M. (1996). *Cultural pedagogy. Once and future discipline.* Cambridge, MA: Harvard University Press.

Corbett, J. (2001). Contrastive rhetoric and resistance to writing. In C. G. Panetta. (Ed.) (pp. 31–46), *Contrastive rhetoric revisited.* Mahwah, NJ: Lawrence Erlbaum.

Cummins, J. & Sayers, D. (Spring 1995). Multicultural education and technology: Promise and pitfalls. *Multicultural Education*, pp. 4–11.

Duff, P. (2001). Language, literacy, content and (pop) culture: Challenges for ESL students in mainstream courses. *Canadian Modern Language Review, 58*(1), 103–132.

Dyson, A. H. (1997). *Writing superheroes: Contemporary childhood, popular culture, and classroom literacy.* New York: Teachers College Press.

Edelsky, C. (1982). Writing in a bilingual program. *TESOL Quarterly, 16*, 211–28.

Ferris, D. (1997). The influence of teacher commentary on student revision. *TESOL Quarterly, 31*, 315–39.

Flecha, R. (2000). *Sharing words: Theory and practice of dialogic learning.* Lanham, MD: Rowman & Littlefield.

Fox, H. (1994). *Listening to the world: Cultural issues in academic writing.* Urbana, IL: National Council of Teachers of English.

Franklin, E. (1999). The fiction writing of two Dakota boys. In Franklin, E. (Ed.) *Reading and writing in more than one language: Lessons for teachers.* Alexandria, Va.: Teachers of English to Speakers of Other Languages.

Franklin, E. (Ed.) (1999). *Reading and writing in more than one language: Lessons for teachers.* Alexandria, VA: Teachers of English to Speakers of Other Languages.

Fu, D. (1995). *"My trouble is my English": Asian students and the American dream.* Portsmouth, NH: Boynton/Cook Publishers.

Gallas, K. (1992). When children take the chair: A study of sharing time in a primary classroom. *Language Arts, 69*, 172–82.

Gee, J. (1993). *An introduction to human language. Fundamental concepts in linguistics.* Englewood Cliffs, NJ: Prentice Hall.

Goldstein, L. (2001). For Kyla: What does the research say about responding to ESL writers. In T. Silva & P. K. Matsuda (Eds.) (pp. 73–89), *On second language writing.* Mahwah, NJ: Lawrence Erlbaum.

Goldstein, L., & Conrad, S. (1990). Student input and negotiation of meaning in ESL writing conferences. *TESOL Quarterly, 24,* 441–60.

Grabe, W. (2001). Reading-writing relations: Theoretical perspectives and instructional practices. In D. Belcher & A. Hirvela (Eds). (pp. 15–47), *Linking literacies. Perspectives on L2 reading-writing connections.* Ann Arbor, MI: University of Michigan Press.

Grabe, B. (2001). Notes toward a theory of second language writing. In T. Silva & P. K. Matsuda (Eds.) (pp. 39–57), *On second language writing.* Mahwah, NJ: Lawrence Erlbaum.

Grabe, W., & Kaplan, R. B. (1996). *Theory and practice of writing.* New York: Longman.

Grabe, W., & Kaplan, R. B. (1997). The writing course, In K. Barrdoovi-Harlig & B. Hratford (Eds.) (pp. 172–97), *Beyond methods: Components of second language teacher education.* New York: McGraw-Hill.

Guerra, J. (1998). *Close to home: Oral and literate practices in a transnational Mexicano community.* New York: Teachers College Press.

Gutiérrez, K., Baquedano-Lopez, P., Alvarez, H., & Chu, M. (1999). A cultural-historical approach to collaboration: Building a culture of collaboration through hybrid language practices. *Theory into Practice, 38* (2), 87–93.

Hayes, C., Bahruth, R., & Kessler, C. (1998). *Literacy con cariño.* Portsmouth, NH: Heinemann.

Hayes, J. (1996). A new framework for understanding cognition and affect in writing. In C. M. Levy & S. Ransdell (Eds.), (pp. 1–27), *The science of writing.* Mahwah, NJ: Lawrence Erlbaum.

Johns, A. (1990). Coherence as a cultural phenomenon. In U. Connor & A. M. Johns (Eds.) (pp. 211–26), *Coherence in writing: Research and pedagogical perspectives.* Alexandria, VA: TESOL.

Johns, A. (1992). Toward developing a cultural repertoire: A case study of a Lao college freshman. In D. Murray (Ed.) (pp. 183–201), *Diversity as resource: Redefining cultural literacy.* Alexandria, VA: TESOL.

Kaplan, R. B. (1966). Cultural thought patterns in intercultural education. *Language Learning, 16,* 1–20.

Krapels, A. (1990). An overview of second language writing process research. In B. Kroll (Ed.) *Second language writing.* Cambridge, UK: Cambridge University Press.

Leki, I. (1995). Coping strategies of ESL students in writing tasks across the curriculum. *TESOL Quarterly, 29,* 235–60.

Li, X. (1996). *Good writing in crosscultural context.* Albany, NY: State University of New York Press.

Lu, M. (1987) From silence to words: Writing as struggle. *College English, 49,* 437–48.

Luke, A., O'Brien, J., & Comber, B. (2001). Making community texts objects of study. In. H. Fehring & P. Green (Ed.) (pp. 112–23), *Critical Literacy. A collection of articles from the Australian Literacy Educators' Association.* Newark, DE: International Reading Association.

Martin-Jones, M., & Jones, K. (2000). *Multilingual literacies.* Philadelphia: John Benjamins.

North, S. (1987). *The making of knowledge in composition.* Portsmouth, NH: Heinemann.

O'Brien, J. (2001). Children reading critically: A local history. In B. Comber & A. Simpson (Eds.) (pp. 37–54), *Negotiating critical literacies in classrooms.* Mahwah, NJ: Lawrence Erlbaum.

Sayers, D. (1993). Distance team teaching and computer learning networks. *TESOL Journal, 3*(1), 19–23.

Scollon, R. (1995). Plagiarism and ideology. Identity in intercultural discourse. *Language & Society, 24,* 1–28.

Spack, R. (1997). The acquisition of academic literacy in a second language: A longitudinal case study. *Written Communication, 14,* 3–62.

Spolsky, B. (1989). *Conditions for second language learning.* New York: Oxford University Press.

Staton, J., Shuy, R., Kreeft Peyton, J., & Reed, L. (Eds.) (1988). *Communication, 107,* 13–142. Norwood: Ablex.

Valdes, G. (1996). *Con respeto: Bridging the distances between culturally diverse families and schools—An ethnographic portrait.* New York: Teachers College Press.

Vasquez, O. (2002). A participatory perspective on parent involvement. To appear in J. Mora & D. Diaz (Eds.) *Research in action: A participatory model for advancing Latino social policy.* Binghamton, NY: Haworth Press.

Vasquez, O., Pease-Alvarez, L., & Shannon, S. (1994). *Pushing boundaries: Language and culture in a Mexicano community.* New York: Cambridge University Press.

Vasquez, V. (2001). Constructing a critical curriculum with young children. In B. Comber & A. Simpson (Eds.) (pp. 55–66), *Negotiating critical literacies in classrooms.* Mahwah, NJ: Lawrence Erlbaum.

Ventola, E., & Mauranen, A. (Eds.). (1996). *Academic writing:Intercultural and textual issues.* Amsterdam: John Benjamins.

Vernon, S., & Ferreiro, E. (1999). Writing development: A neglected variable in the consideration of phonological awareness. *Harvard Educational Review,* Winter, 395–415.

Zamel, V. (1985). Responding to student writing. *TESOL Quarterly, 19,* 79–102.

Zamel, V. (1990). Through students' eyes: The experiences of three ESL writers. *Journal of Basic Writing, 9,* 83–98.

CHAPTER EIGHT

AN INTERACTIVE APPROACH FOR WORKING WITH DIVERSE LEARNERS

THIS CHAPTER WILL FEATURE

- Learner-centered instruction
- Culturally and linguistically diverse students

YOU WILL EXAMINE

- Pedagogical implications for working with diverse students
- The theory of multiple intelligences

INTRODUCTION: SETTING THE STAGE

The past ten to fifteen years has witnessed a simultaneous decline in the number of African American, Hispanic, Asian, and Native American teachers in U.S. schools and an increase in the number of students among these same groups. This decline, unfortunately, also holds true in second/foreign language classrooms. The low number of ethnic minority second/foreign language teachers reflects an overall decline in the number of minority (persons of color) teachers. Both declines pose serious threats to effective education in the twenty-first century. A reduction in the number of ethnically diverse teachers makes our schools less able to reflect the diversity of their students. A shift in the demographics of the United States, coupled with special attention to our nation's educational goals and standards, has created a fertile opportunity for creating change in our teaching force in order to meet the needs of the pluralistic classrooms of the twenty-first century. This chapter will focus on an interactive approach for working with diverse learners. We examine the impact of demographics on classroom diversity and explore pedagogical implications for working with students from multilingual and multicultural backgrounds.

THINK, PAIR, SHARE

Before you begin reading this chapter, complete the following activity with a partner.

1. What are your beliefs about diverse learners?

   _____

   _____

2. In what way(s) do the changing demographics impact classroom diversity?

   _____

   _____

3. How do you define *diverse?*

   _____

   _____

The United States is currently experiencing the greatest level of racial and ethnic diversity since its inception—and 500,000 legal and approximately 200,000 illegal immigrants have contributed to the population increases. By 2010, minorities will constitute one third of the nation (American Council on Education, 1988, as quoted in AACTE, 1990).

With projections that students of color will make up about 46% of the nation's student population by 2020 (Pallas et al, p. 19), greater attention must be given to ensuring that multilingual/multicultural populations succeed in mainstream education. Those involved in decision-making processes must understand how language, culture, and other background characteristics influence performance. Changing demographics in the United States have often been cited as reasons to mandate training in multicultural and multilingualism for pre-service and in-service teachers (e.g., Garcia & Pugh, 1992; Dunn, 1993; Banks, (1997). Bruder (1992) indicated that by the year 2010, California, Florida, Texas, and New York will contain one-third of all United States youth. In Texas and California, 57 percent of those youth will be nonwhite, and in New York and Florida, 53 percent will be nonwhite. **Culturally and linguistically diverse (CLD)** students with special needs should be served by general and special educators who have been effectively trained in how culture and language influence learning. Teacher preparation plays a vital role in providing both pre- and in-service educators with an understanding of cultural, linguistic, socioeconomic, and related variables and their effects on the teaching-learning process. Additionally, training must include methods of using assessment data to plan instruction and to select, adapt, and/or develop curricula to meet the needs of CLD students with special needs.

The demographic characteristics of today's classrooms are very different than they were twenty years ago and according to Banks (1997) by the year 2020 "[w]hites will make up only 54.5% of the nation's population" (p. 5) and students of color will comprise 45.5 percent of that population. This change in population brings new opportunities and challenges for teachers.

The CEC recognizes that changing demographics and cultural and linguistic diversity will continue to increase while the number of culturally and linguistically different professionals entering the field of special education continues to decline. According to the CEC, "Given the pervasive nature of diversity, professional standards are needed that guide professional practice in ways that are relevant to the multicultural populations served in special education. Specifically, these standards reflect the premise that, to design effective interventions, special educators must understand the characteristics of their learners, including factors such as culture, language, gender, religion, and sexuality."

States such as California, Texas, Florida, New York, Massachusetts, Connecticut, Michigan, Illinois, and Ohio, in which the population of CLD students has increased significantly, have initiated Bilingual Special Education programs (Ortiz & Ramirez, 1988). As a result, there has been a push to combine both bilingual education and special education to meet the needs of CLD exceptional students across the nation.

Although literature on CLD students with special needs is now more generally available, research on the impact of literacy occurring with linguistic and cultural differences is scarcer. What is even scarcer is the amount of information on educating teachers to work in school settings with this ever-increasing population of students. The available literature calls attention to such issues as the disproportionate representation (there are more CLD students in special education than maybe there should be) of CLD students in special education and the need for better prepared and trained teachers. There is also a great deal of attention paid to federal legislative compliance with regard to educating special needs students.

FEDERAL LEGISLATION'S INFLUENCE

Shortly after the 2000 presidential election, George W. Bush made plans for reauthorizing the Elementary and Secondary Education Act—"No Child Left Behind." This would serve as a centerpiece for a new domestic agenda. The new law, Title III, is named the English Language Acquisition, Language Enhancement, and Academic Achievement Act. This law requires annual testing of all students in grades 3 through 8. Inherent in this law is the roadblock that is imposed on English Language Learners since these tests are based on a certain level of English Language proficiency.

In the United States during the past ten years many empirical and legal issues related to the education of linguistically diverse students with disabilities have received special attention and litigation. According to Duran (1988) the right for appropriate special education services to linguistically diverse handicapped students was specifically established with the passage of Public Law 93-112, the Rehabilitation Act of 1973.

As a direct result of the implementation of Public Law 94-142 in 1975, the Education Act for all Handicapped (EAH), and the Rehabilitation Act of 1973, Section 504, the individual needs of exceptional bilingual (linguistically diverse) students have received much needed attention (Ortiz & Ramirez, 1988). Consequently, a process for providing special education to meet the individual needs of each student with disabilities was started. Since then, more than 4 million students have been identified as having some type of disability (Ortiz & Ramirez).

Individuals with Disabilities Education Act (IDEA) of 1997 strengthens the concept of least restrictive environment for children with disabilities. It can be argued that the provision of this environment, in the case of linguistically diverse students requires teachers appropriately and effectively trained in both special education and English as a Second Language. IDEA is the first major education law considered by the 108th Congress. English Language Learners who are also disabled should be protected by IDEA.

There are two critical issues at stake here:

1. The language needs of a disabled English Language Learner should be considered in the Individual Education Plan (IEP).
2. Evaluations and assessments of English Language Learners should examine the disability rather than measure the students' language skills.

In spite of these federal laws, the majority of special education programs as presently structured do not meet the needs of limited English proficiency students. IDEA does not address the training or preparedness of teachers or the language of instruction issues. As a consequence, most special education programs are staffed by teachers with little to no training for working with linguistically diverse student populations.

CLASSROOM DIVERSITY: A REALITY IN U.S. EDUCATION

It is quite obvious that the notion of a pluralistic system of education in the United States continues to be undermined by factors such as social, economic, and cultural disparities. These are especially apparent among K–12 student populations. Compare the average test scores from kindergarten through the twelfth grade between a public school with a predominantly white, middle-class population and that of any public, inner-city school, attended primarily by students from low-income families. Weigh the availability of school supplies, the demand for qualified teachers, and the actual condition of the school buildings between a poverty-ridden public school district in Washington, D.C., where white students make up less than 5 percent of the student body (Rivkin, 1994), and one in an affluent neighborhood in nearby Northern Virginia. It is impossible to pretend that the current generations of students are all receiving the same quality of education, the same chances for academic success, and an equal opportunity to develop into self-realized, highly skilled adults. Sadly, educators' beliefs and expectations of children from a lower socioeconomic class or an ethnically diverse background (Wigfield, Galper, Denton & Seefeldt, 1999), and prevalent institutional and social representations of these children (Harklau, 2000) reflect and may exacerbate these educational inequities.

If, in addition to coming from a family background and belonging to an ethnic cultural minority, a child is also not yet fluent in English, his/her chances of receiving an education equal to that of native-born, white, middle-class peers seems even more unlikely. Students who are coming from all over the world enroll in US schools as economic and political refugees. Consequently language instruction must begin with an assumption that all children come to school with varying access to academic environments and materials. However, it is essential to also realize that the classroom potentially becomes richer in resources for linguistic and particularly cultural learning with these students as active members. As a teacher, you can make this a successful and fertile setting for learning by welcoming the children *as contributing members of the group*, varying instruction both directed for their specific needs in separate groups as well as when included. Actively seek out activities and lessons that encourage students to work cooperatively with second language learners.

As individuals, it is our own culture that is the filter through which we interpret and relate to those who come from cultures different from our own. As educators, it is our responsibility to recognize that events in life have no meaning apart from our interpretation of them and our perceptions depend on our frames of reference (Canfield & Siccone, 1995). The school setting in which we teach is itself such a reference: an institution with a defined culture and philosophy (Richards & Lockhart, 1994). Teachers' practices and attitudes are also directly influenced by federal, state, and local policies (Marusza, 1998) that contribute to the type of student expectations they will have. As an educator you will discover that teaching is an activity tremendously influenced by culturally-influenced assumptions about teaching and learning. You will want to be on guard to determine the source of those assumptions and their potential effect on your students.

Preconceived notions made by teachers and administrators are the images held about students' backgrounds, experiences, and needs, and are "the archetypes with which students are labeled which result from attempts to hold a heterogeneous and evolving social world still long enough to make sense of it" (Harklau, 2000, p. 37). Negative stereotypes of what an ESL student is have direct consequences on decisions about curriculum and instructional practices, and affect students' motivation and achievement.

Cummins (1997) determined that low socioeconomic status and minority students are more at risk of negative teacher expectancy effects, and teachers' beliefs about a child are influenced by that child's gender and ethnicity (Wigfield, Galper, Denton, & Seefeldt, 1999). In addition, negative stereotypes that extend to children from other cultures who are learning English as a second language may become internalized by those children (Richard-Amato, 1988) and could undermine their attempts at language acquisition.

PEDAGOGICAL IMPLICATIONS FOR WORKING WITH DIVERSE LEARNERS

It is very likely that you will find yourself in any given school year standing in front of a class comprised of the following: Students who have a) *different linguistic levels*, b) *different languages*, and/or c) *different academic levels*. These same students may be enrolled in bilingual education, English-only, or an ESL class. These are some of the

THINK, PAIR, AND SHARE

1. Think of nonverbal answering practices (body language) that are commonly used in classrooms and brainstorm with a partner to create a list like the following:

   hand raising
   pointing
   standing on line

   _____

   _____

Now think about how these may be integrated into an early phase of a lesson.

2. What other ways could students use the list you generated to signal their comprehension?

   _____

   _____

challenges teachers face every day. How then do you turn these challenges into opportunities via effective instructional and assessment practices?

Different linguistic levels—Because students have a variety of proficiency levels, you will want to provide instruction that allows students to work where they are most comfortable, yet allows them to progress and move forward. Take advantage of the following *opportunities:* Peer tutoring, group work, group projects, cooperative learning.

Different languages—As the teacher you may know one, some, or none of the languages spoken by your students. Therefore, you must ensure that your students learn and understand the material being covered. Take advantage of the following *opportunities:* Visual, auditory, and kinesthetic-oriented lessons. Allow students to use manipulatives and pay careful attention to their preferred learning styles and intelligences.

Different academic levels—You may have students who are newly arrived to the United States and who have little or no formal schooling. Additionally, there may be gaps in their schooling history. Your challenge is to meet the academic needs of every student. Take advantage of the following *opportunities:* Alternating heterogeneous and homogeneous grouping, cooperative learning, and peer tutoring. You will also want to incorporate a variety of teaching methods and approaches.

As discussed in chapter 2, various approaches can be used to instruct second language learners. One approach, which stresses comprehension and does not require learners to use the spoken word until they feel inclined to do so, is Total Physical Response (TPR). Evaluations of this approach have indicated that it is very successful

(Krashen, 1985). You will recall that TPR involves students in physical responses to increasingly complex instructions from the teacher (or fellow student). This approach may be particularly suited to the needs of diverse learners who do well with physical activities and movement or whose verbal abilities are limited in the language. This represents listening and doing and is evident in the Bodily/Kinesthetic intelligence described by Howard Gardner (1983).

The principle of TPR is to find ways in which children can signal their comprehension in nonlinguistic terms and still gradually build up their oral proficiency.

LEARNER-CENTERED INSTRUCTION IN AN INTERACTIVE, CONTENT-BASED CLASSROOM

The principle in this section of the chapter examines ways in which teachers can build on children's diverse abilities. Two directions are provided: a multiple intelligence (psychological) and a multiple resources perspective (sociocultural). Learner-centered instruction is based on the premise that children learn more effectively by becoming active participants in the process. This translates to giving students an environment ripe for discovery and the tools with which to explore it. As their teacher, you are their guide and they are the ones in charge of finding answers or information. This progressive and exciting style of teaching sets the stage for students to not only learn but also think about the way they learn in a fun way.

MULTIPLE INTELLIGENCES

According to Gardner's theory, there are eight intelligences: Bodily/Kinesthetic, Interpersonal/Social, Intrapersonal/Introspective, Logical/Mathematical, Musical/Rhythmic, Naturalist, Verbal/Linguistic, and Visual/Spatial (see table on page 34). Every learner has the capacity to exhibit all of these intelligences, but some are more highly developed than others in certain individuals. Based on multiple intelligences (MI) theory, the challenge in education is for teachers to create learning environments that foster the development of all *eight* intelligences. Balanced instructional presentations that encourage addressing the multiple intelligences benefit all learners and expose students to the appropriate means of strengthening their underutilized intelligences.

Haley (2001) conducted a national teacher action research study that investigated the applications of the Theory of Multiple Intelligences to shape and inform teaching practices and instructional strategies. The purpose of the study was to identify, document, and promote effective real-world applications of MI theory in foreign and second language classrooms. Results indicated that teachers were profoundly affected by the approaches: They felt that their teaching experienced a shift in paradigm to a more learner-centered classroom; they were once again energized and enthusiastic about their pedagogy; and they felt that they were able to reach more students.

The literature on multiple intelligences provides a sound theoretical foundation for an integrated, multidimensional style of education across learning styles and cultures. However, there is a paucity of research in practical applications of MI theory in foreign and second language classrooms.

Bodily/Kinesthetic	Role playing; dancing; TPR, TPRS, hands-on learning, manipulatives; multimedia games or activities; aerobic alphabet; building a model or 3-D project
Interpersonal/Social	Cooperative teams; paired activities; peer teaching; board games; simulations; surveys and polls; group brainstorming; situations or dialogues
Intrapersonal/Introspective	Describe/write about preferred way(s) of spending free time; keep a journal on a particular topic; engage in independent study
Logical/Mathematical	Word order activities; grammar relationships; pattern games; number activities; classifying and categorizing; sequencing information; computer games; cause-and-effect activities
Musical/Rhythmical	Write jingles for a commercial; jazz chants to remember vocabulary/grammar/verbs; musical cloze activities; create music for skits and plays; use music as a stimulator; look for tonal/rhythmic patterns in music of target language
Naturalist	Describe changes in the local environment; debate the issue of homeopathic medicine versus store-bought remedies; plan a campaign drive which focuses on saving an endangered species
Verbal/Linguistic	Debates; storytelling; online communications (E-pals); group discussions; word-processing programs; word games
Visual/Spatial	Using graphs and diagrams; drawing a response; video exercises; computer slide shows; multimedia projects; mind mapping; graphic organizers

FIGURE 8.1   Multiple Intelligences' Instructional Strategies and Activities

Practical applications of MI theory can be found in techniques used in many progressive classrooms today. The key to turning this theory into constructive practice is to present information and skill building in ways that address all kinds of learners. This is especially true when working with second language learners. Figure 8.1 identifies the types of activities best suited to different kinds of intelligence. The following ideas can help you construct an environment conducive to accessible, successful learning for all students. Each idea takes into account the eight intelligences described by Gardner.

1. Centers—These learning areas are the single most powerful classroom tool you can use to reach all different learners in your classroom. Develop brief and pointed activities for each space aimed at teaching a theme or unit. Material should be presented in various ways and require the students to complete an activity for each center. Try to touch on all intelligences, combining them and in some cases highlighting one specific idea.

2. Real-life scenarios/Role play—Pull your students into situations by having them act out stories or content objectives. This method of teaching allows students to once again work in groups and express ideas in their own ways. By doing this, you are making the material come alive for the student and giving them a way to internalize it for individualized comprehension.

3. Cooperative learning groups—Small groups of students at varied levels of learning can be each others' best teachers. Cooperative learning is the foundation for almost all activities in a thriving diverse classroom. The partnerships created by doing activities in this way foster not only fruitful learning, but also lend themselves to becoming a nonthreatening environment where risk-taking can lead to enhanced knowledge development.

The key to using MI theory effectively is to find ways to meld cultural, traditional, and individual learning tendencies together to provide a fresh and horizon broadening learning environment. Gardner's seminal work on this subject, *Frames of Mind* (1983), devotes over 300 pages to explaining and differentiating what were then conceived as six intelligences, but only two chapters (60 pages) to the implications and applications of MI theory in education.

A lively defense of Gardner's theory is presented in the article, "Where Do the Learning Theories Overlap?" (Guild, 1997). The author compares the key features and principles of three learning theories: multiple intelligences, learning styles, and brain-based education. He concludes that these theories intersect significantly, particularly in terms of their intended results. One point in common is that these theories are learner-centered. Another similarity is the teacher's role as **reflective practitioner** and facilitator, with the student acting as a reflective partner. An additional mutual theme of these theories is the concern they have for the education of the whole person. All three theories emphasize curricula with depth and breadth. Additionally, MI theory, learning styles, and brain-based education promote diversity and inclusiveness, rather than the "lowest common denominator" approach to teaching. These three approaches focus on how students learn differently, acknowledging that: "The more diverse learning experiences we provide our students, the more robust their education will be, the more ways they will learn each topic, hence the more they are prepared to succeed in a world marked by increasing diversity and an accelerating change rate" (Kagan & Kagan, 1998, p. xxi).

Learner-centered instruction in a content-based classroom can be greatly enhanced if you are aware of your students' multiple intelligences and can also accomodate their varied learning styles. Multiple intelligences and learning styles are *not* synonymous. Gardner's theory (1983) defines intelligence as "an ability to solve problems, or to create products that are valued within one or more cultures." When working with diverse students instructional planning and assessment will benefit from knowledge of your students' intelligences and learning styles.

LEARNING STYLES

Learning styles refers to each student's pattern of preferences or strengths that affect the ability to "concentrate, practice, internalize and retain new and difficult information" (Marshall, 1997). A **learning style** is a general approach a learner uses to learn a new language (Scarcella & Oxford, 1992, p. 61). This can also be applied to all subjects. Learning styles represent a person's most comfortable way of attaining knowledge.

Learning styles research has provided a context for examining a change in moving from teacher-centered to student-centered instructional strategies and assessments. We are learning that each student's pattern of success is affected by the genetic, cultural, and developmental factors that constitute his or her unique learning style (Marshall).

Learning styles can be categorized into three areas: **global, analytic,** or **integrated.** The table below shows the three areas and corresponding characteristics.

A learning style is a general approach a learner uses to learn a new language (Scarcella & Oxford, 1992, p. 61). Oxford (1990) and Scarcella and Oxford identified five key elements of language learning styles:

1. Analytical-global—demonstrates the difference between a detail-oriented learner and a holistic one. This learner focuses on grammatical details and enjoys looking up words in the dictionary, rather than trying to guess their meaning.

2. Sensory preferences—demonstrates the physical, perceptual ways of learning. These may be visual, auditory, and hands-on (kinesthetic). Visual learners prefer visual cues or an opportunity to read information. Auditory learners like conversations and hearing the lesson's content. Kinesthetic learners do well in environments in which they can physically move around or are provided with manipulatives that aid in comprehension.

3. Intuitive/random and sensory/sequential learning—demonstrates the type of organization a learner prefers in the presentation of material. Intuitive/random learners frequently think in a somewhat abstract way—nonsequential or random. Sensory/sequential learners prefer to learn in an ordered step-by-step linear progression.

4. Orientation to closure—demonstrates those learners who need to reach conclusions and will not tolerate ambiguity. These learners are often characterized by wanting the rules spelled out for them.

5. Competition-cooperation—demonstrates those learners who benefit from competing against or cooperating with their peers. Competitive learners are often motivated by the thrill of winning. Cooperative learners enjoy working with others in a collaborative manner.

CULTURALLY RELEVANT PEDAGOGY

In the past, ethnic communities could be found entirely made of members from one dominant group or another. However, due to globalization and economic changes around the world, immigration to the United States has sharply increased. This movement has resulted in a very diverse student population. Few suburban classrooms remain untouched by this diversity. Now more than ever it is important to recognize each child's cultural and linguistic resources. Harness these resources and use them to

GLOBAL	ANALYTIC	INTEGRATED
Reads for overall idea, skipping details	Concentrates on tasks at hand	
Likes team competitions	Analyzes problem, then decides	
Relates what is taught to own experiences	Prefers to work independently on projects	
Likes working with others	Likes to organize assignments	
Understands thinking "in context"	Prefers options	
Can work on several projects at one time	Remembers details	
Reads between the lines	Consistent with rules, assignments	

Source: Adapted from Marshall (1997)

not only teach democracy but have a classroom that demonstrates it. The struggle many teachers face is how to make this work.

From a sociocultural perspective, every child comes to school with cultural resources. Unfortunately, not all resources are equally valued in schooling. Often it is explained that schools, like all public institutions, become sites of cultural struggles. Conflicts arise when the cultural values of a group are not recognized as important. This is particularly true in a classroom where all students must have equal opportunities to learn in order to be successful. Cultural clashes in a classroom occur over issues such as how to participate appropriately, how to demonstrate learning, and how to apply learning. These essential aspects of the educational process can become major obstacles for students from other cultures. It is important at the onset to help the students become aware of the cultural norms of the school and the classroom. Without these tools, they are less likely to actively engage in the learning and therefore also less likely to achieve. A culturally relevant, diversified learning space, and motivating educational experience will ultimately lead to higher achievement for *all* students.

The following is an example of how a lack of culturally relevant pedagogy can hinder learning. In the Kamehameha schools in Hawaii, native Hawaiian children were expected to take turns telling narratives in a way that went against the lessons they learned through interactions in their homes where instead of one person telling a story, they collaboratively build a narrative in a story talk tradition (Au, 1980). As a result, when called upon to share during sharing time, most students were reluctant to participate. It was culturally awkward and difficult to stand and individually narrate events. Furthermore, when teacher expectations are not met, often students are labeled unwilling or incapable, resulting in remedial education and reduced expectations of students. Additional examples such as differences in sharing time between working-class black children and white children and their middle-class counterparts are also documented by Shirley Brice-Heath (1983).

The most well-known and beneficial means of achieving culturally relevant pedagogy is through multicultural education, which places high priority in valuing what every learner brings to the classroom as a source of knowledge and a capacity for learning. Other curricular strategies are **ethnocentric** in nature. This means that they are focused on the background and norms of one specific culture. A situation like this in a diverse classroom can be detrimental as it does not take into account the pluralistic makeup of the students.

Multicultural education, however, is defined as a curriculum that lends differing perspectives to the learning process. All materials and activities within a truly multicultural classroom should reflect the basic cultural variations and learning styles of every student. In order for a multicultural curriculum to result in culturally relevant pedagogy, the teachers must be trained and well-equipped to instruct in this manner. As a teacher, you can best prepare yourself to teach a multicultural curriculum by doing your own homework about the students in your class. Know something about their backgrounds, native countries, and most importantly their native languages. This information will make your instruction more enjoyable for your students and you.

There are some challenges to multicultural education. One of the most difficult issues is the constant need to maintain a multicultural perspective and pedagogical style. The materials alone do not foster a diversified environment. It is part of your role as a teacher to make the learning encompass the ideas put forth in the materials. Without your wholehearted support, the value of a multicultural learning experience dwindles, resulting in an often ambiguous take on any given academic theme.

Another challenge that must be overcome within a multicultural class is the struggle, for your second language learners and immigrant students, with the concept of assimilation. Many immigrant families feel that their children's best chance at success in the United States is through complete assimilation into English-speaking American culture. From an educational perspective, this philosophy is misguided. Students representing other nationalities and linguistic backgrounds *do* need to adjust and accept many cultural norms of an American classroom; however, this acceptance should not preclude them from preserving their heritage. Therefore, a curricular approach that is multicultural can provide a basis for the students to grow into their new surroundings, while carrying on many of their native cultural traditions. **Multicultural education** takes this idea even further, as all students, even those native to the United States, will learn from the other cultures alive in the classroom. After all, the diversity we are discussing is the fiber upon which American values of democracy and freedom are based. This concept holds exceptionally true in our educational system.

It can also be argued that a multicultural curriculum is as important in a seemingly homogeneous classroom. Even in this type of environment respect for diversity can be cultivated and extended to other types of diversity. The reward is the knowledge your students gain about other people and the more respectful, tolerant way these students react outside the classroom with others.

CULTURALLY AND LINGUISTICALLY DIVERSE EXCEPTIONAL STUDENTS (CLiDES)

Culturally and linguistically diverse exceptional students (CLiDES) is a term defined quite broadly. "Culturally and linguistically diverse" describes persons from a variety of cultural/racial/ethnic backgrounds for whom English is not a first language. For the purposes of this book the term "exceptional" will be used for abilities ranging from gifted to physical, emotional, or learning disabilities.

There are far too many teachers who do not share or know about their students' cultural or linguistic backgrounds and too few have had the professional preparation to work well with these students with special needs. Teachers working in culturally and linguistically diverse school settings have the challenge of determining whether a specific student behavior is the result of cultural differences or evidence of a learning or behavior problem. Teachers need to be especially sensitive to the possibility that what at first appears to be a learning or behavior problem may actually be a difference in the beliefs or customs of the student.

There are additional characteristics that teachers are likely to observe and must be prepared to address with some CLiDES students: (a) delay in language production and reception in both the native language and second language, (b) delay in the acquisition of reading skills in both the native and second language, (c) learning problems related to the lack of instruction and appropriate transition from the native language to the second language, (d) behavior problems associated with experiences of failure either in regular or special education, (e) increasing number of at-risk and dropout students due to the lack of appropriate instruction in the native and second language, (f) cultural identity problems, and (g) poor self-esteem (Omark & Erickson, 1983).

Many CLiDES students have special needs that are inappropriately identified as learning disabilities or mental retardation. They are frequently taught by teachers with minimal training, if any, in both second language acquisition and special education or gifted education. Most of the special education services for these students takes place in self-contained and resource room classrooms.

Furthermore, a disproportionate number of gifted CLiDES students are unidentified and continue to be underrepresented in educational programs for gifted students. This is not because they are any less talented, but rather their different experiences, values, and beliefs have prevented them from fully demonstrating their abilities through forms of assessment commonly used in traditional gifted education programs.

Identifying CLiDES students is the first step toward helping them achieve their full potential. Teachers then need to draw from a repertoire of teaching strategies that not only reflect and respect various cultures and learning styles but that accommodate students' special needs.

Given the diversity of students' abilities and exceptionalities, teachers may need as many strategies to draw from as there are students. The following are additional tips for helping CLiDES students.

GIFTED STUDENTS
- Provide opportunities for them to explore their interests.
- Encourage students to accelerate their progress.
- Allow students to peer tutor, when appropriate.
- Expand assignments according to students' needs and interests.

STUDENTS WITH VISUAL PROBLEMS
- Provide text with large font.
- Orally summarize main points.

- Provide a copy of notes or an oral rendition.
- Provide individualized instruction.
- Provide oral or tactile enhancements.

STUDENTS WITH BEHAVIOR PROBLEMS
- Reduce and restrict stimuli such as loud music, videos with lots of actions, or activities that involve physical activities such as running (classroom games).
- Define clearly and review frequently classroom expectations, for example, "You must raise your hand," "You must ask to get up and walk around," "You must be in your seat when the bell sounds."
- Use role playing to allow students to demonstrate their feelings and provide them with behavior management strategies and conflict resolution tools.
- Review procedural information, e.g., classroom rules.

STUDENTS WITH AUDITORY PROBLEMS
- Provide preferential seating.
- Provide visuals, pictures, maps, diagrams, etc.
- Give short, succinct directions.
- Provide written directions.

STUDENTS WITH LEARNING DISABILITIES
- Use concrete examples.
- Restate directions.
- Break tasks into small, sequential steps.
- Use small groups or pair work to either indicate followthrough or extend whole class work or individual.

WORKING WITH GIFTED STUDENTS IN SECOND LANGUAGE CLASSROOMS

Identifying the Talents of Diverse Students

Emphasis is shifting from what a child knows to how a child learns (Hiatt, 1991; Clasen, 1993). There is recognition that a great diversity exists among the gifted and their expression of talent, and particularly that different cultures express themselves differently (Schwartz, 2000). The result is that evidence of giftedness may be overlooked by evaluators unfamiliar with a child's native culture (Frasier, 1992). Most procedures for identifying gifted students have been developed for use with white middle-class students for whom English is their first and only language. These procedures have led to an underrepresentation of English Language Learners (ELLs) in gifted programs.

Different learning styles may also contribute to the underrepresentation of gifted ELLs. Native Americans are often in conflict with the school's value of independence and the home and community value of interdependence. In school, students generally sit in rows and face the teacher, whereas often in schools where

Native American culture is dominant, everyone would be seated in a circle and decisions would be made collectively (Cohen, 1988).

The body of research on identifying gifted students demonstrates a lack of appropriate procedures. Giftedness is not a trait inherent to native English speakers; however, there is a lack of instruments that can detect giftedness in ELLs (Gallagher, 1979; Llanes, 1980; Raupp, 1988; Renzulli, Reis, & Smith, 1981). The identification of gifted ELLs is complicated since it involves learners who are gifted and from a language or cultural background different from that of white middle-class, native-English speaking students (Cohen).

Gifted students can be described as possessing an abundance of certain abilities that are most highly valued within a particular society or culture. Many ELLs have special talents that are valued within their own cultures; unfortunately these students are often not recognized as gifted and talented (Cohen).

To facilitate identification at school, teacher training programs are now providing an education about cultural and talent diversity among gifted students, particularly to help educators understand how learning style differences can mask evidence of special talents (Balzer & Siewert, 1990). More and more school districts are moving toward an identification model that allows teachers to highlight student talents in specific academic subjects, instead of an all-encompassing identification. This reduces limitations and can open the door for more ELLs to receive gifted services despite linguistic barriers.

Neither poor academic achievement nor limited English language ability indicates a lack of giftedness (Shaklee & Hansford, 1992), for a variety of factors can prevent children from fully demonstrating their intellect. For example, a lack of access to stimulating educational materials and experiences can impede children's early intellectual development, nutritional deficiencies can compromise their ability to concentrate, social isolation can delay their development of interpersonal skills, and trauma from a disadvantaged and dysfunctional home life can depress their overall functioning (Balzer & Siewert, 1990).

Assessment Tools for Gifted Students

■ *Observation*—Teachers, parents, and classmates may play a role in drawing attention to a learner's talents. Teacher and parents' observations can take place over a certain period of time. Classmates can be asked questions about a particular learner to determine how he or she is regarded in the class. In observational assessment, it can be particularly helpful to cooperate with colleagues for more than one perspective.

■ *Self-Identification*—Biographical inventories allow learners to identify their talents in both school and community settings. Although some language learners may feel reluctant to do this, you can make the process more accessible to them through the use of drawing and one-on-one interviews.

■ *Portfolios*—Examining materials that learners select for their portfolios can reveal progress and overall achievement. Portfolios provide assessment of the learner's creativity.

Identifying the special talents of students from diverse backgrounds is just the first step toward helping them achieve their full potential. Educators need to develop programs for gifted students that reflect and respect their cultures and learning styles (Schwartz, 2000).

Programs for Gifted Students

■ *Enrichment program*—Students receive instruction in addition to their regular classroom instruction. Enrichment programs provide learning experiences designed to extend, supplement, or deepen understanding within specific content areas (Dannenberg, 1984).

■ *Parent involvement programs*—Parents help support their child's development at home while the school is used as an additional resource. This encourages a strong link between the home and the school.

■ *Acceleration or honors programs*—These programs may include skipping grades, early entrance, early graduation, credit by examination, nongraded classes, and advanced placement classes (Dannenberg, 1984).

■ *Mentor programs*—Mentors provide role models for the students and thereby give them the opportunity to interact with adult professionals.

Providing appropriate gifted programs for ELLs is a challenge that many school districts face. Since ELLs represent an increasing percentage of the total school population, meeting the needs of these students is vital.

National Clearinghouse for Bilingual Education (NCBE) (1996) discusses the characteristics that define those schools that have been successful in educating highly diverse populations. Many of these characteristics have been noted already but bear repeating. For example, culturally and linguistically different students need to be included in *challenging, core, academic classes*. Curriculum should be arranged in thematic units to allow students to see the relationships across academic disciplines. Additionally, the students' cultures should be incorporated into the curriculum. Other characteristics involved allowing students to study subjects that were relevant to their lives and organizing students into cooperative learning groups.

Finally, the schools communicated with parents on a regular basis, who in turn were actively involved with their children and the school. Berman, Minicucci, McLaughlin, Nelson, and Woodworth (1995) list seven lessons about exemplary practices and schools serving (LEP) students. Those lessons are listed below:

1. A comprehensive school-wide vision provided an essential foundation for developing outstanding education for LEP students.

2. Effective language development strategies were adapted to different local conditions in order to ensure LEP students access to the core curriculum.

3. High quality learning environments for LEP students involved curricular strategies that engaged students in meaningful, in-depth learning across content areas led by trained and qualified staff.

4. Innovative instructional strategies which emphasize collaboration and hands-on activities engaged LEP students in the learning process.

5. A school-wide approach to restructuring schools' units of teaching, use of time, decision-making, and external relations enhanced the teaching/learning environment and foster the academic achievement of LEP students.

THINK, PAIR, SHARE

After reading this chapter, complete the following activity with a partner.

1. After reading, here is what I learned about an interactive approach for working with diverse learners.

   _____

   _____

2. Create listening, speaking, reading, and writing content-based activities that accommodate students' intelligence and learning styles. Explain how they are learner-centered and interactive.

   _____

   _____

---

6. External partners had a direct influence on improving the educational program for LEP students.

7. Districts played a critical role in supporting quality education for LEP students.

All of the above is supported by the study done by Thomas and Collier (1997) in which they, too, discuss the characteristics of effective programs for culturally and linguistically different students. These researchers support allowing students to do their academic work, on grade level, in their first language. According to Thomas and Collier, this will allow students to be more successful in the second/foreign language. They also suggest that these students must be provided a "socio-culturally supportive environment" that is "interactive with discovery learning" that allows students to work cooperatively (p. 50).

HERITAGE LANGUAGE LEARNERS

The term *heritage language learner*, relatively new in language education research, refers to someone who has had exposure to a non-English language outside the formal education system. It most often refers to someone with a home background in the language, but may refer to anyone who has had in-depth exposure to another language (Draper & Hicks, 2000). The key to success in the heritage language classroom, is for the teacher to respect and value the language and cultural experiences that students bring to the classroom (Valdes, 1980; Zentella, 1986; Scalera, 1994). They must understand that there is no "standard" language (Villa, 1996), and that what students bring are the building blocks for future growth in the language (Draper & Hicks). Clearly, teachers also need to know their students.

SUMMARY

In this chapter we have examined an interactive approach for working with diverse learners in content-based classes. The notion of an American "melting pot" in which individuals are expected to eradicate their cultural and linguistic differences in order to conform to some sort of homogeneous "American cultural ideal" has become obsolete and can no longer inform our pedagogical approach to education. Second/foreign language students' self-esteem is jeopardized if the teacher and peers fail to show respect for the first language and the culture of which it is a part (Richard-Amato). All children deserve the chance to succeed in our educational system without having to lose their pride in, or identity with, the culture to which they were born. Our national population is made up of a rich diversity, and a sense of heritage is important to everyone's identity.

> How well we do our jobs as teachers depends, to a great extent, on our ability and willingness to help diverse students make necessary adjustments in their behavior from one peer or home culture to a classroom culture without compromising their essential prized values (Kottler, 1997, p. 8).

EXERCISES AND ACTIVITIES

DISCUSS AND REFLECT

1. What areas in the classroom sociocultural dynamics are you reluctant to take on? Of these, which might have a major impact on your students if you were willing to receive help to develop? Where might you find helpful resources?

2. What are other practices that need to be challenged in your school, community, nation? What are the obstacles? Brainstorm how you can use language or literacy lessons to change the situation and make a difference in your life and that of your students. What resources could be used? What community alliances might you build to help you succeed?

3. Have you had any unsuccessful attempts in teaching for democratic practices in your classroom? What lessons can you draw on that may help to raise others' awareness about the challenges? What alternative methods could be tried?

ASK YOURSELF THESE QUESTIONS

1. What do you believe are the advantages of teaching culturally, linguistically, and cognitively diverse students?

2. What experiences do you have with people whose cultural backgrounds are different from yours?

3. In what ways do your stronger intelligences influence the way you (will) teach?

WHAT DO TEACHERS THINK?

Teaching culturally and linguistically diverse students these past six years has been an incredible learning experience in world cultures and student needs. Each year brings a new group of pupils who not only have diverse backgrounds but also have different learning styles and special needs that I must take into consideration as I develop meaningful and—most important for my class—fun lessons that help prepare my students for eventual entry into grade level classes.

This year I consulted my "first week activities" folder and my "classroom-climate building activities" folder to find ideas for my classroom-climate building activities. It is important for the students to help me define the classroom—even helping to determine the rules, goals, traditions, and units to be studied so that they feel responsible and take ownership over our learning. My students are reminded that I am a student as much as they are. We all teach each other through the use of our prior experiences that come from the diverse make-up of our class.

One student I have this year is a beginning level ESL student from South America. She is a wonderful, highly-motivated sophomore whose dyslexia requires me to rethink my lessons and include different kinds of activities and scaffolding for use in my classroom. She is in both of my beginning level content classes of science and U.S. history where we do a lot of reading and writing activities. One strategy that really helps has been the use of previewing a section before starting the actual reading. All my students have been taught to come up with questions about the section and prepare for note-taking while reading with use of a T-chart. This is done on a piece of looseleaf paper that is folded in half lengthwise (hot dog style). The questions are written on the left side with about five spaces between each, and the answers the students discover as they read are written on the right. Students like this method of guided reading and note-taking. Even my students with learning disabilities feel that this makes reading more focused and they want to continue learning.

Charmaine Spitler, ESL Teacher, Fairfax County Public Schools, Virginia

FIELD-BASED EXPERIENCES

Talk with one or more teachers about student diversity. Ask them the following questions:

1. What differences do you see among culturally, linguistically, and cognitively diverse students?

2. How do you accommodate/celebrate those differences?

3. How do your students differ in the ways they prefer to learn?

4. What do you do to reflect on your current teaching practices with diverse learners? How do you decide when to change instructional practices?

5. What steps did you take to create a community of learners in your classroom?

CASE STUDY
ELEMENTARY BILINGUAL SPECIAL EDUCATION

Luis Galindez is a bilingual special education teacher (Spanish/English) who teaches in a pullout program where fourth-grade students receive instruction in reading, language arts, mathematics, social studies, and science. The students rejoin their classmates for art, music, gym, ESL, and foreign language.

At my school, I am required to show in my lesson plans how I address state standards for each of the content areas. I decided that the best way for the students to learn these areas is to create a thematic unit with social studies, science, reading, and language arts. I try to use at least four different types of writing in my lessons: listing with the whole class, shared writing, guided writing, and independent writing. As an end-of-the-semester activity, my students will be expected to participate in the school's social studies exhibition on the theme ancient civilizations. At this exhibition, they would have to give oral presentations in English and Spanish to school visitors. So I had to prepare them to for public speaking as well.

Since my students decided that they would like to find out about animals in ancient times, I started by taking them to visit the local zoo. There I asked the bilingual zoo keeper to give us a special guided tour, which we taped. The students were allowed to touch some of the animals and to feed others. When we returned, the children reviewed all the animals we saw by listing them on the board in both languages. We grouped the animals into categories by the types of environments they were living in at the zoo. In the following lessons, we named the categories of the animals' habitats, and the children learned new words to describe each, e.g., dry, wet, mountains, valleys, etc., and the children drew a picture of their favorite animal in their habitat. They labeled their drawings with new vocabulary words that we had used earlier. I asked the students to think about their experiences at the zoo, and try to imagine what kinds of zoos might have existed in ancient times in Rome. In pairs they talked, alternating in English and Spanish. When I called "time out," many were still arguing about what animals could be alive then and what kinds of zoos might have existed. Because they had a lot of guesses, I wrote them on overhead transparency sheets. We filled five whole pages with guesses and descriptions!

In the lessons that followed, we read and reread these guesses and made changes. This made them wonder aloud and helped them to ask many questions. I asked each team to write five questions that they really wanted to find out. Then each team read their questions aloud to each other and later to the class. Later the children picked their favorite animal and teamed up to find more information. I selected several CD-ROMS about animals, and I taught the students how to take short notes for their report, similar to the way I wrote their guesses. Later in writer's workshops, I met with each team and the students made the notes longer by using their own words. Later the notes were used to create pictures and then we made posters.

By the time the exhibition came, my students were well prepared to talk about their posters, which had all the animals that they had seen at the zoo and questions that they researched. Guess how the children began—they asked their audience to guess which animals were alive in Roman times and what kinds of zoos could have existed. Then they presented what they learned. The next step we are going to tackle is the drafting of the first paragraph of their written report using their posters.

ANSWER THE FOLLOWING QUESTIONS:

1. How did students' writing help support their inquiries?

2. How did students' use of both languages help their composition processes?

3. How might the oral poster presentations have helped the students prepare for writing their reports?

ACTION RESEARCH

Conduct an Action Research project in which you ask the following question: How will implementation of the eight intelligences into instructional practices and assessments affect second language learners' comprehension and retention in math, science, social studies, or English language arts?

ADDITIONAL RESOURCES

Organizations

Multiple Intelligences Teacher Action Research
http://www.gse.gmu.edu/research/mirs

American Speech-Language-Hearing Association
http://www.asha.org

Council for Exceptional Children
http://www.cec.sped.org

Irlen Institute for Perceptual and Learning Disabilities
P.O. Box 7175, Long Beach, CA 90807

National Information for Handicapped Children & Youth
P.O. Box 1492, Washington, DC 20013

Orton Dyslexia Society
724 York Road, Baltimore, MD 21204

Educational Resources Information Center (ERIC)
http://www.askeric.org

International Dyslexia Association
http://www.interdys.org

LD Online (for learning disabilities)
http://www.ldonline.org

National Center for Learning Disabilities
http://www.ncld.org

Rethinking Our Classrooms: Teaching for Equity and Justice
1001 E. Keefe Avenue
Milwaukee, WI 53212
(414) 964-9646
Toll-free (800) 669-4192
http://www.rethinkingschools.org

National Association for Multicultural Education
733 15th St., NW, Suite 430
Washington, DC 20005
http://www.nameorg.org

GLOSSARY OF TERMS

analytic   one of the three areas of learning styles. Is characterized by: concentrates on tasks at hand; analyzes problems, then decides; prefers to work independently on projects; likes to organize assignments; prefers options; remembers details; consistent with rules, assignments.

analytical-global   one of the five key elements of language learning styles. Demonstrates the difference between a detail-oriented learner and a holistic one. This learner focuses on grammatical details and enjoys looking up words in the dictionary, rather than trying to guess their meaning.

bodily/kinesthetic   ability to use one's mental abilities to manipulate and coordinate movements of one's physical body

competition-cooperation   one of the five key elements of language learning styles. Demonstrates those learners who benefit from competing against or cooperating with their peers. Competitive learners are often motivated by the thrill of winning. Cooperative learners enjoy working with others in a collaborative manner.

CLD   culturally and linguistically diverse

CLiDES   culturally and linguistically diverse exceptional students

ethnocentric curriculum   curriculum that is inclusive of multiple ethnicities

global   one of the three areas of learning styles. Is characterized by reading for overall idea; likes team competitions; relates what is taught to own experiences; likes working with others; understands thinking *in context*; can work on several projects at one time; and reads between the lines.

integrated   one of the three areas of learning styles. Combines **global** and **analytic.**

interpersonal/social   ability to recognize and understand others' feelings and interact appropriately with other people

intrapersonal/introspective   ability to perceive one's own feelings and motivations for planning and directing one's life

intuitive/random   One of the five key elements of language learning styles. Demonstrates the type of organization a learner prefers in the presentation of material. Frequently think in a somewhat abstract way—non-sequential or random.

learning styles   each student's pattern or preferences or strengths which affect the ability to "concentrate, practice, internalize and retain new and difficult information (Marshall, 1997)

logical/mathematical   ability to detect patterns, calculate, think logically, and carry out mathematical operations

mnemonic devices   a formula or rhyme used in aiding one's memory

multicultural education   subject matter that embraces multiple perspectives of varieties of culture

musical/rythmical   the ability to recognize, compose, and remember tonal changes, rhythms, and musical pitch

naturalist   ability to recognize and classify natural surroundings, such as flora and fauna or rocks and minerals

orientation to closure   one of the five key elements of language learning styles. Demonstrates those learners who need to reach conclusions and will not tolerate ambiguity. These learners are often characterized by wanting the rules spelled out for them.

reflective practitioner   teachers/practitioners who reflect on their teaching and make adjustments accordingly

schemata   refers to prior knowledge

sensory preference   one of the five key elements of language learning styles. Demonstrates the physical, perceptual ways of learning. These may be visual, auditory, and hands-on (kinesthetic). Visual learners prefer visual cues or an opportunity to read information. Auditory learners like conversations and hearing the lesson's content. Kinesthetic learners do well in environments in which they can physically move around or are provided with manipulatives that aid in comprehension.

sensory/sequential   one of the five key elements of language learning styles. Demonstrates the type of organization a learner prefers in the presentation of material. Learners prefer to learn in an ordered step-by-step linear progression.

verbal/linguistic   ability to effectively manipulate language to express oneself; allows for the use of language as a means to remember information

visual/spatial   ability to perceive and manipulate images in order to solve problems

REFERENCES

Au, K. (1980). Participation structures in a reading lesson with Hawaiian children. *Anthropology & Education Quarterly, 11*, 91–111.

Balzer, C., & Siewert, B. (Eds.). (1990, July). *Identification: A suggested procedure for the identification of talented and gifted students K–12*. Technical Assistance Paper 1 (revised). Salem: Oregon State Department of Education, Division of Special Student Services. (ERIC Document Reproduction Services No. ED330146).

Banks, J. (1997). *Teaching strategies for ethnic studies* (6ᵗʰ ed.). Needham Heights, MA: Allyn & Bacon.

Berman, P., Minicucci, C., McLaughlin, B., Nelson, B., & Woodworth, K. (1995). School reform and student diversity: Case studies of exemplary practices for LEP students. Retrieved January 14, 2002 from *http://www.ncbe.gwu.edu/mispubs/schoolreform/9haroldwiggs.htm*

Brice-Heath, S. (1983). *Ways with words*. Cambridge, UK: Cambridge University Press.

Bruder, I. (1992, October). Multicultural education: Responding to the demographics of change. *Electronic Learning, 12*, (2), 20–7.

Canfield, J., & Siccone, F. (1995). *101 Ways to develop student self-esteem and responsibility*. Needham Heights, MA: Allyn & Bacon.

Cohen, D. (1988). Teaching practice: Plus ca change . . . . (Issue paper # 88–3). East Lansing, MI: Michigan State University, National Center for Research on Teacher Education.

Clasen, D. R. (1993, September). Resolving inequities: Discovery and development of talents in student populations traditionally underrepresented in gifted and talented programming. In J. Drum (Ed.), *Communicator*. Canoga Park: California Association for the Gifted. (ERIC Document Reproduction Service No. ED365039)

Cummins, J. (1997). Minority status and schooling in Canada. *Anthropology and Education Quarterly, 28*, 411–30.

Dannenberg, A. C. (1984). *Meeting the needs of gifted and talented students: An introduction to issues and practices*. Quincy, MA: Massachusetts Department of Education, Office for Gifted and Talented.

Draper, J. B., & Hicks, J. H. (2000). Where we've been; What we've learned. In J. B. Webb & B. L. Miller (Eds.), *Teaching Heritage Language Learners: Voices from the classroom*. (pp. 15–35). Yonkers, NY: American Council on the Teaching of Foreign Languages.

Dunn, W. (1993). Education diversity. *American Demographics*. April, 38–43.

Duran, E. (1988). *Teaching the moderately and severely handicapped student and autistic adolescent: With particular attention to bilingual special education*. Springfield, IL: Charles C. Thomas.

Fraser, M. M. (1992, March). Ethnic/minority children: Reflections and directions. In *Challenges in gifted educations: Developing potential and investing in knowledge for the 21ˢᵗ century*. Columbus: Ohio State Department of Education. (ERIC Document Reproduction Center No. ED344402)

Gallagher, J. J. (1979). Issues in education for the gifted. In A. H. Passow (Ed.), *The gifted and the talented: Their education and development*. Chicago: University of Chicago Press.

Garcia, J., & Pugh, S. L. (1992, November). Multicultural education in teacher preparation programs: A political or an educational concept? *Phi Delta Kapan*, November, 214–9.

Gardner, H. (1983). *Frames of mind: The theory of multiple intelligences*. New York: Basic Books.

Guild, P. (1997). Where do the learning theories overlap? *Education Leadership, 9* (4), 30–32.

Haley, M. H. (2001). Understanding learner-centered instruction from the perspective of multiple intelligences. *Foreign Language Annals, 34*(4), 355–367.

Harklau, L. (2000). From the 'good kids' to the 'worst': Representations of English language learners across educational settings. *TESOL Quarterly, 34*, 35–67.

Hiatt, E. L. (1991, Spring-Winter). An update on the Jarvits project: Identifying and serving disadvantaged gifted youth. In *Update on gifted education*. Austin: Texas Education Agency, Division of Gifted/Talented

Education. (ERIC Document Reproduction Service No. ED346654)

Kagan, S., & Kagan, M. (1998). *Multiple intelligences: The complete MI book*. San Clemente, CA: Kagan Cooperative Learning.

Kottler, J. A. (1997). *What's really said in the teachers' lounge: Provocative ideas about cultures and classrooms*. Thousand Oaks, CA: Corwin Press.

Krashen, S. D. (1985). *The input hypothesis: Issues and implications*. New York: Longman.

Llanes, J. R. (1980, February–March). Bilingualism and the gifted intellect. *Roeper Review, 2*(3), 11–2.

Marshall, C. (1997). *Learning styles and learning success—What every educator should know*. Draft document: Vocational Home Economics Curriculum, Texas Tech University, Lubbock, TX.

Marusza, J. (1998). An analysis of classroom multiculturalism. *Multicultral Education, 6*, 26–31.

Omark, D. R., & Erickson, J. G. (1983). *The bilingual exceptional child*. San Diego, CA: College Hill Press.

Oxford, R. L. (1990). *Language learning strategies: What every teacher should know*. New York: Newbury House.

Ortiz, A., & Ramirez, B. A. (1988). *Schools and the culturally diverse exceptional student: Promising practices and future directions*. Reston, VA: The Council for Exceptional Children—ERIC Clearinghouse on Handicapped and Gifted Children.

Phillips, S. U. (1972). Participation structures and communicative competence: Warm springs children in community and classroom. In C. B. Cazden, V. P. Johns, & D. Hymes (Eds). *Functions of language in the classroom*. New York: Teachers College Press.

Raup, M. (1988). *Talent search: The Gifted Hispanic student*. Quincy, MA: Massachusetts Department of Education, Office for Gifted and Talented.

Renzulli, J. S., Reis, S., & Smith, L. H. (1981). *The revolving door identification model*. Mansfield Center, CT: Creative Learning Press.

Richard-Amato, P. A. (1988). *Making it happen*. Addison Wesley.

Richards, J. C., & Lockhart, C. (1994). *Reflective teaching in second language classrooms*. Cambridge, UK: Cambridge University Press.

Rivkin, S. G. (1994). Residential segregation and school integration. *Sociology of Education, 67*(4), 279–92.

Scarcella, R. C., & Oxford, R. L. (1992). *The tapestry of language learning*. Boston, MA: Heinle & Heinle.

Schwartz, W. (1997). *Strategies for identifying the talents of diverse students*. (ERIC Document Reproduction Service No. ED410323)

Shaklee, B. D., & Hansford, S. (1992). Identification of young gifted students. *Journal of the Education of the Gifted, 15*(2), 134–44. (EJ 447 211).

Thomas, W., & Collier, V. (1997). *School effectiveness for language minority students*. Washington, DC: National Clearinghouse for Bilingual Education, The George Washington University Center for the Study of Language and Education.

Villa, D. J. (1996). Choosing a "standard" variety of Spanish for the instruction of native Spanish Speakers in the U.S. *Foreign Language Annals, 29*(2), 191–200.

Wigfield, A., Galper, A., Denton, K., & Seefeldt, C. (1999). Teachers' beliefs about former head start and non-head start first-grade children's motivation, performance, and future educational prospects. *Journal of Educational Psychology, 91*, 98–104.

CHAPTER NINE

INTEGRATING TECHNOLOGY IN AN INTERACTIVE, CONTENT-BASED CLASSROOM

THIS CHAPTER WILL FEATURE

- pedagogical implications for using technology
- technology in an interactive content-based classroom

YOU WILL EXAMINE

- traditional technologies
- multimedia

INTRODUCTION: SETTING THE STAGE

This chapter will examine technologies including, among others, CD-ROMs, presentation-enhancing tools, multimedia programs, Internet, online fora, and satellite programs that are available to second/foreign language teachers.

We will examine technology's redefinition of the role of teachers, pedagogical implications for using technology, and sample lessons incorporating technologies, software, telecommunication, and multimedia software.

Under the No Child Left Behind Act (2001), more than $700 million was made available to states and schools through the Enhancing Education through Technology Program, along with $2.25 billion through the E-rate initiative. In addition, under the law, states and schools can use more of their federal funds to make better use of technology.

The goals of the Ed Tech initiative are to:

1. Improve student academic achievement through the use of technology in elementary schools and secondary schools.

THINK, PAIR, SHARE

Before you begin reading this chapter, complete the following activity with a partner.

1. Before reading, here is my opinion of using technology in the classroom.

   _____

   _____

   _____

2. Here is my partner's opinion of using technology in the classroom.

   _____

   _____

   _____

3. Here is what I have learned from my partner.

   _____

   _____

   _____

2. Assist students to become technologically literate by the time they finish the eighth grade.
3. Ensure that teachers are able to integrate technology into the curriculum to improve student achievement.

In July 2002, Secretary of Education Roderick Paige highlighted the importance of harnessing the power of technology to expand access to learning and make sure no child in America is left behind. In discussing technology and e-learning, Secretary Paige highlighted the many attributes of e-learning, including:

■ E-learning promotes local control by expanding opportunities—even in rural and urban areas with limited resources—to tap a vast reservoir of knowledge and expertise online. Schools can increase their repertoire of courses for students, provide professional development for teachers, or share their talented staff with other districts.

■ E-learning increases flexibility for schools and for students so even a living room can be a classroom—and a classroom can be an archeological dig.

■ E-learning promotes individual instruction to meet the needs of each student.

■ E-learning empowers parents to make choices that will help their sons and daughters get the best education possible.

In 1998, President Clinton introduced the Educational Technology Initiative in which he outlined the "Technology Literacy Challenge." Included in this were four areas of emphasis:

1. Modern computers and learning devices will be accessible to every student.
2. Classrooms will be connected to one another and to the world.
3. Educational software will be an integral part of the curriculum and as engaging as the best video game.
4. Teachers will be ready to use and teach with technology. (USDOE, 1998)

Educational research has shown that self-learning and interactive multimedia are particularly effective in facilitating the teaching of English skills (Cates, 1992; Hill, 1988, Laurillard, 1995; Meskill, 1996; Squires & Preece, 1996). As second/foreign language teachers you will want to provide a classroom environment that involves students in authentic, culturally appropriate, and meaningful experiences that stimulate their language proficiency. Technology can provide both a teaching and learning tool that will support and enhance your school's curricula.

Instructors and researchers agree that the use of any technology in the classroom must be integrated into the curriculum as a tool to support and enhance the learning experience rather than serve as the driving curricular force (Armstrong & Yetter-Vassot, 1994; Garrett, 1992; Hughes & Hewson, 1998; Kearsley, 1998; LeLoup & Ponterio, 1996; Patrikis, 1995; Phillips, 1998). Kearsley and Hedderick (1997) warn against the seductiveness of integrating technology as a quick fix to more serious problems.

In the recent past, second/foreign language teachers have utilized such technologies as audio and videotapes, radio, television programs, language labs, films, filmstrips, slides, and the overhead projector. More recently there has been an explosion of newer technologies for classroom adaptability: e.g., computers, CD-ROMs, distance learning, satellite broadcasts, videoconferencing, electronic mail. Now, as never before, students can have access to multiple resources and communicate both orally and in writing with innumerable speakers of other languages.

What impact will technology have on the *role of the teacher?* Throughout this book we have focused on examining the psycholinguistic and sociocultural perspectives. These two must be considered unilaterally when one talks about the influential presence of technology in today's schools. Byrnes (1996) notes that technology such as the Internet "inherently shifts the emphasis from teaching to student learning" thus creating new roles for both learners and teachers, and forcing us to rethink the process of learning. Patrikis points out that computer-based learning individualizes the learning process and gives students more control over both what and how they learn.

Will the computer replace the teacher? Probably not. Will teachers change the way they teach because of computers? Probably. Because of the growing use and popularity of new technologies, teachers find themselves being urged to keep up. More and more states and school districts are implementing a technology competence requirement as part of students' standards of learning. Similarly, schools of education are requiring educational technology courses in teacher licensure programs. Thus, the role of the teacher has been and will continue to be redefined in part by new technology.

One direct influence of technology has been seen in teachers moving from whole class to small group instruction, as well as a shift from students all learning the same things to learning different things. This affords teachers the opportunity to move from verbal thinking, to the integration of visual and verbal thinking. According to Cummins (2000), ". . . our task as educators in general, and as language educators in particular, should be to assess the potential of Information Technology (IT) to improve the human condition. As educators, we are committed to drawing out the potential of the students we teach; as language educators, we strive to increase students' capacity to use language to fulfill their personal goals and contribute to their societies."

PEDAGOGICAL IMPLICATIONS
FOR USING TECHNOLOGY

Integrating technology successfully begins with explicitly defining the pedagogical role for that technology (Ragan, 1999). Every individual teacher must choose why, how, and when to use technology. This choice is often influenced by access, ease of comfort in using technology, and knowledge of *how* to use existing resources. Access to information technology differs among and within countries, states, and school districts. The digital divide is clearly visible. According to Cummins (2000), "I believe that IT also has considerable potential to promote language learning in a transformative way when it is aligned with a pedagogy oriented towards promoting collaborative relations of power in the classroom and beyond."

Garrett (1991) cautions us that using the computer does not replace methodology, since the computer is nothing more than a tool. According to Garrett, the more critical issue is the quality of the software material available, and the ways teachers use the material to achieve the desired learning outcomes. ". . . Teachers must learn to use the new technology to allow students to interact more effectively with the same 'old' material. The change must be carefully and thoughtfully crafted, for we cannot continue to ask teachers to use the 'newest' devices if we continue using pedagogical practices that are no different from those previously used" (Moore, 1999).

Computer technologies can play a crucial role in facilitating the objectives of L2 instruction in at least four ways. Whether the learner is located in the classroom, computer laboratory, home office, or any other location for learning, computer technologies can facilitate L2 language instruction by providing:

- diverse structure-focused activities with learner-specific evaluation and feedback;
- complex multimedia input to the learner;
- a variety of forms of dynamic, monitored interaction with that input;
- diverse environments for interpersonal communication, both dynamic (synchronous) and delayed (asynchronous).

APPROACH	METHOD	IT APPLICATIONS
Behaviorist	**ALM**	Electronic workbook, drill practice, application activities, dialogues, stimulus response, transformation drills
	Grammar Translation	Tutorials, writing assistance, information resources
	Direct Method	Videos and tapes/CDs for listening practice; students can create and view classmates' own videos
Rationalist	**Cognitive Anti-Method**	WebQuest
	Cognitive Code	Video texts, CD-ROMs
Functional	**CALLA**	Internet to research a topic, followed by Inspiration software to create graphic organizers and outlines to organize information, and presentation software (PowerPoint, Apple Works) to summarize and present information on a particular topic
	Communicative Language Teaching Approach	Video e-mails, creations of videos, videoconferencing with other students/others
	TRP/TPRS	Videos of original stories, Inspiration to organize idea of story and to add pictures to stories
	Natural Approach	Games to assess listening comprehension, e-mail, keypals, chatrooms, and videoconferencing for "real" language use, simulations
Humanistic	**Communicative Language Learning (CLL)**	Presentation software, slide shows, student created videos and "movies"
	Silent Way	Tutorials, drill practice, electronic workbook
	Suggestopedia	Watch and create videos of role plays
	Rassias	Internet research, teacher created online activities (examples can be found at *http://www.quia.com*), create and watch videos, CD-ROMs

FIGURE 9.1   Information Technology Approaches and Methods

In chapter 2, we discussed behaviorist and rationalist methods, and functional and humanistic approaches. Figure 9.1 is a graphic organizer that shows the approaches, methods, and possible IT applications.

Using IT with a pedagogy more oriented toward project-based learning has been documented in case studies as highly successful (Brown, Cummins, Figueroa, &

FOCUS ON . . .		
MEANING	**LANGUAGE**	**USE**
• Making input comprehensible • Developing critical literacy	• Awareness of language forms and uses • Critical analysis of language forms and uses	Using language to: • Generate new knowledge • Create literature and art • Act on social realities

FIGURE 9.2   Instruction for Language Learning and Academic Achievement

Source: Cummins (2000)

Sayers 1998; de Klerk, 1998). When students are provided with both people resources and information resources via technologies, they are exposed to reading in a wide variety of genres. (See chapter 5.) Furthermore, students are engaged in higher-order thinking skills, resulting from exposure to comprehensible input and these transform into critical literacy. The three examples of language use presented in Figure 9.2 (generate new knowledge, create literature and art, act on social realities) are meant to illustrate important components of critical literacy.

Cummins (2000) outlines a framework for promoting academic language learning and describes how IT can be used to facilitate access to people resources and information resources that are specific to extending and deepening learners' knowledge of academic language. Cummins describes this as a *transformative pedagogy*. Transformative pedagogy aims to create patterns of educator-student interaction that effectively challenge and transform the ways in which schools have traditionally reproduced social and economic inequalities (Cummins, 1996; Nieto, 1999).

Digital Literacy

Using the computer as a reading medium is becoming more evident in today's foreign/second language classrooms. Teachers and students are more likely than ever to be "drivers" on the information highway. However, one potential problem in language pedagogy may already be present—analog materials replaced by digital forms. Teachers must be aware that some online material is not suited for sequential reading. First, print-based reading skills, skimming, and scanning, mentioned in chapter 3, are not easily accomplished when there is a fair amount of scrolling required to get through a text. Second, the teacher must constantly alter reading pedagogy, depending on on-and-off line media.

The following are recommendations for ways to alter reading pedagogy:

1. Shorten the amount of online print-based text presented at a given time. For instance, rather than requiring students to read a ten-page text, ask students to skim or scan two pages at a time. Thus by breaking the text into manageable chunks, learners are not overwhelmed with trying to scroll through the entire text.

2. Select reading on-line print-based texts based on learners' interest and degree of second/foreign language proficiency. Once the level of proficiency and genre have been determined, the teacher can provide appropriate pre- and post-reading skills and strategies.

REFLECT AND RESPOND

1. How has technology changed the way you teach or learn?

   _____

   _____

   _____

2. In what ways will you likely incorporated technology in your classroom?

   _____

   _____

   _____

3. Make a list of three activities that you use/might use that incorporate technology.

   _____

   _____

   _____

TECHNOLOGY IN AN INTERACTIVE CLASSROOM

Interactive Learning/Technology/Constructivism

Technology, an inherently active medium, provides students interactive learning experiences. Students may be required to give input, make choices, think, and act. Audiotape or videotape are certainly improvements over exclusively print-based language instruction, but students can still "tune out," whereas computer-based instruction requires active attention which, according to Vygotsky, "is a correlate of the structure of what is perceived and remembered" (Vygotsky [1934] 1986, p. 169).

The inherent interactivity of the computer also enhances learning because the reaction of the computer to the student's action allows learning to continue by providing information or evaluation, whether in the browsing or tutorial mode (Frommer, 1998). Additionally, the interactive nature of the computer allows it to be used independent of a teacher.

Constructivism refers to a collection of different theories, from a wide range of disciplines, forming a common approach to education. According to Driscoll (1994), there is no single constructivist theory of learning; rather, "there are researchers in fields from science education to educational technology and instructional technology who are articulating various aspects of constructivist theory."

Constructivist researchers have two primary foci of particular importance to language learning: (1) learning is an [inter]active process, and (2) learning takes

---

PRACTICAL APPLICATIONS OF CONSTRUCTIVISM AND TECHNOLOGY

DESIRED LEARNER OUTCOMES	LESSON CAN INCLUDE
Learners use vocabulary, themes, topics	Tasks requiring reading of online resources
Analyze similarities and differences between two settings, people, objects, or events	Research opportunities in which aspects of two entities are compared and contrasted
Investigate a topic from multiple perspectives, synthesize them, and modify their views in response to feedback	Create groups to research and collect data from different genres and work collaboratively to write a report or present a demonstration

Source: Adapted from Richard Harrison (1998)

---

place in social contexts. Interactive learning allows learners to construct their own meaning and use their existing knowledge to make sense of a situation. Learners provided opportunities to collaborate in the learning process can socially negotiate meaning. Constructivists believe that learners construct their own meaning and impose their own structure on any situation they encounter, no matter how complex (Harrison, 1998).

Traditional and Newer Technologies

In the following section we will discuss a few of the traditional and newer technologies available to second/foreign language. Some of the more traditional technologies include:

- Films, audio- and videocassettes, language labs
- Tool software (word processing, desktop publishing, databases, spreadsheets)

Some of the newer technologies include:

- Telecommunication (narrative, WWW, distance learning programs, TV programs), e-mail
- Multimedia software (CD-ROMs, HyperStudio, PowerPoint)

The last twenty years has seen an increase in the use of computers in second/foreign language learning as the range of tools available to teachers and students has increased (Debski, 1997). The kind of tools Debski refers to can be summarized in the following:

1. *Tools for natural language processing:* online dictionaries, concordance programs, thesauri, and machine translation software
2. *Tools for communication:* e-mail, bulletin boards, and videoconferencing
3. *Tools for gathering information:* World Wide Web (www) browsing tools

4. *Tools for creativity:* www provides an environment for learners to publish their own information
5. *Tools for collaboration:* collaborative learning between second/foreign language learners is made possible with WWW publishing tools and Internet tools such as e-mail

TECHNOLOGY AND SECOND/FOREIGN LANGUAGE LITERACY

With the advent of widespread computer use and global communications networks, technology continues to affect how we read, how we write, and how we use written language to learn and to communicate with others. The most profound effects of computer technology on literacy and language learning will likely arise not from language pedagogy software but from the new forms of information dissemination and social interaction made possible by local and global computer networks (Kern, 1998).

Selecting and Accessing Authentic Texts

Selecting and accessing authentic texts can sometimes be very challenging, given the wide range of resources available. Authentic material used in the classroom not only contains limited and sometimes biased and incorrect cultural information, it also presents rather limited written language samples (Moore). According to Rings (1986), the most authentic language samples are the spontaneous, unrehearsed utterances of speakers in real-life contexts.

However, the value of using authentic texts in a second/foreign language classroom is paramount to students' being able to learn to negotiate meaning about the target language and culture. Galloway (1990) recommends the following criteria for selecting authentic texts:

- Topic should be accessible to the learner.
- Length of text should not be intimidating to beginning readers.
- Linguistic level should be slightly above the reader's own level (Krashen's *i + 1* theory) unless the tasks are closely structured to involve focused listening/reading.
- Clues to meaning should be abundant—contextual, verbal, pictorial, linguistic, etc.

As students work with authentic texts they may find it difficult to comprehend everything they see and hear. Once careful attention has been given to the selection of authentic texts, teachers will want to provide students with strategies that can help them organize, synthesize, and relate new information to their existing knowledge. See chapter 5 for suggested reading strategies.

The Royal Tombs of Ur.

Go to the website: http://www.mesopotamia.co.uk/tombs/home_set.html for an interactive high school ESL world history activity. Students will research the tombs or graves of the kings and queens of the city of Ur.

PREREADING STRATEGY
Instructions: Before you begin the reading selection, skim the text for general ideas.

1. _____

2. _____

3. _____

DURING-READING STRATEGY
Instructions: Click on "Story" and make 3 predictions about the text from the picture.

1. _____

2. _____

3. _____

Next click on "Explore" and answer the following questions:

1. Of what were the walls made?

   _____

2. Who was buried in the tomb?

   _____

3. What objects were found here?

   _____

4. What was found inside the chest?

_____

5. What kind of vehicle was this?

_____

6. What was this object?

_____

7. What did the body have around its neck?

_____

8. What was it made of?

_____

9. What musical instruments did the Sumerians bury with them?

_____

AFTER-READING STRATEGY
Instructions: Retell what you have learned about The Royal Tombs of Ur.

_____

_____

_____

_____

_____

_____

_____

Selected Types of Programs Used in Computer Assisted Language Learning (CALL)

TYPE OF SOFTWARE	TYPES OF PROGRAMS
Generic: supplemental software not based on a text	**Drill and Practice:** use word level exercises like fill-in-the-blank and multiple-choice to focus on discrete grammar skills
Text-based: textbook-specific software easily integrated into curriculum	**Simulations:** make the users' responses have specific consequences to the character or story line of the program
Course-based: software that serves as the basis of a course	**Tutorials:** offer users pre- and posttests, exercises, and explanations for improving linguistic skills
Course-adapted: software adapted from various sources to serve a specific course	**Games:** utilize the elements of competition, challenge, and problem solving to teach and/or reinforce learning
	Writing Assistants: are word-processing programs that provide learners with on-line aids for writing
	Authoring Programs: provide the teacher with the ability to alter or create lessons for specific classes or commercial use
	Information Resources: are collections of information such as dictionaries, atlases, galleries, and encyclopedias
	Information Management: are database and spreadsheet software packages used to track student grades, progress, and more

Source: Kassen & Higgins, 1997

COMPUTER ASSISTED LANGUAGE LEARNING (CALL)

Note: Subsumed under Computer Assisted Language Learning (CALL) are Computer Assisted Language Instruction (CALI) and Technology Enhanced Language Learning (TELL).

Warschauer (1996) claims that teachers must learn to harness the educational capabilities of technology; one way to do this is by developing integrative approaches to Computer Assisted Language Learning (CALL). As you will see later in this chapter, many of the recent developments in CALL are based on two technological advances—multimedia computers and the World Wide Web (WWW). Also, according to Warschauer (1996) **Multiple-user-domains Object Oriented (MOOs)** best allow for real-time communication, simulation, and role playing. The highly interactive nature of CALL utilities, like MOOs, can facilitate the teaching of culture by providing immediate, ongoing contact with native speakers in the second language (Moore, Morales, & Carel, 1999).

GAMES AS INTERACTIVE ACTIVITIES

Computer games can be defined as instructional activities that provide motivation, entertainment, competition, and reinforcement while presenting a superficial or simulated reality (Herselman, 1999). Computer games could play an important role in ensuring automaticity of skills (Anderson, 1980, p. 76; Gagne, 1985, p. 90). Computer games could be particularly useful in schools where English as the medium of instruction is not the mother tongue of learners (Stern, 1990, p. 118). With the great diversity of learners, particularly in terms of available resources, it becomes important to determine the extent to which computer games can augment the learning process, both for the resource-deprived and resource-advantaged learners (Herselman).

Jones (1997) describes two types of games: **strategy games** and **twitch games.** **Strategy games** require higher-order thinking skills and problem-solving skills for successful completion. The learner must comprehend the larger problem and plan strategies to solve it. Examples of these games are:

- logic games
- role-playing games
- board games

Twitch games require quick reaction to stimuli. Movement in these games is usually lively and feedback is instantaneous. Examples of these games are:

- psychomotor games
- arcade games
- games of chance

In today's second/foreign language classrooms computer games are a fun way to actively engage and involve all students. The exact proficiency learners should develop varies with the content (Salisbury, 1990, p. 45). Another perk to computers and games is a low affective filter. There may be an initial tension until the program, keys, joystick, ticks, and tricks are familiar. For cognitive skills, one expects learners will be able to retrieve factual information effortlessly from their memories (Herselman). For procedural skills, one expects learners to perform quickly, smoothly, and with few errors (Grabe & Grabe, 1996, p. 92). With quick and clear feedback, enjoyment and intrinsic motivation can be optimized (Quinn, 1997, p. 9).

CONTENT-BASED LANGUAGE TEACHING THROUGH TECHNOLOGY (COBALTT)

In 1999, the Center for Advanced Research on Language Acquisition (CARLA) introduced the Content-Based Language Teaching Through Technology (CoBaLTT) initiative. The initiative offers a resource center and technology-based professional development. The professional development program meets each year with a group of foreign and second language teachers who participate in institutes and workshops that focus on:

- curriculum development and teaching strategies for content-based instruction
- best practices in using technology for teaching and learning
- creation of authentic tasks that meet national and state foreign and second language standards
- measurement of student proficiency through performance-based assessment

Lessons completed by the program participants are posted at the online resource center: http://carla.acad.umn.edu/cobaltt.

WORLD WIDE WEB RESOURCES FOR LANGUAGE TEACHERS

Debski has described teachers using computers and the World Wide Web in two ways: agentive and instrumental.

Agentive computer use means that the computer delivers rote practice, often contextually and linguistically impoverished, since it must be close-ended due to computers' limited ability to process natural language. In this approach, computer activities are added peripherally to support the instruction of certain curricular elements, or to reinforce them following a classroom session. (1997, p. 45)

Instrumental computer use refers to situations in which learners use the computer as a tool for carrying out certain learning tasks, such as linguistic research for linguistic exploration (e.g., concordances), and the employment of word processors and spreadsheets as tools helping to organize thought and discourse in the foreign language classroom. . . . Computers used instrumentally place technology at the disposal of learners who use them as tools of communication, activity, and creativity, as these engage in language learning and teaching driven by real communication tasks. (1997, p. 46)

There are numerous approaches to using the World Wide Web in today's second/foreign language classrooms. Teachers and learners alike have discovered that the Web is a wonderful resource for language instruction. Numerous sites contain authentic materials such as online newspapers, transportation schedules, movie reviews, music recordings, and live Web cam videos, to name but a few. See Additional Resources at the end of the chapter.

Creating tasks on the Web may include activities such as WebQuests. **WebQuests** are structured tasks, based on the principle tenets of constructivism

---

ACTIVITY FOR VIDEO CLIP

Answer the following questions after viewing the video clip.

1. Describe how the teacher utilizes a one-computer classroom for this activity.

   _____

   _____

   _____

2. In what ways does the teacher connect this lesson to the national standards?

   _____

   _____

   _____

3. What assessment activity can this teacher use for this WebQuest activity?

   _____

   _____

   _____

---

discussed earlier. These are designed to (1) guide learners in using the WWW as an environment in which they can gather information on a topic, (2) help them to think about that information in a critical manner, and (3) transform the information into some meaningful form (Harrison).

A WebQuest is defined as "an inquiry-oriented activity in which some or all of the information that learners interact with comes from resources on the Internet" (Dodge, 1995). A WebQuest is a learning activity that can focus on either a single topic or can be multidisciplinary. There are two types of WebQuests: *short-term* and *long-term*.

A short-term WebQuest is one in which the goal is knowledge acquisition and integration. Students are asked to seek and process a certain amount of information from the Web and make sense of it usually in the form of some completed task or project. Short-term WebQuests are generally designed to be completed in one to three class periods.

A long-term WebQuest is one in which the goal is to challenge students to extend and refine the information they discover online. Students are asked to analyze a particular body of knowledge, integrate it into their own knowledge base, and then present this to the class in the form of a task or project. Long-term WebQuests are generally designed to take between one week and one month to complete.

Now view the video clip of a teacher using a WebQuest.

CONSIDER THESE SAFEGUARDS
WHILE USING THE WEB

    1. Whacking or **cache:** Terms used to indicate that a site taken from the server is copied, downloaded, and stored on local storage (either hard drive or local server). If you consider whacking a site, you must gain permission to copy the site and to store it. Whacking a site requires particular software be installed. Two advantages to whacking Web sites is that the sites do not disappear and students are limited to these sites. Therefore, students are not tempted to go off into undesirable sites.

    2. Blocking Programs: Programs such as NET Nanny, Surf-Watch, CyberPatrol, or CYBERsitter block certain sites and prevent students from going out of predesignated areas.

    3. Bookmarking: Bookmark those sites which are to be used on a particular project/assignment. This keeps the sites you have located marked and identified so you can easily access them.

    4. Internet contracts: Have students sign a contract that outlines their responsibility as an Internet user.

VIRTUAL FIELD TRIPS

    Thanks to the WWW, you can plan field trips with a lot more frequency for your students—a **virtual field trip!** The Internet offers links for hundreds of museums and zoos. Students can actually take a guided tour on many of these sites. For instance, at *http://wwar.com/museums.html* there are links to over 10,000 museums all over the world. Teachers can plan for their students to tour the Louvre in Paris or the Prado in Madrid, to name only two. Or if you would like for your students to experience a scavenger hunt at the Smithsonian in Washington, D.C., you can go to *http://www.si.edu.*

    Zoos around the world have Web sites that are available for virtual tours. We suggest the following sites: *http://www.trinizoo.com* (Emperor Valley Zoo—The Zoological Society of Trinidad and Tobago), *http://www.zooreach.org* (Zoo Outreach Organization), and *http://www.bronxzoo.com* (largest metropolitan zoo in the United States).

E-MAIL

    E-mail, a form of asynchronous computer-mediated communication, has been called "the mother of all Internet applications" (Warschauer, Shetzer, & Meloni, p. 3). This section will include multiple uses of e-mail in second/foreign language learning. E-mail offers learners the opportunity to extend the time and place where foreign/second language occurs. This may include one's own room, public library, or cyber café. Additionally, when students are connected to speakers of the target language outside the classroom, authentic communicative situations are enhanced. E-mail also allows for communication between students in a context where the teacher's role is no

COMPARISON OF FEATURES OF WRITTEN COMMUNICATION VIA PEN AND PAPER AND E-MAIL TECHNOLOGIES IN FOREIGN LANGUAGE CLASSROOMS

PEN AND PAPER WRITING	ELECTRONIC MAIL
Normally limited audience (teacher)	Contact with real people outside the classroom
Often limited communicative purpose (display of competence)	Wide range of communicative purposes (informing, persuading, etc.)
Tends to be perceived as relatively permanent and "on record"	Tends to be perceived as relatively ephemeral and disposable
Intensive, recursive process that fosters elaboration and development of ideas	Emphasis on speed and succinctness of expression
Adherence to formal norms (language, genre, style) generally plays more important role	Adherence to formal norms tends to be relaxed (e.g., mixing of oral/written genres, grammar/spelling mistakes)

Source: Kern, 1998

longer at the center (Patrikis). This also empowers learners to take more control over their own learning. E-mail allows students to communicate with native speakers of the target language without the cost of traveling abroad (Hedderick; Roakes, 1998).

Among the advantages, e-mail offers a relatively simple way of bringing learners into regular contact with native speakers. Such contact can provide real purpose and motivation for learning vocabulary and grammar and foster a deep personal involvement with the language (Kern).

Finally, teachers need to be aware of the work involved in using e-mail as an instructional tool. Technical glitches and the amount of time consumption are important factors to be considered. Students have to be prepared for using e-mail and they must be given a clear explanation of the task that has been assigned.

Easy Ways to Implement E-Mail in the Second/Foreign Language Classroom

Group E-mail Exchanges   There are many ways in which students can gain written communication practice by using e-mail. The following list provides several suggestions:

Intraclass e-mail interaction: Ramazani (1994) describes an activity called "The Weekly Essay." A few days before his class meets, the students e-mail each other essays written on a particular reading. Students come to class better prepared for class discussion of the essays. Another suggestion is for the teacher to assign a debate topic and ask students to begin to discuss it via e-mail. When students come to class they will have some knowledge of both sides of the issue.

Interclass e-mail interaction: may involve a project in which two groups of native speakers collaboratively compose a bilingual slang dictionary via e-mail. *Independent groups outside of class:* Students take part in e-mail projects beyond a regular interclass or intraclass activity. This is especially useful for independent study assignments.

One-on-One E-mail Interaction.   In *e-mail between teacher and learner,* learners may gain self-confidence and self-assurance in their language skills. An exchange with the teacher "may serve as a transition toward the use of foreign language in a real-cybernetic-world context" (Gonzales-Bueno, 1998, p. 55). Teachers may require students to send them periodic messages, offer feedback to students on writing assignments, or correspond using dialogue journals.

In *e-mail between two individual second/foreign language learners,* penpals who correspond using the computer are often referred to as **keypals.** There are numerous lists on the Web containing names of sites where teachers can go to identify keypals for their students. Robb's (1996) online article, "E-mail Keypals for Language Fluency" is a very useful tool. This is particularly beneficial when all correspondence is conducted in the target language.

Listservs.   A **listserv** is an electronic mailing list program that links e-mail users who share a mutual interest, belong to a particular group, or speak a common language (Gonglewski, 1999). Thanks to e-mail, teachers can create listservs that provide direct communication and access to whole groups of students. Typically this is set up by class, thus enabling the teacher to post announcements and homework, and to send and receive information to and from individual students. While instructors can participate in this discourse, their role as primary L2 input source vanishes, and students are "exposed to much comprehensible input in the form of each others' interlanguage" allowing them to engage in meaningful negotiation within their own discourse community (Beauvois, 1995). Teachers may have students submit assignments and/or homework electronically and this can then be graded either by peer assessment or the teacher.

Teachers can take advantage of the numerous professional listservs now available. There are two international listservs which have grown in popularity very recently: **FLTEACH,** administered by LeLoup and Ponterio at SUNY Cortland and **Language Learners and Teachers International (LLTI).** The process for subscribing to these listservs is quite easy and they provide an exchange of information on teaching practices, assessment, employment opportunities, texts, and materials.

Chatrooms.   Chatrooms are similar to listservs in that they provide an environment for students to interact through written communication. This venue is very close to real-time communication. Rankin (1997) points out that chatrooms give students additional valuable "conversation" practice in the target language outside of the classroom, where students can get as little as ten minutes to talk in one week.

Another benefit to chatrooms, MOOs, or similar virtual classrooms is that often during real-time chat, when the teacher poses a question it is taken as a far more personal question, i.e., the student has more of an impression that he or she, and the entire class, is being addressed. This often results in a more active and productive session.

Newsgroups.   Newsgroups are electronic bulletin boards where messages grouped topically are posted and responded to any time (Gonglweski). Using this application, the teacher and student can select a certain number of groups and then read those messages posted.

VIDEO CONFERENCING/DISTANCE EDUCATION

Distance education is instruction delivered to students who are physically and/or geographically separated from the teacher. Communication therefore, is mediated between the teacher and student through some form of technology in synchronous (real) or asynchronous (delayed) time. Distance education is a very useful tool for filling gaps for reaching students who may be in remote geographical areas or who otherwise do not have access to a teacher on-site. It can also be helpful for supplementing the number of courses or levels available to students.

There are many models of distance education that have been applied to the field of second/foreign language instruction. Satellite, microwave, radiowave, and cable broadcast, distributed canned video (used independently or in conjunction with telephone, facsimile, photophone, and other technologies) are used for reaching distant learners.

Distance education is widely used throughout the world, thanks in large part to the ever-increasing availability of technology and multimedia. Distance education is used by colleges and universities, community colleges, K–12 schools, corporations, government and military training programs, and numerous health-care agencies. Teaching through distance education is not exactly the same as teaching face-to-face. Many adaptations need to be made to lessons, activities, and pedagogy in general, and pre- and in-service training for teachers is imperative.

Lynn Fulton-Archer (2000) is a Spanish teacher with South Carolina Educational Television and describes her program by saying:

> "My program, *Descubre el espanol*, began six years ago for rural schools that did not have enough student demand for a full-time teacher. My students are spread across many states. This year's class includes two students on an island off the South Carolina coast, four in a rural school in the western part of the state, and six more at a residential school with a student population of fewer than fifty.
>
> Each day at 11:30 A.M. and 1:30 P.M., I walk into my classroom—a television studio—and teach. My students talk with me live through a multischool conference call, view pictures and language-learning videos showing native-speaking students on classroom TVs to help them learn vocabulary, and converse with their distance classmates hundreds of miles away."

CLASSROOM MODELS FOR DISTANCE EDUCATION
One-way video/Two-way Audio
Two-way video/Two-way Audio

DELIVERY SYSTEMS FOR DISTANCE EDUCATION
Instructional Television Fixed Service (ITFS)
Digital Satellite System (DSS)
Asynchronous Transfer Mode (ATM)—fiber optics
T1—compressed video using existing phone lines
ISDN—newly installed telephone lines

MULTIMEDIA TECHNOLOGY

The term *multimedia* refers primarily to computer applications that include not only text but also other media in digital format. Multimedia provides both teachers and learners a variety of media, e.g., text, graphics, sound, animation, and video. Through prelistening activities and guided listening tasks, beginners can even engage successfully in specified listening comprehension exercises using online live or prerecorded radio programs (Lafford & Lafford, 1997). These can all be accessed on a single computer. The most common multimedia environment consists of multimedia PCs or audio-visual Macintoshes with digital speakers and CD-ROM or DVD drives. This can also include **hypermedia,** which means that the multimedia resources are all linked together. This affords the learner great freedom in moving about at his or her own desired pace and direction. Additionally, teachers can easily accommodate and include the four skills (listening, speaking, reading, and writing) as well as the three modes of communication (interpersonal, presentation, interpretive).

Computer-Mediated Communication

Computer-mediated communication can be asynchronous through e-mail or it can be synchronous using programs such as MOOs, which allow people all over the world to have simultaneous conversations simply by typing on their keyboards. Two popular ways for teachers and students to use CMC via real-time audio- and audio-visual chatting are NetPhone and CU-SeeME.

Videos and Videotexts

Video is at best defined as the selection and sequence of messages in an audio-visual context (Canning-Wilson, 2000). Interactive language learning using video, CD-ROM, and computers allows second/foreign language learners the opportunity to view and actively participate in lessons at their desired pace. While relatively little research has been done to demonstrate how audio-visual aids enhance the language learning process, there are a few that address the issue. Baltova (1994) posits that unlike a student who listened in sound-only conditions, students who used video *and* sound conditions were more consistent in their perception of the story, in the sense that difficult and easy passages formed a pattern. Further, this study indicated that scenes in which utterances were backed up by an action and/or body language, were considered easier to understand by students. Research conducted by Herron, Hanley, and Cole (1995)

LEVEL OF PROFICIENCY	VIDEO VIEWING TIME
Beginning	3–5 minutes
Intermediate	5–7 minutes
Advanced	8–15 minutes

Source: Hall Haley, 2002

suggests that visual support like descriptive pictures significantly improved comprehension scores with language videos for English speaking students who were learning French. This study's results indicated that extensive listening was facilitated by the richness of the context visual organizers, such as language videos, provide.

Canning-Wilson in a large-scale survey suggested that students like learning a language through the use of videos. One of the results of this survey showed that learners preferred action/entertainment films to language films or documentaries in the classroom.

Target language video can and should be used at each level of second/foreign language study. We recommend that the amount of time allotted for viewing videos be determined by the learners' level of proficiency.

Videotexts can be used as highly effective teaching tools in the classroom. As the teacher you will want to preview videos ahead of time to determine their appropriateness (age and language proficiency). Many school districts have their own video libraries from which you can select materials that have already been evaluated.

PRACTICAL IMPLICATIONS FOR USING VIDEO IN A SECOND/FOREIGN LANGUAGE CLASS

- Is a basic form of communication that can be achieved without the help of language

- Provides visual stimuli, such as the environment, which can lead to and generate prediction, speculation, and a chance to activate background schemata

- Allows the learner to see body rhythm and speech rhythm in second language discourse through the use of authentic language and speed of speech

- Allows contextual clues to be offered

- Can act as a stimulus or catalyst to help integrate materials or aspects of the language

Source: Adapted from Canning-Wilson (2000)

Using video provides second/foreign language learners the opportunity to improve their ability to understand comprehensible input. Teachers who opt to use videos can ask **display** and/or **referential questions**. Display questions are those which are based on what the learners interpret visually. This is sometimes referred to as **visual literacy**. Whereas **referential questions** address learners ability to comprehend aural input, display questions may be "spiraling" questions that might stated as the following:

1. yes/no
2. multiple choice

3. one-word answer
4. multi-word answer

Additionally, teachers may wish to utilize graphic organizers and other visual realia to enhance comprehension. Software programs such as Inspiration or Kidspiration allow students to create their own graphic organizers.

Examples of referential questions are those that:

1. make inferences
2. are based on fact or opinion
3. require critical or higher order thinking skills
4. draw conclusion(s)

Electronic Texts

Electronic texts provide information displayed electronically on a computer screen and offer teachers and students tools such as multimedia and telecommunications for second/foreign language and literacy instruction. Language and literacy are socially mediated and socially constructed phenomena. Technology may be regarded as a venue for independent, nonsocial activities. However, utilization of technologies in conjunction with national standards, goals, and effective planning can lead to dynamic interactive classrooms where students take control of their own meaning-making, while teachers scaffold and guide the process. Meskill, Mossop, and Bates (1998) cite the following as pedagogical advantages of using electronic texts:

1. autonomous learning
2. self-pacing
3. increased motivation
4. efficiency in productivity and record-keeping

TECHNOLOGY AND ASSESSMENT

Technology can be a great help to assessment. Some ways to use traditional technologies can include taping students' performance on audiocassette and/or videotape recording a skit, simulation, or dialogue.

Alternative assessment is different from traditional testing in that it actually asks students to show what they can do. Students are evaluated on what they integrate and produce rather than on what they are able to recall and reproduce. Alternative assessment that utilizes technologies may include: journals, reading logs, videos of role plays, audiotapes of discussions, self-evaluation questionnaires, or anecdotal records.

Authentic assessment describes the multiple forms of assessment that reflect student learning, achievement, motivation, and attitudes on classroom activities. The rubric is one authentic assessment tool which is designed to simulate real-life activities

REFLECT AND RESPOND

1. How can the second/foreign language learner benefit from the use of video in the classroom?

   _____

   _____

   _____

2. What are some ways the teacher can assess the learner's comprehension of the video?

   _____

   _____

   _____

3. Select a video segment from a content-based text, e.g., math, science, social studies, English language arts. Give examples of one *display question* and one *referential question*.

   _____

   _____

   _____

in which students are actively engaged in solving real-world problems. Table 9.3 is an example of a rubric designed for authentic assessment of a Web lesson adapted from http://members.aol.com/maestro12/web/evalform.html.

The evaluation rubrics that follow can be used for foreign language Web lessons.

Other Interactive Technology-Based Assessment Tools

One example of proficiency assessment using technology is the Test of English as Foreign Language (TOEFL), which is produced by the Educational Testing Service. Used by over 4,300 institutions of higher education in the United States, it is an indicator of a prospective student's ability to be successful in academic work in which English is the language of instruction. The TOEFL consists of sections on listening comprehension, grammatical accuracy, written expression, reading, and vocabulary. Candidates may opt to take the computer-based test (CBT), which consists of four sections: listening, structure, reading, and writing.

The **Computerized Oral Proficiency Instrument (COPI)** is a multimedia, computer-administered adaptation of the tape-mediated **Simulated Oral Proficiency Interview (SOPI)**. Both the COPI and the SOPI are oral proficiency tests which are based on the Speaking Proficiency Guidelines (see www.actfl.org) of the American Council on the Teaching of Foreign Languages (ACTFL). Oral proficiency assessments such as the SOPI and COPI use simulated real-life tasks to elicit speech that is rated according to the ACTFL guidelines' criteria. The purpose of the COPI is to use the advantages

Class_____ Language Level_____
Web site (URL)_____
Circle all that apply: 1 = poor, 5 = excellent

TYPE OF INSTRUCTION

Individual at computer	Small group at computer	Whole class—one computer			
Skills Addressed					
Listening	Speaking	Reading	Writing		
Thinking Skills					
Recall	Comprehension	Application	Analysis	Synthesis	Evaluation
Standards Addressed					
Communication	Cultures	Connections	Comparisons	Communities	
1 2 3	1 2	1 2	1 2	1 2	
Intelligences Addressed					
Verbal/Ling	Log/Math	Visual/Spatial	Bod/Kin		
Intra/Intro	Mus/Rhythm	Naturalist	Inter/Soc		
Learning Styles					
Visual	Auditory	Kinesthetic		.	
Communicative Mode					
Interpersonal	Interpretive	Presentational			
Reading Strategies					
Pre-reading	Skimming	Reading introduction & conclusion	Semantic mapping		
During-reading	Predicting main idea of each paragraph	Skipping unknown words	Create sentences to demonstrate comprehension		
After-reading	Retell what the writer has said	Relate text to own experiences	Respond to text		
Type of Lesson					
Content-based	Web Quest	Scavenger hunt	Guided reading		

FIGURE 9.3   Evaluation Rubric for Foreign Language Web Lessons

Circle 1 = poor, 5 = excellent						
Appropriateness for level	1	2	3	4	5	
Integration into curriculum	1	2	3	4	5	
Use of target language	1	2	3	4	5	
Enjoyment level for students	1	2	3	4	5	
Advanced preparation by teacher compared to student benefit	1	2	3	4	5	
Appeal to a diverse student population	1	2	3	4	5	
Overall rating	1	2	3	4	5	Excellent Lesson

FIGURE 9.3   (*continued*)

of multimedia computer technology to improve the SOPI by giving examinees more control over various aspects of the testing situation and increasing raters' efficiency in scoring the test (Malabonga & Kenyon, 1999).

TECHNOLOGY AND STANDARDS

In chapter 3 we discussed the role of standards in today's second/foreign language classroom. Here we will discuss the relationship of the ESL and ACTFL foreign language standards as they relate to technology (see www.actfl.org and www.tesol.org). More and more second/foreign language teachers see the resources of the Internet as a way to expand the study of second/foreign language beyond the boundary of the classroom, we must determine how this technology addresses the demands of the standards (Gonglewski). According to Waltz (1998), the Web offers teachers one answer to the challenge of implementing the national standards—". . . the Web must be considered the single best source for all the languages we teach." Having to interact with materials on the Web and independently make discoveries through links to other topics or disciplines contributes to the retention of knowledge (Kost, 1997). Both of these aspects fit nicely with meeting the objectives of the national standards.

Second/foreign language teachers recognize that technology provides ideal means for students to reach out of their own world to another and be able to communicate with the people of that world in multiple languages. The Internet, the Web, and e-mail provide an environment for language learning by supporting the goals set forth in the Foreign Language Standards and the ESL Standards. In the Foreign Language Standards, the goals are grounded in real-world language use. They require students to interact with other speakers. Utilization of e-mail and other Internet resources makes this possible.

The ESL Standards "define the content area for ESL by focusing on the language skills English language learners must master to function successfully in classrooms at all grade levels, as well as in the wider community" (Katz, 1999).

Technology and Diverse Learners

Technology and multimedia are excellent resources for teaching culturally, linguistically, and cognitively diverse students in an interactive content-based classroom setting. As highlighted in chapter 8, working with diverse learners requires you to be an astute observer and record-keeper. By doing so you will be able to note your students' interests, strengths, and weaknesses and provide instructional assistance accordingly. Additionally, you will find that an added benefit of integrating technology into your planning is that it will allow you to reach more students whose learning styles and multiple intelligences are at various levels.

TECHNOLOGY AND TEACHING CULTURE

The sparse work done on computer-enhanced culture learning focuses primarily on products and practices and follows the same model of interacting with native speakers for the purpose of getting information on holidays, celebrations, food, celebrity figures, music, and so forth (Lee, 1997). Such a model may not be effective for providing students with the investigatory tools by which they can come to an understanding of the perspectives of speakers of the second language. Furthermore, such a model raises concerns about native speakers' socioeconomic status, education level, gender, and ethnicity as they relate to other cultures (Moore, Morales, Carel).

If we view language less as a formal or structural system with a fixed set of vocabulary and grammatical rules and more as interaction and discourse in context (Kramsch & Anderson, 1999), we see that language use itself reflects culture, and language learners can gain sociocultural competence by recognizing and decoding signs in the target culture contexts. Multimedia technology allows us to transform context into text so that it can be made learnable in the classroom (Kramsch & Andersen), so that students can view authentic interaction on the screen and incorporate appropriate cultural practices into their own interaction in the target language.

Pusak and Otto (1990, p. 40) state that "by far the most compelling medium for presenting cultural content is video." They also express the belief that the lack of pedagogically sound software may discourage widespread use of interactive media (Moore, Morales, Carel).

WORKING IN DIFFERENTLY EQUIPPED TECHNOLOGY FACILITIES

The Multicomputer Classroom

If you are among the fortunate who teach in a multicomputer classroom, consider yourself lucky. Multicomputer classrooms provide an endless amount of rich resources for both teachers and learners. In such an environment the teacher can provide a varied repertoire of instructional strategies and assessments that can range from learner-centered to teacher-centered. Multicomputer classrooms offer increased opportunities for students to work at varying proficiency levels, preferred learning styles, and multiple intelligences.

The Computerless Classroom

If you find yourself in a classroom in which there is no computer, don't despair. You can still incorporate technology in one form or another. As mentioned earlier, technology in the classroom before computers included overhead projector, cassette recorder, TV monitor, VCR, slide projector and shortwave radio, to name a few. These remain highly effective teaching tools. Other ways to bring technology to a computerless classroom include shortwave or multiband radio and the use of a telephone (land line or cellular). Shortwave or multiband radios can be used for corresponding with target language countries. Additionally, telephones can creatively be used by utilizing the resources of native target language speakers who are willing to telephone students directly in the classroom.

The One Computer Classroom

second/foreign language teachers often find themselves being told to implement technology and though quite willing to do so, are all too frequently faced with the following:

- inadequate staff development on technology
- students who are more technologically literate than they are
- required to use a textbook with accompanying ancillary materials but a lack of appropriate hardware and/or software
- scheduling time in the computer lab is often reserved for other disciplines and not second/foreign language classes
- faced with one computer in the classroom, the teacher must cleverly devise ways to incorporate technology

Should you find yourself in any of the above situations, you can still incorporate technology into your daily lessons. One way to do this is with a lightweight portable scan converter. This enables the teacher to use one computer and convert VGA signals for TV monitors, LCD projectors (these are useful when/if the TV screen is too small for a large group), and VCR. The computer is thus connected to the TV monitor and the entire class can see the same screen.

Another way to remedy this problem is to arrange learning stations around your classroom that utilize not only the computer but other forms of technologies.

Learning stations provide an optimal experience in interactive learning. Clearly, the teacher's role is redefined from that of "knower" to that of "facilitator." This can sometimes be a little unsettling for teachers and it moves the position of the teacher to the periphery, thereby instilling a feeling of loss of control over the class. When you are considering setting up learning stations, you might want to consider the following checklist.

LEARNING STATIONS

Reading	This station can have reading materials such as magazines, TV-guides, short stories, or newspapers. There might be a prerecorded cassette tape to accompany texts, allowing students to listen while they read. Worksheets direct students to requirements for completing tasks.
Listening	This station can include cassette recorders and headphones. Students may be asked to complete a musical cloze activity (see chapter 3) or listen to a news or weather report and discuss it with classmates.
Speaking	This station can include speaking prompts for students that elicit oral response on preselected topics, e.g., describe a typical day; give directions from school to the city library. Students work in pairs or up to four persons.
Writing	This station can include open-ended text activities or ancillary materials, e.g., worksheets, transparencies on an overhead projector.
Games	This station can include logic, role-playing, board, psychomotor, arcade, or games of chance (explained earlier in this chapter).
Culture	This station can include authentic realia such as post cards, menus, money, stamps etc. Student would be asked to compare/contrast and make inferences.
Technology	This station can include exploring the WWW, e-mailing key-pals, developing flashing cards for vocabulary/grammar practice, word-processing activities, or using a CD-ROM for drill and practice.

TEACHER'S CHECKLIST FOR LEARNING STATIONS

Each learning station is numbered and has clearly printed directions taped to a desk/table top.	
Rubrics assessing students' work are in folders at each learning station. These should include a mixture of self- and/or peer-assessment.	
Have a timer in place to move students from one station to the next.	
Create and maintain a "master" notebook with copies and answers to all activities.	
Explain all rules and procedures *before* students begin station work.	
Devise a method for creating groups, allowing for students to work with different combinations.	

REFLECT AND RESPOND

1. How can technology assist teachers in identifying and meeting the individual learning needs of all students?

   _____

   _____

   _____

2. How can technology assist in utilizing different teaching and learning styles to help students meet national standards?

   _____

   _____

   _____

3. Create an action plan describing how a teacher can use technology to improve collaboration between parents and teachers to improve student learning.

   _____

   _____

   _____

DEVELOPMENTS AND TRENDS IN TECHNOLOGY

Information technology is, to say the least, a fluid field. It seems there are always new trends and developments. One can hardly keep pace with the rapid changes in what's new and popular. At this writing, we decided to try and capture just a few of the latest developments and trends that can be implemented as effective instructional practices in K–12 classroom settings.

- voice recognition
- devices for Internet access
- wireless Internet and Web—to use on field trips or scavenger hunts
- handheld digital devices—to create skits or projects
- e-books
- scanners—broadens teachers' access to and variety of materials and ability to share
- education Web portals
- machine translation—take students to online translator

THINK, PAIR, SHARE

After reading this chapter, complete the following activity with a partner.

1. After reading this chapter, this is what I think is important about integrating technology in an interactive, content-based class.

   _____

   _____

   _____

2. After reading, here is what I learned from my partner. Listen to what your partner has written and write down what you learned.

   _____

   _____

   _____

SUMMARY

In this chapter you have examined traditional technologies and multimedia. We have also discussed the pedagogical implications for using technology and its use in an interactive classroom. In the decade of the 1990s and into the millennium second/foreign language education witnessed the use of technologies as commonplace. The computer and other technologies will increase exposure to multi-languages and cultures. This, hopefully, will enhance second/foreign language learning and cultural understanding. Technologies can play a significant role in shaping the instructional discourse and dynamics within carefully planned learning environments. second/foreign language teachers' utilization of technologies provides cross-curricular opportunities in which activation of learning strategies can easily be carried over to other disciplines. ESL teachers can create activities that use software that focus on reading, writing, vocabulary, and grammatical expansion that will coincide with students' content area subjects, and foreign language teachers can provide a vast exposure to authentic texts in mixed genres.

Everyone must remember, however, that technology should never be used just because it is there. Technology must be used only when it enhances the language learning experience (Meloni, 1998). The computer can serve a variety of uses for language teaching. It can be a medium of global communication and a source of limitless authentic materials.

EXERCISES AND ACTIVITIES

DISCUSS AND REFLECT

1. For the purposes of lesson planning, curriculum development, and program implementation, what factors should be considered that will ensure teachers and learners are effectively using technology as a teaching and learning tool?

2. How can technology extend learning time beyond school hours?

3. How can technology decrease the need to build additional school facilities?

4. What can states, school districts, administrators, and teachers do to ensure that a digital divide does not exist in schools?

ASK YOURSELF THESE QUESTIONS

1. How will the second/foreign language learner benefit from the use of multimedia in the classroom?

2. How does technology support the national standards?

3. How is video used in a classroom context?

4. What is the overall educational purpose for implementing technology?

WHAT DO TEACHERS THINK?

My Thoughts on Technology

Technology can truly be a useful tool for a classroom teacher. As a foreign language teacher with six years of experience, I've found technology, from the simple (overhead projectors, videos) to the complex (Internet research, WebQuests) to be a useful tool for my students to use in the classroom.

I am currently fortunate enough to teach at a school in which technology is abundant and easily available. I have four computers in my classroom, which are all linked to the school's computer network and have Internet capabilities. My school also has an LCD projector as well as a piece of equipment called a "focus box," which allows us to connect a computer to the television, so the class can view what we are doing on one computer.

I am the type of teacher who likes to try new technology and finds it fun to try out new things with the technology available in my classroom. I recognize, and know, however, many teachers for whom technology is a bit scary. The main suggestion I have for those who find technology intimidating is to talk to either the technology teacher in your school (if you have one; in my school, we have one TRT [Technology Resource Teacher] and two technology assistants) or if that's not possible, ask a colleague who is more technologically savvy to help. Another possibility is to ask your students; I have found new information, on more than one occasion, from a student.

Teacher Technology Standards

Standard A	Operate a computer system and utilize software.
Standard B	Apply knowledge of terms associated with educational computing and technology.
Standard C	Apply productivity tools for professional use.
Standard D	Use electronic technologies to access and exchange information.
Standard E	Identify, locate, evaluate, and use appropriate instructional technology-based resources to support SOL and other instructional objectives.
Standard F	Use educational technologies for data collection, information management, problem solving, decision making, communications, and presentations within the curriculum.
Standard G	Plan and implement lessons and strategies that integrate technology to meet the diverse needs of learners in a variety of educational settings.
Standard H	Demonstrate knowledge of ethical and legal issues relating to the use of technology.

www.loudoun.k12.va.us/schools/farmwell

The TRT where I teach is wonderfully helpful. The whole technology staff is always willing to help and in addition, they offer classes frequently for teachers in the building. This availability is a huge help! As an example of what is offered to teachers, see the school's Web site at *http://www.loudoun.k12.va.us/schools/farmwell*.

As mentioned early in your chapter, many school districts are holding students accountable for technology as part of their standards of learning. In Loudoun County, Virginia, teachers are also held to a technology standard. For each evaluation cycle every teacher and administrator is required to complete a technology portfolio that is evaluated by both the TRT and the principal. I have included the Teacher Technology Standards of Loudoun County in the following table.

Internet Research and Presentation

One of the major lessons in which I incorporated technology was when I was teaching a unit on French-speaking countries. We identified the countries in class and briefly discussed where the countries were located. The students were then tasked to create a travel brochure to entice people to visit one of the French speaking countries. In order to do this, they had to first choose a country and then research it and then finally create a slide show highlighting the best aspects of their chosen country.

All of the research the students completed was done on the Internet. Before going to the computer lab, I had spoken with the TRT about the project (this is key; the technology teachers can help with finding appropriate Web sites and directing the research). They found a handful of Web sites with various information through which the students could search. The students did have a handout to help guide them on the types of information that would be best to gather.

After they completed their research, which included saving pictures to use in their presentation, the students used a presentation program to create a slide show highlighting their country. When all of the slideshows were complete, the class viewed each one and voted on the most desirable country to visit.

WebQuest

I have used a WebQuest in order to have the students find information about Paris. As stated before, this could be done for any other city that could be useful for an ESL class. This was not a WebQuest that I created, but one that was available through the Loudoun County Public School's Web site (which has many teacher resources). I was able to use the WebQuest, however, as it fit nicely into my curriculum and lesson plan.

I divided the students into groups and each student was assigned to be a member of a family. Each member of the family had different interests, and therefore had to research different places to go and sights to see. After the students completed their WebQuest, each group had to come back together and create a poster (including pictures) of what their "family's" trip would look like, incorporating each family member's wishes.

This activity was nice because it allowed the students to complete their own research and then share the knowledge they had gained with the other members of their group. It was also a nice mix of technology (the WebQuest) and nontechnology (the posters).

Kathy Seaholm is an ESL and French teacher, Loudoun County, Virginia.

I have always thought that the limitations of computers included their lack of human qualities and their inability to provide meaningful support and encouragement: their lack of flexibility and creativity in making instructional decisions, their inappropriateness for extensive amounts of text. In addition to this, many second/foreign language teachers have embraced Internet technologies as effective resources that enhance instruction and consequently student learning, but many more have not done so for a variety of reasons. Lack of knowledge, lack of access, and inadequate role models contribute greatly to the underuse of communications technology in the second/foreign language classroom. The result is many preservice teachers marching through their language curriculum seldom, if ever, seeing technology implemented in the classroom. They therefore are little inclined to include communications technology as part of their own teaching. I personally think that we must make a concerted effort to educate our students in the utilization of communications technology resources. Teachers should be assisted in the creation of sample plans that integrate second/foreign language communications technologies in their curricula. In this respect, and as an example, students will work on their reading and writing skills in the target language via electronic mail. Teachers must be able to integrate technology into their curriculum in meaningful and beneficial ways.

Nour-eddine Bouchtia is an ESL teacher, Prince William County Schools, Virginia.

	TEACHER USE	STUDENT USE
Computers, scanners, printers, etc.	Create worksheets for student use	CD-ROMs to review language (e.g., Rosetta Stone)
	Present information to students using PowerPoint or similar program (AppleWorks, etc.)	Create presentations on a variety of topics—example: after researching home country, create presentation to present to class and perhaps to other classes. About home country (using Internet research, pictures from Internet or home (scan them in); also could create presentation about family (family album); student could have choice of real family or made-up one (nontraditional families)
	Inspiration program for graphic organizers for students	Internet research—variety of topics can be researched (see example above)
	E-pals	Internet e-pals—correspondence with other students from schools in same district or across country or even in another country (might also help with research)
	Games	Games to enhance learning and supplement curriculum: example—Number Munchers for Math, similar type of game for English language skills; dissection programs for animals (many schools have these, perhaps on the network; these are examples from where I work), Story Builder to help write stories
	Draw programs	Use Draw programs to create original drawing and to describe in English; example—body parts, colors, clothing, house, combinations of above, etc.
	Teachers could record students to track progress	Some computers have recording capabilities—students could record themselves and listen back to self-assess and improve speaking skills
Overhead projector & transparencies	Presentation of material given in written form for students to see	Students could use transparencies to present group projects; write out explanation and present to the class. (They love writing on transparencies!)

	TEACHER USE	STUDENT USE
	Flyswatter game (can also be done on chalkboard); various words and answers, written mixed up on transparency; two teams; one member from each team comes to board, teacher asks question, first person to hit the correct answer projected on the board with the flyswatter gets point for team	Students can also create flyswatter games for review and lead the game for the rest of the class
Tape recorders, tapes, CDs	Use tapes/CD for listening activities; example—conversations, music	Have students pick out words they know; stop tape/CD and have them tell you next word (following along with text); cloze activities (fill in missing words—with or without word banks); students can learn words to a song and sing the song, analyze song for grammar concepts (a teacher I had for English in 7th grade did this with a Supertramp song and I still remember it; it was great fun!)
Digital cameras	Take pictures of classes, students, hang up in the room (although students, especially middle schoolers, tend to complain about having their pictures taken, they do enjoy seeing theirs and others' pictures in the room/hallway!)	Students could take pictures for projects; examples—geometric items in various kinds of topography, famous landmarks
Video Cameras	Teachers could record conversations, debates, etc., for use in the classroom	Students could use cameras to film themselves and others in school; interviews; make "movies" using cameras and then software such as I-Movie (Apple)
	Teachers could record student presentations and analyze students' progress.	Students could record, view selves and self-analyze progress
LCD projectors	If short on computers for student use, can use to present material on computer	
TV-Ator/ Focus Box	If short on computers for student use, can use to present material on computer	

Kathy Seaholm
Ideas for Use of Technology in ESL classroom

FIELD-BASED EXPERIENCES

1. Arrange to observe three foreign or second language classes with different teachers during lessons/activities that incorporate technology. Observe how each teacher approaches technology. Reflect on what worked and what didn't work in the lesson/activity.

2. Interview three different foreign or second language teachers and ask them how they incorporate technology in their classroom. How has it, changed the way they approach instruction, if at all?

3. Interview students (or classmates) to identify technology activities that they have used successfully. Have them describe the activity, how to use it, and how they know it works.

CASE STUDY

Ms. Bernier is a second-year ESL teacher. She currently is teaching beginner ESL students; she originally started out with twenty students and now has twenty-nine. Her room, which is extremely small, comes equipped with two computers and no ESL specific software. The school does have two computer labs, but time in the labs is hard to come by. Ms. Bernier would like to include technology in her lessons, but is unsure of where to start.
Answer the following questions:

1. How could the teacher incorporate technology in her lessons?

2. How could she overcome the limitations of having only two computers in her classroom?

3. What help could Ms. Bernier request from her administration in order to help her incorporate technology?

ACTION RESEARCH

1. Create a lesson plan that incorporates technology and try using it in the classroom. What worked? What didn't work? Make revisions and reteach the lesson. How was it different?

2. Design an action research project that will allow you to monitor how the use of different types (or one type in particular) of technology will affect your students' success.

APPLICATION ACTIVITIES

1. Create a graphic organizer that summarizes the different types of technology and their uses in the classroom.

2. As part of your field experience, student teaching internship, or in your own classroom, select three different activities that incorporate technology. Keep notes on what worked well and what didn't. Ask students their opinion of what worked and what didn't.

3. Begin to compile a portfolio, or include in your current portfolio, examples of lessons and/or activities that incorporate technology.

4. Create or find a WebQuest to use in your classroom. After creating and using the WebQuest, reflect on what went well and what didn't go well. If you didn't create a WebQuest, work on creating one that is specifically tailored to your instruction.

5. Arrange to interview technology teachers in different schools/school districts. During your interview, ask them their view on technology, how they support administrators, teachers, staff, etc., what staff development they provide for their teachers, and how they align with local, state, and national standards.

ADDITIONAL RESOURCES

Journals

CALICO Journal
Duke University
014 Language Center, Box 90267
Durham, NC 27708-0267 USA
http://calico.org

Computer-Assisted English Language Learning Journal
1787 Agate St.
Eugene, OR 97403 USA
iste@oregon.uoregon.edu

Computer Assisted Language Learning
P.O. Box 825
2160 SZ Lisse
The Netherlands

Teaching English as a Second or Foreign Language e-journal
TESL-EJ (available on the WWW)
http://www-writing.berkeley.edu/TESL-EJ/about.html

Electronic Mail Lists

EST-L (Teachers of English for Science & Technology)
listserv@asuvm.inre.asu.edu

JALTCALL (Japan Association for Language Teaching CALL)
majordomo@clc.hyper.chubu.ac.jp

LLTI (Language Learning and Technology International)
listserv@dartmouth.edu

NETEACH-L (Using the Internet for teaching ESL)
listserv@thecity.sfsu.edu

TESL-L (Teachers of English as a Second Language)
listserv@cunyvm.cuny.edu

FLTEACH
http://www.cortland.edu/flteach/

CALL: Computer Assisted Language Learning
Many listservs are available. Search on *computer assisted language learning*.

Creating Language Interactivity
http://mld.ursinus.edu/~jarana/Colby/index.html

Organizations

AACE (Association for the Advancement of Computers in Education)
P.O. Box 296
Charlottesville, VA 22902 USA
AACE@virginia.edu

EUROCALL
CTI Centre for Modern Languages
University of Hull
HULL HU6 7RX, UK
Cit.lang@hull.ac.uk

MUESLI (Micro Users in ESL Institutions)
C/o IATEFL
3 Kingsdown Park
Tankerton
Whitstable, Kent
England CT5 2DJ

TESOL CALL Interest Section
C/o TESOL
1600 Cameron St., Suite 300
Alexandria, VA 22314 USA
Tesol@tesol.edu

Other Online Resources

http://www.elsabio.com—K–12 education online content that can be also used offline. Contains interactive tools and activities for teachers and students

http://escuelaelectronica.com—for adults and students wanting to complete their high-school equivalency diplomas

http://electronic-books.com—digital library

http://www.gutenberg.net—free online books in multiple languages

http://epals.com—EPALS Classroom Exchange lists more than 5,900 classrooms from 73 countries

http://ericir.syr.edu/Virtual—Ask ERIC virtual library. Site offers lesson plans and information guides

COMPUTER-ASSISTED LANGUAGE LEARNING

POSTCARD GEOGRAPHY

Cross-Curricular Project

Resources: The Internet and the E-mail
Materials: ESL Science Textbook, *Destinations in Science*, Unit E, Chapter 3
Count Areas: Science, Geography, Language Arts—*cross-curricular*
Objectives: Students will perform the following tasks:

- designing and sending (i.e., e-mailing) geographical postcards on the Internet;
- practicing summary skills in paragraph format *(for review purposes);*
- describing the geography of the Colorado Plateau *(for review purposes);*
- exchanging specific information with an *e-pal* on the Internet via e-mail.

Instructions:

1. Turn to **Unit E, Ch. 3** in your book.
2. Read and review your knowledge about "**plateaus**" (pg. E52–E57).
3. Pick only *one* of the parts of the **Colorado Plateau** below:
   a) **Grand Canyon**
   b) **Bryce Canyon**
   c) **Zion Park**
4. List *3 facts* that you learned about this landform. Provide definitions for vocabulary words such as **plateau, canyon, erosion,** etc.
5. Now you are ready to work on your **e-postcard.**
6. Go to one of the addresses below on the **World Wide Web** (Internet): *www.Corbis.com* or *www.Webshots.com*
7. Search for a ***picture*** that depicts your choice of geographical place.
8. Click on "**send as an e-card**".
9. Type in your **name,** your **e-mail address,** and your **e-pal's email address.**
10. In the message box, type your **message** to your e-pal.
11. Your message should have the following items in order:
    I. **Today's Date**
    II. **Salutation** (Dear . . . .,)
    III. **The Body,** containing the 3 facts you listed above.
    IV. **Closing** (Love, /Your Friend, etc), and
    V. **Signature**
12. Now you can **email your e-card to your e-pal.**

CONGRATULATIONS!

EVALUATION FORM FOR WEB LESSONS

Lesson name _____ Intended language level _____

Web address _____

Circle all that apply.

Type of instruction:					
Individual at computer	small group at computer	whole class - one computer			
Skills addressed:					
listening	speaking	reading	writing		
Thinking skills:					
recall	comprehension	application	analysis	synthesis	evaluation
Which standards are addressed:					
Goal 1	Goal 2	Goal 3	Goal 4	Goal 5	
Which intelligences are addressed:					
verbal-linguistic	logical-math	visual-spatial	bodily-kinesthetic	musical-rhythmic	interpersonal
Senses utilized:					
auditory	tactile	olfactory	visual	gustatory	
Type of communication required:					
written	oral				
Reading strategies employed:					
pre-reading activities:					
during reading:	skimming	cognates	guess meaning in context	careful reading	other
application:					
Type of lesson:					
form-based:	language learning				
meaning-based:	simulation	role play			
uses authentic document	scavenger hunt	research	guided reading		

339

Circle one: 1=minimal, poor, 5=maximum, exemplary

Appropriateness for level	1	2	3	4	5	very appropriate
Integration into curriculum	1	2	3	4	5	integrates perfectly
Use of target language	1	2	3	4	5	exclusive/very appropriate
Enjoyment level for students	1	2	3	4	5	very enjoyable
Advanced preparation by teacher compared to student benefit. (sow/reap)	1	2	3	4	5	minimum teacher preparation; maximum student benefit
Appeal to a diverse student population	1	2	3	4	5	very appealing to all students
Overall rating	**1**	**2**	**3**	**4**	**5**	**exemplary lesson**

Would you use this in your classroom? _____

Could this lesson be presented as well or better in another medium (book, computer program, tapes, etc.)?

_____

How would you modify it?

_____

Other comments:

_____

_____

A RUBRIC FOR EVALUATING WEBQUESTS

The WebQuest format can be applied to a variety of teaching situations. If you take advantage of all the possibilities inherent in the format, your students will have a rich and powerful experience. This rubric will help you pinpoint the ways in which your WebQuest isn't doing everything it could do. If a page seems to fall between categories, feel free to score it with in-between points.

	Beginning	**Developing**	**Accomplished**	**Score**
Overall Aesthetics (This refers to the WebQuest page itself, not the external resources linked to it.)				
Overall Visual Appeal	0 points There are few or no graphic elements. No variation in layout or typography. OR Color is garish and/or typographic variations are overused and legibility suffers. Background interferes with the readability.	2 points Graphic elements sometimes, but not always, contribute to the understanding of concepts, ideas and relationships. There is some variation in type size, color, and layout.	4 points Appropriate and thematic graphic elements are used to make visual connections that contribute to the understanding of concepts, ideas and relationships. Differences in type size and/or color are used well and consistently. See *Fine Points Checklist*.	
Navigation & Flow	0 points Getting through the lesson is confusing and unconventional. Pages can't be found easily and/or the way back isn't clear.	2 points There are a few places where the learner can get lost and not know where to go next.	4 points Navigation is seamless. It is always clear to the learner what all the pieces are and how to get to them.	
Mechanical Aspects	0 points There are more than 5 broken links, misplaced or missing images, badly sized tables, misspellings and/or grammatical errors.	1 point There are some broken links, misplaced or missing images, badly sized tables, misspellings and/or grammatical errors.	2 points No mechanical problems noted. See *Fine Points Checklist*.	

Introduction

Motivational Effectiveness of Introduction	0 points The introduction is purely factual, with no appeal to relevance or social importance OR The scenario posed is transparently bogus and doesn't respect the media literacy of today's learners.	1 point The introduction relates somewhat to the learner's interests and/or describes a compelling question or problem.	2 points The introduction draws the reader into the lesson by relating to the learner's interests or goals and/or engagingly describing a compelling question or problem.
Cognitive Effectiveness of the Introduction	0 points The introduction doesn't prepare the reader for what is to come, or build on what the learner already knows.	1 point The introduction makes some reference to learner's prior knowledge and previews to some extent what the lesson is about.	2 points The introduction builds on learner's prior knowledge and effectively prepares the learner by foreshadowing what the lesson is about.

Task (The task is the end result of student effort . . . not the steps involved in getting there.)

Connection of Task to Standards	0 points The task is not related to standards.	2 points The task is referenced to standards but is not clearly connected to what students must know and be able to do to achieve proficiency of those standards.	4 points The task is referenced to standards and is clearly connected to what students must know and be able to do to achieve proficiency of those standards.
Cognitive Level of the Task	0 points Task requires simply comprehending or retelling of information found on Web pages and answering factual questions.	3 points Task is doable but is limited in its significance to students' lives. The task requires analysis of information and/or putting together information from several sources.	6 points Task is doable and engaging, and elicits thinking that goes beyond rote comprehension. The task requires synthesis of multiple sources of information, and/or taking a position, and/or going beyond the data given and making a generalization or creative product. See *WebQuest Taskonomy*.

Process (The process is the step-by-step description of how students will accomplish the task.)

	0 points	2 points	4 points
Clarity of Process	Process is not clearly stated. Students would not know exactly what they were supposed to do just from reading this.	Some directions are given, but there is missing information. Students might be confused.	Every step is clearly stated. Most students would know exactly where they are at each step of the process and know what to do next.

	0 points	3 points	6 points
Scaffolding of Process	The process lacks strategies and organizational tools needed for students to gain the knowledge needed to complete the task. Activities are of little significance to one another and/or to the accomplishment of the task.	Strategies and organizational tools embedded in the process are insufficient to ensure that all students will gain the knowledge needed to complete the task. Some of the activities do not relate specifically to the accomplishment of the task.	The process provides students coming in at different entry levels with strategies and organizational tools to access and gain the knowledge needed to complete the task. Activities are clearly related and designed to take the students from basic knowledge to higher level thinking. Checks for understanding are built in to assess whether students are getting it. See: • *Process Guides* • *A Taxonomy of Information Patterns* • *Language Arts Standards and Technology* • *WebQuest Enhancement Tools* • *Reception, Transformation & Production Scaffolds*

	0 points	1 points	2 points
Richness of Process	Few steps, no separate roles assigned.	Some separate tasks or roles assigned. More complex activities required.	Different roles are assigned to help students understand different perspectives and/or share responsibility in accomplishing the task.

Resources (Note: you should evaluate all resources linked to the page, even if they are in sections other than the Process block. Also note that books, video and other off-line resources can and should be used where appropriate.)

	0 points	2 points	4 points
Relevance & Quantity of Resources	Resources provided are not sufficient for students to accomplish the task. OR There are too many resources for learners to look at in a reasonable time.	There is some connection between the resources and the information needed for students to accomplish the task. Some resources don't add anything new.	There is a clear and meaningful connection between all the resources and the information needed for students to accomplish the task. Every resource carries its weight.
Quality of Resources	0 points Links are mundane. They lead to information that could be found in a classroom encyclopedia.	2 points Some links carry information not ordinarily found in a classroom.	4 points Links make excellent use of the Web's timeliness and colorfulness. Varied resources provide enough meaningful information for students to think deeply.

Evaluation

	0 points	3 points	6 points
Clarity of Evaluation Criteria	Criteria for success are not described.	Criteria for success are at least partially described.	Criteria for success are clearly stated in the form of a rubric. Criteria include qualitative as well as quantitative descriptors. The evaluation instrument clearly measures what students must know and be able to do to accomplish the task. See *Creating a Rubric*.

Total Score   **/50**

Original WebQuest rubric by *Bernie Dodge*.

This is Version 1.03. Modified by Laura Bellofatto, Nick Bohl, Mike Casey, Marsha Krill, and Bernie Dodge and last updated on June 19, 2001.

GLOSSARY OF TERMS

agentive computer use means that the computer delivers rote practice, often contextually and linguistically impoverished, since it must be close-ended due to computers' limited ability to process natural language (Debski, 1997)

alternative assessment asks students to show what they can do. Students are evaluated on what they integrate and produce

authentic assessment multiple forms of assessment that reflect student learning, achievement, motivation, and attitudes on classroom activities

blocking programs programs such as NET Nanny, Surf-Watch, CyberPatrol, or CYBERsitter block certain sites and prevent students from going out of predesignated areas.

bookmarking marking a site on an Internet browser, enabling the user to return access the site more quickly

cache term used to indicate that a site taken from the server is copied, downloaded, and stored on local storage (either hard drive or local server)

CALL Computer Assisted Language Learning

CD-ROM Compact Disk Read-Only Memory

chatroom chatrooms are similar to listservs in that they provide an environment for students to interact through written communication. These are generally real-time conversations.

computer-mediated communication examples include e-mail and synchronous (live or real-time) communication via the Internet.

constructivism refers to a collection of different theories, from a wide range of disciplines; learners construct their own meaning and impose their own structure on any situation they encounter, no matter how complex (Harrison, 1998)

COPI Computerized Oral Proficiency Instrument, a multimedia, computer-administered adaptation of the tape-mediated Simulated Oral Proficiency Interview

display question questions that are based on what the learners see

e-mail a system for sending and receiving messages electronically over a computer network, as between personal computers

FLTEACH international listserv where teachers can share teaching tips, materials, successes/failures, and sources of information

HTML Hypertext Markup Language; programming language used to create Web pages.

hypermedia a computer-based information retrieval system that enables a user to gain or provide access to texts, audio, and video recordings, photographs, and computer graphics related to a particular subject

instrumental computer use refers to situations in which learners use the computer as a tool for carrying out certain tasks, such as linguistic research for linguistic exploration, and the employment of word processors and spreadsheets as tools helping to organize thought and discourse (Debski, 1997)

key pal a pen pal reached through the Internet

LLTI Language Learners and Teachers International listserv where teachers can share teaching tips, materials, successes/failures, and sources of information

LCD a digital display that uses liquid crystal cells that change reflectivity in an applied electric field, used for portable computer displays and watches

listserv an electronic mailing list program that links e-mail users who share a mutual interest, belong to a particular group, or speak a common language (Gonglewski, 1999)

MOOs Multiple-user-domains Object Oriented: an interactive CALL utility that allows for real-time communication, role playing, and simulation

referential question questions that address learners ability to comprehend aural input

SOPI Simulated Oral Proficiency Interview, oral proficiency test based on the *Speaking Proficiency Guidelines* of the American Council on the Teaching of Foreign Languages (ACTFL)

strategy game require higher-order thinking skills and problem-solving skills for successful completion

TELL technology enhanced language learning   refers to the use of some means of technology to improve the flow or quality of the message between second/foreign language teachers, learners, and users (Shrum & Glisan, 2000)

twitch game   requires quick reaction to stimuli. Movement is usually quick and feedback is instantaneous.

URL   uniform resource locator: an Internet address, most often designated by beginning http://.

VCR   video cassette recorder; an electronic device for recording and playing back video images and sound on a videocassette

videotext   videos that can be used to supplement your content-based teaching. Because of the wide variety available, you will find videos in just about every content area.

virtual field trip   using the WWW, guided tours can be taken to visit far-reaching places of the globe

visual literacy   refers to learners' ability to answer questions based on what they see in a video, pictures and images

Web   the array of computer systems that can read HTML (see HTML) allowing users to navigate a variety of connected sites on the Internet. (Also known as the World Wide Web.)

WebQuest   an inquiry-oriented activity in which some or all of the information that learners interact with comes from resources on the Internet (Dodge, 1995)

whacking   term used to indicate that a site taken from the server is copied, downloaded, and stored on local storage (either hard drive or local server)

WWW   refers to the World Wide Web, a complex set of computers spread throughout the world, all connected to one another via software

---

REFERENCES

Andersen Kramsch, C., & Andersen, R. (1999). Teaching text and context through multimedia. *Language Learning and Technology*, 2, (2), 31–42.

Anderson, R. (1980). *Cognitive psychology and its implications*. New York: W. H. Freeman.

Armstrong, K., & Yetter-Vassot, C. (1994). Transforming teaching through technology. *Foreign Language Annals*, 27 (4), 475–86.

Baltova, I. (1994). Impact of video on the comprehension skills of core French students. *Canadian Modern Language Review*, 50 (3), 506–31.

Beauvois, M. (1995). E-talk: Attitudes and motivation in computer-assisted classroom discussion. *Computer and the Humanities*, 28, 177–90.

Brown, K., Cummins, J., Figueroa, E., & Sayers, D. (1998). Global learning networks: Gaining perspective on our lives with distance. In E. Lee, D. Menkart, & M. Okazawa-Rey (Eds.) (pp. 334–54), *Beyond heroes and holidays: A practical guide to K–12 antiracist, multicultural education and staff development*. Washington, DC: Network of Educators on the Americas.

Byrnes, H. (1996). The future of German in American education: A summary report. Available at: http://www.aatg.org/futfr.html

Canning-Wilson, C. (2000). Role of video in the F/SL classroom. In S. Riley, S. Roudi & C. Coombe (Eds.), *Teaching, Learning and Technology*, TESOL Arabia 1999 Conference Proceedings, March 8–10, 1999.

Cates, W. (1992). Fifteen principles for designing more effective instructional hypermedia/multimedia products. *Educational Technology*. 32 (12), 5–11

Cummins, J. (1996). *Negotiating identities: Education for empowerment in a diverse society*. Los Angeles: California Association for Bilingual Education.

Cummins, J. (2000). Academic language learning, transformative pedagogy, and information technology: Towards a critical balance. *TESOL Quarterly*, 34(3), 537–48.

Debski, R. (1997). Support of creativity and collaboration in the language classroom: A new role for technology. *The Australian Review of Applied Linguistics. Occasional Papers*, 16, 39–65.

de Klerk, G. (Ed.). (1998). *Virtual power: Technology, education, and community*. Long Beach, CA: Pacific Southwest Regional Technology in Education Consortium.

Dodge, B. (1995). Retrieved from http://webquest.sdsu.edu/about–webquests.html

Driscoll, Marcy Perkins. (1994). *Psychology of learning for instruction*. Needham Heights, MA: Allyn & Bacon.

Fast, M. (1998). In Judith Muyskens (Ed.) (pp. 117–42), Remote access for foreign or second language acquisition: New interpretations of distance learning. *New ways of learning and teaching: Focus on technology and foreign language education.* Boston: Heinle & Heinle.

Gagne, R. M. (1985). *The conditions of learning.* New York: Holt, Rinehart and Winston.

Garrett, N. (1992). Technology in the service of language learning: Trends and issues. *Modern Language Journal, 75,* 74–96.

Gassin, M. Smith (Eds.), *Language learning through social computing: Applied Linguistics Association of Australia occasional working papers,* No. 16. ALAA & Horwood Language Centre, University of Melbourne, pp. 39–66.

Gonglewski, M. R. (1999). Linking the Internet to the National Standards for Foreign Language Learning. *Foreign Language Annals, 32*(3) 34–61.

Gonzalez-Bueno, M. (1998). The effects of electronic mail on Spanish L2 discourse. *Language Learning and Technology, 1* (2), 55–70.

Grabe, M., & Grabe, C. (1996). *Integrating technology for meaningful learning.* New Jersey: Houghton Mifflin.

Harrison, R. (1998). The evolution of networked computed in the teaching of Japanese as a foreign language. *Computer Assisted Language Learning,* 11 (4), 437–52.

Hedderich, N. (1997). Peer tutoring via electronic mail. *Die Unterrichtspraxis Teaching German, 2,* 141–7.

Herron, C., Hanley, J., & S. Cole. (1995). A comparison study of two advance organizers for introducing beginning foreign language students to video. *Modern Language Journal, 79* (3), 387–94.

Herselman, M. (1999). South African resource-deprived learners benefit from CALL through the medium of computer games. *Computer Assisted Language Learning,* 12 (3), 197–218.

Hill, B. (1988). Developments in interactive video. *Die Neueren Sprachen,* 87(6).

Hughes, C., & Hewson, L. (1998). Online interactions: Developing a neglected aspect of the virtual classroom. *Educational Technology, 38* (4), 48–55.

Jones, M. G. (1997). *Learning to play; playing to learn: Lessons learned from computer games.* Retrieved March 7, 1997, from *http://intro.base.org/docs/mjgames* [To access this paper, search on title.]

Kassen, M. A., & Higgins, C. J. (1997). Meeting the technology challenge: Introducing teachers to language-learning technology. In M. D. Bush & R. M. Terry (Eds.) (pp. 165–84), *Technology-enhanced language learning.* American Council on the Teaching of Foreign Languages. Lincolnwood, IL: NTC/Contemporary Publishing Group.

Katz, A. (1999). Standards-based assessment for ESOL students. ERIC Vol. 22, No. 2. Retrieved from http://www.cal.org/ericll/news/199903/main.html.

Kearsley, G. (1998). Educational technology: A critique. *Educational Technology, 38* (2), 47–51.

Kern, R. (1998). Technology, social interaction, and literacy. In Judith Muyskens (Ed.) (pp. 57–92), *New ways of learning and teaching: Focus on technology and foreign language education.* Boston: Heinle & Heinle.

Kost, C. (1997). Landeskunde im internet: Eine computergest tzte unterrichtseinheit. *Die Unterrichtspraxis/Teaching German, 2,* 210–13.

Lafford, P., & Lafford, B. (1997). Learning language and culture with Internet technologies. In M. D. Bush & R. M. Terry (Eds.) (pp. 215–62), *Technology-enhanced language learning.* American Council on the Teaching of Foreign Languages. Lincolnwood, IL: NTC/Contemporary Publishing Group.

Laurillard, D. (1995). Multimedia and the changing experience of the learner. *British Journal of Educational Technology, 26* (3) 179–89.

Lee, L. (1997). Using technology to enhance culture. *Foreign Language Annals, 30* (3), 410–26.

LeLoup, J., & Ponteiro, R. (1996). Choosing and using materials for a 'net' gain in FL learning and instruction. In V.B. (Ed.), *Reaching out to the communities we serve.* NYSAFLT Annual Meeting Series 13.

Malabonga, V., & Kenyon, D. (1999). Multimedia computer technology and performance-based language testing: A demonstration of the computerized oral proficiency instrument. *Association for Computational Linguistics Proceedings—1999.*

Meloni, C. (1998, Jan/Feb). The Internet in the classroom: A valuable tool and resource for ESL/EFL teachers. *ESL Magazine, 10* (16).

Meskill, C. (1996). Listening skills development through multimedia. *Journal of Educational Multimedia and Hupermedia, 5* (2).

Meskill, C., Mossop, J., & Bates, R. (1998). *Electronic texts and learners of English as a second language.* Paper presented at the American Educational Research Association. San Diego, CA, April 13–17, 1998.

Moore, Z. (1999). Technology and teaching culture in the L2 classroom: An introduction. *Journal of Educational Computing Research, 20* (1), No. 1–9, 1–9.

Moore, Z., Morales, B., & Carel, S. (1999). Technology and teaching culture: Results of a state survey of foreign language teachers. *CALICO Journal, 15* (1–3), 109–28.

Nieto, S. (1999). *The light in their eyes: Creating multicultural learning communities.* New York: Teachers College Press.

Patrikis, P. (1995). Where is computer technology taking us. *ADFL Bulletin, 26* (2) 36–9.

Phillips, J. (1998). Media for the message: Technology's role in the Standards. *CALICO Journal, 16* (1), 25–35.

Pusak, J., & Otto, S. (1990). Applying instructional technologies. *Foreign Language Annals, 23* (5), 409–17.

Quinn, C. N. (1997). *Engaging learning.* Retrieved from *http://www.addressneedscompletingplease:* Itforum: *listserv@uga.cc.uga.edu* [To access article, search on title.]

Ragan, L. (1999). Good teaching is good teaching: An emerging set of guiding principles for the design and development of distance education. *Cause/Effect, 2* (1). Available at *http://www.educause.edu/ir/library/html/cem9915.html*

Ramazani, J. (1994). Student writing by e-mail: Connecting classmates, texts, instructors. Retrieved on December 8, 2001, from http://www.virginia.edu/~tre/tcemail.htm

Rankin, W. (1997). Increasing the communicative competence of foreign language students through the FL chatroom. *Foreign Language Annals 30* (4), 542–46.

Roakes, S. (1998). The internet: A goldmine for foreign language resources. Retrieved on December 7, 2001, from *http://www.call.gov/resource/essays/internt.htm*

Robb, T. (1996). E-mail keypals for language fluency. Retrieved on December 8, 2001, from *http://www.kyoto-suacjp/~trobb/keypals.html*

Salisbury, D. F. (1990). Cognitive psychology and its implication for designing drill and practice programs for computers. *Journal for Computer-Based Instruction, 17* (1), 23–30.

Squires, D., & Preece, J. (1996). Usability and learning: Evaluating the potential of educational software. *Computers and Education, 27* (1), 15–22.

Stern, H. H. (1990). *Issues and options in language teaching.* Oxford, UK: Oxford University Press.

United States Department of Education. (August 3, 1998). The Technology Literacy Challenge. Office of Educational Technology. Retrieved December 30, 2001, from *http://www.ed.gov/Technology*

Vygotsky, L. (1986). *Thought and Language.* Cambridge, MA: MIT Press.

Waltz, J. (1998). Meeting standards for foreign language learning with World Wide Web. *Foreign Language Annals, 31,* 103–14.

Warschauer, M., Shetzer, H., & Meloni, C. (2000). *Internet for English teaching.* Alexandria, VA: TESOL Publications.

Warschauer, M. (1996). Computer-mediate collaborative learning: Theory and practice. *The Modern Language Journal, 81* (4), 470–81.

Warschauer, M. (1996). Computer-assisted language learning: An introduction. In S. Fotos (Ed.) *Multimedia language teaching.* Tokyo: Logos, International.

CHAPTER TEN

COMPREHENSION EXERCISES

CHAPTER 1

How Languages Are Learned and Acquired

I. CHAPTER REVIEW

1. Define *language*.

_____

_____

_____

2. Define *language learning*.

_____

_____

_____

3. Differentiate between *language learning* and *language acquisition*.

_____

_____

_____

4. What are some pedagogical implications for psycholinguistic theories and practices?

_____

_____

_____

5. What are some pedagogical implications for sociocultural theories and practices?

_____

_____

_____

II. REFLECTING ON WHAT YOU'VE READ

1. How do you ensure that your lessons are both interactive and content-based?

_____

_____

_____

2. Given that you will undoubtedly have multilevel proficient students in your classes, how will you design instructional strategies that provide comprehensible input, namely _i + 1?_

_____

_____

_____

3. What kinds of print material will you make available to students in your classroom? What will guide your selection?

_____

_____

_____

4. How will you use resources from your students' L1 to help them learn English?

_____

_____

_____

III. GRAPHIC ORGANIZER

Use the graphic organizer below to illustrate similarities and differences between socio-cultural and psycholinguistic theories and practices

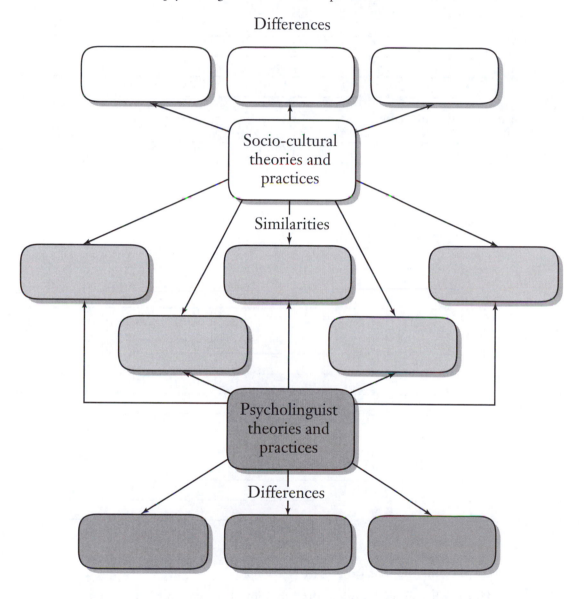

IV. APPLICATION ACTIVITIES

Write an activity for second language learners that incorporates each of the five attributes of interaction:

Meaningful Interaction

_____

_____

_____

_____

Authentic Interaction

_____

_____

_____

_____

Relevant Interaction

_____

_____

_____

_____

Reflection and Action

_____

_____

_____

_____

Feedback

_____

_____

_____

_____

V. KWLA

Use the following KWLA activity to summarize what you've learned.

This is what I now **know, wanted** to know, **learned,** and how I'll **apply** how languages are learned and acquired:

_____

_____

_____

_____

CHAPTER 2

Methods and Approaches in Language Teaching

I. CHAPTER REVIEW

1. List and describe the *behaviorist* methods.

_____

_____

_____

_____

_____

2. List and describe the *rationalist* methods.

_____

_____

_____

_____

_____

3. List and describe the *functional* approaches.

_____

_____

_____

_____

_____

4. List and describe the *humanistic* approaches.

_____

_____

_____

_____

_____

5. Describe one interactive activity each for a beginner, intermediate, and advanced ESL class for #s 1–4.

_____

_____

_____

_____

_____

II. REFLECTING ON WHAT YOU'VE READ

Review your second/foreign language experience as you described it on p. 34. (Reflect and Respond).

1. Are there methods or approaches that you would probably *not* use? Why?

   _____

   _____

   _____

   _____

2. How did your experience as a second/foreign language learner influence your preference for a method or approach?

   _____

   _____

   _____

   _____

III. GRAPHIC ORGANIZER

Fill in the four graphic organizers below using what you've learned from this chapter.

IV. APPLICATION ACTIVITIES

1. Select an ESL textbook that you may use/are using. What methods or approaches would work best?

   _____

2. Observe ESL classes or view videotapes and describe the methods and approaches used by the teacher(s). Describe what worked best and with whom.

   _____

V. KWLA

Use the following KWLA activity to summarize what you've learned in this chapter.

This is what I now **know, wanted** to know, **learned,** and how I'll **apply** what I learned about methods and approaches to teaching second languages:

_____

_____

_____

_____

BEHAVIORIST METHODS

	GRAMMAR TRANSLATION	DIRECT METHOD	ALM
Characteristics			
Interactive Content-Based Application			
Interactive Content-Based Activity			
ESL Standards			
Learning Styles			
Multiple Intelligences			

RATIONALIST AND MENTALIST METHODS

	COGNITIVE ANTI-METHOD	COGNITIVE CODE METHOD
Characteristics		
Interactive Content-Based Application		
Interactive Content-Based Activity		
ESL Standards		
Learning Styles		
Multiple Intelligences		

FUNCTIONALIST APPROACHES

	CALLA	CLT	TPR	TPRS	NATURAL APPROACH
Characteristics					
Interactive Content-Based pplication					
Interactive Content-Based Activity					
ESL Standards					
Learning Styles					
Multiple Intelligences					

HUMANISTIC APPROACHES AND METHODS

	CLL	SILENT WAY	SUGGESTOPEDIA	RASSIAS METHOD
Characteristics				
Interactive Content-Based Application				
Interactive Content-Based Activity				
ESL Standards				
Learning Styles				
Multiple Intelligences				

CHAPTER 3

Planning for the Standards-Based Classroom

I. CHAPTER REVIEW

1. List three types of planning.

2. Describe FLES, FLEX, and immersion education.

3. What is meant by reflection in the planning process?

4. Explain the concept of differentiated instruction.

5. Explain how the time of day influences your planning.

II. REFLECTING ON WHAT YOU'VE READ

1. How does prior knowledge influence planning in an interactive standards-based classroom?

2. What are some of the criteria you would use to analyze and select a textbook for a content-based beginning level ESL class?

3. When planning, how can or should standards be a part of the process? To what degree should they direct your planning?

4. How does cultural awareness play a role in planning?

5. Why is it important to meet with multiple-content teachers and or other team members on a regular basis regarding planning?

III. GRAPHIC ORGANIZER

Building a thematic or unit plan. Use the following organizer to develop a one-week unit plan. You may base the plan on either a thematic subject or on a required standard.

SUBJECT, THEME, OR STANDARD

	MONDAY	TUESDAY	WEDNESDAY	THURSDAY	FRIDAY
Activity Description					
Objective					
Resources Needed					

IV. APPLICATION ACTIVITIES

One of the many challenges that new teachers face is planning appropriately, based on curriculum requirements as well as student need. You should teach content in a way that assists the students academically as well as with second language acquisition. The following is a class scenario with which you can practice planning lessons that suit the group's dynamics. Note that the group is not homogeneous, reflecting real-life situations.

The class has been set up to indicate each student's age, gender, home language, L2 level, and learning style. Use this information during preplanning, when choosing materials, and for developing both lesson plan structure and assessment models.

ELEMENTARY LEVEL
CLASS A
GRADE 5

STUDENTS	M/F	HOME LANGUAGE	LEVEL	LEARNING STYLE
Hyung	M	Korean	Beg	Auditory
Byung	M	Korean	Beg+	Kinesthetic
Claudia	F	Spanish	Int	Visual
Samantha	F	Spanish	Beg	Auditory
Rosalva	F	Spanish	Beg	Visual
Hasan	M	Urdu	Int	Spec Need
Henry	M	Spanish	Beg	Kinesthetic

1. Situation 1: The fifth-grade team comes to you and informs you that the class is beginning a unit on the three branches of the U.S. government. How will your planning reflect the needs of the students in this class, assuming it is a pullout

situation? Pullout indicates that the ESOL teacher works independently with students in a separate location than mainstream students. *Write a sample lesson for this student group using the following questions as a guide.*
  a. What do you want your students to know?
  b. What do you want your students to be able to do?
  c. Can you measure it? (How?)
  d. How will you differentiate instruction to meet the needs of all your learners?

2. Situation 2: Prepare a reading lesson where the skill taught is identifying the main idea. Choose a book you think would be appropriate for this group and explain how you would differentiate instruction for students in your class.

3. Situation 3: Prepare a writing prompt and describe a writing lesson you would plan that encourages students to share attitudes and information that reflect their culture.

4. Plan a lesson that would introduce and prepare students for one of the following: reading and comprehending calendars, bus and train schedules; filling out job applications, or developing banking skills.

V. KWLA

Use the KWLA activity below to summarize what you've learned in this chapter.

This is what I now **know, wanted** to know, **learned,** and how I'll **apply** what I learned about planning for a standards-based classroom:

_____

_____

_____

_____

CHAPTER 4

Creating Interactive and Content-Based Assessment

I. CHAPTER REVIEW

1. What is assessment? How does it differ from evaluation?

_____

_____

_____

2. Describe three ways assessment can be used.

_____

_____

_____

3. Define alternative assessment and describe one example.

_____

_____

_____

4. What is a standardized test? Name one standardized test in your school district. What content is measured?

_____

_____

_____

5. Compare an analytic rubric to a holistic rubric.

_____

_____

_____

II. REFLECTING ON WHAT YOU'VE READ

1. What assessment tools could you use to determine a student's ability to comprehend text read aloud and the content-based concepts within the text? How would the information gained enable you to meet the student's needs?

_____

_____

_____

2. Given that assessment and instruction need to be aligned, what are the multiple ways of assessing content that could be matched with teaching practices?

_____

_____

_____

3. Describe how the use of portfolios enhances the students' abilities to self-assess their work.

_____

_____

_____

III. GRAPHIC ORGANIZER

Developing an assessment plan

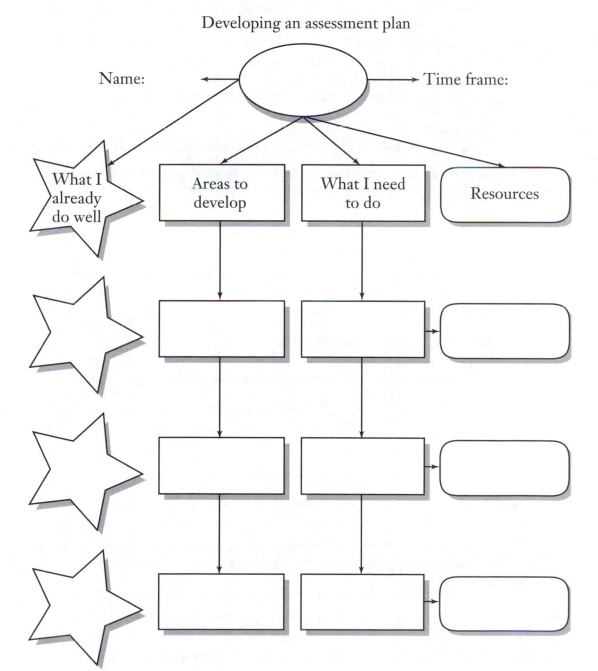

IV. APPLICATION ACTIVITIES

1. When creating or choosing a writing assessment tool for use with a diverse group of students, what criteria should you use to determine the best instrument for gathering information? Write four criteria or essential ideas to consider.

2. Using the ESL standards for writing, create a holistic rubric to be used as an assessment tool in a diverse ESL class. Keep the objectives or goals for your students clear, so the rubric can also be used as a self-assessment tool for the students.

V. KWLA

Use the following **KWLA** activity to summarize what you've learned in this chapter

This is what I now **know, wanted** to know, **learned,** and how I'll **apply** what I learned about interactive and content-based assessment:

_____

_____

_____

_____

CHAPTER 5

Interactive Listening and Reading

I. CHAPTER REVIEW

1. What does listening mean in the context of second language learning?

_____

_____

_____

2. Define literacy. How is it different from reading?

_____

_____

_____

3. What is the purpose of the ESL standards?

_____

_____

_____

4. List the differences between foreign and second language learning.

_____

_____

_____

5. List types of media used in teaching how to interpret oral communication.

_____

_____

_____

6. List and define reading skills and strategies.

_____

_____

_____

_____

II. REFLECTING ON WHAT YOU'VE READ

1. How would you use reception strategies in an ESL classroom?

_____

_____

_____

2. How would you integrate listening and reading skills into content area learning in the classroom?

_____

_____

_____

3. What is the value of social interaction in the negotiation of meaning in the context of a reading classroom?

_____

_____

_____

4. Why is cultural validity an important aspect of literacy?

_____

_____

_____

III. GRAPHIC ORGANIZER

Complete the following table with definitions of reading skills.

READING SKILL	DEFINITION
Intensive reading	
Extensive reading	
Skimming	
Scanning	

1. Complete the following Venn diagram comparing and contrasting listening and reading comprehension.

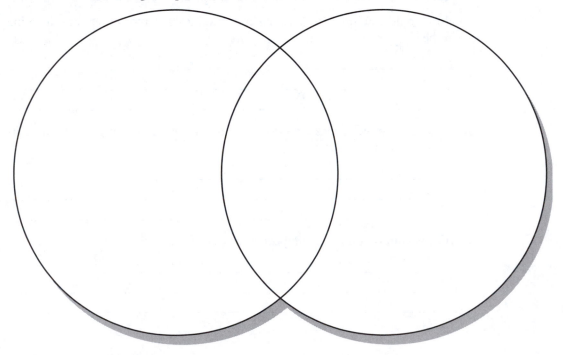

IV. APPLICATION ACTIVITIES

1. Observe two ESL classes or view videotapes and describe how the teacher integrates listening and reading skills in his or her classroom. Describe what worked best. Compare and contrast the teaching methods implemented in each class.

_____

_____

_____

2. Select a content area objective. Then create a brief text-based activity that will enable students to develop knowledge or skills associated with that objective (e.g., science—The earth revolves around the sun and rotates on its axis). Be sure that the activity you choose will allow you to assess the students' reading comprehension and strategies.

V. KWLA

Use the following KWLA activity to summarize what you've learned in this chapter.

This is what I now **know, wanted** to know, **learned,** and how I'll **apply** what I learned about interactive listening and reading:

_____

_____

_____

_____

CHAPTER 6

Foregrounding Oral Communication

I. CHAPTER REVIEW

1. What are some characteristics of good learners in terms of oral communication?

_____

_____

_____

2. Define acquisition.

_____

_____

_____

3. In what ways can an ESL content-based program improve overall student learning and academic skill development?

_____

_____

_____

4. Explain strategic competence.

_____

_____

_____

5. Define the difference between interference and fossilization.

_____

_____

_____

6. What is subtractive bilingualism and how is it detrimental to second language learners?

_____

_____

_____

7. Explain the processability theory.

_____

_____

_____

II. REFLECTING ON WHAT YOU'VE READ

1. In language development, why does oral development usually come after listening comprehension?

_____

_____

_____

2. Explain the value of cultural norms to the bilingual child.

_____

_____

_____

3. Why is it essential to involve early or emerging bilinguals in consistent, sustained oral language practice?

_____

_____

_____

4. What instructional strategies or learning activities could you use to help a student express personal views and values interactively?

_____

_____

_____

III. GRAPHIC ORGANIZER

The following organizer can be used as a concept map. Choose an idea from the chapter (e.g., dialogic communication, critical language awareness, strategic competence) and write it at the top in the oval as your concept. Then, complete the map by defining specific goals, objectives, and activities to work on this concept with students.

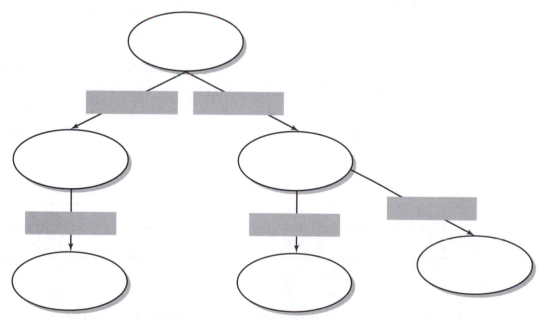

IV. APPLICATION ACTIVITIES

1. Write a role-play scenario for middle school ESL or FL students. Clearly define the setting and the linguistic or conversational goals or requirements for the students.

2. Observe a mixed proficiency level ESL class and write a brief analysis of how gender, ethnicity, and race play a role in the students' participation or oral communication.

3. Observe and assess a group of ESL or FL learners in a communicative situation based on the interview scale in chapter 6.

V. KWLA

Use the following KWLA activity to summarize what you've learned in this chapter.

This is what I now **know, wanted** to know, **learned,** and how I'll **apply** what I learned about foregrounding oral communication:

_____

_____

_____

_____

CHAPTER 7

A Focus on Written Language Communication

I. CHAPTER REVIEW

1. Define interactive writing.

_____

_____

_____

2. List some important skills students need to develop for written communication.

_____

_____

_____

3. How does cultural perspective affect writing development?

_____

_____

_____

4. What is the difference between the psycholinguistic and sociocultural perspectives on writing for second language learners?

_____

_____

_____

II. REFLECTING ON WHAT YOU'VE READ

1. Why is writing the last component of language communication to develop in most second language learners?

_____

_____

_____

2. How does the sense of audience help a second language learner improve writing skills?

_____

_____

_____

3. Why is written communication development a different process for older second language learners as contrasted with elementary learners?

_____

_____

_____

III. GRAPHIC ORGANIZER

The following organizer can be used as a planning tool for writer's workshop. Define a genre and the information you want students to understand about that genre. Next list some actual examples used in real life of this style of writing, and, finally, describe a possible activity to develop student writing in this area.

Genre			
Characteristics: What students should know			
Real-Life Examples			
Possible Activity			

IV. APPLICATION ACTIVITIES

1. Write an interactive writing lesson for an ESL class to teach the skill of paragraph development. Be sure to use topics and ideas relevant to your students.

2. Observe a writers workshop activity or lesson in a standard classroom. Take notes on what you see and describe it. Then explain how you would adjust or scaffold that lesson to use in an ESL environment and meet the writing needs of ESL students.

V. KWLA

Use the following KWLA activity to summarize what you've learned in this chapter

This is what I now **know, wanted** to know, **learned,** and how I'll **apply** what I learned about written language communication:

_____

_____

_____

_____

CHAPTER 8

An Interactive Approach for Working with Diverse Learners

I. CHAPTER REVIEW

1. How does the increase in diversity among students in the United States contrast with the current changes in the demographics of teachers? Why is this an issue for the educational system?

_____

_____

_____

2. What constitutes a diverse learner?

_____

_____

_____

3. As a teacher, what are some essential things you need to learn about your students? How will this knowledge affect their education?

_____

_____

_____

4. Explain the importance of training special educators on the subject of ESL.

_____

_____

_____

5. What factors contribute to the inequality of education across districts and around the nation?

_____

_____

_____

6. Define the term *learner-centered instruction.*

_____

_____

_____

7. How can instruction be made culturally relevant? What are some challenges to this process?

_____

_____

_____

II. REFLECTING ON WHAT YOU'VE READ

1. Briefly describe how you learn. What is your learning style? How do you know this? What types of learning activities are most comfortable for you? What activities are more difficult?

_____

_____

_____

_____

2. What are some approaches you can use to identify a gifted second language learner whose English proficiency is limited?

_____

_____

_____

3. Federal legislation describes a "least restrictive environment" for special needs students. Other than the physical ability to move comfortably in the classroom, how else could this term be applied to diverse learners?

_____

_____

_____

4. What aspects of classroom dynamics in a diverse population seem most challenging to you? Of these, which might have a major impact on your students if not appropriately developed? Where might you find helpful resources on this subject?

_____

_____

_____

5. Consider your own education and other school experiences you have had. Describe a practice in the school that needs to be adjusted to accommodate diverse learners. What can be done to change the situation? What community alliances might help any adjustments be successful?

_____

_____

_____

III. GRAPHIC ORGANIZER

1. Multiple Intelligence (MI) Theory—Practical Usage Organizer
   Using the two organizers shown here, choose two of the eight intelligences and
   complete the diagram with ideas for activities that apply to that intelligence for
   each area of learning.

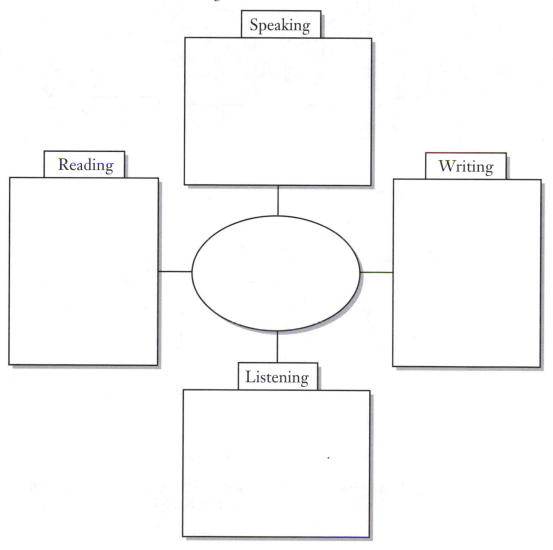

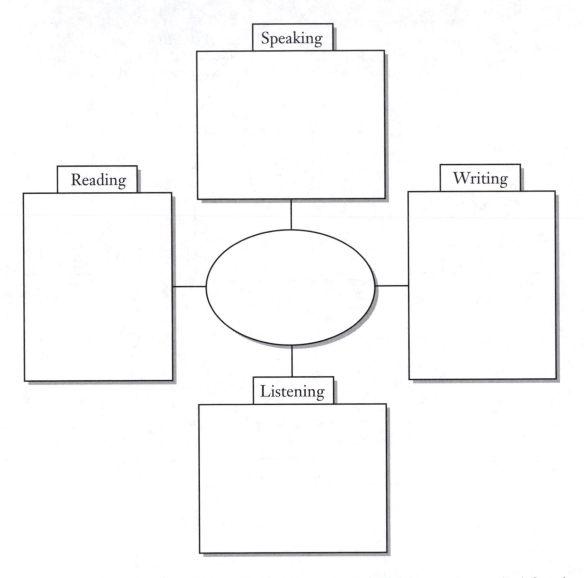

2. Using the following *T*-chart, list each of the learning styles on the left and describe an interactive content-based activity that accommodates it on the right.

LEARNING STYLES	ACTIVITY

IV. APPLICATION ACTIVITIES
CLiDES—Culturally and Linguistically Diverse Exceptional Students

Complete these activities to further your understanding.

1. Based on Gardner's Theory of Multiple Intelligences, create a learner-centered activity that includes all students in a diverse class. Your plan should incorporate several ways for students to learn the information while working on the same topic. Use the chart of multiple intelligences and the outline below as a guide.

   Topic:

   Intended Audience:

   Activity Description:

Complete the following activity and question.

1. Joanna is a second language learner in third grade. She speaks both Spanish and English at home and is receiving ESL assistance and native language support in school. However, she seems unable to succeed in completing most individual tasks in the classroom. Each task takes her an inordinate amount of time. Her responses to questions often seem inappropriate to the topic. She seems to depend heavily on peer assistance.

   As Joanna's teacher, you are responsible for identifying that a problem exists and communicating this to a student study committee. In addition you need to explain strategies you will use to accommodate some of her needs in the classroom. Using the information about CLiDES in the chapter, write a brief letter to the student study committee expressing your student's learning issues and what you have implemented to address her needs.

V. KWLA
Use the following KWLA activity to summarize what you've learned in this chapter.

This is what I now **know, wanted** to know, **learned,** and how I'll **apply** what I learned about approaches to working with diverse learners:

_____

_____

_____

_____

CHAPTER 9

Integrating Technology in an Interactive, Content-Based Classroom

I. CHAPTER REVIEW

1. Other than computers, what are some technology resources that can be used in a classroom?

_____

_____

_____

2. Describe how constructivist theories apply to language learning and technology.

_____

_____

_____

3. What is transformative pedagogy?

_____

_____

_____

4. How can you decide if information within a technological resource is authentic text?

_____

_____

_____

5. Explain the use of games in a technology-rich classroom. What functions do they serve?

_____

_____

_____

6. What is a WebQuest and how can it be used as an effective teaching tool in a content-based ESL classroom?

_____

_____

_____

II. REFLECTING ON WHAT YOU'VE READ

1. How do you think technology will affect/has affected your role as a teacher of second/foreign language? How do you see this role as differing from the teacher's role when you were a language student? What are the pros and cons of technology's effect on the teacher's role and on the student?

   _____

   _____

   _____

2. With which technology described in this chapter are you most familiar/comfortable? How would you incorporate it in your second/foreign language classroom? Which teaching method(s) or approach(es) would you use with this technology?

   _____

   _____

   _____

3. With which technology described in this chapter are you most unfamiliar? How would you go about improving your knowledge of this technology? How could you employ it in your classroom?

   _____

   _____

   _____

4. Choose one method each from the behaviorist and rationalist methods and one approach each from the functional and humanistic approaches discussed in chapter 2. Select a technology that could be employed for each method or approach and describe how it might be used in support of that method/approach.

   _____

   _____

   _____

III. GRAPHIC ORGANIZERS

1. Using a Venn diagram, choose three technologies you might use in your classroom and depict which instructional practices could be applied in the overlapping segments.

2. Create a graphic organizer to depict how you could use technology for alternative assessment versus how you could use it for more traditional testing.

IV. APPLICATION ACTIVITIES

1. Describe how you could make use of e-mail in your second/foreign language classroom. What type of teacher planning and preparation would be necessary before

you employed this technology? What language skills would you hope your students would develop through this technology? How would you measure progress?

2. Browse through at least three of the online resources listed in this chapter. Describe one or two ideas you found for using technology in the content area and how you would implement them.

3. Think about and describe what types of technology learning stations you might employ in your classroom. Select both traditional and newer technologies. For each learning station describe which learning styles it would best apply to and which method/approach it would be used for. Describe various methods of selecting the groups to work at your technology stations. What would be your rationale for each grouping and what would be the pros/cons for each?

4. Search the Internet and select one authentic text each that you could use for a beginning, intermediate, and advanced level. How would you need to adapt the texts you found for use by the language learners?

V. KWLA

Use the following KWLA activity to summarize what you've learned in this chapter.

This is what I now **know, wanted** to know, **learned,** and how I'll **apply** what I learned about planning for a standards-based classroom:

_____

_____

_____

_____

SUBJECT INDEX